ADVANCED
Media: Communication and Production

Joe Nicholas, John Price
& Ben Moore

Nelson

Thomas Nelson and Sons Ltd
Nelson House   Mayfield Road
Walton-on-Thames   Surrey
KT12 5PL   UK

Thomas Nelson Australia
102 Dodds Street
South Melbourne
Victoria 3205   Australia

Nelson Canada
1120 Birchmount Road
Scarborough   Ontario
M1K 5G4   Canada

© Joe Nicholas, John Price, Ben Moore 1996

First published by Thomas Nelson and Sons Ltd 1996

I(T)P   Thomas Nelson is an International Thomson Publishing Company

I(T)P   is used under licence

ISBN 0-17- 490001-5
NPN 9 8 7 6 5 4 3 2 1

All rights reserved. No paragraph of this publication may be reproduced, copied or transmitted save with written permission or in accordance with the provisions of the Copyright, Design and Patents Act 1988, or under the terms of any licence permitting limited copying issued by the Copyright Licensing Agency, 90 Tottenham Court Road, London W1P 9HE.

Any person who does any unauthorised act in relation to this publication may be liable to criminal prosecution and civil claims for damages.

Acknowledgements:
Acquisitions: Alex Bridgland/Steve Berry
Administration: Jenny Goode
Editorial: Simon Bell
Marketing: Jane Lewis
Production: Liam Reardon
Staff Design: Maria Pritchard
Design/Typesetting: Hardlines

Printed in Spain

The Advanced GNVQ Media: Communication and Production Team

Joe Nicholas is Head of the Division of English, Media Studies and Perfoming Arts at Oaklands College, St Albans. He has been involved with local working groups developing the GNVQ specifications since their inception.

John Price is a former secondary school Head of English and Deputy Head who now manages the Newspapers in Education department at the *Sunderland Echo*. He is co-writer of Unit specifications for GNVQ Media at Advanced and Intermediate Levels, and has written specifications for Optional Units for the RSA. His previous publications include the *Newspaper Study Pack* for Macmillan.

Ben Moore has taught Media Studies at levels through from Primary to Higher Education. He is a former Media Education adviser to Newcastle Local Education Authority, and has been an Assistant Examiner for the Welsh Joint Examinations Council. He has also been manager of Newspapers in Education at the *Newcastle Evening Chronicle and Journal*.

Acknowledgements

Illustrations and other printed matter

The authors and publishers are grateful to the following for permission to reproduce copyright material. If any acknowledgement has been omitted, this will be rectified at the earliest possible opportunity.

Figure in introductory section, page 11: reproduced from *Big!* magazine, by permission of EMAP Metro
Figures 1.1, 1.2a, 1.9, 3.4, 3.7, 3.8 and 3.9 reproduced by permission of the *Guardian*
Figures 1.2b, 1.5, 1.6, 1.7, 1.8, 1.10, reproduced from the *Sun* by permission of Newscorp
Figures, 2.4, 2.5, 2.6, 2.8, 2.9 and 2.10, reproduced from *More!* magazine by permission of EMAP Elan
Figure 3.5 reproduced from *TV Times*
Figure 3.6 reproduced from the *Daily Mail* by permission of Associated Newspapers
Figures 3.10 to 3.18 reproduced by permission of North Eastern Press/*Sunderland Echo*
Figures 3.19, 3.20, 3.22 and 3.24 reproduced by permission of The Press Association
Figures 4.10a-c reproduced by permission of David Sparrow
Figure 4.16 reproduced by permission of Lauren Cairns, Julie Watson and Joanne Hughes
Figure 4.17 reproduced by permission of Sue Maidens, Manor School, Hartlepool
Figures 5.1 to 5.5, 6.15, 6..25, 6.29 and 6.30 reproduced by permission of DC Thompson Ltd., Dundee

Figures 6.1 to 6.4 reproduced by permission of Suzy Varty
Figures 6.8, 6.16 to 6.24 and 6.26 to 6.28 based on images in *Comics – the Invisible Art* by Scott McCloud, published by Harper Collins.
Figures 7.1, 7.3, 7.4, 7.8 7.10 and 7.12 reproduced by permission of the British Film Institute
Figures 7.6 and 7.7 reproduced by permission of Channel 4 Films
Figures 8.2, 11.4 and 11.5 reproduced by permission of the BBC
Figure 13.4 reproduced by permission of RAJAR
Figures 14.1 to 14.14 based on material supplied by Richard Lawson of Martin Tait Advertising Agency, Newcastle-upon-Tyne
Figures 4.2, 4.8, 4.9, 6.7, 6.9, 8.7, 8.10, 8.11, 8.12, 8.13, 9.2, 9.3, 9.4, 9.5, 9.6, 9.11, 9.12, 9.13, 9.14, 10.1, 10.4 to 10.14, 10.16 a and b, 11.1, 12.1, 12.2, 12.6, 12.7, 12.8, 13.1 and 13.6 were taken by David Sparrow at West Kent College, Brook Street, Tonbridge, Kent. The authors and publishers gratefully acknowledge the assistance of Celia Nelson, Norrie Wallace and the students and members of staff who were involved.
Extracts from *Victoria Station* by Steve Chambers, © Steve Chambers, reproduced by permission of Michelle Steinberg, literary agent
The authors gratefully acknowledge the help provided by Jennifer Miller, Information Technology Manager, Newcastle-upon-Tyne LEA, for her guide to producing CD-ROMs

Contents

Introduction	2
How to use this book	2
Finding information in the book	2
How GNVQ works	3
The scope	3
Unit tests	4
Assignments	4
Assessors	4
Assessment, grades and grading themes	4
How does GNVQ compare with other qualifications?	5
GNVQ terminology	5
Building a portfolio	6
The qualification in Media: Communication and Production	7
0 The basic toolkit	10
Analysing the media	10
Why analyse?	10
Group interaction	10
Image analysis using a semiotic approach	10
Spoken and written language	13
Genre analysis	13
Analysis of narrative structure	14
Production	15
Group and individual work	15
Industry standards	15
Audience	16
Audience segments	16
1 Analysing a tabloid newspaper	18
Introduction to analysing a tabloid newspaper	18
Preparation	19
The production history of the *Sun*	21
The competitive market and the *Sun*	22
Cover price	23
Circulation and advertising	24
Readership	24
Textual analysis	25
Analysis of a popular tabloid news story	25
Analysis of an editorial	30
Analysis of the *Sun*'s sports coverage	32
Assignment: Analysing a tabloid newspaper	39

2 Analysing magazines — 40
- Introduction to analysing magazines — 40
- What is a magazine? — 41
  - The production history of the magazine — 41
- How to analyse a magazine — 44
  - Basic information — 44
  - Type of content — 44
  - Advertising — 45
  - Layout and cover page — 45
  - Language — 46
  - Images — 46
  - Relationships between language and images — 47
  - Conclusion: the 'character' of a magazine — 48
- An analysis of a female teenage magazine — 48
  - Basic information — 48
  - Type of content — 48
  - Advertising — 49
  - Layout and cover page — 50
  - Language — 52
  - Images — 52
  - Conclusion — 56
- An analysis of a male teenage magazine — 57
  - Match — 57
- Assignment: Analysing a magazine — 61

3 Planning and developing print material — 62
- Introduction to planning and developing print material — 62
- Generating, developing and evaluating ideas — 63
  - Is it practical — 63
  - Is it suitable? — 64
- Finding ideas for writing feature articles — 65
- Organising research — 66
  - Primary sources – interviewing — 66
- Writing features — 68
- Getting the style right — 69
- Case Study: Writing a feature — 70
- Thinking about representation — 71
- Understanding legal and ethical issues — 74
  - Libel — 74
  - Copyright — 76
  - Ethics — 76
- Producing visual material — 77
  - Photographs — 77
  - Graphics — 82
- Profile: Newspaper reporter — 86
- Assignment: Design a graphic — 87

4 Producing newspapers and magazines — 88
- Introduction to print production — 88
- Evaluating product ideas — 89
  - Target audience — 89
  - Objective — 90
  - Production — 90
  - Distribution — 90
  - Content — 91
  - Information sources — 91
  - Finance — 91
  - Production — 92

Planning the production process	92
Product design	93
Checklist of design features	93
Typography	94
Using photographs	96
Case Study: *Babe*	99
Case Study: *Manorisms*	100
Assignment: Setting up communications	100

5 Analysing comics 102
Introduction to analysing comics	102
The *Beano*: production history and marketing context	103
Publishers' view	105
Critics' views	106
Artist's view	106
Analysis of comics by genre	108
The narrative structure of 'The Bash Street Kids'	110
Case Study: Calamity James	111
Assignment: Analysing a comic	113

6 Making a comic 114
Introduction to making a comic	114
Case Study: *Lasses' Night Out*	114
Finding a client and an audience	116
Research	116
Production	117
Equipment	119
Comic conventions	120
The use of icons	120
Framing	120
Selection	122
Passage of time	122
Movement	122
Assignment: Make an educational comic	127

7 Analysing film fiction 128
Introduction to analysing film fiction	128
Looking at film genre and production context	128
Introduction: how film genres developed	128
How to analyse a film genre	129
Analysis of the horror film genre	129
Production context	133
Analysis of film images	133
Sample analysis of a film image	134
Analysing film as narrative	135
Film openings	135
Endings	139
Films as fairy tales	144
Case Study: *Four Weddings and a Funeral*	145
Assignment: Analysing film fiction	149

8 Analysing and producing quiz shows 152
Introduction to analysing and producing quiz shows	152
Analysing quiz shows	152
Textual analyses of quiz shows	155
Assignment: Analyse a quiz show	159
Studio production of a television quiz show	161
Writing the formula and script	161

Planning for production	163
Roles	164
Set design and floor plans	164
Planning meetings	165
Finalise the script and prepare a shooting script	166
Run through the complete programme	166
Production	167
Assignment: Producing and filming a quiz show	168

9 Planning a video production — 170

Introduction to planning a video production	170
Generating and developing ideas	170
Assignment: 'Teenagers now and then'	172
Generating ideas: 'Brainstorming'	172
Evaluating ideas	173
Product specification	174
Carrying out research	174
Case study: Video assignment report	175
Contract issues	176
Developing production scripts	176
Treatments	177
Case Study: Treatment: Video assignment	178
Synopses and scripts	178
Planning the shots	179
Planning the production process	184
Production and post-production roles	184
Action planning and shooting schedule	185
The reconnaissance	187

10 Producing a video — 188

Preparation	188
Equipment	188
Practice shoot	189
The shoot	189
Shooting for editing	189
Shooting for continuity	190
The edit	196
Editing tips	198
Making multimedia	199
Assignment: Produce a video	202

11 Analysing radio programmes — 204

Introduction to analysing radio programmes	204
Critical listening	205
The nature of radio	205
The listeners	206
Format radio	207
Radio presenters	208
Radio genres	210
Phone-ins	211
Radio drama	211
Assignment: Analysing a radio format	223

12 Producing radio programmes — 224

Introduction to producing radio programmes	224
Setting up a radio station	216
Planning audio productions	217
Factual programming	217

viii

Equipment	219
Portable tape recorder	227
Microphones	227
Microphone technique	229
Profile: Radio journalist	230
Assignment: Producing a radio programme	231

13 The purposes and methods of media research 232

Introduction to the purposes and methods of media research	232
Who needs research?	232
Industry research organisations	233
BARB (Broadcaster' Audience Research Board)	233
The National Readership Survey	234
Academic research	238
How to conduct research	239
Pitfalls	239
Research techniques	239
Case Study: Focus groups	233
Assignment: Conducting your own research	244

14 Marketing 246

Introduction to marketing	246
Marketing activities of a regional newspaper	246
Case Study: The *Herts Herald*	250
How to prepare a marketing plan	251
Case Study: Northern Electric – Super Tariff Campaign	251
Marketing a film	257
Merchandising	258
Marketing your own product	258
Assignment: Marketing a video	259

15 An overview of United Kingdom media industries 260

Introduction to media industries	260
Print media	261
Newspapers	261
Magazines	264
News Agencies	265
Broadcasting	265
The BBC	266
ITV	267
Channel Four	268
Satellite and cable broadcasting	268
Independent radio broadcasters	269
Film and video	270
Access and regulation	271
Access	271
Regulation	271
Assignment: The company game	274

16 A historical sketch of mass media in the United Kingdom 278

Before 1914	278
1914-1949	280
1950-1969	283
1970 onwards	285
Conclusion	288

Index 289

Introduction

How to use this book

This book shows you how to analyse and produce media products: video and radio programmes, films, newspapers, magazines and comics. You can follow the book closely or you can dip into it for help. The chapters are written and organised so that you can look at them in any order you wish.

The book aims to help you in your work, increase your enjoyment and understanding of the media as well as to give you practical advice.

Chapters with advice on analysing media texts give worked examples of different types of analysis so that you can see the kind of knowledge and critical insights you need to acquire. There is an emphasis in the analyses on popular culture which reflects the authors' own interests and enthusiasms. They would like to think that you will follow their example. However, it is the methodology which is important and you can apply the same critical techniques to whatever media products you yourself find of interest.

Some chapters give you practical advice on production, showing you how to achieve a 'standard approaching professional practice'. They lead you step by step through the production process, giving you advice on techniques, equipment and methodologies. This advice is sometimes illustrated with case studies of students' work and examples of professional work.

The chapters on research, marketing and industry give you important information illustrated with examples of professional practice.

The activities are either suggestions for things to do or group discussions, which will develop your thinking, knowledge and skills. They encourage the active learning style which the GNVQ seeks to promote. They all provide some opportunity to meet the GNVQ requirements expressed in performance criteria and range statements.

Assignments are more complex and challenging than activities and are designed to help you produce work for your portfolio to satisfy the evidence indicators of particular Units.

Finding information in the book

There are three ways in which you might find the information you need in this book:
- the contents list at the front
- the index at the back
- by 'pressing' the appropriate button to another section.

Buttons in the margin direct you to relevant sections, or to further reading in other useful titles. They form a cross-referencing system which allows you to find the information you need quickly. When you do look something up don't forget to mark your place in the book so that you can get back to it.

Buttons look like this:

▶ Audience segments, page 16

How GNVQ works

GNVQ stands for General National Vocational Qualification.

The qualification is general because you have to acquire and develop a wide range of skills, knowledge and understanding. In Media terms this means working with sound, vision and print.

It is national because the qualification is recognised throughout the nation and it will be the same standard whether you study in Plymouth, Portadown or Peterlee.

It is vocational because the methods of working are largely practical and linked to careers in the media industries.

The scope

To be awarded an Advanced GNVQ you must complete fifteen units (i.e. topics):
- eight mandatory units
- four optional units
- three mandatory core skill units.

There is a wide range of optional units with different titles offered by different awarding bodies, but they are all designed to give students a chance to pursue some of the activities in the mandatory units in more depth.

The optional units differ according to which awarding body your school or college uses. There are three awarding bodies: the Royal Society of Arts (RSA), City and Guilds and the Business and Technical Education Council (BTEC).

These bodies are responsible for checking that colleges and schools organise and deliver their courses properly, for setting unit tests and awarding certificates at the end of the course.

The core skills are:
- Application of Number
- Communication
- Information Technology.

Application of Number is about gathering and working with data (which is particularly relevant in the chapters in this book on research and marketing), solving problems (such as working out budgets for media productions) and presenting and interpreting data (which you will do when you analyse target markets).

Communication is about talking and writing effectively, both of which you will need to do when you give presentations, work in groups in planning and producing media products, or interview members of the public as part of your media research.

Information Technology is about word processing and handling databases which you will be doing as part of your print production work.

Unit tests

Unit tests are multiple choice tests which check whether you have understood the main concepts and acquired the necessary knowledge outlined in the *Unit specifications*. This book helps you to understand those concepts and develop the knowledge you need but does not give you specific training in test techniques.

Assignments

GNVQ courses are taught through *assignments*. During an assignment you are asked to complete a number of tasks. The tasks will enable you to complete reports and/or products (in the form of print, audio, video or multimedia products). The assignments will have deadlines for the completion of tasks and a final deadline for the handing in of all the evidence for that assignment, including any product.

During assignments you will work in different roles, sometimes as an individual, sometimes in pairs and often in production teams. Teamwork is an important skill on a vocational course and is assessed on GNVQ assignments.

Each assignment will be given a grade as an outcome of the process called assessment. Your assignments build up into a body of work which gives evidence of what you have achieved on the course. This body of work is collected and organised into a portfolio of evidence on which you are assessed and given your final grade at the end of the course.

At the end of each assignment a teacher or lecturer, or a group of them, will explain why you got the grades you did and discuss with you how you might have done anything better. Comments on this from you and the teacher will be recorded. This is part of the assessment process which is explained below.

In this book you will find ideas and outlines in the form of sample assignments. These will help you and your teachers or lecturers to develop your own ideas.

Assessors

Who will assess your work? Teachers and students should work together so that students understand how they are being assessed and have a realistic idea of their own performance. There are two or three key people who make sure that work is assessed fairly and in a way comparable with other schools and colleges (or *centres*). Your course tutor is an important key person. The *internal verifier* (who may be the same person as your course tutor) acts as an adviser within your institution. A person who comes from outside, and is appointed by your lead body, is the *external verifier*. The external verifier visits a number of centres and works with the internal verifier. When the external verifier visits, you may be asked to exhibit your work and individual students may have discussions with the external verifier.

Assessment, grades and grading themes

On every GNVQ course you can gain one of three grades: Pass, Merit or Distinction. If you do not pass your work will be referred and your teachers will tell you how you may try again, or *re-submit*.

You will gain your grades on the basis of an assessment not only of what you produce at the end (the *outcome*), but also how you work through the assignments from start to finish (the *process*). This is organised under four headings called *grading themes*. There are three headings under process:

- Theme 1: Planning
- Theme 2: Information
- Theme 3: Evaluation.
  There is one outcome theme:
- Theme 4: Quality of outcomes.

How does GNVQ compare with other qualifications?

One advanced level GNVQ is the equivalent of two A-levels. It is meant to be more broadly based than an A-level which is why it takes longer to do. It is different from A-level because it gives more emphasis to the vocational or work-related aspects of education.

On the other hand, it is also different from NVQ (National Vocational Qualification) because it requires more understanding of theory and it does not oblige you to spend time in a workplace. The qualification is designed to let you progress either into a job or into higher education.

GNVQ terminology

The GNVQ specifies the skills you need to develop and what you should understand by the end of your course. It tells you and your teacher what the outcomes of the course should be. It does not specify how you should achieve those outcomes. It is up to you and your teachers to work out how best to achieve them. This means that alternative learning approaches and contexts can be developed to suit local circumstances and particular students' needs.

The subject has been divided into *Units* each one covering a specific *topic*. There are eight compulsory Units at advanced level, usually having a title like this 'Investigating and Carrying Out Media Marketing'.

Each Unit or topic is subdivided into *Elements*. These tell you *what you have to do* or study. These often follow a chronological pattern such as 1 Plan the production process...; 2 Produce printed product; 3 Edit ...printed product; and 4 Review and evaluate printed product.

Each element is then divided into *performance criteria* which give more detail about what you have to do. So that, for instance, in reviewing and evaluating a printed product you have to:
- distribute it
- test audience response
- analyse feedback
- evaluate the planning and production.

The *range statements* tell you *how much you have to do*. Thus if the phrase 'describe your target audience' is in the performance criteria, the *range statements* should tell you what that involves as you could describe a target audience in almost endless depth by describing every individual in it. So the range might say 'in terms of age, social class, gender'. The range therefore clarifies and limits. You know that here, anyway, you do not have to describe your audience in terms of ethnic origin, IQ scores, geographical location, occupation or buying habits, though each of these could have been included.

It is important that you cover all Range statements in your work, but notice that you only have to do 'in depth those aspects of the range which are the focus of the project and other activities' which you select for each unit. That means some range statements only need to be done in outline. The Unit Tests will be set on the whole of each Range, however.

Introduction

The *evidence indicators* tell you *how you show what you have done*. Usually you have to produce a complete product or a report on something you have learned about. The evidence indicators are meant to describe the minimum amount of evidence you have to produce. But they are indicators and you may offer alternative forms of evidence. So if you are asked to produce 'an edited copy of the print product, supported by draft page layout design', you might be able to submit photographs of computer screens showing the development of your page, arguing that with electronic make-up it is not necessary to have draft designs. The design may emerge as you work. The important thing is not to be a slave to the evidence indicators.

Amplification is meant to explain key words and phrases where necessary. It often gives examples to clarify certain terms in the elements.

Guidance provides advice for teachers or students in the design or management of the learning process. It can tell you how you might tackle the element and perhaps suggest the kinds of equipment that you will need.

Building a portfolio

The evidence of your work on the GNVQ in Media: Communication and Production, apart from your performance in the unit tests, will be presented in the form of a collection of your work called a portfolio.

What is a portfolio? A portfolio is a set of records of work completed. These records include not only the media products you make, on your own or in groups, but also evidence of how you made them and what you learnt in the process. The portfolio will be organised to show the assignments that you have covered with your teachers. It will show that you understand the course and what you have studied. It also shows what you have achieved and what you have done well.

Your portfolio will also show that you have covered the course as described in the units from the standards for the GNVQ. It will be important to complete paperwork to keep track of your progress, and to help the teachers who assess your achievement find their way around the portfolio. Your teachers will show you how to do this.

How should you build your portfolio? Collect everything you can which shows what you have done on the course – this is the evidence. You will build your portfolio throughout your course, and should review your progress in doing this with your teachers and course tutor. Although some things may not go into the finished portfolio, it is better to make the final decisions about how to select or edit the finished portfolio later on.

You may be surprised by what counts as evidence. You may collect evidence in writing, on tape, on video and in other visual forms such as photographs. It is very important to log in some details about the date, time and situation in which these took place. Course handouts, recorded conversations, debates, diary entries, essays, exhibitions, letters, notes, phone calls, questionnaires, questions and answers and role plays can all count so long as you produce the evidence. Any record of your work can count as evidence. If you hold a meeting make sure that you make a record of it in minutes or some other form. What will not count is simply your assertion that you did something without some kind of record. In addition, you may agree with your teachers to collect evidence that you have covered certain requirements of the course from experiences outside, such as work experience, school activities or work for the student union. This can be particularly useful for evidencing skills. You can suggest to your teachers ways in which you might give evidence of your skills and achievements.

Finished pieces of work and the final products you make as part of a group, or on your own, are very important. Things which show how you worked, or the process by which these products were made, are also important. It is usually a good idea to present the products and the evidence of the process separately.

In order to collect all this evidence you must organise yourself. You will need materials such as files and folders in which to collect your evidence.

The most common types of portfolio used include:
- lever arch files – useful for holding large amounts of work securely
- artist's portfolios – display visual materials such as drawings, paintings and posters well, but not very secure for written work
- box files – hold a combination of flat work such as reports and drawings, and 3D objects such as models and video tapes, if necessary.

You will find that aids to organising your work, such as dividers, labels and lists of contents (indexing), are essential. You may find it helpful to use colour coding to identify which evidence belongs to which assignment or unit.

▶ BTEC, 1994, *Getting GNVQs Right: Building Portfolios*, BTEC Publications

Let's conclude with some further advice. Do not be put off by the paper work involved in building a portfolio, or the amount of work it involves. Remember that portfolio building is not something which can be achieved in a day. You will build up your portfolio step by step over your course. In order to achieve a well built portfolio, you will plan your time and work, meet deadlines and concentrate on achieving your best at each stage of the process. The final product is your personal property, and something you will be able to show interviewers or even prospective employers, and may keep for the rest of your career.

The qualification in Media: Communication and Production

The qualification in Media is designed to cover a broad range of skills that are needed by those working in the media industries. The emphasis is on production, but you have to make different products across a range of media. The minimum length of these products is specified in the introduction to the GNVQ Media specifications. You then have to design an advertising campaign for one of the products so that you become aware of the prime importance of marketing and distribution in media industries, large or small.

While you are making your media products you are expected to broaden your awareness of how professionals go about the same sorts of tasks. This means you will have to analyse media texts (e.g. newspapers, magazines or comics, radio and television programmes) to see how they have been constructed and what effects they have on their audiences or what uses the audiences make of them.

You need also to understand the industrial and commercial background of media production as this affects the style, content and purpose of media products.

The introduction to the specifications for Media: Communication and Production stresses that the Units need not be done in sequence. Course leaders and students are encouraged to work out 'the manner and organisation of delivery' of the qualification.

The figure opposite is a model outline syllabus based on a theme of popular culture. If a detailed syllabus were constructed on this model you would need to check back to the Performance Criteria, Range statements and Evidence Indicators to make sure that each one had been covered, either in depth or in outline as mentioned above; but the model, or one of your own devising, gives you some control over the qualification and shows how the more theory-based units can be used to support and inform the production work which takes precedence. In this way schools and colleges can organise courses to suit their strengths and special interests, and give practical work the emphasis that was intended when the unit specifications were drawn up.

GNVQ Media: Communication and Production - A Popular Culture Model					
		TV/Film	**Radio**	**Print Media**	
Production	Produce five media products (two moving image, two audio and one print) working with other people	a) Video of an extract from soap episode, original script based on actual characters from a soap (fiction) b) Video of your own quiz show (non-fiction)	a) Radio magazine programme aimed at teenage audience (non-fiction) b) Scenes from a radio play (fiction)	a) Community newspaper or magazine aimed at catchment area of school/college (non-fiction)...	...or b) Fun comic for juvenile audience in local schools (fiction)
Marketing	Choose one of the above and design an advertising campaign to market it, again working with other people		Look at marketing activities of: commercial and public service radio stations e.g. a local radio station and Radio 1, with particular attention to one programme from each	Look at marketing activities of: a national tabloid newspaper: e.g. *Sun's* cover price war, TV adverts, games and prizes etc. compared with the marketing of a local paper	
Analysis	Concepts: genre; representation; narrative structure; media languages	Analyse TV quiz shows (e.g. *Fifteen to One*) or a popular film	Analyse radio shows aimed at younger audience (e.g. *Chris Evans Breakfast Show*)	Analyse example of the tabloid press (e.g. the *Sun*) or a popular teenage magazine	Analyse Juvenile Comics (e.g. the *Beano*)
Research	Conduct research into audience responses to your own media product	Conduct research into audience 'participation' in quiz shows (depth interviews) or into perceptions of representation of minority groups in one film. Report on work of BARB (Broadcasters' Audience Research Board)	Organise a quantitative survey of teenage radio consumption. Report on work of RAJAR (Radio Joint Audience Research). Account for changes in audience reach of two radio programmes	Report on work of National Readership Survey. Analyse trends in newspaper/magazine sales	Research into male/female attitudes to a particular comic
Industry	Interview media professionals about jobs and report your findings	Describe relationship of BSkyB to Murdoch press. Summarise development of TV quiz show genre and sub genres or the development of one film genre	Describe changes in public service broadcasting. Give account of work of The Radio Authority	Describe growth of News International. Give account of work of Press Complaints Commission	Investigate the production and history of a genre of comic (e.g. sci-fi, horror, juvenile, adventure, girls'.)

0 | The basic toolkit

Analysing the media

Why analyse?
By analysing media products which have been made by professionals you will learn more about how to make your own products. You should also become a more independent and discerning consumer of the media. As Len Masterman says in *Teaching the Media* (Routledge, 1992) 'The acid test of any media education programme is the extent to which the pupils are critical in their own use and understanding of the media *when the teacher is not there.*'

Group interaction
Analysis can be a group activity as well as an individual exercise. By sharing observations and testing out ideas on others you can think more sharply about what you are analysing. By having to explain to others what you are thinking, your own thoughts become clearer: 'How do I know what I mean until I hear what I say?'

It is a good idea for your group to develop the habit of discussing, with or without a teacher, media products which several people have watched, heard or read. The discussions should go beyond the 'did you see so-and-so last night?' kinds of conversations that people frequently have as part of their social interaction.

You can develop the discussions by asking questions which will encourage analysis. From talking about what happened in *Eastenders* last night you can wonder why it happened and speculate on how the story will develop in future episodes. A description of a memorable interview on radio can lead to considering why it worked so well and what techniques the interviewer used.

It would be useful to organise common media experiences so that these discussions can include everyone. The group can agree to watch or hear particular programmes or to circulate and read a specific magazine article. For media students analysis should become a habit rather than an occasional exercise.

In GNVQ Media you are asked to concentrate on three kinds of analysis: image analysis, genre analysis and narrative structure analysis.

Image analysis using a semiotic approach
Semiotics is the study of 'signs' and the rules that govern their use. It asks

Introduction

how meaning is created rather than what meaning is. 'Signs' are made up of an image, object or sound and the concept or emotion it represents. The image, object or sound is called the *signifier* and the concept the *signified*. For instance, the tolling of a single church bell (sound as signifier) could suggest mourning and death (signified).

When you use this technique you need to be aware that signifiers all depend on their history and cultural context for their meanings, so that a semiotic reading of an image can lead to very detailed analysis. In semiotic theory all communication is considered 'partial, motivated, conventional and biased' (Ellen Seiter, 'Semiotics, Structuralism and Television', from *Channels of Discourse Reassembled* ed. Allen) so that to understand any media product we need to know how it was produced, who produced it, when it was produced and where.

Semiotics has introduced to media analysis the concepts of denotation and connotation which are useful when you are analysing media images - e.g. stills or moving excerpts from films or television, articles from newspapers (with or without accompanying pictures), jingles, extracts from radio programmes or any kind of advertisement.

▶ Allen, J., (ed), 1992, *Channels of Discourse Reassembled,* Routledge

You should begin by describing as objectively as you can whatever it is you see, hear or read.

This image is taken from *Big!* magazine, published to cover the dates 16 to 29 November 1994, where it appears just inside the front cover. It shows a publicity shot of Kym Wilson for her debut appearance in *Heartbreak High*.

When you analyse an image you should separate out what is literally in the picture from the meanings you associate with it. The *denotation* of an image is what it actually shows, such as a colour. The *connotation* of an image is the set of meanings which we associate with what is shown; for example, red can *connote* danger.

The photograph denotes a young woman standing by a wall-mounted phone. She is holding a strand of hair in her right hand. Her left hand is clasping the earpiece of the phone to her left ear, with her index finger upraised to support the receiver. She is leaning on a wall alcove, turned slightly to the left of the picture, with her eyes looking upward to a point to her right. The wall-mounted part of the telephone with black push buttons is positioned to her left, above her head. She is dressed in jeans and a see-through blouse, underneath which she is wearing a bra. Her hair is in pigtails, with two metal hairslides. She has a chain bracelet on her right forearm.

SUBJECT: KYM WILSON — HEARTBREAK HIGH BABE
LOCATION: A Sydney photographer's studio. MODEL: Kym Wilson. ASSIGNMENT: Publicity shots for Kym's debut appearance in Heartbreak High. Kym will hit our screens next year. CREDENTIALS: Cover girl Kym is one of Australia's top stars, she's appeared in A Country Practice, E Street and she also presents a Saturday morning music show called Video Smash Hits. HOT RATING: Sizzling.

You can list individual signs in the image, their denotation and the connotations which they might have. For example:

Denotation	Connotation
strand of hair held in right hand	this could indicate either thoughtfulness or flirtatiousness or both
closed lips	she is listening, feeling serious
telephone flex behind left arm	this could indicate an intimate conversation as if she were clasping the line and conversation to herself
polka dots on blouse	indicates a desire in the wearer for decoration, and to be noticed

The appearance and body language of the young woman have many possible meanings or connotations. For example, her pigtails connote girlishness. There is a strong contrast between the connotations of the setting and the connotations of the way in which the girl has dressed. The telephone has rather formal or institutional connotations and a public context, such as a college. The transparent blouse has connotations of sexuality and a display of the body. The hairslides have connotations of intimacy.

You should also bring in aspects of the *treatment* of the picture. In a photograph, where is the camera. How is the shot framed? For example, in this image the camera is positioned facing the woman, although she is looking off to her right with the object of her gaze outside the frame. This has two possible meanings: she is looking at something, or she is lost in thought. The framing cuts off the woman at the waist below the waistband of her jeans. This sort of view strengthens the idea of an interaction between the person in the shot and other participants. There is the conversation on the phone, and the point of view, or positioning, of the viewer, us.

You can find possible stories around images: these are their narrative possibilities. You can also find evidence of the type, or types, of media product they are likely to be used in. This image gives evidence of a soap opera type of setting. There is a look about the image of everyday reality, apart from the quality of the photograph and the lack of clutter in the background. The action of soaps takes place largely through talk – indicated here by the telephone. However, the quality of the image, and the lighting in particular, indicates another possibility which is confirmed in the written text underneath the image in the magazine, namely that it is a publicity shot.

Images have so many possible meanings that you do not know where or when to stop. The writing, which you find with images in magazines and other print media, limit and tie down certain meanings in the image. This tying down of meaning is called *anchorage*. You should note how words or writing do this. This will then tie in to the media product in which the image is found, and the use that is being made of the image.

The nature of the hot shots image is altered, or *anchored* considerably by the text. The flirtatious and sexual possibilities of Kym Wilson's appearance are anchored by the final 'hot rating': 'sizzling', a word which has connotations of food. The fictional possibilities of the image are altered by the 'assignment' category in the text: 'Publicity shots for Kym's debut appearance in *Heartbreak High*' which highlights that this is publicity *hype* for a potential star, a shot which has been posed as if part of a soap narrative.

Thus elements of soap and elements of the publicity shot are mixed together in the image. The text and the image fit into the identity of *Big!* as a teenage magazine which promises to let its readers see behind the scenes of the media they follow and watch the hype being created.

Spoken and written language

The language we hear and read in media products (usually the English language) is also important for analysis. You can look for important topics and the type of language used. You can analyse the vocabulary (the stock of words being used) and the denotations and connotations of the words used.

For example in an analysis of *Big!*, the magazine's topics cluster around those areas of the media world which appeal to the target audience, in particular music, soaps, films and young stars with a female audience. Other connected topics include relationships, romance and sexuality. Keywords commonly repeated include: 'gossip', 'stardom', 'love', 'date', 'boy', 'girl', 'film', 'album', 'best' and 'worst'. The language used is close to spoken English. Sentences are usually short and simple. Sometimes the language used includes slang, often with an American influence, used by teenagers and *youth media*. Examples include 'a tad too long'; 'this is pony' (in a review of a video); 'pop crumblies M-People'; 'megababes'.

▶ How to analyse a magazine, page 44.

▶ An analysis of a female teenage magazine, page 48

A Activity

Discuss with members of your group what the connotations of this image are. Compile a list of meanings that are shared by most of the group and those which are individual.

Genre analysis

Genre analysis is about putting things into categories, finding common elements in different media products. The assumption behind this process is that we will more clearly understand the structure and purpose of the object of study.

Genre study is usually defined by *critics*. In theory critics are free to construct any genre they wish. For instance, the genre known as *film noir* was a way of describing common features of certain gangster, thriller and detective films. The genre was identified by French film critics, particularly Nino Frank, though the concept is now used by film directors and producers who are making *neo-film noir* films.

Genre is also based on *industry practice*. Genre offers a way for film and television industries to control the tension between similarity and difference inherent in the production of any cultural product. If every film were unique they would be more expensive to produce and audiences would not know what to expect. Genres provide media producers with an easy-to-use creative toolbox and they are a way of predicting audience popularity.

Genre analysis involves recognising certain elements in a media text which both the sender of the message and the receiver of the message have come to understand as *normal*. These elements are sometimes called *codes*. One of the codes of television news presentation, for instance, is that the reader sits behind a desk and is shown in medium close up. One of the current codes of tabloid newspapers is to have large headlines, a picture and small amounts of text on the front page. The important thing to be aware of when recognising and describing codes is that they are not absolute and fixed, but have come to be accepted by choice.

A Activity

Try to describe the characteristics of small scale sub-genres such as Australian soap operas (how are they different from British and American?); red masthead tabloids (how are the *Mirror*, *Sun* and *Star* different from the *Mail* and *Express*?); humorous radio shows on current affairs; adult comics (such as *Viz*).

Analysis of narrative structure

Storytelling is everywhere in the media which present a vast range of narratives that share certain similarities and yet have important differences.

It is important to realise that narratives are not just confined to fiction. There are storytelling techniques used in news reporting, in documentaries and in advertising – indeed in almost every media text.

How do you go about analysing these narratives? First realise what narrative structure is not about. It is not about the industrial processes which produced the text being studied; nor is it about the effects of the text on the audience. It is about a study of the formal characteristics of texts and there are two central questions that have to be asked: i) What happens to whom? and ii) How is the story told? A third important question which applies to television is how the narrative is affected by its place in a schedule. That is how is it affected by the narratives around and within it (e.g. adverts).

▶ Films as fairy tales, page 144

What happens to whom? can be broken down into:
- how things change from one state of affairs to another
- how characters perform certain functions (e.g. hero, villain, helper, false hero)
- how events are caused
- how suspense is created
- how stories have a state of affairs followed by a complication and then a resolution (or a beginning, a middle and an end).

(Be careful when looking for patterns that you do not force the details to fit with certain theories such as Vladimir Propp's (referred to on page 144)).

'*How is the story told?*' can be broken down into:
- *types of storyteller*, for example, are they characters (personally involved) or observers (detached)? Are they telling stories in someone else's story (embedded)? How reliable are they? Whatever they are they need to be examined closely, for, as Walter Benjamin put it: 'Traces of the storyteller cling to the story the way the handprints of the potter cling to the clay vessel.'
- *the time of the storytelling*: this involves the sequence in which the events are related. They do not have to be told chronologically. So in films there are techniques such as previews and flashbacks, the one to tease the other to remind the viewer. It is also possible to stretch time as with slow motion replays on television. The job of the person analysing the text is to consider what lies behind the choices among ways of presenting time.
- *types of story*, for example, predictable, following a formula or multiple storylines wound together as in soap operas.

A Activity

Record a television news story which contains film of a controversial incident such as an industrial strike or a protest march. Have members of your group write alternative narrations of the event. People should try different ways of speaking, dressing and 'broadcasting' from different settings. How would a newsreader dressed as a tramp and lying on a bench tell the story and with what effect on the viewer? Video the different narrative styles and discuss how and why the story changes.

Production

In GNVQ Media you have to produce a variety of media texts:
- one print product such as a newspaper or comic
- two audio products such as a radio magazine programme and a music programme
- two moving image products, such as an extract from a studio-based quiz show and an extract from a documentary
- material for a marketing campaign about one of your products.

The purpose behind these demands is to give you a chance to try a variety of tasks using different media. You may then have a clearer idea of which branch of the media you want to specialise in or what particular aspects of the media you would like to study in more depth.

Group and individual work

Teamwork is expected in all of the production work undertaken as consultation and co-operation are so important in the professional production environment. The roles in teams should be shared and rotated and you should take on as many roles as possible during the course. It is important that an accurate record is kept of all the contributions that individuals make to a production as in the end assessment is of individual achievement.

Industry standards

A far as possible you should follow industry procedures in your work. You may not have industry standard equipment to work with but you can still follow the methods which professionals use.

There are some general procedures in production which are the same whatever medium you are working in. These are *origination*, *specification*, *research*, *budgeting*, *recording* or *writing*, *editing* and *distribution*.
- origination: coming up with ideas of what to produce and how to produce it
- specification: writing down precise details about what is to be produced, how, by whom, to what deadlines and at what cost
- research: several types – into the market for the product, into the circumstances of making the product (making sure that the right equipment is available, for instance), into the subject matter of the production (identifying people who are experts and obtaining information from them, for instance)
- budgeting: revenue anticipated; costs expected – including materials, time, distribution costs etc

- recording/writing: the raw material of the product
- editing: refinement of the raw material, so that it meets the standards expected by its audience
- distribution: making sure that the product reaches its audience at the appropriate time.

There are differences of detail which vary according to what you produce and these are described in the chapters dealing with specific production processes.

Audience

After the *Panorama* interview with Princess Diana in November 1995 there was considerable media debate and analysis. The news programmes the next day reported that the audience of 21 million was the largest television audience ever for an interview. John Humphrys on radio's *Today* programme asked the BBC's media correspondent if there were not 'two audiences in Diana's mind' – the general public and the Royal Family. The *Sun* newspaper, like many others, reported how individuals had watched the programme and what they made of it as well as the results of a readers' phone-in expressing support for or disapproval of the princess. The feedback included information about how her son, William, watched the programme 'alone' and quoted the responses of a 'heroin junkie', a 'coma survivor' and a girl who had written 'to Superman actor Christopher Reeve after breaking her neck'. They also recorded the responses of various politicians, Barbara Cartland, the editor of *Majesty* magazine and the editor of Burke's Peerage as well as *Sun* readers who rang the newspaper.

This illustrates three different approaches to the notion of 'audience'. First, there is the quantitive approach which involves calculating the numbers of people who see, hear or read a media product. This information is important for media producers and the advertising industry. Advertisers would be interested in the total numbers of readers, viewers or listeners of particular media texts as well as the charges producers of texts are asking so that they can negotiate the best deal for their advertising. Producers of media products need to know how popular their products are and why so that they can change their products to satisfy consumer demands.

Audience segments

Second, there is the notion that an audience is not homogeneous, but is composed of groups or segments – at a crude level the general public and the Royal Family, but at more sophisticated levels involving age, gender, lifestyles, interests and so on. Again this information is important to both programme producers and advertisers, who in a sense are 'buying' audiences. Advertisers need to know how effectively the messages they want to get across to the public are reaching their target audiences. So a research organisation like the National Readership Survey can give specific information about audiences such as which publication has the highest number of readers from the higher social classes (ABC1) who 'usually look at beauty and personal health topics', which would be the kind of information cosmetics manufacturers would be interested in.

Third, there is the notion that audiences are also made up of individuals, each one making his or her own interpretation of a programme. Increasingly academics are interested in how individuals interpret and make use of media texts. Their work has shown that we should not work on the assumption that any text has an absolute meaning which we have to try to understand and puzzle out, but that meaning is produced by the person receiving the text as well as the author of the text. Academic research is increasingly concerned with the environment in which the audience receives media texts and how this affects their interpretation. (See especially the work of David Morley in works such as *Family Television* published by Comedia.)

▶ Morley, D., 1986, *Family Television*, Comedia

Classification by socio-economic groups

This is a way of dividing an audience of people into groups according to their jobs. Media producers and advertisers are interested in such classification because people's buying patterns are closely linked to the work they do and therefore the amount of money they earn.

AB grades (about 15% of the working population) are people in professional and managerial positions.

C1 grade (about 28% of the working population) are people in skilled non-manual jobs, sometimes referred to as lower middle class.

C2 grade (about 31% of the working population) are people in skilled manual jobs, sometimes referred to as upper working class.

DE grades (about 25% of the working population) are people who are semi-skilled or unskilled manual workers. State pensioners and the unemployed are classed as grade E.

A Activity

Find out from a random sample of 40 people which are the most watched Saturday evening television programmes, the most read newspapers and the most listened to radio music programmes. Conduct a similar survey amongst teachers/lecturers and compare the findings (here you are looking at overall consumption figures).

Investigate the popularity of particular radio programmes, comparing sudents with pensioners, car owners with people who mainly use public transport, Walkman owners with non-Walkman owners. Produce charts to show your results. (Here you are looking at different groups or segments of audience.)

Choose a current television advert which contains images and messages about which there is some dispute or confusion. Record the responses to it of a wide variety of people, for example, a young child, a visitor to this country who is not familiar with its culture, a person who would obviously have no use for the product or service being advertised, the kind of person you think the advert is mainly aimed at, people with very different attitudes towards advertising and so on. Try to divide the responses into those who are most clearly in tune with what you take to be the advertiser's message, those who make a more personal interpretation of the message and those who make no sense of the message, reject it altogether or have a highly individual interpretation. (Here you are looking at how individuals make different meanings from the same material.)

1 | Analysing a tabloid newspaper

This chapter will help you to analyse a national newspaper, looking in particular at:
- its format
- the images it presents to its readers
- the relationship between text and images
- its narrative structures
- the way it represents people and issues.

The chapter shows how to analyse the *Sun* and is organised into the following sections:
- Introduction to analysing a tabloid newspaper
- The production history of the *Sun*
- The competitive market and the *Sun*
- Textual analysis.

Introduction to analysing a tabloid newspaper

Analysing a tabloid newspaper, in this case the *Sun*, is not as simple as it sounds. You need to define what you mean by the *Sun*. Do you mean one issue of the newspaper, a week's issues, several issues taken over a span of time? The more issues you analyse, the more complete your overall critical picture will be, but you are limited by the amount of time you spend on this. This chapter takes a close look at some parts of the *Sun* newspaper over one week's publications. It focuses on one news story, an editorial and the way the paper reports sport.

As long as you are covering the analytic concepts mentioned in the GNVQ specifications, you are free to examine those aspects of a newspaper which interest you. You should make it clear, however, what the scope of your analysis is.

By a close dissection of one or more news stories you can begin to see how the writer has constructed the story and so learn conventions which might help you as a writer. You can understand, for instance, how to produce snappy lead paragraphs and how to build your story around personalities rather than issues. You can also benefit as a reader because you will see more clearly what journalists consider important, and you can identify the techniques they use to hook your interest and manipulate your feelings and opinions. You can become more independent.

The chapter also maintains that, before you start any textual analysis, it is important for you to know something of the history of the publication and something about the commercial pressures which govern its existence. It is useful to know, for instance, that the *Sun*, which claimed that it won a general election for John Major and the Conservatives, was born from an ailing newspaper belonging to the Trades Union Congress. The fact that it is now owned by Rupert Murdoch, who also owns Sky television, affects the way sport, for example, is reported in the paper, and unless you are aware of this connection you might miss detecting some bias.

The purposes of critical analysis generally are outlined in the section entitled 'Analysing the media' in the introduction.

Preparation

A Activity

Before you begin your analysis, discuss in your group what people's perceptions of the *Sun* newspaper are. Ask group members to express their opinion (with a reason) of the *Sun* in one sentence. Find out if people are regular *Sun* readers, casual *Sun* readers or not *Sun* readers. Now read and discuss the following comments and then after the discussion see if people have modified their original opinions.

- 'People who don't buy the *Sun* just don't understand it.' (Kelvin MacKenzie, former editor)
- 'The *Sun*, a coarse and demented newspaper.' (The *Daily Mirror*)
- 'The *Sun* is the lackey of its financial boss.' (Sir Edward Heath)
- 'Those ideas which were associated with Fascism of the 1920s and 30s are now appearing day after day in the *Sun*.' (Tony Benn)
- 'I see it as a branch of showbiz. It recognised for the first time the need for entertaining the reading public. The front pages even look entertaining, rather like the front of a theatre, all stars and bright lights beckoning you inside. There's so much glitz and razzmatazz about the *Sun*' (David Banks, former employee of the *Sun*)
- 'That tawdry little journal, the *Sun*, written for morons by morons.' (The *Sunday Express*)
- 'We acknowledged what many journalists were at the time anxious to forget – that the basic interests of the human race are not in politics, philosophy or economics, but in things like food and money, sex and crime, football and television. But we did not deal with these things to the exclusion of all others...We tried ceaselessly to make the *Sun* a newspaper which cared, and a newspaper which mattered. A newspaper which got it first, and got it right. A newspaper for people, not for Fleet Street.' (Larry Lamb, former editor of the *Sun*)
- 'I do think we speak for middle-England common sense and we understand working class values. It's a mixture of morality and hedonism: it sounds contradictory but we want them to have a good time yet have very strong values.' (Rupert Murdoch)

▶ Roslyn Grose, 1989, *The Sun-sation*, Angus and Robertson

(These were taken from *The Sun-sation* by Roslyn Grose, published by Angus and Robertson.)

- 'By tradition the *Sun* speaks in the crotchety and capricious tones of the put-upon braggart propping up one corner of the public bar and complaining that it's all the fault of the bleeding Frogs and the effing Krauts and the sodding poofs and the bloody unions.' (John Diamond writing in the *Guardian*.)
- 'We are in favour of *everybody* getting on with their lives, going to school, doing well, or a bit better than their parents. It is optimistic, but there is a price to pay if all you do is have a good time. We don't believe the state should have anything but the smallest part to play.' (Kelvin MacKenzie, Former editor.)

Figure 1.1 *Former* Sun *editor Kelvin MacKenzie, pictured as a sewer dweller – a reference to the 'Teenage Mutant Ninja Turtle' craze of the time. What meanings, both overt and implied, does the cartoon have and how closely do they accord with your perceptions of the paper?*

As your group discuss their attitudes to the publication, it is worth reflecting on how these attitudes will affect any analysis of the paper. As well as examining preconceived ideas about a publication and its readers, it is useful to have some *historical awareness* of the product's development and knowledge of its place in a *competitive media market*. If you know how the newspaper has developed and changed in character over the years, you are more likely to understand its current attitudes and style and you will be aware that it is constantly adapting itself to different political and social conditions. This will lead you into making more subtle judgements about it. The same is true of being aware of the commercial forces which affect a publication. If you understand that a newspaper has to please its readers and advertisers above all else, or it will not survive financially, then this will lead you to produce a more informed analysis.

The production history of the *Sun*

The paper was once owned by the Mirror group, but its circulation was low by national standards – 850 000 in 1969. Before that it had been a Trades Union Congress paper known as the *Daily Herald*.

Rupert Murdoch, who already owned several newspapers world-wide and had recently purchased the *News of the World*, bought the *Sun* for £600 000 in 1969. Murdoch is boss of News International which also owns *The Times*, *The Sunday Times*, the *News of the World* and BSkyB as well as newspapers and television stations around the world.

Murdoch appointed Larry Lamb, northern editor of the *Daily Mail*, as the *Sun*'s new editor. Under his guidance the paper concentrated on 'sex, sport and sensation' and competed directly against its 'parent' the *Daily Mirror*. At first other newspapers were scathing about it. The *Morning Star* called it 'less like a sun than a paraffin lamp in a brothel' and *Daily Mirror* editor Hugh Cudlipp said it was 'no threat to anybody'. But by the third day of its publication its sales had risen to 1 650 000.

The contrast between Cudlipp and Murdoch is interesting. Cudlipp relied on market research to help him position the *Sun* in 1964. Marketing experts had detected hordes of upwardly mobile young people who wanted a paper that was an easier read than the *Daily Telegraph* but less 'common' than the *Daily Mirror*. Like many other newspapers, the *Sun* did not find the market the researchers had described. The problem was partly due to Cudlipp's belief that working-class people were essentially virtuous and anxious for self-improvement. Murdoch was different. He relied on gut feelings rather than on market research. He believed that readers mainly wanted entertainment.

The *Sun*'s first nude page 3 picture appeared on 17th November 1970. The policy of printing pictures of bare-chested women shocked some people. The Sowerby Bridge library committee banned the *Sun* from its reading room. The newspaper took advantage of the decision, and perhaps the name of the Yorkshire village, by running a series of stories about it. The headline 'The silly burghers of Sowerby Bridge' suggests the tone of the 'campaign'. This tactic of making news out of complaints against it has long been a *Sun* characteristic.

The *Sun* covered its first election in 1970 and it was firmly in favour of the Labour party.

'In the past few weeks the *Sun* has kept its promise to bring you all the Election news. Our coverage has been, as we promised, detailed, analytical and non-partisan. We also promised that we would tell you, when the time came, which way the *Sun* would vote. The time has come and the *Sun* would vote Labour.'

By 1974 it had 'reluctantly, and as a choice of evils' come out in favour of the Tories. In 1979 Rupert Murdoch declared that, 'We were all Labour-inclined when we started the *Sun* but I think we grew pretty disillusioned like the rest of the country.' Tory Central Office did its best to seek the *Sun*'s approval and Margaret Thatcher tried to influence both Murdoch and Lamb. Murdoch liked the new-style Tories because he felt they would 'break with the old school tie, the people with an inherited right to govern'. This time at the election the *Sun* said 'Vote Tory. Stop the Rot. There may not be another chance.'

20 things you didn't know about the Sun

1 In 1969 Larry Lamb took circulation from 650,000 to 1.5 million in 100 days

2 First exposed nipples (1969) belonged to model Uschi Obermeier

3 First topless Page 3 girl appeared on the new paper's first anniversary, in 1970

4 Kelvin MacKenzie appointed 1981, but doubled on the Daily Express for two months

5 MacKenzie was instantly nicknamed MacFrenzie

6 Murdoch banned MacKenzie from further TV appearances after he raved on News At 10

7 GOTCHA! headline (on the sinking of the Belgrano) was Wendy Henry's idea, not MacKenzie's

8 Henry and MacKenzie regretted it – but Murdoch approved

9 MacK's definition of political story: "Who's Maggie got her leg over, eh?"

10 Murdoch's typical rebuke: "You're a political pygmy, Kelvin."

11 Sun photographers called snapping the Royals "Whacking the Germans"

12 MacK's first thought for the infamous Hillsborough headline: YOU SCUM!

13 Initial Elton John story was MacK's brother Craig's idea

14 Last thought as Elton edition rolls: "We're all going down the pan"

15 MacK's pet name for paper: Currant Bun. Later: Curranticus Bunnicus

16 MacK's term for zipping into action: "Ferret down trousers!"

17 Ditto for crash change of splash: "Reverse ferret!"

18 Ditto for a Sun personal smear campaign: "Ferret up bum!"

19 MacK's term for hyping up a story: Scamulate

20 MacK's term for the Guardian: the World's Worst

10 THINGS THEY WISH THEY'D NEVER SAID

1 Former U.S. vice-president Dan Quale, asked if he would become a Jehovah's Witness, said no, because he "didn't see the accident".

2 The late Tory Dame Irene Ward, angry at sailors getting new uniforms ahead of Wrens asked MPs: "How long will you hold up Wrens' skirts for sailors' convenience?"

3 Harold Wilson, then PM, called Aussie leader Gough Whitlam "Whit Goughlam."

4 Richard Nixon, then President, called Mr. Wilson "Prime Minister Macmillan."

5 Quale said "bondage" was important for families.

6 Tory MP Geoffrey Dickens planned "to do a favour for every woman in the UK."

7 Quale told a group of Samoans: "You look like happy campers to me!"

8 Tory Jeremy Hanley called a riot "exuberance".

9 Ex-Tory MP Tim Jarman, jokingly addressing cattle, thanked "the village cows" for their vote. His audience was packed with Tory women.

10 Quale (again) told mourners: "Have a nice day!"

Figure 1.2 *The* Guardian *mimics a* Sun *technique.*

▶ More details of the *Sun*'s development to the end of the eighties can be found in *Stick It Up Your Punter – The Rise and Fall of The Sun* by Peter Chippindale and Chris Horrie, published by Heinemann, 1990.

Kelvin MacKenzie was appointed as editor in 1981 with the brief to fight off the challenge of the newly launched *Daily Star*, according to Roy Greenslade, a *Sun* insider, 'It is only under Kelvin's idiosyncratic and autocratic leadership that the *Sun* gained its reputation.' That reputation Greenslade describes variously as 'a byword for modern society's ills', 'a symbol of working class alienation', and 'a positive manifestation of working-class hostility to the establishment'.

Another *Sun* writer, Sean Macaulay, summed up MacKenzie's influence by saying: 'His peculiar genius is his ability to instinctively capture and, to a great extent, embody the tastes, opinions and prejudices of the English working class. When the more sanctimonious broadsheets ignore the sheer good humour and wit of the *Sun* and attack it for being crass and barbarian, what they're really attacking is most of the working class.'

Under MacKenzie the *Sun* became an enthusiastic supporter of Thatcherite policies. It took pride in claiming in the 1992 election that it had played a crucial part in the defeat of the Labour party under Neil Kinnock, especially with its dramatic front page on election day urging the last one to leave the country if Labour won to turn out the lights.

MacKenzie left in 1994 to work for Sky News, owned by Murdoch, after a circulation drop which could only be halted by a huge price cut.

The competitive market and the *Sun*

A newspaper's main commercial aim is to maintain and improve its circulation (sales). If it loses circulation it loses revenue not only from its sales price, but also from its advertising. As the total sales of all newspapers are declining, individual titles have to compete more aggressively against each other for a bigger share of a shrinking market.

Cover price

Cover price is a significant factor in newspaper purchase. Since 1969 newspaper cover prices have risen by over twice the rate of price increases in other consumer goods. At the same time retirement and redundancy among the working class has meant that there is less money for newspaper buying and if people are cutting back one of the first economies is in the weekly newspaper bill. Working patterns have also changed, with traditions such as the reading of a newspaper during a communal tea break disappearing.

One of the tactics tried by News International titles has been to cut their cover prices. News International is able to subsidise this price cut with profits from elsewhere in its empire. Titles which cannot afford to reduce prices suffer falling circulation and a drop in advertising revenue. If this continues for long enough such titles go out of business, and the survivors gain some of their readers. This means the survivors can increase their cover prices once more. There have been substantial rises in the circulation of The *Times* and the *Sun* because of their price reductions and both have been able to offset the reduction in revenue from the cover price by increasing their charges for advertisers.

TITLE	Cover Price	Circulation	% Yr-on-Yr Change	S.C.C. Rate	Colour Rate	Readership's 000's	Readers Per Copy
The Sun	23p	4,064,301	+5.5	136.00	39,700	9,999	2.5
Daily Mirror	27p	2,476,518	−1.9	100.00	32,800	6,492	2.6
Daily Star	25p	745,177	−0.8	38.50	15,092	2,001	2.7
Mirror + D. Record	-	3,235,744	−1.1	129.50	42,700	8,623	2.6
N.o.W.	50p	4,826,741	+2.4	150.00	46,400	11,913	2.5
Sunday Mirror	5op	2,550,567	−0.8	110.00	36,250	7,798	3.0
The People	50p	2,066.002	+4.0	77.00	27,300	5,185	2.5
Today	25p	594.121	+5.3	24.00	6,188	1,766	2.9
Daily Mail	32p	1,760,888	+2.6	90.00	32,760	4,400	2.5
Daily Express	32p	1,292,888	−7.5	85.00	31,500	3,250	2.5
Sunday Express	65p	1,434,309	−11.7	105.00	38,623	4,122	2.8
M.o.S.	65p	1,952,732	+0.9	107.00	38,350	5,568	2.9
The Times	20p	614,311	+36.8	39.00	23,000	1,558	2.6
D. Telegraph	3op	1,069,583	+5.1	80.00	43,500	2,659	2.5
The Guardian	45p	405,170	+0.9	36.00	16,000	1,286	3.2
The Independent	30p	287,347	−7.6	32.00	18,000	886	3.1
Financial Times	65p	389,800	−0.5	66.0	37,200	680	2.4
Sunday Times	£1	1,288,254	+3.3	105.00	55,000	3,918	3.1
S.Telegraph	70p	670,142	9.2	58.00	30,500	2,061	3.1
Observer	90p	489,957	−1.4	51.00	28,100	1,498	3.1
I.o.S.	£1	312,815	−12.3	32.00	18,000	989	3.2

Figure 1.3 Newspaper readership and circulation figures. Today *ceased publication in November 1995.*

Analysing a tabloid newspaper

Figure 1.4 Analysis of the readership of leading titles by various categories. Today is no longer published.

Circulation and advertising

The data in Figure 1.3 show how the *Sun*'s circulation compares with those of other newspapers, and how readership figures are closely related to the amounts of money charged for advertising. The daily paper with the lowest circulation, *Today*, charged the least for a page of colour advertising – £6 188 per page. The most expensive colour advertising among dailies is in the *Daily Telegraph*, £43 500 per page, but these are broadsheet pages, which are bigger than tabloid pages.

Coverage and Profile Demographic Analysis NRS JULY – DECEMBER 1994

	The Sun 000's	% Profile	Daily Mirror 000's	% Profile	Daily Star 000's	% Profile	Today 000's	% Profile	Daily Mail 000's	% Profile	Daily Express 000's	% Profile
ALL ADULTS	9,999		6,492		2,001		1,766		4,400		3,250	
SOCIAL CLASS												
C2DE	6,955	70	4,352	67	1,481	74	888	50	1,495	34	1,256	39
BC1C2	6,059	61	3,930	61	1,092	55	1,330	75	3,549	81	2,603	80
BC1C2D	8,566	86	5,593	86	1,712	86	1,614	91	3,970	90	3,000	92
ABC1	3,044	30	2,140	33	520	26	878	50	2,905	66	1,994	61
AGE												
15–24	2,153	22	1,026	16	435	22	314	18	608	14	404	12
25–34	2,343	23	1,271	20	552	28	441	25	545	12	397	12
35–44	1,561	16	928	14	401	20	308	17	639	15	463	14
45–54	1,420	14	1,051	16	274	14	277	16	915	21	587	18
55–64	1,101	11	842	13	157	8	212	12	657	15	509	16
65+	1,421	14	1,374	21	182	9	214	12	1,036	24	891	27
15–44	6,057	61	3,225	50	1,388	69	1,063	60	1,792	41	1,264	39
44+	3,942	39	3,266	50	613	31	703	40	2,608	59	1,986	61
AGE AND CLASS												
BC1C2 15–44	3,874	39	2,119	33	811	41	842	48	1,518	35	1,038	32
BC1C2 45+	2,185	22	1,811	28	281	14	488	28	2,031	46	1,565	48
ABC1 15–44	2,026	20	1,225	19	389	19	566	32	1,250	28	793	24
ABC1 45+	1,018	10	915	14	131	7	312	18	1,656	38	1,202	37
SEX												
MALE	5,514	55	3,545	55	1,306	65	1,042	59	2,220	50	1,708	53
FEMALE	4,485	45	2,947	45	696	35	724	41	2,180	50	1,542	47
MAIN SHOPPERS												
ALL MS	5,860	59	3,846	59	1,058	53	1,087	62	2,747	62	1,979	61
FEMALE MS	3,696	37	2,473	38	588	29	620	35	1,867	42	1,332	41
REGION												
LONDON & SE	3,648	36	2,147	33	403	20	712	40	2,208	50	1,125	35
MIDLANDS	1,935	19	1,156	18	290	14	298	17	579	13	474	15
SW & WALES	1,271	13	880	14	199	10	243	14	574	13	409	13
SCOTLAND	922	9	59	1	140	7	62	4	116	3	297	9
NORTH WEST	801	8	1,058	16	436	22	295	17	543	12	462	14
NORTH NE	1,423	14	1,191	18	533	27	156	9	379	9	483	15
WORKING STATUS												
FULL TIME WORK	4,806	48	2,817	43	1,148	57	971	55	1,978	45	1,396	43
FT WORK UNDER 45	3,571	36	1,950	30	947	47	697	39	1,115	25	795	24
EARNING £12,000+	2,756	28	1,743	27	587	29	733	42	1,944	44	1,317	41

Readership

Figure 1.4 shows a breakdown of the *Sun*'s readership compared with that of its closest competitors. The paper has a wide social appeal and in fact more ABC1s read the *Sun* than read any of the 'quality' broadsheets. The total readership of the *Telegraph* is just over two and a half million, whereas the *Sun* has an ABC1 readership of over three million. It is also apparent that its sales are very much higher in the South East than in other parts of the UK. Although the *Sun* is often thought to be a 'man's paper', and in fact it has more male than female readers, nevertheless it has twice as many female readers as the *Daily Mail*, which boasts a strong female readership.

▶ Audience, page 16

Newspapers compete with television in providing people with news. Most people now get their news from television. Almost every home has at least one television set and on average people watch for 24 hours a week. Television viewing is especially popular with the very people that form the main readership base of the tabloids – under 35s in the C2, D and E social classes.

The creation of habit is especially important in building future sales, yet children are drawn to television rather than newspapers for leisure and information. Popular newspapers tend to react by exploiting this interest rather than fighting it, so they provide information and opinion about television programmes and feature stories about television personalities, real and fictional.

Another marketing problem which is difficult to measure but is probably important has to do with the level of literacy. The Adult Literacy and Basic Skills Unit (ALBSU) says that 25% of people between the ages of 16 and 20 report having reading difficulties. 9% of that sample never read newspapers. The figure rises to 13% among twenty-year-olds. The *Sun* responds to the problem of low literacy levels by keeping the reading age of its contents to 12.

If you want to find out about the production history of a publication and its marketing context to help with your analysis, the sales and marketing departments of most publications will provide basic information about these issues. It is better if they have to respond to just one request per institution, rather than to individual requests. The information can then be disseminated.

Textual analysis

Here are three analyses of *Sun* material which are designed to help involve you. The analyses show how stories are put together and the way they are told (i.e. their *narrative structure*), how they are typical of popular tabloid newspaper style (i.e. their *genre*) and how they represent individuals, groups and ideas.

The first analysis is of news story, the second is of an editorial and the the third is of the *Sun's* sports coverage. These are seen as sub-genres of the main genre of popular journalism.

Analysis of a popular tabloid news story

A *broadsheet* newspaper has large pages which are the size of a rotary printing press. A *tabloid* newspaper is made of pages which are half the size of broadsheet. The word tabloid came from the name of a medicine sold in tablet form. It was then applied to any thing that was compressed or concentrated. The term 'Tabloid' applied to newspapers is often used to indicate that the contents of the paper are in a popular style with sensationalised reporting. It is sometimes used sneeringly. However, many 'quality' newspapers now have tabloid sections and a broadsheet format does not guarantee a good quality product.

Sensationalism has been defined in an interesting way by an ex-editor of the *Daily Mirror*, Silvester Bolam: 'Sensationalism does not mean distorting the truth. It means vivid and dramatic presentation of events so as to give them a forceful impact on the mind of the reader. It means big headlines, vigorous writing, simplification into familiar, everyday language and the wide use of illustration by cartoon and photograph.'

If you are analysing the story as an example of a genre you need to specify what that genre is. You could look at the story as an example of a newspaper genre and compare it with stories in books, for instance. Or you could analyse it, as here, as an example of popular tabloid journalism and contrast it with 'quality' broadsheet journalism – the kind you would find in *The Times*, the *Telegraph*, the *Independent* and the *Guardian*, for instance.

THINNA GAZZA OUT ON RAZZA WITH SHEZZA

EXCLUSIVE by MARK WOOD

SLIMLINE Paul Gascoigne is back wooing Sheryl Kyle — after ten months apart.

The soccer ace and leggy Sheryl looked "very lovey-dovey" as they enjoyed a romantic dinner at a swanky restaurant.

A fellow diner said: "Paul seemed to hang on her every word and Sheryl was equally captivated by him.

"Paul seemed to be making a special effort and sticking to mineral water."

Ex-model Sheryl, 29, looked dressed to kill in a minidress at London eaterie Langan's on Tuesday.

The couple swept away at midnight in a stretch limo.

Yesterday Gazza, 27, left Sheryl's home at Stanstead Abbots, Herts, wearing the same jeans and waistcoat he had on at Langan's the night before.

The England star, who has lost three stone, swore at reporters who asked if the couple were back together.

He yelled: "That's a load of b*******s. Now f*** off. If you stay there I'll get something to tip over you." Earlier he pelted a photographer with stones while out jogging.]

He and mum-of-two Sheryl left the house in a convertible B.M.W. Their stormy two-year affair ended last May. Two months later Gazza broke down and wept as he admitted bullying and beating Sheryl.

The star is due to be back playing with Rome team Lazio next season after recovering from a broken leg.

Fat . . . a year ago

Weight to go . . . streamline Gazza and mini-skirted Sheryl leave Langan's after their romantic dinner

STONE ME, HE'S SLIMMER THAN EVER, SEE PAGES 46 & 47

Figure 1.5 A typical Sun *news story*

In this case you could begin by simply describing the layout and appearance of the story. As a lead story on a *Sun* page it has a prominent headline in capitals printed white on black. Sometimes subsidiary headlines will be included, either above or below the main one, but not here. The picture is bigger than the story, which is quite short, about 250 words. It is labelled to look special – the word 'exclusive' is often used and is a claim that no other paper has this story. The pictures have captions which are produced in a *house style*, that is to say a style determined by the newspaper. The paragraphs are short, with the first one in bold print. The story is printed in thin columns with five or six words to a line.

> **A** **Activity**
>
> Find a lead (main) story from any page of a 'quality' broadsheet, such as the *Telegraph*, and compare it with these characteristics, noting similarities and differences. For instance, popular tabloids and 'quality' broadsheets will each have headlines over stories but the size and style will differ.

If you are looking at narrative structure, first ask what the story is about: in other words, look at its content.

This one is about a personality well known to readers. It is told as a dramatic tale involving conflict. It is about sex or romance and there are references to affluence and expensive lifestyles.

The conflicts centre on a flawed hero, Paul Gascoigne, whose fortunes have been followed by the popular press for years, and in this sense it is a continuing or 'running' story. The conflicts are both external and internal.

The main external conflict involves a sexual relationship. The story is more interesting because there is an element of mystery too. Are Paul Gascoigne and Sheryl Kyle 'back together'? The relationship also has an historical dimension to it, mentioned in the second last paragraph: 'Their stormy two-year affair ended last May.'

The second main conflict is internal. It is about Gascoigne's struggle to regain fitness. Gascoigne is newsworthy because his behaviour is contentious. He is a hero in that he can win matches for his club and country by his exceptional footballing skills. But he is flawed. He is temperamental and has been described in the past as leading a lifestyle which does not allow him to keep fit. The fact that he seems overweight and that this is due to excessive self-indulgence has made news before.

A third conflict is between Gascoigne and the media. His aggressive reactions to reporters and photographers are mentioned.

The story also touches on wealth, with references to expensive restaurants and cars.

There is also an element of suspense in the story. The story ends, as many newspaper stories do, by referring to possible future developments. 'The star is due to be back playing with Rome team Lazio next season after recovering from a broken leg.' The readers will have to wait to find out whether the footballer has retained his skills after an injury and whether the man is changed enough to sort his private life out.

Representation

A second way in which you can consider narrative structure is to look at the way in which the story is written.

There is a tendency to use descriptive words and phrases to portray people and their actions. Gascoigne is described as 'slimline', 'streamline', 'soccer ace', 'England star' and 'star'. These emphasise his appearance (in terms of fitness), his job and his importance. Sheryl Kyle is described as 'leggy', 'miniskirted', 'ex-model' and 'mum-of-two'. These emphasise her appearance in terms of sexuality, her job and her position as a member of a family.

It can be illuminating to collect such descriptions from several stories to see if men and women are represented in different terms in the *Sun*. See the suggested activity at the end of this chapter.

Language

Tabloid journalism tries to use ordinary, everyday language in its reporting. There are several words in the Gascoigne story which are colloquial: 'very lovey-dovey', 'swanky' and 'dressed to kill', for instance. But the constructions used are not those of everyday speech. 'Ooh look, there's mini-skirted Sheryl and slimline Paul Gascoigne coming out of that London eaterie', does not sound authentic.

The direct speech of Gascoigne, however, does. And the inclusion of direct speech is used to give colour and liveliness to a story. The characteristic of printing asterisks in swearwords is curious and typical of tabloid style, combining a desire to shock with a desire to appear 'respectable'.

The headline and opening paragraph are important to attracting readers into stories.

Headlines are used as labels to tell a reader quickly what stories are about, or they can provide a mystery that readers then need to explore, or they can shock.

This headline labels and surprises. It does this by being unconventional. 'Gazza' is a nickname recognised by most readers and the *Sun* often uses such nicknames. Here the headline writer is playing around with language to surprise and amuse the reader. 'Shezza' is an invented name, similar to the *Sun*'s 'Hezza' for Michael Heseltine. 'Razza', invented because of its sound, suggests razzle or razzmatazz, while 'Thinna' is mis-spelled to fit in better with the nicknames. The overall effect suggests the rhyming and the repetition of similar sounds. These are effects which you find in poetry and novels. This combination of the colloquial and the literary is typical especially of the *Sun* style of journalism. The overall effect is amusing, fitting in with the newspaper's declared policy of entertaining its readers and debunking celebrities, letting you know that the paper is not taking these people very seriously. There is also an element of self-mockery, telling you that it is not taking itself seriously.

Is this irony important in a newspaper that identifies with 'ordinary people'? Is it subverting the successful, those with wealth and power and fame? If so, which types of people does the *Sun* try to subvert? And, just as important, whom does it not subvert?

Lead paragraphs

The lead paragraph or opening of a news story is crucial. It should tell the essence of the story as succinctly as possible. It is meant to hook the reader by arousing interest and curiosity. In this case the lead is expressed in twelve words and the journalist has decided that the story is a love story.

There is a hint of another story in the word 'slimline' and there is some history ('after ten months apart'), so there are three things to arouse the reader's curiosity – why are the couple back together, why have they been apart and how come Gascoigne is slim?

Personalisation

The *personalising* of stories, which you have seen in the Gascoigne story, is an important tendency in the press, especially the popular press. The individual reference is heightened, by the supplying of personal details such as age, residence, job and personal appearance – with a liberal use of photographs.

But in his book *Language in the News*, Professor Roger Fowler says that the world presented by the popular press is not one of a collection of unique individuals but 'a culturally organised set of categories'. He sees three main categories:
- Important (elite) people doing something either spectacular or ordinary, e.g. Princess Diana re-marrying or wearing an unusual hat.
- Ordinary people if something unusual happens to them, e.g. a named person winning the National Lottery.
- Anonymous people caught up in some more general process, e.g. refugees in Rwanda.

The way a publication *categorises* people tells much about the paper's beliefs and attitudes. Here is a list of category labels taken from one issue of the *Sun*:
- Occupational: top Tory ; Cabinet MP; wealthy MP; £35 000-a-year Avon council accountant; rip-off plumbers; presenter; telly newsman; shop-owner; pensioner; medical director.
- Family roles: hard-up mums; mum-of-two; bachelor; dad-of-two; ex-wife of telly star.
- Physical appeal: stunning supermodel; £5 000 per day model; stunning schoolgirl; society beauty.
- Violence with heroes and villains: hero; louts; rioting English soccer thugs; mindless thugs; vandals.

A Activity

Collect category labels from a week's issues of the *Sun* and note what types of label appear and how frequently. Which category labels do not appear? Decide from this research what the preoccupations of the newspaper appear to be. You can try the same exercise with a range of one day's papers to see if there are any general patterns or individual differences. It would also be useful to compare a 'quality' broadsheet with a popular tabloid. This can be relevant to the study of genre characteristics and representation.

Image analysis

Here is an image analysis of the main picture that forms part of Figure 1.5.

The picture is not posed. It has the appearance of catching someone unawares. Gascoigne is not only not looking at the camera, he is walking away from it as if dismissing it. The camera seems to be helping us to intrude into someone's private life. The people being pictured seem to be resisting this process. They are not posing and smiling; one is striding purposefully away, the other is looking at the ground.

The fact that the picture was taken at night and outside a famous restaurant, we are told, seems to add to the sense of mystery and intrigue. The posture and relationship of the two people does not seem to fit with the story that they are 'back together' again. There is no contact at all between the two people in the picture.

The lighting of the photo seems odd. The woman is in the background and in a dark entrance, yet her white clothes stand out clearly. This suggests that the picture could be made up of two pictures, taken at different times but now joined together. Another possibility is that Sheryl's image could have been computer enhanced before being passed to the production department.

Figure 1.6 *The* Sun *Says*

THE SUN SAYS

Blame game

BARINGS knew something odd was going on.

The Financial Times says Nick Leeson's Singapore operation was investigated by the bank's head office last August because it had made an exceptional profit of £20 million in seven months.

The report warned of a "significant risk." But the big boys at Barings seem to have done nothing about it.

Could that be because he was making them a mint?

Leeson may have broken the bank . . .

But shouldn't someone else be taking the blame, too?

Danger ahead

RAISING a child is hard at any age. At the age of 14, it's nigh-on impossible.

That's why the future for Vicky Reid and Barry Grubb fills us with dread.

Their mums say they were "shocked and worried" when they learned the news of Vicky's pregnancy.

Let's hope other teenagers read our story and feel the same way.

They should realise that under-age sex is no game. It can wreck your life.

It's a Ken-up

WE all make mistakes . . . but the Chancellor's was particularly daft.

He praised Consett steelworks as one of the best and the most modern in Europe.

But it closed 15 years ago.

Come on, Ken. You must do your homework better.

By the way, have you read that Maastricht treaty yet . . .

Or are your views on a single currency another silly mistake?

Bad example

EVERY eight minutes there is bad language on TV.

Half the programmes include acts of violence.

Those are the disturbing findings of new research.

There'll be experts, of course, who'll say TV doesn't influence behaviour.

If so, why does it show adverts?

And finally . . .

THEY'VE got a brilliant new law in California

Commit three violent offences and you get 25 years in jail.

We should try it here.

Only trouble is there'd be fewer people at football matches.

On AND off the pitch.

Analysis of an editorial

In terms of genre characteristics an editorial in a newspaper can be recognised because it expresses the opinions and values of the newspaper as an institution. Although in practice it is written by the editor or some other senior writer from the staff, an editorials is deliberately unsigned. If it were seen as one person's opinion, it would carry less authority, and be easier to dismiss.

The editorial is always about topical issues regarded as important by the editor, though sometimes trivial issues can be the topic of an amusing or comic section. Editorials do not have pictures to illustrate them. They follow the pattern of a statement of a topical issue or problem, an analysis of that issue and suggested action, advice or moral guidance. The editorial is usually placed alongside other opinion pieces in the middle of the paper. On rare occasions an editorial can make the front page if the issue examined is significant enough.

Editorial techniques

Various narrative techniques are used to give the illusion of an authoritative speaker. The speaker addresses the readers directly and tries to persuade them to identify with the 'us' in an 'us versus them' conflict.

Look at Figure 1.6. The title of the editorial itself introduces the idea of the newspaper speaking. Compare it with 'The *Sun* Writes'.

The *typography* is used to stress certain words by using bold, underlined and italicised words. This mimics the way in which emphasis is used in speech.

The editorial uses *pronouns* (words such as 'I', 'we', 'you', 'they') to suggest it is talking directly to the reader: 'We all make mistakes', 'We should try it here'. The reader is enticed into feeling like 'one of the gang' by agreeing with what the paper is saying. The enticement is reinforced with the matiness of the language. The editorial uses phrases and words which would not be out of place in relaxed but polite conversation among friends: 'making a mint', 'nigh-on impossible', 'particularly daft', 'Come on Ken', 'silly mistake', 'by the way'.

The colloquial style of the piece is also apparent in the use of *contractions* which are mainly used in the recording of direct speech: 'it's' for 'it is' and so on. Examples from the *Sun* editorial are: 'let's', 'they've' and 'shouldn't'.

The frequency of *commands and questions* is another characteristic of spoken language. Three of the items in the editorial end with rhetorical questions; that is to say, the reader knows what answer the writer is expecting to the question. Then there are commands (orders) – 'They should realise', 'You must do your homework better', 'We should try it here'.

Another characteristic of conversational style is the use of incomplete sentences: 'On and off the pitch', for instance. There is also the unusual technique of using the second half of a sentence as a complete paragraph:

'Leeson may have broken the bank...

But shouldn't someone else be taking the blame too?'

A Activity

Re-write the editorial as a dialogue between two people having a casual conversation in a pub. Make as few changes as possible. Discuss any alterations you have to make.

Structure

The structure of most newspaper editorials is:
- statement of a problem or dilemma
- analysis of its causes
- a suggested solution.

In 'the *Sun* Says' there seems to be very little analysis, if any. The pattern is to refer briefly to a news item, personalising it where possible, and then to suggest a simple solution or reaction either directly or by implication. So in the editorial quoted here the pattern looks like:

1. Problem: a bank goes bust/one fairly insignificant man blamed.
   Solution: blame someone higher in the hierarchy.
2. Problem: being a very young parent.
   Solution: don't have under-age sex.
3. Problem: ministerial gaffe.
   Solution: do more research.
   (Tagged on to the structure here is an anti-European bias which explains why the *Sun* criticises Kenneth Clarke, a politician in favour of closer links with Europe.)
4. Problem: television is a bad influence.
   Solution: not one really – but there is an implication that readers should distrust experts who deny a causal connection between TV watching and bad behaviour.
5. Problem: violence.
   Solution: more severe punishment.

An analysis like this can lead to some conclusions about the newspaper's values and how it chooses to represent particular issues. In problems 1 and 3 there is the *Sun*'s tendency to support the little person against the system, to humble the mighty; in 2, 4 and 5 there is its rather simplistic or fundamentalist attitude to behaviour: television is bad for you, don't have too much sex, treat criminals harshly and don't trust experts or foreigners.

A Activity

Analyse ten *Sun Says* items for statement of problem, analysis of problem (if any) and suggested resolution of problem.

Examine a series of *Sun Says* editorials over a period of time to see what the newspaper's preoccupations, attitudes and values are. This evidence can be used in a study of the representation of an issue such as Britain's relationship with Europe.

Between the 10th and the 17th of February 1995 these were the items covered in *Sun* editorials:
- European law over-riding British law; dangers of closer ties with Europe; attack on single European currency; attack on European attitude to immigration (twice); attack on European policy on sexual harassment.
- Authority being too soft with scroungers; authority being too soft with Eric Cantona; authority being too tough with British soldier accused of murdering a joyrider.
- Criticism of bribes in sport; criticism of violence of English football followers (twice).
- Inequalities of pay and remuneration; excessive profits.
- Space exploration.
- The lack of security in hospitals.
- Attack on the BBC for wasting money.
- Support for commemorations of bombing of Dresden.
- Weakness of opinion polls.
- Opposition to an interest rate rise.
- Praise for British actor nominated for Oscars.
- Attack on 'cowboy' plumbers who exploited an old lady.

This is an example on a small scale of a technique called content analysis. It aims to describe short or long term trends in any aspect of media by quantifying and describing a particular characteristic. You could for example study over a period of time the amount and nature of violence shown on prime time television to see if there are any changes.

The example above shows the high priority given to persuading the readers that closer ties with Europe are undesirable. Secondly there is a concern for justice, with (usually) a demand for 'tougher' punishments. This is coupled with injustice stories (in a wide sense) where ordinary people are exploited. There is also a concern with money, how it is distributed, how it is wasted, but nothing, surprisingly, about sex. The overall impression given of the *Sun*'s 'voice' is that it expresses the attitudes of conservative, working class, urban England. It attacks greed and exploitation, especially by the powerful, but it accepts the conventional political structure – it is not revolutionary. It is suspicious of and hostile to foreign things. It is patriotic. It likes fun and scandal, but it expresses traditional moral attitudes. It favours strictness in treating law breakers. It dislikes the BBC.

Question this interpretation and compare it with your own findings. And remember, when editors change, so inevitably do editorials.

Analysis of the *Sun*'s sports coverage

The *Sun*'s sports coverage is extensive and aimed mainly at a youngish, male audience. The back page, which is always devoted to sport, is designed like a front page with a big headline and prominent picture accompanying a lead story. As many people start reading from the back of the paper the back page needs to perform the same role as a front page.

The coverage aims to complement television coverage of sports rather than compete with television. There is consequently less reporting of events and more emphasis on background stories.

> **A** **Activity**
>
> Analyse the content of the sports section of the *Sun* to determine the amount of space given to different sports. Collect information for a complete week's papers in the winter and another week's in the summer. Measure the coverage in column centimetres (a column centimetre is the space occupied by one centimetre's depth of a single column. Make sure you include information such as race cards or league tables in your calculations. Count pictures and headlines as well as body text.
>
> Now list all the sports covered. Next, find out how popular these sports are among males aged 15–25 in a sample group of people you know. How closely do the profiles of the two sets of figures correspond?

In the winter, coverage of sport in the *Sun* follows a predictable pattern. There is racing coverage every day with results, race cards, betting forecasts and form guides. The pages attract a good deal of related advertising, from bookmakers and fortune tellers, for instance. On Saturday the coverage is extensive enough to form a coloured supplement with extra copy such as a special guide to races on television.

The bulk of the rest of the coverage is of football, with rugby league, rugby union, motor sports and boxing given secondary coverage. The pattern seems to be to cover the most popular spectator sports and to address the reader as if s/he (but mainly he) is a spectator rather than a participant.

After having an overview of the sports coverage over a period of time, you can look more closely at the coverage of one sport to see if there are any conventions of reporting and how that sport is represented.

Analysing football coverage in the Sun

Saturday's *Sun* previews the weekend's fixtures. Prominence is given to Premiership matches, though there is some reference to Endsleigh League matches as well.

Structure and style

Here (Figure 1.7) is a typical preview from the *Sun* of Saturday, 11th February 1995.

The piece is *personalised* in the lead paragraph. Although the contest is between two teams, the writer chooses to focus on the *angle* of Mark Hughes' reinstatement to the Manchester United team. The other previews on the same page start in a similar way, focusing on a well-known player or a manager:

'Norwich boss John Deehan will end defender Carl Bradshaw's two-month injury nightmare...'

'Tony Adams believes Leicester will be made to suffer...'

'Lee Chapman returns to Elland Road with a chilling message...'

'Aston Villa Boss Brian Little has ordered his £2 million striker Tommy Johnson to show he has no need to buy to replace John Fashanu.'

'Best pals Kevin Gallen and Robbie Fowler are ready for a goalscoring showdown at Anfield.'

'Sol Campbell cannot forget his Spurs debut against Chelsea – he scored and was dropped for six months.'

Analysing a tabloid newspaper

ON YER MARKS

By JOHN RICHARDSON

MARK HUGHES roars back into action today alongside Andy Cole – the £7million man bought to replace him.

Soccer's unlikely alliance will be hitched up by Manchester United boss Alex Ferguson with orders to demolish the old enemy.

It will be an emotional return for Hughes, who believed his Old Trafford career was up in January when United signed Cole and he suffered his sickening knee injury.

Almost a month later Hughes returns in full battle dress, signed up to the United cause for another 2½ years.

He admitted: "I have to be honest and say I felt the Newcastle game was going to be my last for United. I said to myself before kick-off 'Let's go out with a bang.' I didn't expect it to actually happen the way it did.

"But, if I hadn't have been injured then, it would have been my last game for the club. I was never a believer in fate, but certainly am now."

Now Hughes, the cult hero of the United masses, readily admits a debt of gratitude to the supporters.

He adds: "I'll have a lump in my throat when I run out in front of the fans again.

PREMIERSHIP							
	P	W	D	L	F	A	Pts
Balckburn	27	18	5	4	58	24	59
Man Utd	27	17	6	4	48	21	57
Newcastle	27	13	9	5	45	29	48
Liverpool	26	13	8	5	45	21	47
Nottm F	27	13	7	7	40	29	46
Tottenham	26	12	6	8	44	37	42
Leeds	26	10	9	7	24	28	39
Sheff Wed	27	10	9	8	36	33	39
Wimbledon	26	10	6	10	31	40	36
Norwich	26	9	7	10	25	29	34
Arsenal	27	8	9	10	30	31	33
Chelsea	26	8	8	10	34	37	32
Man City	26	8	8	10	65	41	32
A Villa	27	7	10	10	32	36	31
Southmptn	26	6	12	8	37	42	30
C Palace	27	7	9	11	21	26	30
QPR	25	8	6	11	38	44	30
Everton	27	7	9	11	27	36	30
West Ham	26	8	4	14	24	33	28
Coventry	27	6	10	11	25	45	28
Ipswich	27	5	5	17	29	55	20
Leicester	26	4	6	16	24	45	18

They've been fantastic and have helped me get an extra year.

"The players are having a laugh about things, but I think they are pleased it has all been sorted out as well."

Fergie has an embarrassment of attacking riches, with Cole determined to add to his first goal for the club last week against Aston Villa and wingers Ryan Giggs and Andrei Kanchelskis biting at the bit.

City have not won in 10 derbies and suffered a humiliating 5-0 thumping at Old Trafford earlier this season.

Boss Brian Horton demanded: "I want my players to stand up and be counted, I want them to be strong. We don't want any repeat of the Old Trafford game. That was an absolute nightmare.

"We have to match United physically. That doesn't mean going out there to kick them, but it does mean competing."

Andy Dibble will be back in goal, with Tony Coton still suffering from the knee problem he picked up last weekend at Southampton.

KEY MAN: Mark Hughes (United).
LAST SEASON: 2-3

CREATIVE SPARK....Hughes is back in harness

Figure 1.7 'On Yer Marks'

The stories seem to hinge on *personal dramas and aggression*. In the case of the Hughes story it is the player's recovery from injury, which ironically prevented Manchester United from transferring him, which is the main interest. The irony of the fact that Hughes is to play alongside the player who was bought to replace him, Andy Cole, adds to the *emotional appeal* of the story, further enhanced by the mention of the player's rapport with the United supporters.

Conflict is introduced with the phrase 'with orders to demolish the old enemy' and the comments of the Manchester City manager about standing up and being counted and competing.

A perspective is given with the mention of City not having won in ten derbies and there is a reference to the earlier derby match which Manchester United won 5–0. A game is sometimes put into perspective in terms of its relevance to the teams' league positions, to a manager's future, or to recent performances.

The piece ends with *information*: team news and last season's result together with a judgement about a 'key player', part of the personalising process and linked with the star player feature of the match report in Monday's paper.

So the narrative pattern seems to be:
- personalise
- dramatise
- appeal to the emotions
- highlight conflict
- put match in context
- inform.

The world of sport is seen in terms of individuals rather than teams (stressing individualism, not collectivism) and conflict rather than co-operation.

PETER PUTS 'EM ALL IN SHADOW

By PETER FITTON

Man City 0 Man Utd 3

WHEN Peter Schmeichel stands up to be counted, it suddenly goes dark for the rest of football.

He is the John Wayne of goalkeepers – a massive hulk of a man who simply shuts out the light, and the goals.

Manchester United take on a different aura when he is around. They look and play like true-grit champions.

And that has not been the case during a winter campaign when even manager Alex Ferguson's closest admirers would seriously question his team.

For much of this season, Schmeichel has been missing. Lying flat on his back, wracked with pain and wondering if his career was over.

But he emerged from a derby success talking soccer sense.

The great Dane spoke in glowing terms about the impregnability of his defence and the sharpened killer instinct that left City close to the relegation ditch.

But the actions of the man speak loudest. In 23 games Schmeichel has managed an astonishing **FOURTEEN** clean sheets, lost just twice and been a winner 16 times.

Carry that through until May and Blackburn's Kenny Dalglish might be spluttering over his cornflakes.

Schmeichel cautioned: "Blackburn will get a lot of points in the weeks ahead, but we are getting our act together again.

"We haven't had the best first half. We lost and drew too many games and didn't play as well as in the past two seasons.

"In this game, though, we started to play our entertaining, high-class football again. It proved the confidence is back.

"We were attempting things again we wouldn't have tried two months ago. Now I feel we can clinch a hat-trick of titles."

City boss Brian Horton compared United to a well-run machine. His own team are still bits and pieces on the garage floor.

They did not have the full-back cover to resist Ryan Giggs and Andrei Kanchelskis. Or an experienced ball-winner able to sit and hold when the going got tough.

United skipper Steve Bruce said: "Once we scored we just ran over the top of them. Defensive discipline was abandoned as City lost their heads."

The growing concern in the City camp is that Horton might lose his permanently after collecting just four points from the last 30.

Andy Cole notched his second goal in a week and helped create the other two for Kanchelskis and Paul Ince. Schmeichel kept a clean sheet. Now the race **IS** on.

DREAM TEAM

★ **star man** ★

BRIAN McCLAIR (Man Utd). Self-sacrificing star recognised more in team than on terraces.

★ ***Sun* ratings** ★

MAN. C: Dibble 6, Summerbee 6, Brightwell 5, Gaudino 6, Curle 7, Kernaghan 6, Brightwell 6, Walsh 6, Rosler 6, Flitcroft 7, Beagrie 5, (Quinn 6), Subs not used: Burridge, Hill. Booked: Beagrie, Quinn, D. Brightwell.

MAN UNT: Schmeichel 7, Irwin 7, Bruce 7, Sharpe 6, Pallister 8, Ince 8, McClair 9, Giggs 8, Kanchelskis 7 (May 6), Cole 8, Neville 6 (Scholes 6). Subs not used: Walsh. Booked: Ince.

REF: P Don (Hanworth Park) 6:

REMAINING FIXTURES

FEBRUARY 18 Arsenal (h), **Feb 22** Norwich (a), **Feb 25** Everton (a).

MARCH 4 Ipswich (h), **Mar 7** Wimbledon (a), **Mar 11** Tottenham (h), **Mar 18** Liverpool (a).

APRIL 1 Leeds (h), **APR 8** Southampton (h), **Apr 15** Leicester (a), **Apr 17** Chelsea (h), **Apr 29** Coventry (a).

MAY 6 Sheff Wed (h), **May 13** West Ham (a).

I'M YOUR MAN . . . striker Andy Cole wheels away after notching his second United goal of the week Picture: BRIAN WILLIAMSON

The match **report** on Monday follows the same kind of pattern (see Figure 1.8.) It is accompanied by two pictures, a large one taken from behind the goal, with the ball, which looks as though it has been pasted on to make the picture more dramatic, nestling in the net and Andy Cole wheeling away in triumph after scoring. A Manchester City defender lies despairingly on the ground in the mud. It captures an *emotional climax* in the game, with the dejection of the loser and the elation of the winner. Another picture shows two United players celebrating a goal.

The report under the headline 'Peter Puts 'Em All In Shadow' *personalises* the story by focusing on United goalkeeper Peter Schmeichel. What happened to 'key man' Mark Hughes? He wasn't even playing, which shows that if you are going to personalise a story you need to pick the right person. There is no mention in the report of Hughes' absence.

Figure 1.8 'Peter Puts 'Em All In Shadow'

The report begins as most do by *focusing on one player*, showing the media's liking for and reinforcement of the star system. It does not pretend to be factual and objective. On the contrary, it uses a literary style which is typical of *Sun* feature writing. 'When Peter Schmeichel stands up to be counted, it suddenly goes dark for the rest of football.' This exaggeration is more typical of fiction than of factual reporting. Then there is a metaphor (a direct comparison) – Schmeichel is John Wayne (the hero) – followed up in the third paragraph with a reference to one of Wayne's films: 'They look and play like true-grit champions' when Schmeichel is playing for Manchester United.

The language of the first part of the report is *emotionally charged* with phrases like 'take on a different aura', 'the great Dane', 'wracked with pain', 'sharpened killer instinct'.

But then the tone changes with the reference to Manchester City being close to the 'relegation ditch'. It is interesting that the report might well have focused on City's struggle against relegation, which for some people is a more important story than Manchester United's fight for the championship, but the convention of tabloid sports reporting is to concentrate on success.

After the glowing tributes to Schmeichel, the quotations from him are mundane, close to cliche. The imagery becomes more *down-to-earth* or *homely* with an image of Kenny Dalglish, manager of Blackburn Rovers who United were challenging for the championship, spluttering over his cornflakes and the Manchester City team like a car in bits and pieces on the garage floor. It descends to football *jargon* in the second last sentence with Schmeichel keeping a 'clean sheet'.

The report ends with the nomination of a star performer and the marking of individual performances, emphasising the newspaper's preoccupation with *individuality and personality*.

A Activity

You can compare this style of report with one from a broadsheet on the same match (see Figure 1.9) but presenting a very different view of the game. What are the similarities and differences in relation to:

- match events
- individual players and managers
- the significance of the game
- the conditions and atmosphere the match was played in
- the supporters
- Schmeichel's role in the game?

As well as analysing particular stories, you should take a close look at the coverage of sport over a period of time, say a week. Try to discover patterns in what you read. In the week beginning February 14th it was obvious that

Analysing a tabloid newspaper

stories involving conflict, or reported in a way which emphasised conflict, took precedence. There was, for instance, a prominent picture of a goalkeeper being shown the red card and a story about his manager 'fuming' over his suspension. There were stories about a boxer threatening to pull out of a fight because of a tax bill, an argument between Manchester United and the professional footballers' union leader, Gordon Taylor and even a fishing story involving allegations of cheating. The language of the stories emphasised conflict with words like 'crackdown', 'clash', 'smashed', 'giving the bullet', or 'boot' and sentences such as 'Wales will have to walk over Dean Richard's dead body if they are to derail England's Grand Slam bandwaggon.'

Then when serious conflict did occur and a football match in Ireland had to be abandoned because of the violent behaviour of English supporters, the coverage became emotional and angry. On the front page a child's bewildered face appeared with the headline 'Why are they all doing it dad, it's only a game?' On the sports page, however, John Sadler, who 'gives it to you straight' began angrily: 'It starts today. The silent war. And it is a war of attrition that we must win.' He called the people who were responsible for the violence at the soccer match, 'urban terrorists', 'vermin', 'scum', 'right-wing rabble' and 'thugs'. The rugby writer joined in the outrage against the 'unemployed or menial trash who band together for England soccer matches and drag the Union Jack into the gutter'. And letter writers were selected who expressed the same sentiments: 'Castrate the yobs and all who follow them.'

The *Sun* sports writers seem to want to report and even invent conflict in their stories, but then to condemn it with a self-righteous outrage and in aggressive language when it actually happens.

A Activity

How is football represented in the *Sun*?

Look at one week's football stories and the pictures that accompany them.

Look at the topics of the background stories and the angles chosen by the writers.

Consider the captions and think about how they determine the meanings of the pictures.

Analyse the language of the reporting and consider the kinds of conflict and the types of emotions that are predominant.

You can compare this with the football coverage of a broadsheet newspaper such as the *Guardian*, *The Times*, the *Independent* or the *Telegraph*.

You could also compare national coverage of specific games with local or regional coverage of the same games. In this way you will also build up a picture of the genre of popular national tabloid sports journalism and be able to analyse the narrative patterns of stories.

Figure 1.9 'United Deliver a Dose of Salts'

Manchester City 0, Manchester United 3

United deliver a dose of salts

Commentary
David Lacey

LOCAL derbies, by tradition, are a law unto themselves, owing more to the conflicting passions of the day than to form and league position. Regular meetings of the Old Firm are still no places for the infirm, no matter how well Rangers or Celtic appear to be doing at the time.

Other examples of the derby syndrome are too numerous to mention. But in one English city convention has been abandoned. Here, derby days are no longer occasions for close encounters of the bilious kind. Rather they have become bi-seasonal victory parades put on to remind any lingering doubters who is in charge.

On Saturday, Manchester United resumed their game of leapfrog with Blackburn at the top of Premiership by beating Manchester City 3-0 at Maine Road, having already over-whelmed them 5-0 at Old Trafford in November. In the league City have not defeated United at home for five seasons, and they last beat them away in 1973-74.

The latest reminder of Mancunian inequalities was delivered less in the spirit of Epsom Downs than Epsom Salts, the latter being a reasonable analogy for the ease with which Alex Ferguson's attack eventually moved through Brian Horton's defence. Even without Cantona, Hughes and Keane, the champions looked worthy of their title as they achieved their biggest away victory of the season so far.

Naturally the winning manager was all aglow. Ferguson had not been top since November. "All we need to do is keep reaching our capabilities," he said. "Today our performance in the second half was outstanding."

With this it was difficult to argue, and the manager of City was not in an argumentative mood. "United play the same way whether they are winning 1-0 or losing 1-0," Horton enthused. "Bruce and Pallister have been outstanding for them in both our games this season. They're playing the ball across the back like the Liverpool of old. We play one ball across the back and we've got to go forward. They kept the ball, we gave it away; that was the difference."

Apart from consoling himself that City had shaded the first half, which in terms of possession was undeniable even if this did merely emphasise their shortcomings near goal. Horton's was hardly a discordant voice amid the general chorus of praise with which United's apparent return to better form was greeted.

Certainly Giggs has regained almost all of his old desire to destroy defences and on Saturday inflicted on the right-hand side of City''s defence the punishment its left had suffered against Kanchelskis at Old Trafford. In this Giggs was ably assisted by Cole, who once Scholes had been introduced to the United attack frequently moved wide to display the vision and awareness which Ferguson always insisted he had.

Gary Lineker said on Match of the Day that Cole was always taking up positions between defenders. True enough, but surely that was what the pundits were saying about Romario, and his destruction of Bruce and Pallister, when United were bundled out of the European Cup by Barcelona rather in the manner that City were beaten on Saturday.

A sense of proportion would appear to be essential where matches such as this are concerned. United did play with consummate authority once Ince's shot had gone in off Summerbee, and though Kanchelskis's goal owed something to Dibble's error in allowing the ball to sneak in at the near post, the passing and movement which saw Cole complete the victory could hardly have been bettered.

Yet the shambolic state of a City defence playing with a reserve goalkeeper and make-shift full-backs was hardly a yardstick by which to judge championship, let alone European, potential. Horton's players have not won a league fixture since the beginning of November and are now two points off the bottom four.

Ferguson thought Horton's approach to the match had been positive. As the rain swept across Maine Road and it became obvious that City were being hung out to drip dry, the home supporters began to go home in droves. The name of Horton was mentioned in conjunction with several adjectives and adverbs. But positive was not among them.

SCORERS: Manchester United: Ince (58 min), Kanchelskis (74), Cole (77). **Manchester City:** Dibble; Summerbee, Curle, Kernaghan, D. Brightwell, Gaudino, I. Brightwell, Flitcroft, Beagrie (Quinn, 63), Rosler, Walsh. **Manchester United:** Schmeichel; Irwin, Bruce, Pallister, Neville, (Scholes, 53), Kanchelskis (May, 82), Ince, McClair, Sharpe, Cole, Giggs. **Referee:** P Don (Hanworth Park).

37

Analysing a tabloid newspaper

Figure 1.10

GAZZA'S SHAZZA HAZZA BIG NEW BRAZZA

She's up for 34C cup after star buys £3,000 boob job

Now... Sheryl with a 34C chest   Then... 34A Sheryl and Gazza

By ANDY COULSON

PAUL Gascoigne's girlfriend Sheryl Kyle was over the moon yesterday as she admired her new £3,000 assets.

Gazza paid for her boob-enlargement op. An now Sheryl, like the soccer star, has plenty of front after going from a 34A to 34C. Gazza, 27, forked out for the implants to make up for cruelly nicknaming the blonde ex-model "Sheryl No-Boobs."

And the day after the op the cheeky England star sent a bunch of roses to her home in Stanstead Abbots, Herts, addressed to "Dolly Parton."

Brilliant

A friend said: "Sheryl has wanted to have her boobs done but has always backed out.

"Paul used to take the mickey out of her something rotten, calling her Sheryl No-Boobs.

"She always laughed but deep down she longed for a bigger chest. When he offered to pay for the operation she was thrilled and the results are really brilliant.

EXCLUSIVE

"Sheryl is so proud of the implants. They look terrific – like two halved footballs."

The pal added: "Paul's had a good look at Sheryl's new chest. He thinks it was money very well spent.

"She was agonising over going for a 34B or a 34C but decided to go for the big one."

Gazza and mum-of-two Sheryl, 30, are back together after breaking off their engagement last May following a series of violent rows.

Further activities

Collect descriptions of men and women from ten *Sun* stories and contrast the ways in which gender is represented. You can also collect pictures and analyse these in the same way. In particular you could look at the images of page 3 women and compare these with the images in the women's supplement. Don't neglect the captions as you have to study the way text and image relate to each other and captions are often used to guide the reader into a particular interpretation of an image (sometimes referred to as *anchorage*).

In *Stick It Up Your Punter* Horrie and Chipperfield compare the *Sun*'s attitude to royalty with a gamekeeper who nurtures pheasants so that they can be brought out and shot for sport when desirable. Study the *Sun*'s coverage of one the following to determine groups who can be 'shot for sport':
- Royalty
- left-wing councils
- soap stars
- lesbians and homosexuals
- social workers
- teachers
- pop stars.

Are these groups always criticised?

For the picture of Gascoigne and Sheryl write alternative captions for these interpretations: Gascoigne has had an argument with Sheryl; Sheryl is pursuing him; Gascoigne has been thrown out of a restaurant for being too casually dressed; others of your own invention, the more bizarre the better.

Analyse the follow-up to the Gascoigne story: 'Gazza's Shazza Hazza Big New Brazza' (see Figure 1.10).

Assignment

Analysis of a tabloid newspaper
Select one of these to study:
- Downmarket (aimed mainly but not exclusively at the lower social classes) tabloids – the *Sun*, the *Daily Mirror*, the *Daily Record*, the *Daily Star*.
- Middle market tabloids (aimed mainly but not exclusively at the middle classes) – the *Daily Express*, the *Daily Mail*.

Read several copies of the selected title over a period of time – at least a week.

Choose extracts for comparison from broadsheet papers such as the *Guardian*, the *Independent*, the *Daily Telegraph*, *The Times* or the *Scotsman*.

Obtain information from the publishers and library sources about the production history and marketing circumstances (such as circulation figures) of the title.

Choose a topic for genre and narrative structure study from:
- news stories
- features
- sports reporting
- editorials
- columnists
- gossip
- comic strips and photo stories
- politics.

Image analysis
Compare different newspapers' picture coverage of the same event. Find examples of captions giving different interpretations of similar pictures.

Study repeated images on the same theme, such as sport, entertainment or politics. Try to describe any patterns and formulae you notice.

Representation
Choose one of these topics in detail:
- continental foreigners
- women
- men
- criminals
- sport
- protest groups
- teachers
- health workers
- trades unions
- teenagers
- homosexuals
- the armed forces
- any group, ideology or major event which is receiving current news coverage.

2 | Analysing magazines

▶ Why analyse?, page 10

This chapter shows you how to analyse magazines, and magazines aimed at teenage audiences in particular. In GNVQ you have to analyse media images and print formats. In this analysis you are expected to understand how the meaning of any text depends on the text itself, the audience and the industry which produces the text. See the general introduction section on analysis.

This chapter is organised into the following sections:
- Introduction to analysing magazines
- What is a magazine?
- How to analyse a magazine
- An analysis of a female teenage magazine
- An analysis of a male teenage magazine

Introduction to analysing magazines

If you decide to study magazines, you need to explain the surface meaning and the implied meanings found in them. You will also have to show that you understand: how the meaning of any text depends on the text itself, the audience and the industry which produces the text; and how the format of teenage magazines is distinctive – how it differs from, say, a newspaper or from a gardening magazine. You are in addition expected to look at the way stories are told in teenage magazines.

The analytic technique used here is only one of many possible strategies. You should refer to the section in the introduction to this book which gives others.

▶ Why analyse?, page 10

The emphasis here as elsewhere in the book is on the analysis of popular media products. By definition, these are likely to be influential on contemporary culture and, in analysing them, you should develop your understanding of how mass media can influence society and how individuals can make use of the media products available to them.

A Activity

Write down your own definition of the word 'magazine'. In a group, discuss your definition and those of other members. Then look up the definition in a dictionary. Discuss how your group's definitions differ from the one in the dictionary.

What is a magazine?

Print magazines may be distinguished from newspapers by the following characteristics:
- They have less 'news' than newspapers.
- They have features of more permanent interest, so that they are kept around longer.
- They tend to use more colour, illustrations and photographs than newspapers.
- They tend to be more specialised than newspapers. Magazines are aimed at specific audiences more narrowly defined in terms such as age, gender, lifestyle and interests.
- They are not normally printed on newsprint paper, and tend to use more glossy paper.
- Magazines usually appear less frequently, i.e. they appear weekly, fortnightly, monthly or quarterly.
- Magazine pages are usually bound together, by staples or glue.

Often 'magazine', 'periodical' and 'journal' refer to much the same item. The term 'magazine' suggests a colloquial and popular publication, whereas 'journal' suggests a 'serious' periodical with an up-market, minority audience. 'Periodical' is the more general term which librarians use.

The production history of the magazine

The origins of mass-circulation magazines in Britain go back to the first materials produced on the printing press in the sixteenth century which were intended to make money by being 'popular'. Many publishers in the sixteenth and seventeenth centuries saw business opportunities in subjects which would attract the interest of the wider public. The materials produced were published in a wide range of forms: single sheet, pamphlet, and cheaply bound books. What they had in common with the popular magazine of more recent times was their relatively low cost, and their informal, sometimes 'naughty' tone. Where they were different was in the fact that they concentrated on a single subject, and were 'one-off' publications. They might be sensational accounts of 'real events' or stories, or songs and jokes, medical advice of dubious value, or calendars of events. In the seventeenth century, 'chapbooks' (cheap books) with a greater mixture of items appeared. These were small, paper-covered booklets with items such as ballads, fortune telling, jokes, stories and other bits and pieces which appealed to a wide audience. The main limit on their appeal was that the majority of the population could not read or write.

Figure 2.1 A seventeenth-century woodcut

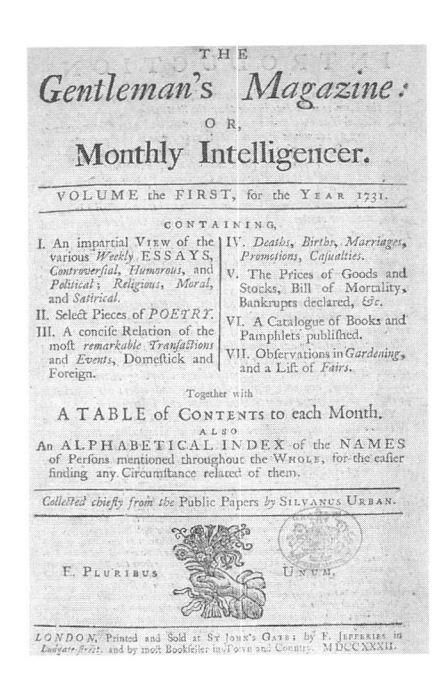

Figure 2.2 Cover page and contents page from the Gentleman's Magazine.

Figure 2.3 An early front cover from The Ladies' Mercury.

From early in the seventeenth century, the first publications which could be called newspapers or magazines began to appear, although such distinctions were not made at the time. The circulations of all newspapers and periodical publications were small by comparison with today. Some of the first periodicals to appear were publications called 'serials'. They originated in publisher's lists of books for sale, which developed to include extracts from books, reviews and illustrations printed from woodcuts. The first 'women's magazine' was *The Ladies' Mercury* (1693). This included advice on marital relationships and asked readers to write in with their own questions.

During the eighteenth century periodicals developed in their use of advertising, and in their range of content. In the early eighteenth century the periodical titles, Tatler and the Spectator, which are still used today for magazines, first appeared. It is estimated that at this time the total circulation of all newspapers and magazines published was under 50 000. The first periodical to use the word 'magazine' was the *Gentleman's Magazine* (published between 1731 and 1907). The first issue was laid out like a book and had a table of contents at the front to assist the reader. The contents included reviews of books and essays, advertisements, an item on witchcraft, poetry, prices of goods and stocks, lists of bankrupt persons, a list of fairs and some comments on gardening(see Figure 2.2). The first issue of the magazine opened with 'A View of the Weekly Essays and Public Controversies' written by Dr Samuel Johnson which criticised the poor level of debate in Parliament.

In the nineteenth century different types of magazine, such as political magazines, women's magazines, boy's magazines and professional magazines (e.g. *The Lancet*, the journal of the British Medical Association), developed and became established types. The first mass-circulation women's magazine, *The Englishwoman's Domestic Magazine* (first published in 1852), reached a circulation of 50 000 copies. It included cookery, fashion, dressmaking patterns, competitions and a problem page. Magazines also built up wider audiences and became more popular. The *English Illustrated Magazine* in 1884 was one of the first popular illustrated magazines to use photographs as illustrations. Developments in education for all from 1870 meant that literacy improved, and by the end of the century the mass of the population could read and write. The first real mass-circulation magazines appeared towards the end of the century. *Titbits*, a popular entertainment publication in the form of stories and competitions became the first magazine to sell a million copies.

During the twentieth century, magazines continued to grow in popularity, and 'pulp' magazines from the United States, named from the cheap paper pulp which was used in their manufacture, began to influence the medium. 'True confessions' and crime story magazines were introduced from America. Film magazines reached a peak of popularity in the 1920s and 1930s. *Photojournalism* magazines such as *Life* (in the US) and *Picture Post* (in the UK) appeared in the late 1930s.

The first magazines for the teenage market appeared in Britain in the 1950s with titles such as *Boyfriend, Marilyn, Mirabelle, Romeo, Roxy* and *Valentine*. These magazines featured romantic stories and used line-drawn picture stories. The spread of television into homes in the late 1950s and early 1960s drove down the readership of many magazines. Newspapers also began to borrow ideas for their contents from magazines in order to compete with television. The first newspaper colour supplement magazine was the *Sunday Times Magazine* (1962). *Private Eye*, the satirical magazine, originated as an alternative magazine in the 1960s.

Representation

The way that men and women are shown in magazines has changed over the years. In modern magazines, for example, these representations reflect the changes in the relations between the sexes in the late twentieth century. Women's magazines in the 1950s were very much about 'the home'. In the 1960s fashion was more emphasized. In the 1970s and 1980s more varied and independent roles for women were represented. In the 1990s topics and issues such as recreational sex, sexual harassment, rape, equal rights and women at work are dealt with in ways which are more 'open' than would have been considered acceptable in the past. At the same time, this new openness about sexuality has been used to promote consumerism and 'sell' goods. Men's magazines have also been a developing area. Men's magazine titles such as *Arena* and *GQ* appeared in the 1980s, recognising that representations of masculinity were changing, and new titles continue to appear.

This brief and partial history shows that the answer to the question, 'what is a magazine?' has changed over time. It also shows that magazines are part of national and popular culture. Nowadays, the magazine market is very varied. The number and variety of magazine titles is astonishing, as a browse among the shelves of any large newsagent will tell you. Interestingly, nobody seems to keep count of absolutely all the titles produced. The number of business and consumer titles which take advertising was estimated at over 6 600 in 1993. Business and professional magazines account for the greatest number of titles, although individual consumer and lifestyle magazines have larger mass audiences. Magazines are some of the fastest changing media; titles change hands, new titles are born and old titles die more frequently and more rapidly than in the newspaper industry.

Teenage magazines

One of the most volatile markets is that for teenage magazines. EMAP plc, which among many others owns the titles *More!* and *Match*, examined on pages 48–60, is the second largest magazine publisher in the UK. It owns most of the top teenage magazines including *Smash Hits*, *Just Seventeen*, *Looks* and *Big!* Teenage magazines are very widely read: according to EMAP, 96% of teenagers read at least one a week. Teenage magazines are worth considering as a specialist medium. They offer particular attractions to teenage audiences. For example, it has been pointed out that the problem page is probably used by most readers as a source of entertainment, although it can also be an important source of information and advice to many readers. Teenage magazines may be further classified according to their appeal to male or female audiences. Female-orientated magazines for young women and girls such as *Just Seventeen* and *More!* concentrate on heterosexual relationships and their problems, gossip about the media, showbiz (young stars in particular) and fashion features. Male-orientated magazines tend to avoid the areas of emotions and relationships. Magazines for teenage males are often focused upon topics which are 'informative' and which they can discuss, such as sport, computer games and music.

Examples include *Match* and *Nintendo Magazine System*. There are also magazines such as *Smash Hits* which cater for both female and male teenagers in a more equal way.

> ### A Activity
>
> In this activity, you are encouraged to consider your own experience of magazine reading, and how these magazines relate to audiences, beginning from your own experience of reading magazines. Use the following questions to help you consider these points before you move on.
>
> 1 What magazines do you read, when do you read them, where and how often?
>
> 2 Why do you read these magazines? In other words, how do you find them enjoyable, or useful?
>
> 3 What language and images do you expect to find in teenage magazines which are:
>
>   a) female-orientated?
>
>   b) male-orientated?

How to analyse a magazine

There are many different ways to analyse a magazine. The method which is used in this chapter is just one way, and you do not have to follow it exactly.

Basic information

When you start to analyse a magazine you need to establish the basic information about the title of the magazine, what type of magazine it is, who produces it, how many copies it sells (its circulation), at whom it is aimed, how often it comes out, how much it costs, how many pages it has.

A copy of the magazine will tell you most of what you need to know, but some further background information about the producer and the circulation is also important. You can find background information of this kind in various guides, such as *Benn's Media Directory*, the *Guardian Media Guide* and *Willing's Press Guide*, usually available in the reference sections of libraries. *The Magazine Writer's Handbook* by Gordon Wells is also useful; although much of it is out of date, it gives an overview of the magazines in more detail than you will find in the more up-to-date directories. The entries in these reference books will give you reliable information about circulation, and an objective description, without hype.

The magazine itself will give you the basics of frequency, cost, number of pages and the company which is the producer/publisher. You will find the information about who produces the magazine at the foot of one of the pages at either the back or the front of the magazine.

Type of content

Reference books classify magazines by their contents in terms such as business, professional, consumer, lifestyle, outdoor activities, music, computers, women, teenage etc. One of the best guides to the content of a magazine is the categories it uses on its contents page.

▶ *Benn's Media Directory*, Benn, published annually

▶ *Guardian Media Guide*, published annually

▶ *Willing's Press Guide*, British Media Publications, published annually

▶ Wells, G., 1986, *The Magazine Writer's Handbook*, Allison and Busby.

Looking at the contents of mass circulation magazines of the 'consumer and lifestyle' type, there are certain predictable features. 'Factual' material will predominate, although there may be some fiction, nearly always in short story form. Some features will follow a regular format which is repeated each week such as a day in the life of somebody, or a page giving readers' feedback on previous issues. A substantial amount of material will be about personalities in various forms based on interviews. Features which are led by consumer products vary from those which resemble advertisements to those which show some choice or evaluation of the products. Features which are based on issues may cover causes for concern, scandals, social and health problems. The following will also crop up in some form or other: advertising; layout and selling devices such as the cover, contents page and headings; reviews; news; comment or gossip. Other types of feature which may appear include serialisations, diaries, humour, letters, advice columns and problem pages, features concerned with health, fashion and appearance ('beauty' in women's magazines), horoscopes, quizzes, games, competitions and crosswords.

When you look at a magazine you can usually pull out certain titles and features as 'characteristic' of the general content and style. For example, 'fashion and beauty' items, such as a feature about beachwear, might be typical of a mainstream female-orientated teenage magazine. A feature about gadgets, such as personal stereos, or stop-watches, might be more typical of a male-orientated magazine.

Advertising

Advertising pays profits for the magazine publisher, and can help keep the cover price of the magazine down. Magazine producers tell companies who make products of interest to their readers about their target audience, and sell them advertising space.

You can tell a lot about a magazine and its relationship with its readers by looking at the advertising it contains, the language and images used, and by taking note of categories of products which are frequently advertised. Advertisers buy space in magazines because they can reach a more precisely defined target audience than in wider cast media forms. It is noticeable from the analysis of *Match* on pages 57–60 that mail order firms selling football sportswear and shoes are attracted to the magazine audience.

Magazine advertising grabs attention by offering a 'hook', such as something unexpected. It will usually go on to offer the reader either something they need or something they find interesting and/or amusing in itself. The advertisement may then give some detailed information for the reader who wants to buy the product offered.

Layout and cover page

In the simplest terms, layout is the look of the page. Are columns used, and if so, how many? How are images organised on the page? Are they double, full or part page? If an image 'bleeds off' the page it extends over or across the margins of the page. How are headlines and sub-headings used? The size, case and typeface of headlines are important. Headlines may have lead ins, explanations or elaborations above or below them, called 'straplines'. What are the effects of the layout adopted, and why are they there?

Front covers are the 'shop window' for any magazine. They tell the casual browser about the product, and are intended to motivate the target audience to purchase. Their use of images is aimed to appeal directly to the target audience, persuading them to buy with sensational titles or 'sell lines'.

Language

You can analyse written language in terms of words, phrases, sentences, punctuation and typeface. For example, popular lifestyle magazines will often use bold typeface, and punctuation in the form of exclamation marks and question marks to attract attention to their contents. For similar reasons, they will use words with sensational connotations to attract attention to their contents. You can also describe the kind of language used, and how it relates to the images, subject matter, and other factors, such as audience. For example, subject matter and audience in computer magazines are reflected in a rather technical kind of language, with many jargon words, directed at a male audience.

Language is always in a process of change, with new ways of speaking and new vocabulary gaining ground. Teenage magazines often reflect these changes, and challenge ideas of what is 'correct' in writing. It is useful to be able to compare the language of magazines with what is 'normal' in writing generally, or the rules taught by teachers and described in grammar books. The kind of writing which is usually taught in schools and described in grammar books is called 'standard English'. In general, and overall, most magazines use more 'standard English' than 'non-standard English'. However, when magazine texts do show the use of 'non-standard forms' it is important to observe and describe these in detail since they can tell us a lot, not only about the character of the magazine, but also about its attempts to suit the language to the target audience and the subject. Popular magazines often use the written language in ways which copy how their audiences speak. Teenage magazines, for example, vary in how much slang they use, but where it appears it often reflects the ways that teenagers speak.

Images

The *denotation* of magazine images, or in other words, 'what is shown', can be put into simple categories, such as pictures showing people and pictures showing objects. People can be further categorised in terms of the type of shot (e.g. head and shoulders/full figure/group) and/or other distinctions such as age, gender and ethnic group.

▶ Image analysis using a semiotic approach, page 10

Once you have worked out the common categories of image which recur, you can count up the number of images in each category. This type of analysis is called 'content analysis'. Begin by looking through the images in the magazine to be analysed. Make a note of the categories which the images break down into, such as:
- photographs/illustrations
- people/objects
- male/female
- models/celebrities etc.

You can count through all the complete images in the magazine keeping a running total, and at the same time a tally of all the images in particular categories. Content analysis can be useful in providing evidence of the importance of certain images, and any significant omissions. For example, it will be significant if you find that only one sex is represented, or that one sex is more frequently represented in a magazine. Content analysis can also be used to show the existence of stereotyping, as where images frequently represent a group engaging in certain types of activity. For example, a car magazine which shows only males engaging in car mechanics is following, or reinforcing, a stereotype.

Two researchers called Masse and Rosenblum published a study in 1988 which analysed 564 advertisements from the 1984 editions of three male-orientated and three female-orientated magazines. They found that in the advertising images in male-orientated magazines, males were unlikely to be touching one another or gazing at others. By contrast, in the images in female-orientated magazines, they found that males were more likely to touch one another and gaze at others.

▶ See Masse and Rosenblum, 1988, 'Male and female created they them...' *Women's Studies International Forum* *II* (2), 127–144.

▶ Also quoted in Craig M., (ed), 1992, *Men, Masculinity and the Media*, p. 16.

You will notice that 'content analysis' is a good technique for sorting a large amount of information. You may also notice that the decision about what category to put an image into is almost a matter of personal decision. This is a weakness of most content analyses, since the decision about what categories to use, and how to fit the information into those categories is arbitrary, and often subjective.

When you carry out 'image analysis' you take apart an image and take note of everything which affects the appearance and meaning of the image. It is useful to organise your analysis under concepts such as *denotation* and *connotation*. For example, the painting of the *Mona Lisa* carries the denotation of a woman smiling. The connotations, or 'what is meant', include 'mystery' (why is she smiling?) and the high status of 'fine art'.

▶ Image analysis using a semiotic approach, page 10

Relationships between language and images

The following terms are useful in helping to describe relations between images and text:
- picture-led
- text-led
- anchorage.

When the written language in a feature is there just to support or 'explain' the image, the feature can be said to be *picture-led*. When the images are there purely to support or illustrate the writing, then the feature is *text-led*. Teenage magazines, in general, are often described as picture-led, although they usually contain some features where the written text is leading, and pictures are in a secondary, illustrative role.

When you look at an image or read a piece of writing, a number of interpretations are possible. However, images tend to be more open to a greater number of different interpretations than writing. The way in which the writing which accompanies pictures 'ties down' certain meanings, as when a caption 'explains' an image, is referred to as *anchorage*.

Teenage magazines are dominated by images of young people. In female-orientated magazines these images repeat such connotations as 'beauty', 'celebrity' and 'having a good time'. The caption, or accompanying text, will anchor the meaning of such images, indicating purposes such as to indulge in gossip about a celebrity, or gain information about the clothing a model is showing off.

Conclusion: the 'character' of a magazine

If you ask people to describe their favourite magazine they will come out with descriptions such as 'stylish', 'friendly', or 'it makes me laugh'. These refer to judgements on the character of a publication. Magazine producers will sometimes use and record discussion groups of their readers in order to measure their responses to the magazine product.

An analysis of a female teenage magazine

In this section we will analyse some different types of teenage magazine, starting with female-orientated teenage magazines. The first magazine analysed in detail here is *More!*. The analysis of *More!* will be organised under the following headings:
- basic information
- type of content
- advertising
- layout and front cover
- language
- images
- relationships between language and images
- conclusion: the 'character' of the magazine.

Basic information

More!, which bears the banner slogan at the top of the cover page 'Smart girls get *More!*', is published fortnightly by EMAP Elan, part of EMAP Metro, which is in turn part of the huge EMAP group of magazine publishing companies. *More!* is the most successful female teenage title; in June 1994 it had a circulation of over 39 000 (source: ABC). *More!* is aimed at young women who are interested in boyfriends, relationships, articles about sex and emotional problems. *More!* appears to appeal to young women older than teenagers, but in fact it is bought by teenagers of 16 upwards. The magazine has 100 pages and costs £1.15.

The example analysed here is *More!* magazine, issue 184, 12–25 April 1995. This issue came with a 'free gift' of a 'Sex and Scandal' pocket book of stories in the genre of 'true life dramas' concerned with relationships, sex and personal dilemmas. This 'free gift' is an important sales ploy, but is excluded from the rest of the analysis here since it is a one-off gimmick, and not a regular feature.

Type of content

The contents pages provide an instant analysis of what is in the magazine, the purpose of which is, together with the cover page, to entice and guide the reader through the magazine.

The contents page of *More!* has four sections. 'Celebrities' includes news, reviews and interviews. 'Fashion & Beauty' is self explanatory. 'Features' includes gossip, stories and articles about relationships and their problems. 'In every issue' is a further section which lists regular features including reviews, problem pages for both young women and young men, offers ('Freebies'), letters, crossword and horoscopes.

On the contents page, the titles of each item are often followed up by a short explanation or 'strapline'. One original feature which resembles 'youth' television magazine and game shows is titled, 'Which of these men

Analysing magazines

Figure 2.4 Contents page from More! 12–25 April 1995

has had the most lovers?' followed by the question, 'Can you tell a slapper from a shy boy?'

Advertising

In issue 184 of *More!*, there are 22 full pages and 7 part pages of advertising in a magazine of 100 pages. In other words 22% of the magazine is full-page advertising, and 29% of all pages have advertising.

The most frequent type of advertisement is that concerned with careers, education and jobs. There are five advertisements in this category, including two advertisements for au pair agencies, and one for NVQ qualifications. This reflects the fact that *More!* is aimed at single teenagers of 16 and over either working or studying, or looking for career opportunities, as well as attracting younger teenagers.

Arguably, the most frequent advertisements in *More!* are those concerned with products which improve appearance and personal hygiene. These reflect the female orientation and what these teenagers are likely to spend their disposable income on. There are three advertisements for shampoo and three advertisements for panty liners. It may be significant

49

that two of the adverts for panty liners are positioned next to the problem pages. There are also advertisements for contact lenses, mail order clothes, shoes, eye drops, moisturiser and perfume. Another frequent category is mass media leisure products such as films and popular music albums. These tend to be placed close to the features reviewing film and music releases. There is a full-page advertisement for the next issue of More!

Figure 2.5 Advert for next issue in More! 12 April 1995

Layout and cover page

More! has a compromise between the teenage magazine convention of dropping page numbers and the convention of numbering pages. 54 of the 100 pages are numbered. Full-page adverts and other full-page images are not given page numbers.

Not all of the customers for More! will buy every issue. Many of the readers of this issue will have bought the magazine on an impulse which may have been triggered by the attractions of the cover page. The style of the cover page for More! follows the codes and conventions of the women's magazine cover page, possibly connoting a 'more mature' type of teenage

Analysing magazines

Figure 2.6 More! cover page. Issue 184 12–25 April 1995.

reader. Short, slogan-like titles, called 'cover lines', down the left- and right-hand borders of the cover page overrun the cover photo and inform the reader about the actual features in this magazine. The cover lines make references to 'boys', relationships, female models and showbiz gossip ('Hollywood Sleaze'). These include teasers like 'HELLO TOY BOYS!' in upper case, with 'Why men like to play with themselves' underneath. Sex as intercourse is implied or referred to in double meanings, rather than directly.

Inside, *More!* also has a fairly conventional layout. Single images for adverts and fashion features may fill one or two pages. Advertisements may occupy a half or a quarter page. Written text is usually organised in columns of up to four or five columns per page. Some feature pages use a 'cut-and-paste' appearance, with blocks of image and text across a variable number of columns which, together with the use of bold colour and different typefaces, gives the page a more informal appearance. The effect is not as 'anarchic' as some of the louder youth magazines. The overall effect is one of variety with a number of different page layout options.

▶ Typography, page 94

Language

The language of *More!* is very informal and speaks directly to the heterosexual female reader. Take these two items from the cover page: 'Meet the models with bodies like yours (Wobbly bits and all!)', 'How Many Lovers Has He Had?' Punctuation such as exclamation marks (also called 'screamers' by journalists) and question marks are used for emphasis or to grab attention. On the cover page of issue 184 there is frequent concern not only with heterosexual sex and relationships, but also with the male sex, from the female point of view: 'Hello Toy Boys!', 'Meeting Mr Right', 'It's over . . . So why can't you tell him?' are all features to which the cover draws attention.

The use of non-standard and colloquial language contributes to the informal, 'friendly' relationship *More!* cultivates with its readers. A gossip item on page 3, for example, begins with 'And we thought Wet Wet Wet were such shy retiring lads', breaking the formal rule that you should never begin a sentence with 'And'. The vocabulary of the magazine occasionally includes teenage slang. The Wet Wet Wet item also uses the adjective 'lairy' to refer to the group's nature, and translates their euphemism 'intimate moment' as 'a shag'.

The title 'How many lovers has he had?', on the cover page has the subtitle 'Spot a slapper at a hundred paces'. The image of *More!* is that of a magazine which is unafraid to talk frankly about sex. The vocabulary of the magazine constantly refers to sex as a topic which cuts across all the other major topics of celebrity and showbiz, fashion and appearance, and 'problems'. An interview with Adam Ant is 'on the bed with Adam Ant' and contains the profound quote from Adam:

'If guys took as much care of their willies as women do of their faces, it would be a better world.'

'Sex talk' is a regular feature, with letters asking information and advice about women having wet dreams and a reader with a boyfriend who wants her to call his penis 'Harry'. Words such as 'love', 'lover' and 'love life' are sometimes used but usually in the context of relationships and emotional problems and not usually in the context of romance.

The section about looking after clothes and appearance, 'Fashion and Beauty', is scattered over half the magazine in this issue and the vocabulary of consumerism, clothes, make up, modelling and appearance is prominent. *More!* does not exclude the world of work, and although the coverage is limited, there is a 'Working Girl' section and an article in the Features section about 'Careers in the caring professions'.

Images

At a casual glance, the most prominent images in *More!* are stars and celebrities, and young female models intended to represent real-life people.

We put the magazine through a simple content analysis, by counting all images and putting them into categories. Objects were separated from people, and images of people were defined by sex into the three categories of female images, male images and those which were mixed. These categories for people were further sub-divided into advertising images, and the remaining 'editorial' material into models, celebrities, magazine personnel and 'other' which in a sense were 'ordinary people' featured in the magazine. Nearly all images were photographic and there was a separate category for drawn illustrations. The results were put into a table which is reproduced below.

categories	total (rows)	advertisements	models	celebrities	drawn illustrations	magazine personnel
female only	135	23	52	32	2	10
male only	58	7	8	32	0	0
female and male	55	8	11	27	3	0
objects	51	18 (+ 5 'freebies')	n/a	n/a	0	n/a
other	15	1 (dog)	n/a	n/a	12 (star sign symbols)	n/a
total (columns)	314	62	71	91	17	10

There were 314 complete images in the magazine, roughly three per page on average. There were far more images of people than of objects alone. On this count, 248 of the total of 314 images were of people: in other words, over 80% of the images included people. The most common single category of image was female models, of whom there were 52 instances. Female images, in general, outnumbered male images. Interestingly, images of females alone or in groups outnumbered images of females and males together. Images of celebrities outnumbered images of models in total.

The conclusion from this content analysis of one issue is that *More!* is packed with images of young men and women and provides very different images of male and female. Although one purpose of the magazine is to sell advertisers' products, images of people and personal appearance are much more important than objects. Images of females are much more common than images of males. The main representation of what is female is provided by 'glamorous' young models. The most frequent image of the male is the male star or celebrity. Images of young males picked as representatives of those from more ordinary walks of life are of limited importance (at a frequency of 16 instances – not shown in the table).

Nearly all of the images were of white, conventionally attractive young people under 25. If older people are represented it is either because they appear as famous stars, or often in the form of an uncomplimentary stereotype.

The ages of the young women featured in the fashion images are often difficult to determine: certainly many of the models could be as young as 16. The 'child-woman' image, which harks back to the 1960s and is fashionable at present, is in evidence, notably in a feature called 'Pool Hall Queen' (see Figure 2.8).

The images in *More!* accommodate the gaze of both male as well as female readers. *More!* might be seen to be a more alternative publication where its male readers are concerned, however, there is evidence of old fashioned sexism. The 'Fashion and Beauty' item, 'Even models aren't perfect', includes fairly sexist comments from a young male panel. For example, a young man, Mike, comments:

Figure 2.7 *Table showing results of analysis of images in* More! *magazine 12–25 April 1995. Key: n/a = not applicable, or no category.*

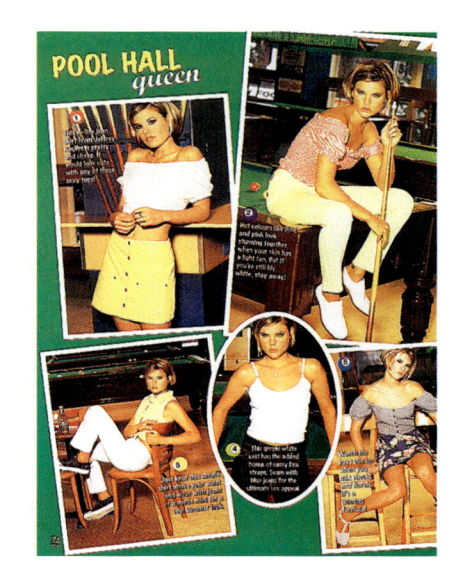

Figure 2.8 *'Pool Hall Queen' from* More!, *issue 184*

Analysing magazines

'You can park a bike between her legs. She's much too thin – you can see what she's had for dinner. I'd snap her – she's not a big boy's toy.'

There are a number of significant absences. Images of parents are either absent or make a rare appearance, likely to be in the stereotype of the unfashionable or embarrassing parent. Although there are instances of images of black people they are arguably so few as to have been included only as a gesture, or 'tokenism'. In issue 184, the images of black males could have been described as supporting a stereotype of the promiscuous 'black stud'. The feature 'which of these men has had the most lovers', illustrates this.

Figure 2.9 *Pages 50 and 51 of More! magazine 12–25 April 1995*

▶ Typography, page 94

▶ Image analysis using a semiotic approach, page 10

Image analysis of the cover page

A typical cover page for *More!* is shown on page 56. The colours used are dark blue, yellow, red and white against a light blue background, which contribute to the impact and attention grabbing effect of the cover. The image of the cover girl is framed and blended with text. The title block at the top across the model's forehead is *More!* in bold yellow lower case, sans serif type, with a tall exclamation mark.

The cover is dominated by the photographic image of a conventionally attractive, unnamed young model. The cover girl fills the page, and the printed text wraps around her image. In fact, the image 'bleeds off'; in other words, it reaches the outer edges of the page. The image of the model appears to confront the reader's gaze with a direct gaze of her own which looks the viewer in the eye. Her eyes appear to be slightly narrowed and her top lip is very slightly lifted so that the lips are just parted. Her left eyebrow is lifted. The suggestion of this facial expression is sensual and engages the viewer. The model's hair is tousled, suggesting a certain casualness or 'untidiness'. Her arms are upraised, the left hand on the top left of her head, and the right cradling the right side of her face with the fingers under her hair. The pose as usual in such cover images *connotes* the sensuality of the model, but the meaning of this look is complex and ambiguous. For the gaze of the female viewer it is not passive and seems to invite the respect of the female reader. As far as the male gaze is concerned, the look could connote either a challenge or a 'come-on', or both.

Relationships between language and images
We find four kinds of item in terms of language and image in *More!*:
  1 Fashion and beauty shots with images of models.
  2 Celebrity stories.
  3 Articles and stories with images acting as 'illustration'.
  4 Advertising images.

The frequency of images in *More!* means that the magazine appears, like other teenage magazines, to be led by pictures rather than writing. However, we can make a simple distinction between features which are 'picture-led' and those which are led by written language.

Fashion and beauty shots in *More!* are usually picture-led. To a large degree, the images of the models wearing the products 'tell the story'. The written language gives important information about the product being worn such as price and the outlet where it may be found, but the most important information is given in the image of the model wearing the product and showing how it might look. An example of this is 'Babe watch', a fashion shoot which shows off 'neon bright sportswear' in both female and mixed male and female images of models on the beach. Interestingly, there is one image of males only without a caption.

Longer articles and stories are predominantly written text, where the image is provided by a model simply acting out a 'part' as illustration to the story. In issue 184 there is an article on unwanted pregnancy titled, 'Warning! Pregnancy can ruin your relationship'. This headline acts as a caption to a photograph of a couple on a bed in their underwear, the male looking troubled and a female attempting to talk to him. Here the image draws attention to the article, and illustrates the story, possibly adding some visual realism to the authenticity of the problem, but it adds little or no information to the piece.

Images are important in celebrity stories and advertisements, but usually the relationship between pictures and writing is more equal, in the sense that the written text gives the reason why the images are there. The celebrity images are often 'library pictures' with many possible uses and the written text gives an 'anchorage' which pins the image down to that particular story. In the case of the most 'newsworthy' stories there are often photographs more strongly linked to the stories themselves. For example, the feature on 'Hollywood Scandal' has news images of stars 'in trouble'. The most dramatic of these is a photograph of Victoria Sellers in handcuffs with a female police officer, which is captioned, 'Victoria Sellers was jailed for possession of amphetamines'. The guts of the story are in the written text, however.

Figure 2.10 More! *title block illustration*

- title in lower case, sans serif
- attractive cover image
- printed text wraps round image
- image 'bleeds off' page
- different techniques to make cover text grab the reader's attention

▶ Milloy & O'Rourke, 1991, *The Woman Reader*, Routledge.

Conclusion

The language and images of *More!* are gossipy, trendy, 'sexy' and provocative. It aims to entertain, amuse and inform a female reader who is working out her self image. It offers pleasures which allow female readers to look at images of attractive young men and women, and to fantasise.

More! is successful because it succeeds in combining material about the concerns and obsessions of teenage life within a package which is bright, positive, attention grabbing and 'not too serious'. Although the magazine is preoccupied with the subject of sex there are also wider concerns about relationships, identity and self-image, and how other people live and work. The magazine does not only use sex as a means to sell and present content. It is obsessed with appearance and the values of the attractive which models represent. It connects most closely with other media forms in its obsession with fame and gossip. The result is an excess of 'personalities'.

Female readers of magazines like *More!* may have rejected the passivity and unreality of the relationship with the male heroes of romantic fiction. But in their place have come images of young males in the form of celebrities and models, with gossip and news about the celebrities' lives. The relationship of the reader with these images is less passive and they are probably felt to be more 'real', but they are also idealised and rather distant or 'safe' to fantasise about. *More!* has a kind of politics of everyday life which celebrates the pleasures of sexuality in order to promote consumerism (in other words, to sell things). In commercial terms the magazine is a platform for advertisers who want to speak to a precisely defined audience of teenagers. *More!* delivers these consumers through a publication which has a direct, friendly and intimate approach to its readers.

A Activity

Have a look at an issue of *More!* and/or any other female-orientated magazines and consider how it relates to the needs of the female reader. Read the following quotation, and see how far your opinions are represented in what it says.

'We were all struck by how much the magazines featured royalty, film stars and celebrities. Women like the magazine's readers were almost entirely absent, so the magazine provided fantasy and gossip rather than guidance about everyday life and problems or role models. There was quite a heated debate about what the magazines should offer. One side of the argument saw them as trivialising the readers' own lives and inculcating an unhealthy attitude of envy and admiration for the very wealthy. The other side thought women knew the reality of their own lives far too well and were entitled to be taken out of themselves if they wanted to be.'

(Milloy & O'Rourke *The Woman Reader*, Routledge, 1991.)

Does your opinion come down on one of the 'sides' in the quotation, or do you have another point of view?

An analysis of a male teenage magazine

Male teenage magazines are often more specialised in terms of the topics each covers than female teenage magazines. An analysis does not have to be broken down under sub-headings. This analysis follows the same structure as the analysis of *More!*, but it is written in the continuous form of an article or essay.

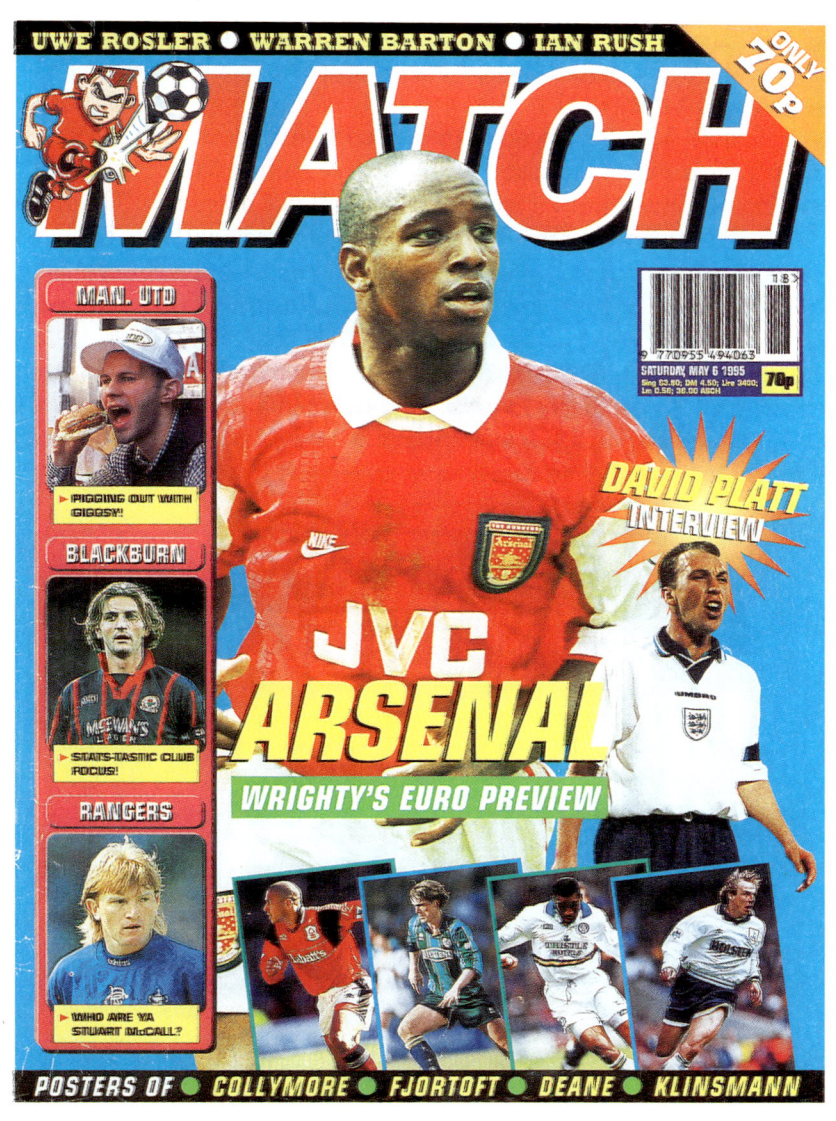

Figure 2.11 *Cover page of* Match

Match

Match is the biggest selling boy's magazine, aimed at a wide spread of younger males. It is weekly, has 56 pages and is priced at 'only 70p'. The magazine is produced by EMAP Pursuit which publishes outdoor pursuit titles. *Match* boasts a circulation of over 185 000 copies a week, growing from 110 000 in 1993 and overtaking its IPC rival *Shoot*. 55% of the target audience is in the 10–14 age range, but 25% of its customers are older teenagers.

Match is, to use the title of one of its features, 'football mad'. All the features are about football or football celebrities and their lives. Typical contents include football news, posters, fact files about footballing stars, longer interviews, team profiles, information about fixtures, results and league tables. A frequent feature is the 'questionnaire interview' with not only footballers and managers, but also football presenters (in a feature called 'TV Times').

In the issue examined in detail here, dated Saturday 6th May 1995, advertisements covered 10 full pages and one third-part page out of the 56. There were 21 advertisements in all, including one double page advertisement for mail order sports shoes and one page of 11 small ads. The advertisements by category included 7 for strategy games and competitions, 5 for sportswear and 4 for magazines (including 2 full-page promotions for *Match* itself).

The pages in *Match* have no numbers, contents list or index to break up the 'flow' of features and images. This 'flow' suggests a 'fast forwarding' reader who becomes familiar with the layout of the magazine. Those pages which are led by text are laid out in columns, up to 5 per page. There are 4 poster pages which have conventional action images of celebrity footballers, previewed in 4 small images at the bottom of the cover page. Two of the poster pages are double page spreads. The magazine is laid out and organised in such a way that it can be taken apart. There is a 16-page centre section, '*Match Facts*', which can be pulled out with the posters (see Figure 2.12. '*Match Facts*' is a magazine in itself laid out in columns packed with information, tables and statistics.

Figure 2.12 *Page from 'Match Facts'*

Like other teenage magazines, *Match* is about personalities, celebrities, news and gossip, and links itself with other media forms, particularly television. The difference, of course, is that it is all centred upon football. The stories and the language used tend to centre around action, competition, and the game of football itself. For example, the footballers talk about 'kicking', 'heading it in', 'scoring', 'playing' and 'showing off'. There are discussions about relegation, winning, beating and defeat. The terminology of 'fouls', 'penalties', 'bookings', 'sending off' and 'goals' refers to the rules of football.

The language used has some unusual or characteristic features. Colloquialisms, slang and non-standard language are used, as this opening sentence from 'football mad' demonstrates.

'Check it out y'all! Matchman's slammin it in ya face once again with the newz and viewz from the man that knows the score. No, not the referee dummy, me good self of course!'

The stars and celebrities are usually referred to by either their surnames or their full names, not first names. There is also a tendency to add '-y' to surnames as in 'Giggsy', 'Platty' and 'Wrighty'. Words are often shortened or 'clipped': statistics becomes 'stats', football becomes 'footy', European becomes 'Euro', favourite becomes 'fave'. There are aspects of the style and language of *Match* which are stereotypically 'male'. Take, for example, this story, 'The Day I Turned', from page 3.

'It wasn't a case of going red, more like going green! I threw up on the pitch against Tottenham just after I signed for Villa! I felt really embarrassed at the time and the lads gave me loads of stick when the game finished. It must have been down to nerves and all I can remember when I was crouched down was Andy Townsend kicking the sick back into the mud and laughing!'

As you can see, the magazine tends to have a boyish sense of humour. For example, in another story, headlined 'Fun and Games', we are told about Trevor Sinclair taking a corner and 'kicking the flag by mistake'.

Match is 'picture-led'. On a rough count there are 198 images in *Match* including 2 double-page and 3 full-page poster images. There are fewer images in *Match* Facts, at 28 an average of less than 2 per page (1.75). In *Match* Facts these include 9 graphics which present statistics. In the main body of the magazine there are an average of 4 per page (4.25). The overwhelming majority of images (160) are of footballing males, of whom most are the star footballers themselves. Most of the images do not have captions as such, but illustrate features or advertisements.

The female sex is significantly absent from both images and text in *Match*. The only image which includes women shows two young girls lifting up Ian Rush. The jokey caption is 'Show some leg girls, I want to get in the paper!' The legs, of course, are his.

Match is the '*Smash Hits* of Football'. It has most of the features of the '90s teenage magazine: pin ups, media news and gossip about stars and celebrities, interviews with stars, readers' letters, a crossword, quizzes etc. *Match* treats 'big name' footballers as the heroes, stars and celebrities of boys' culture. It gives these celebrities similar treatment to the ways in which female magazine treat pop stars, with glimpses into, and trivia about, their personal lives. On the other hand, *Match* is male-dominated and represents the world of professional football in terms of traditional images of a 'laddish' masculinity. This kind of sports journalism allows boys to gaze at photographs of males. Unlike the female readers of magazines like *More!*, male readers of *Match* can look at pictures of their own sex who are not measured against standards of 'model' looks, but are there by virtue of their success in competitive sport. Male fans are given information about 'behind the scenes' and the 'horseplay' their team gets up to, which allows them to feel 'one of the lads'. According to the editor of *Match*, Chris Hunt, the producers of the magazine are aware that they have female readers too. The female reader is not, however, included in the language or images the magazine presents. Its way of speaking to its audience is gendered in terms of traditional 'one of the lads' masculinity, which excludes women from its world.

A Activity

Form a group of people who have read the same magazine in order to answer the following questions. Write a short report of your findings.

1. What do you find enjoyable about this magazine?
2. What are its weaknesses?
3. How would you describe this magazine:
    a) if it were a person?
    b) if it were an animal?
    c) if it were an item of furniture?

From the point of view of magazine publishers, the strengths of a magazine will be judged in terms of its success. A large, or rising, circulation will indicate success, and attract advertisers. Weaknesses will show in a declining readership. As a student of the media you will need to look for other strengths and weaknesses. How far does the magazine under study meet your own needs, or those of others? You will also want to draw conclusions on the 'house style' of the publication from the observations made in the analysis.

Assignment

Analysing a magazine

Analyse a magazine of your choice by doing the following and then writing or recording a report:

1. Obtain at least three issues of the magazine over a period of time so that you can see if there are any changes in content or style over time or in response to seasonal interests.
2. Obtain other magazines of a similar format so that you can compare the magazine you are analysing with the market competition.
3. Obtain information from the publishers of the magazine about target audience, sales figures and advertising rates.
4. Note basic information about the magazine such as cost, circulation, frequency of publication and so on.
5. Study the contents of the magazine closely, reading every page carefully.
6. Produce tables showing categories of contents (e.g. fiction, 'real life' stories, medical advice etc.) and how the contents are divided up amongst the categories in pages or column centimetres.
7. Categorise the advertising in the magazine (e.g. food, hygiene, cosmetics) and study the link between editorial content and advertising (e.g. adverts for music CDs on a page of reviews).
8. Examine the images in the adverts and discuss the messages they are intended to give. You might also note the different interpretations of the images among your group.
9. Look carefully at the cover page and comment on the images used. What effects are they meant to have? Do they help to sell the magazine? Comment on the styles of print used and the use of colour.
10. Examine the language used in the magazine. Is there evidence of a 'house style'? What are the levels of formality of language?
11. How is the text used to limit or alter the meaning of images in captions and headings?
12. Categorise the images in the magazine to see if you can detect any patterns over time. You might find, for instance, that there are more active images of males than there are of females.

3 | Planning and developing print material

Unit 2 of the Advanced GNVQ specifications describes what you have to do to prepare your material for the making of a print product. Unit 2 can be referred to as a *pre-production* unit, though that term is used more commonly in audio and visual media than in print media. It is best to think of the print sections of Units 2 and 3 as a continuum.

To achieve your GNVQ, you need to:
- come up with and develop ideas for stories and visual material (graphics and photographs)
- evaluate these ideas in terms of their practicality and relevance to the target audience
- identify sources of information and contacts
- conduct research into the needs and attitudes of the target audience
- conduct research for information for news or feature stories, involving interviewing and desk research
- understand the main legal and ethical restraints on writers.

This chapter is organised into the following sections:
- Introduction to planning and developing print material
- Generating, developing and evaluating ideas
- Finding ideas for writing feature articles
- Organising research
- Writing features
- Getting the style right
- Thinking about representation
- Understanding legal and ethical issues
- Producing visual material.

Introduction to planning and developing print material

This chapter guides you through the process of preparing individual material for a publication and will suggest ways of coming up with ideas for both fiction and non-fiction articles and stories. It is very important that the planning stages of the writing process are done thoroughly and that your specification is thought through, otherwise you can waste time and money trying to do something that turns out to be irrelevant, impossible or inappropriate.

The chapter will also advise on how to prepare for and conduct interviews as part of your research. It emphasises the need to match the style of your writing to the needs of your audience.

You need to be aware of the various legal and ethical constraints on your writing and the chapter highlights those that are the most relevant to student journalists.

It is always helpful if illustrators, photographers and writers work closely together so that they understand each others' problems and opportunities, and the chapter ends with some basic advice about taking effective pictures and designing informative graphics.

While there is opportunity here to do considerable individual work, you should also bear in mind that eventually you will have to work in a team to make a joint print product. It will save effort if the material you produce for Unit 2 could be used in your final product. This will, of course, involve discussion and negotiation and you should keep a record, in note form, of all such discussions.

Generating, developing and evaluating ideas

This is what you have to do:
- Come up with ideas for stories/articles for publication.
- Come up with ideas for visual material, one of which should involve photography. These could be linked with the text ideas.
- Discuss these ideas with your group and make a detailed evaluation of each one (see Figure 3.1).

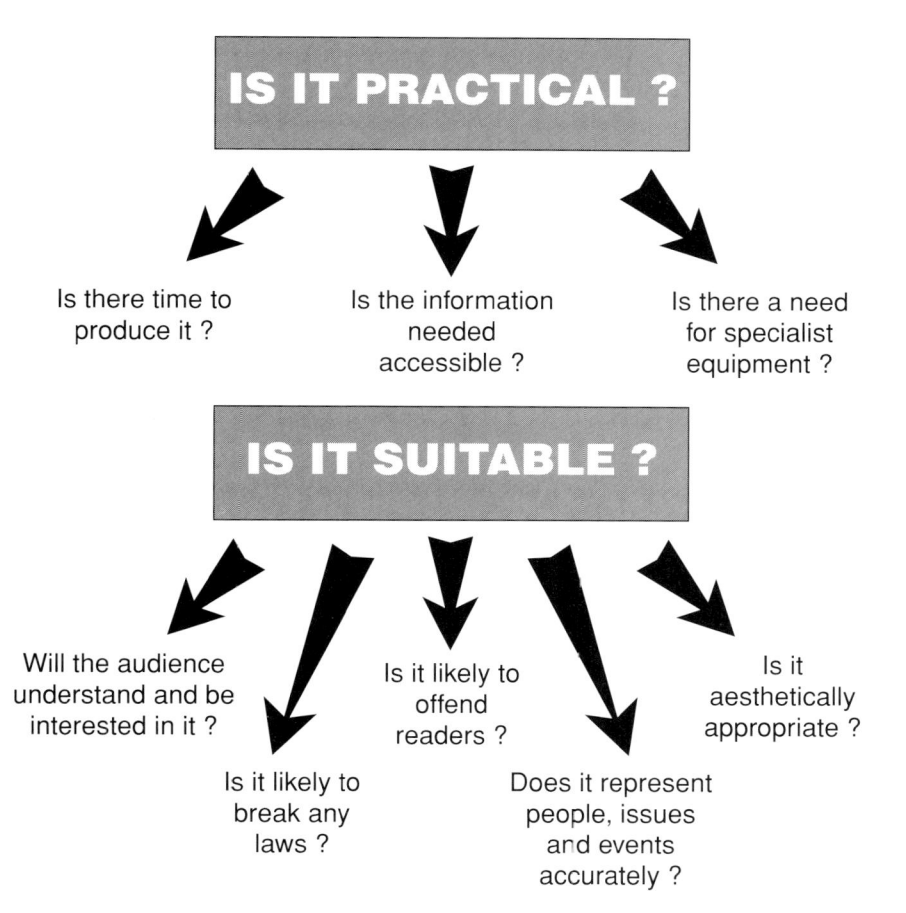

Figure 3.1 *Evaluating an idea*

IS IT PRACTICAL?

- Is there time to produce it?
- Is the information needed accessible?
- Is there a need for specialist equipment?

IS IT SUITABLE?

- Will the audience understand and be interested in it?
- Is it likely to offend readers?
- Is it aesthetically appropriate?
- Is it likely to break any laws?
- Does it represent people, issues and events accurately?

Is it practical?

That is – is there time to produce it? Is the information needed accessible? Is there a need for specialist equipment (e.g. a portable tape-recorder for interviews, lighting equipment for portrait photography)?

Planning and developing print material

Is it suitable?

That is – will the people who read/view it understand it, be interested in it? Is it likely to break any laws? (E.g. is it libellous?) Is it likely to offend readers? If it is, is it still justifiable to publish it?

Does it represent fairly and accurately the people, issues and events it is about? Can you justify any bias?

Is it aesthically appropriate for its intended publication? (E.g. would the size and shape of photos fit the space available?)

Once you have decided which ideas are to be developed you should write out a specification like the one in Figure 3.2.

Figure 3.2 *A sample specification*

```
                    Barbecues
Medium: general interest magazine.
Purpose: to inform readers about new equipment for barbecues.
Text to be a guide to new equipment, recipe ideas,
characteristics of a successful barbecue party.
Audience: young home-owners, especially C1s and C2s with high
disposable income living within a five-miles radius of
college/school.
Content: two-page colour spread for an A4 magazine. 350 words of
text, four coloured photos, two line drawings.
Aesthetics: warm, cheerful colours; affluent settings for
equipment; young, happy and healthy couples entertaining friends
and having fun; use of cut-outs to suggest informality and
spaciousness. Liberal use of sub-heads and white space for same
effect.
Technical: Barbecue equipment for pictures provided by Smithers
Ltd, 'Freshair' Ltd. and 'Conway's Campers'.
        Locations: 77 Sunset Avenue and 80 Glebe Crescent.
        Models: Students still to be named.
        Equipment: 35 mm camera, tripod and stepladders.
        Date for photo session: May 17th or 18th, depending on
        weather.
Information sources: advertising material from Barbie, Partytime
and Great Outdoors; returns for questionnaire on barbecue likes
and dislikes; interview with Stephen and Susan Cullen (barbecue
fanatics); library - for recipe ideas and brief history of
barbecues..
```

A Activity

Write a specification for a feature article using a Blind Date format. You have to arrange for couples to go out on a date with facilities provided by companies or organisations which would welcome the publicity. The participants need to be photographed and interviewed. You will have to think up a print equivalent to the initial question and answer session of the TV programme.

Finding ideas for writing feature articles

Where do editors turn if they want ideas for their publications?

Figure 3.3 shows which sources of information editors think are most useful (source MORI). The percentages refer to the proportion of editors who think that the source is useful. So 86% of editors think that reading articles in newspapers is useful for gathering ideas, whereas only 19% of editors think that public relations officers are useful.

Articles in newspapers	86%
Own journalists	81%
Informal meetings	58%
Articles in magazines	56%
Interviews with officials (not PRs)	56%
Radio	50%
Telephone conversations with officials (not PRs)	47%
News agencies	39%
Friends	31%
Press releases	22%
Company press relations officers	19%

Figure 3.3 *Information sources*

Here are some categories of newspaper and magazine articles to help you produce your own ideas.

'How to...' articles

These are very useful as they:
a) Deal with practical problems (e.g. organising a student loan; selecting the most suitable course; making the most of your money)
b) Show how to make things (e.g. a garden pond)
c) Deal with personal problems (e.g. coping with exam pressure; being at ease with the opposite sex).

You don't have to be an expert yourself, but you need to find experts who can give authoritative advice.

Personal experience

This could be your own – 'How I survived a disastrous holiday' – or someone else's that you collect, such as two separate and contrasting accounts of being unmarried fathers.

Surveys

These involve providing consumer information and, perhaps, opinion. For example, value for money at local cinemas; a guide to places for families to visit during the Easter holidays.

Travel

Come up with a new angle on a familiar place, for example where to find Bank Holiday solitude in the Lake District, or else write about somewhere not often visited.

Achievements

Think about different types, such as sporting, intellectual, overcoming misfortune, financial.

Changes
Investigate new building/demolition. Find out what's happening and why. Look into changes in procedures (e.g. re-classifying benefit allowances for disabled people).

Moans
Listen to and investigate the things people complain about (e.g. discontinuation of public transport after dark because of violence).

Organising research

At one level all of a writer's, photographer's or graphic artists's life is research. This is a question of habitual curiosity: listening to people's stories, anxieties, hopes, frustrations; looking at how people dress, their mannerisms, their movements, their off-guard behaviour. It is also about being curious about places, finding out why somewhere is cordoned off, why somewhere else is being 'done up', noticing details of the environment that are significant. Although you can keep notebooks recording this kind of casual 'research', you might just want to store it in your memory. The important thing is to become more alert and responsive to the people and places around you.

In practice this might lead (to use actual examples) to an investigation into low pay for teenagers, after hearing several complaints from different 'exploited' individuals; to a photo essay on collecting sea coal from Durham's beaches (what are those sacks the men are pushing on their bikes?); to a feature on a deserted gunpowder factory 'discovered' on a walking holiday in Scotland.

Primary sources – interviewing

Most features for newspapers and magazines are based on interviews. The writer is in the position of the inquisitive observer who needs to find out information from the 'experts' – those who know most about the event or topic. The ability to conduct effective interviews is at the heart of good journalism.

Whenever possible some *preliminary research* should be done on the topic to be discussed and the person being interviewed. For example, it is not uncommon for student reporters to interview professional footballers from their local team. If the interviewer does his/her preliminary research it becomes possible to ask an effective question such as how well the player has settled in after his £1 million transfer from a lower division team than to ask naively which other teams he has played for.

A student reporter interviewing Lord Young, who was at the time a cabinet minister, was able to break the ice because she had read about his interest in golf in 'Who's Who' and knew his handicap was 1. A brief and cheerful conversation about golfing prowess established a rapport that helped the serious political interview along.

The more facts you can learn before the interview the better, so that you can concentrate on the interviewee's thoughts, opinions and feelings.

It also helps if you can focus your investigation on a particular *angle or theme*. In other words you need to have an idea of what your article will be about before you start the interview. If you are to talk to a fellow student about her impending expedition to the Himalayas you do not want to waste time asking about her GCSE results.

Once you have a clear idea of what you want to learn, you should prepare your questions. Assuming you know the basic facts before the interview, most of your questions should be open rather than closed. A question that allows a 'yes/no' answer is closed.

It is useful to use the word 'how' at the start of a question – 'How did you first come to decide to join an expedition to the Himalayas?' or 'How do you feel about the potential dangers of the expedition?' It is also useful to simply say 'Tell me about...'

A Activity

It is quite useful to organise an interviewing session for your group. Hotels at non-peak periods are a good choice. You need to arrange with the management for a group of students to interview a range of employees and perhaps guests. You should do some preliminary research on the hotel itself. See if there is a file on it in the local newspaper office. Think of possible lines of enquiry. Are there any stories about particular rooms being unlucky? Which customers are most likely to cheat on paying their bills and how do they do it? Are there any 'awkward customer' stories? Which groups are the worst behaved at conferences? And so on.

Think of the story lines of *Fawlty Towers* and use these as your starting points. Of course an exercise like this can lead you up some blind alleys, but it would be unusual if you did not end up with at least one good story.

Arranging an interview

If you are intending to interview a well-known personality you may well have to organise things through a *publicity agency*. If, for instance, you want to interview a pop star, you will probably have to contact his/her record company and ask to speak to whoever is handling the publicity.

You need to say something about your publication, its target audience, its circulation, date of publication and the type of story you want to write.

It is obviously best to interview someone who is visiting your region in the near future if you want a face-to-face interview. You should also ask about any *press conferences* which are being organised and see if you are able to attend. Sometimes your local newspaper, radio or TV station will be able to help you with arrangements and contacts.

If you can't arrange for a face-to-face interview, ask if you can organise a telephone interview or if that fails, a postal interview. Whoever you contact, always ask for an up-to-date press pack and publicity pictures as they might be useful.

This is all very hard work and if you were working for a newspaper or magazine there would be a bank of information and contact lists available. Ideally your college or school should try to set up its own communications *resource bank* with contacts, addresses, photos and cuttings. A useful starting point would be to buy a copy of the *Guardian*'s annual *Media Guide* which has, among other valuable information, a section on 'contacts' with telephone numbers of pressure groups, sporting organisations, official bodies and so on.

The interview

Once the ground is prepared, you have to make sure that the interview goes smoothly. Be prompt if you are visiting someone. It helps to arrive early and to take in your surroundings. You can pick up some telling details from working environments which you might be able to use in your article – the family photo on the desk, the Animal Rights poster on the wall, the caged parrot in the corner of the room!

It should go without saying that you have checked the exact location of the interview venue, but students have been known to turn up at the wrong St Joseph's school, there being two in the town, or the Empire Theatre rather than the Theatre Royal.

Use a portable battery-driven tape-recorder if you do not know shorthand as you will need to use accurate quotations in your article. Don't leave things to chance. Check batteries, amount of tape, volume settings. Ask if it is all right to record the interview. Use a notebook as well and jot down key phrases and words during the interview. If something is particularly significant and possibly controversial, check that you have understood what is being said and ask if you can use the quotation in your article.

If you have any controversial or especially challenging questions, keep them towards the end of your list and use them once you have the confidence of the interviewee.

You can soften the impact of any difficult questions by attributing any implied criticism to other people – 'How do you react to people who say that expeditions to the Himalayas are polluting the environment?'

Writing features

Once you have collected your raw material you need to shape the article. First set yourself a *word limit*. If you are writing for a publication you should know what space there is for your article. If you know how many words you have to produce, write 20% more and then edit the work down. This is much easier than having to add material which could distort the balance of your piece. It is also true that most people tend to over write to begin with and revision reveals redundancy.

Think about your *audience*. Imagine a group of typical readers and write as if you are talking to them in language that they will understand. But think also of being an entertainer, a raconteur, someone who can enthral an audience.

Decide what the *main purpose* of your feature is. Write this down in one short sentence and change it until you are happy about the direction your writing will take. Once you start to write keep referring to this purpose. Modify it if you need to, discard it and start again if you must, but always have a clear theme in mind.

Pay special attention to the *opening paragraph*. It should invite the reader to read on, as these do:

'After the furore of Princess Diana's gym pictures is a voluntary press ombudsman on the way?' (*Media Guardian*, 22/11/93)

This has a topical peg, a question to involve the reader, and a famous name.

'Michelle Pfeiffer, who has been described as one of the ten most beautiful women in the world, is standing amongst a crowd of strangers. As they hurry past, she notices they are staring at her. She looks down and is mortified to see that she has no clothes on.'

A famous name, a strange predicament needing explanation and an embarassment that anyone can identify with.

▶ Audience, page 16

Willies for peace

P.S.

Brandon Robshaw

HERE'S an anecdote. A young woman, 18 weeks pregnant, had just been for an ante-natal checkup. Everything was fine, the midwife told her. "Good," said the woman. "Now I'd better go and see my boyfriend in casualty." "What did you do to him?" enquired the midwife humorously.

"I poured boiling water over his willy," said the woman and added, as the nurse gazed at her dumbstruck, "He deserved it. He doesn't understand a thing about pregnant women." I was told this story by the nurse concerned. The reaction of the assembled company when we heard it was perhaps predictable; women as well as men, we clasped our crotches, performed comical grimaces of mock agony, cracked jokes about it. The feeling seemed to be that the woman had some something outrageous but not that she had done something outrageously cruel.

It's a commonplace that we laugh at what frightens us. But is laughter really appropriate in a case like this? Similar reactions were observable in the case of the Filipino woman who castrated her husband with a machete, with people writing jokey letters to this newspaper about it; and still more so in the celebrated John Wayne Bobbitt case. Suzanne Moore wrote that in lopping off (note that casual unfeeling verb) her husband's penis, Mrs. Bobbitt had discovered a "novel solution" to the heterosexual spread of Aids. But this is wrong. What Mrs. Bobbitt did was a cruel, violent act and no solution to anything.

Of course, willies, like breasts and bottoms (though not vaginas) have always been funny. But when it comes to deliberate mutilation, isn't that where the fun stops?

I'm not suggesting that women have declared open season on men's genitals. Women still have more cause to fear violence from men than from women; in fact, men have more cause to fear violence from men than women do. I'm not one of those paranoid loonies who think that all feminists are out to castrate men, though Moore's flippant remarks don't do much to dispel this myth. It's the levity with which these rare cases are treated that I don't like.

Symbolically, an assault on a man's penis is an assault on masculinity, on privilege, on patriarchy, and seen in this light (and John Wayne Bobbitt's macho forenames rather encourage one to see it thus) it's possible to treat it as an almost praiseworthy gesture of rebellion, rather like knocking off a policeman's helmet. But forget the symbolism. In itself, the act of damaging or destroying somebody's private parts has nothing to commend it. And I should have been every bit as appalled to hear of a woman's getting scalding water over her genitals as I was to hear of its happening to a man.

Both in the way we treat each other and in the way we talk about the way we treat each other, it's time we showed more respect for each other's bodies.

Figure 3.4 *Willies for peace' from the Media Guardian, 14/1/94*

A Activity

Make a collection of effective opening paragraphs and write brief comments on why they work.

The *main part* of the article should be *logical* and answer the kinds of questions an intelligent reader would ask. Make sure that you link cause and effect. If you look at 'Willies for Peace' (Figure 3.4) you know an effect – someone's girlfriend poured boiling water over his willy. What caused that? The writer, Brandon Robshaw, tells us it was because the man 'doesn't understand a thing about pregnant women'.

What caused Robshaw to tell this anecdote? He says the reaction of the people who heard this story was to laugh. He then introduces his *main theme* – 'But is laughter really appropriate in a case like this?' This may sound like a puny theme and a small peg on which to hang some scatalogical anecdotes, but that's a separate issue.

The rest of the article has examples of vengeful mutilation by women on men. A plea for greater respect in the way we treat each other and the way we talk about the way we treat each other brings the article to a *clear conclusion*.

Getting the style right

The style in which you write will depend on the nature of the publication you are writing for. In this unit you can try a variety of styles if you wish, but bear in mind that some of your work will appear in your final print product. It might be helpful, therefore, if your group works out a 'house style' which will be appropriate for the publication's intended audience.

Here are some extracts from a newspaper publisher's style book:

Taken from *North East Press Stylebook*, North East Press, 1994

> 'Remember that short simple words are best, if they are the right ones. Use them accurately and precisely. Few words do exactly the work of others. Watch jealously their varying shades of meaning and choose the shortest one if it fits.
>
> Use "very" sparingly; "good" is usually enough. Split an infinitive only when you know you are doing so and can explain why. Avoid the double negative in all its forms.
>
> Keep paragraphs short, but do not slavishly confine them to a single sentence.
>
> Never use commas and other punctuation marks unnecessarily.
>
> Write the story as you would like to have it told to you; keep to the point and do not over-write.
>
> Use adjectives sparingly, words of more than three syllables and superlatives only when nothing else will serve.'
>
> In general you should aim to:
> - be precise;
> - be concise;
> - be clear;
> - be interesting;
> - be aware of the rhythms your sentences make;
> - vary the length of your sentences;
> - use appropriate language (for audience/content/publication).
>
> Most first drafts benefit from cutting unnecessary words. Substitute single words for phrases where you can:
> - "At this moment in time" – "now";
> - "blue in colour" – "blue";
> - "small in size" – "small";
> - "quite unique" – "unique" (if it is).
>
> Get rid of repetitions:
> - "he repeated it again" – "he repeated it";
> - "people have a nostalgia for things of the past" – "people are nostalgic";
> - "a local man from this area" – "a local man".

CASE STUDY Writing a feature

To give you some idea of how professionals go about preparing for, researching and writing a feature, here's how one article was produced. (The highlighted words refer to the specification of material range statements in Unit 2 of Advanced GNVQ Media.)

The writer working for *TV Times* (**medium**) had to produce a piece to accompany the launch of a new programme, *Press Gang*, about teenagers making their own newspaper (**purpose**). It had to attract young readers as they would be the ones most likely to watch the programme (**audience**).

The writer, Andrea Kon, contacted the Newspaper Society in London (**information source**) to find out which schools produced the most ambitious newspapers where the pupils took most of the responsibility. She was directed to Crossgates Junior School in Rochdale, where junior pupils produced their own freesheet, and to the *Sunderland Echo* which produced a paper written and designed by pupils from different schools and had a circulation of 67 000.

The writer completed this initial background research by telephone interview with people at the Newspaper Society.

She next had to arrange to visit the school and the local newspaper to interview the people involved (**information sources**). The visits were arranged (**technical**) for two separate days because of the amount of travelling involved. In the case of the visit to the *Echo*, the writer asked if a special editorial meeting could be arranged for her to attend and see the pupils 'in action'.

The logistics of the visits were organised. The writer and a photographer (Ron McFarlane) had to fly from London to Newcastle, collect a hire car and drive to Sunderland. The next day she had to visit Rochdale via Manchester airport and another hire car.

These technical details are most important. The journalists had to fit their planned visit into the production schedule of the magazine, leaving themselves enough time to write the story and develop and edit the pictures. They would be given budget limits which would take into account travelling, subsistence and time (i.e. wages per hour).

Such organisation may be beyond your college/school resources (heavy irony), but the basic method (substituting public transport for planes and hire cars) still applies.

Thinking about representation

You are required to consider issues of representation in your work. This is perhaps best done in consultation with others and in the context of a complete publication.

According to Professor Stuart Hall, the media exercise 'the power to represent the world in certain ways. And because there are many different and conflicting ways in which meaning about the world can be con-structed, it matters profoundly what and who gets represented, what and who regularly gets left out, and how things, people, events, relation-ships are represented' (*Bending the Reality: the State of the Media*, 1986).

As a media producer, however humble, you are caught up in this process. You need to become aware of its complexities and its significance, so that your decisions are informed.

Examples might help to illustrate something about the process. The *Daily Mail* published a two-page centre spread (Figure 3.6) about Kylie Minogue in December 1989. One was a version of an interview approved by Warner Brothers (who were responsible for Minogue's publicity) and the other was 'what reporter Sara Barrett wanted to write'. In an introduction the newspaper explained why it was doing this:

'In the world of pop and showbusiness, the gap between image and reality is growing ever wider. What follows is a classic example of how media manipulation can result in reporting the image rather than the true picture. The *Daily Mail*, in common with other newspapers, was given the opportunity to interview Kylie Minogue to coincide with pre-publicity for her new film, *The Delinquents*. We had to sign an agreement with the distributors, Warner Brothers, accepting two conditions. First we should submit our completed article for vetting by Miss Minogue's representatives; secondly, that we should publish no earlier than today to assist publicity for the film.'

Figure 3.5 The resulting article

Figure 3.6 *(on the next page)* The Daily Mail's *spread on Kylie Minogue*

In a bid to head off the latest wave of media manipulation, the

The two faces of

IN the world of pop and showbusiness, the gap between image and reality is growing ever wider. What follows is a classic example of how media manipulation can result in reporting the image rather than the true picture. The Daily Mail, in common with other newspapers was given the opportunity to interview Kylie Minogue to coincide with pre-publicity for her new film, The Delinquents. We had to sign an agreement with the distributors, Warner Brothers, accepting two conditions. First, we should submit our completed article for vetting by Miss Minogue's representatives; secondly, we should publish no earlier than today to assist publicity for the film. These conditions are not uncommon. But in order to highlight this trend in PR practice, the Mail has decided to carry two articles on Kylie – the version below, which was accepted by Warner Brothers without alteration, and the version on the right which was what writer Sara Barrett wanted to write.

A pint-sized piper who calls the tune

AUTHORISED VERSION

THERE once was a little girl from the boring suburbs who dreamed of being rich, famous and treated like a princess wherever she went.

The little girl grew bigger (but not much – at 21 she's just 5ft 1in and 6½ stone), won a part in a popular TV soap, was spotted singing at a football benefit and the dream came true.

She was whisked into a recording studio, sold platinum albums all round the world and then traded in her Miss Goody-two-shoes image for a raunchy part in film about teenage runaways.

The girl is Kylie Minogue, one of the success stories of the decade. A woman feted, mobbed and adored wherever she goes. Even the igniting of the Regent Street Christmas lights – a role usually assigned to royalty – was hers this year and, incredibly, was postponed so Kylie could combine it with her promotional tour for her film, The Delinquents.

There was a red carpet in Regent Street and scenes of mayhem, as crowds strained against crash barriers when she stepped into the blaze of popping flashbulbs. Kylie for the first time was truly amazed. She really had become the Princess of Pop. 'I felt like royalty, I just can't believe the way England has reacted to me,' she says.

And here is Kylie, dressed like a tomboy, her famous wavy blonde hair stuffed into an oversized mariner's hat, her elfin frame dwarfed in a palest mauve leather bolero jacket in which she thrusts tiny hands with short, unvarnished nails. She wears loose trousers, flat shoes and no make up.

SHE is the antithesis of the sleek groomed, kiss-curled beauty queen who wowed the crowds at her film premiere in that black side-split dress with the natty little hot pants underneath and says of it: 'Sometimes I think people imagine I sit down and say "OK, I'm only going to wear these sorts of clothes from now on." But I don't ask myself "How's this outfit going to affect my career?" because I think the best feeling is a gut feeling, and if I feel like wearing a see-through dress, so be it.'

The Delinquents, which opens here on Boxing Day, is about two runaway lovelorn

by SARA BARRETT

teenagers in dullest Australia in the Fifties. Unloved by their families, they experiment prematurely with sex and get into trouble. Lola, played by Kylie, is seen topless, in bed with her lover Brownie (played by Charlie Schlatter) and giggling with him over the mechanics of contraceptive devices.

And the contraceptive bit is no laughing mater for Lola. Earlier in the film she is forced by her mother into having an abortion. The film is 12 Certificate. Would Kylie, I asked, feel happy taking a 12-year-old daughter to the film?

'That's an interesting question,' she says thoughtfully. 'Yeah, I would. I think that kids shouldn't be shielded. They're going to see more violence by watching the television and I'd rather have my kids see The Delinquents than Rambo. Parents might think "Uh oh! This film will give kids ideas" but on the other hand the young viewers are seeing what life is like; that it's not romantic and glamorous to run away.'

Did she, I wondered, think long and hard about the two swear-words that the film includes? 'No, not at all. With going topless, it wasn't embarrassing to film but when I saw the rushes I totally cringed. I certainly wouldn't go any further than that in future films – not at this stage, anyway.'

Kylie is clearly deeply sympathetic to the characters of Lola. 'People ask me,' she continues, 'if I was like that when I was 16' and I say "Yes, I was a pretty rotten 16-year-old like most are, rebellious and arguing, sneaking out of school, but Lola and Brownie loved each other so much because they had no love from anywhere else. God! I can't imagine like that. My family is so close.'

Kylie, in raunching-up her image for the film, has faced some criticism that she may be 'selling out' on her very young fans. She thinks long and hard and tells me with great deliberation: 'No, I'm not really but I can't tiptoe through the tulips like a careful little square. I am growing up and my audience is too, but I'm not forgetting about the kids, I've still got my records; I still do kids' shows and interviews.'

Kylie, the epitome of girl-next-door safety until The Delinquents is seen looking dangerously sexy on the film poster. Does

she see herself as sexy?

'More so recently,' she confesses to me, 'my image has changed.' She points to a magazine on the coffee table in front of her in which she is photographed pouting and dressed in a black leather jacket. 'For example, I wouldn't have done that sitting there a while ago, but then I am growing up! With my looks, I am so critical of myself.'

At the film premiere, Kylie arrived escorted only by minders. She was sad not to have friends and family from Australia there – in particular, I suggested, rock star boyfriend Michael Hutchence from INXS.

Kylie laughs. 'Well he's just a friend at this stage. It would have been nice for him to come to the film and I wish my parents had been, too, but it's a long way to come and hopefully they will be at the Australian premiere.'

ON the touchy subject of boyfriends, Kylie continues mischievously: 'I am pretty good at saying nothing about those things but what I say and what I do could be completely different! I do go out on dates with different people. In fact I love going out on dates! It's such fun.

'In the future . . . I'll definitely have children . . . although whether or not I'll get married, I don't know. Marriage is kind of a piece of paper. It's fair way off now, anyway.'

Miss Minogue earns a reputed £1million a year, but, she confesses, is really not terribly good at spending money. 'I'm better than I used to be but I can't help being a bargain hunter. It's in my blood. I couldn't tell you exactly how much I earn but it is a lot – especially for someone my age.'

Kylie's manager, Terry Blamey, arrives and shows Kylie a watch with her face on it. 'Good, much better,' she says, turning to me and confiding: 'You're in the midst of a decision here. That watch came to me and I hated it so I chose the picture and said 'put it this way with the name on the side'. Half the time I design my own stuff, like the invitation to the movie, and the T-shirts and other merchandising.'

No talk with Kylie would be complete without a mention of Neighbours (her character Charlene has left the series and will not be seen again). Would she like to have lived in Ramsay Street? 'No, not at all,' she replies. I'm glad I moved out! I would rather live in Italy or somewhere else romantic like the South of France.'

Our time was up. Kylie had a host of other people to see, other things to do. As I left the room, she stretched her arms toward the ceiling in a gesture of childish exuberance and, smiling, called through to her manager: 'What next?'

It's tough at the top, but one thing's for sure, Kylie Minogue can handle it.

'With my looks, I am so critical of myself . . . '

PIPE OF HYPE: She's the pop and soap princess,

Mail presents the contrasting sides of a showbusiness phenomenon

Kylie Minogue

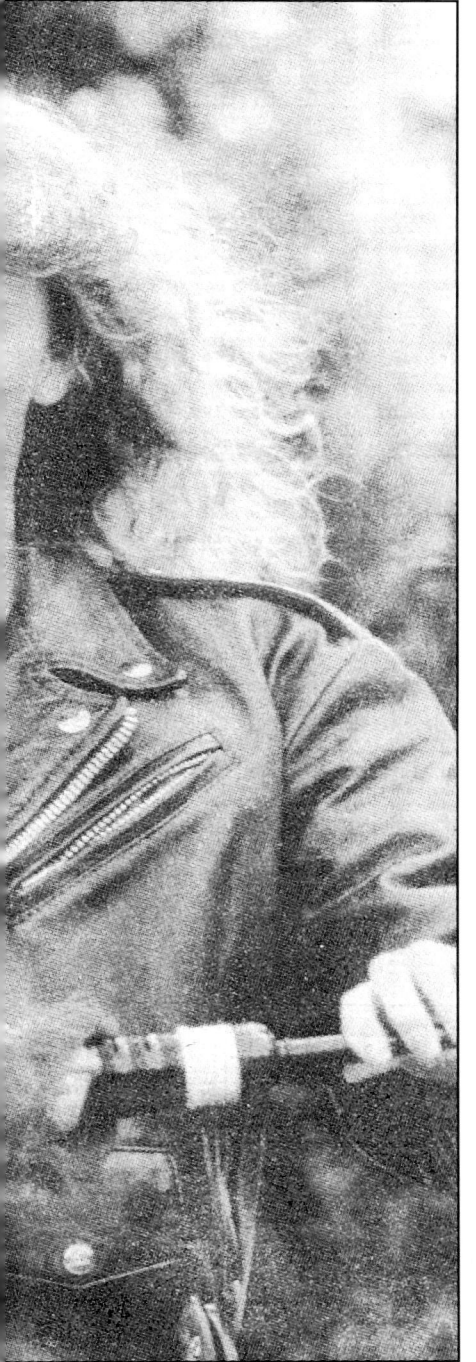

She is a little girl for whom too much has happened too quickly

The article you have just read on the left appears by arrangement with Miss Kylie Minogue's representative. What I wrote was scrutinised and approved on her behalf.

Not only was our interview carefully screened, to give Kylie's entourage the opportunity to sift out even the slightest hint of anything that could be construed as detrimental, but also the date we were 'permitted' to run the interview in the Daily Mail was made a condition of Kylie speaking to us as well.

Actually the interview was done some time ago, but we were forbidden to publish until today, presumably to achieve maximum publicity for Kylie's film (we won't bother to mention the name again).

We were also not allowed to take any photographs of Kylie. Instead, we were told that there would be plenty of material to do with the film made available to us. No new pictures would be necessary. And what if the Mail had not agreed, in writing, to all these terms? Bye-bye interview.

Ridiculous

The interview took place in highly impersonal circumstances with journalists kept herded out of sight in a dark library in a West End club, then allowed their magic 30 minutes with Kylie (and that didn't include the time it took to go up in the lift to her suite or any interruptions) before being politely but firmly ushered out.

There was a copy of the one newspaper which gave a rave review to Kylie's film opened at the appropriate page and displayed on the coffee table downstairs in the 'waiting room'. During the interview, a woman from the aptly named Sharp Ends, Kylie's public relations people in London, remained present.

When I asked politely, as we waited for the lift, if I could do the interview alone with Kylie, the woman looked suspicious and said briskly: 'Well there's no need for that, is there, and why should it make any difference?'

The questions I asked were mindful of the fact that the interview would be supervised by the eagle eyes of her publicists. They were as daring as I could make them, but nothing like the kind of things I really wanted to know.

I would like to have told her that I found it a little difficult to accept her assurance that she just has good friends. And what about all the ridiculous speculation that has surrounded her relationship with Neighbours co-star Jason Donovan over the past two years. Had it ever been on, or was

Does she really have only 'just good friends'?

UNAUTHORISED VERSION

by **SARA BARRETT**

it just another marketing man's stunt to titillate the public appetite for the sickly-sweet Neighbours and the syrupy songs she and Donovan did together?

But most of all I wanted to talk to her at length – impossible in my authorised and chaperoned 30 minutes – about whether she thinks it's really suitable for her, as an idol and role model for very young girls, to take part in a film with a 12 Certificate that shows abortion, sex below the age of consent, and running away from home and makes it all right in the end because true love lasts. Would Kylie really sit happily through that with a 12-year-old daughter?

The hyping of Kylie and the dynamics of the Minogue machine (of which I suspect dear little Miss K is very much an integral part, although her sweet smile and baby blue eyes suggest otherwise) are a salutary lesson to us all in manipulation, marketing and how pop stars can be picked up and made heads of multinational corporations one day, and dumped on the rubbish heap the next in many cases.

Vulnerable

Kylie, like so many before her, is a product. A soap powder to be packaged and pointed at a defined target audience who've been carefully researched. The audience are young and vulnerable. They want posters on their bedroom walls, Kylie pencil case, ruler and rubber sets, and even (and God knows why the Minogue Machine, which earns £25 million a year from record sales alone, hasn't thought of it yet) a Kylie dress-up doll, if it were available.

Grey men in grey suits sit round boardroom tables tapping their pencils and thinking about how this particular product can most effectively grab its share of the household purse. And Kylie thinks too.

The Minogue machine decides, presumably, when the product must be 're-packaged'. In Kylie's case, after two years of being safely sweet, it was decided she should become dangerously sexy. Suddenly, to stop her becoming 'old hat' she must be wrenched from her pinnacle as the inspirational, clean girl next door into tawdry adulthood.

At the film premiere Kylie, despite the fact that the theatre was only three quarters full, was brimming with confidence as she welcomed everybody. 'Hope you enjoy it as much as we did making it,' she said. If she noticed the empty seats then she was too well rehearsed to show it.

At the interview, it was the Kylie image which was all-important. The creation was even allowed to be slightly risqué with references to marriage and children. The ever-watchful PR woman was quite happy to let her giggle over gorgeous Michael Hutchence (Kylie's much-pictured recent beau) and even imply that what Kylie says and does might be two quite different things. Tee, hee naughty Kylie. Last year's marketing strategy would surely never have permitted such brazen indiscretions.

Gruelling

But like all publicity machines, the Minogue machine is meticulously reverential to the figurehead. I was made to feel by Michelle, a public relations girl from the film company, that I was really very lucky indeed to be seeing 'Herself'.

There was a huge appointment book layed out in the hotel containing a carefully typed-out Kylie itinerary for each day, with different things to do, every half hour. When my time came, one of the PR's knocked at the door saying, 'Right, here we are, we're here now, right, in we go,' in the slightly breathy, clipped tones of a nun who's spent her life doing good works and was about to be presented to the Pope.

When the door to the interview room swing upon I hovered, unsure where to sit down. Kylie grinned and bounced on to a green velvet-covered sofa and patted the side of it with her hand, and the PR girls said excitedly, 'there you are! She's saying you can sit beside her!'

They were determined Kylie would not be hassled.

Publicity machines, are of course, expert at all this. They keep a star's relatives, who might express concern at the gruelling schedules, at a discreet distance. They ensure exposure of their precious commodity is carefully controlled, because every merchandising expert will tell you that with too much over-exposure, the thing goes pop.

Kylie is a tiny little girl for whom too much has happened too quickly and she has never been allowed to grow up.

It would be charming to think of her as a manipulated victim, but she's not. It was Kylie herself who declined by request for photographs.

One thing Kylie Minogue should remember about her Machine. When the now apparently insatiable public appetite for her begins to pall, it is she, not her Machine who will be the casualty. The managers and PR people will slink off and try to find someone else to manage and the 'machine' will form around someone new.

but when will the bubble finally burst for Kylie?

So the *Mail* is revealing part of the process of representation which is normally concealed from the reader.

However, the newspaper is doing its own manipulation in the way it chooses to represent Kylie Minogue. It labels two juxtaposed pieces as 'Authorised Version' and 'Unauthorised Version' giving an appearance of balance but implying 'the lie'/'the truth'. The preferred reading of the pages is suggested by a large unflattering picture of Minogue going cross-eyed as she plays the bagpipes, captioned 'PIPE OF HYPE: She's the pop and soap princess, but when will the bubble finally burst for Kylie?'

It looks as though an editorial decision has been made to injure two birds with one journalistic stone. The unathorised version is severely critical of both Kylie Minogue ('Kylie is a tiny little girl for whom too much has happened too quickly and she has never been allowed to grow up') and publicity 'machines' ('Our interview was carefully screened to give Kylie's entourage the opportunity to sift out even the slightest hint of anything that could be construed as detrimental').

This is an illustration of how people and issues are consciously represented, but you also need to think about the publication's selection of material. The *Mail* could have rejected the opportunity to interview Kylie Minogue. Which 'personalities' would they consider worth interviewing? Why 'personalities' anyway? How far do readers' interests influence choices? Over a number of issues of the same publication is there a pattern? Are some kinds of people more likely to be represented than others and if so why?

A Activity

Look at Figure 3.7 'Di finds a worm in the Big Apple' (Guardian 3.2.89) and Figure 3.8 'Gosh, is it 9 years?' (Guardian 26.6.89).

How and why is the representation of Princess Diana in the New York press different from that in the British press?

How does Debrett's represent the Princess? Why?

How do the views of the respective reporters become apparent? How far are they stated and how far implied?

If Princess Diana were visiting your area how would you choose to represent her in a local paper selling to a family audience? How far would you use/subvert the PR machinery?

Understanding legal and ethical issues

Libel

The law of libel protects people from unfair attacks and accusations which are published. Writers must not write anything defamatory about an individual unless it is justified (which might be difficult to establish). Defamation means damaging a person's reputation in the eyes of a community. The kind of situation where this could arise would be if you express your view of the standards of teaching in a college or school and criticise the competence of an identifiable individual. Or you could be reporting what seem to you to be very genuine complaints by aggrieved employees about their harsh and tyrannical boss. In both cases you need to be careful.

Planning and developing print material

Figure 3.7

Figure 3.8

Di finds a worm in the Big Apple

Martin Walker in New York

THE Princess of Wales wiped her hand on her skirt in New York yesterday morning, and probably lost whatever chance she had of taking this hard and cynical, but deeply sentimental, city by storm.

She had just made a brief and evidently token foray into the small crowd of poor people from the lower East Side housing estates, had smiled and chatted and pressed a little New York flesh which was almost deep-frozen after awaiting her arrival for over an hour in the chill wind.

As she turned away, the Princess wiped her hand none too discreetly on her skirt. She then marched past the massed lenses of the city's press and television corps and replied to their beseeching questions about whether she liked the Big Apple with a brisk: "Morning."

"That lady sure don't take no prisoners," the chap from the Daily News muttered.

In the city's tabloid newspapers yesterday, the royal family's superstar had to share the front-page billing with a shock-horror story about a three-year-old tot used as a human shield in a drugs-deal shoot-out.

The New York Times reported the Princess's arrival with an extremely cool and brief caption beneath a photograph tucked away on a page inside. Newsday raged on its front page at the way city employees were scraping chewing gum off the pavement where Princess Diana might step when the city had so many better things to do.

Pete Hamill, who has made his soft-hearted, touch-guy column in the Daily News into a minor art form, greeted her as "the most famous welfare mother in the world, a permanent recipient of British dole.

"She does not work, has no known talents and derives her celebrity entirely from the man she married." All that is true, and fair comment, but it started considerable quivering among the stiff upper lips of the royal-image controllers yesterday.

They are so accustomed to the easy successes of public relations from the practised servility of the British, the politeness of the Commonwealth, and the snobbish sycophancy of the Reagan White House that the hardboiled curiosity of New York has come as a blunt surprise.

This city know about real celebrities. It gave its heart to Mikhail Gorbachev last December, even though he strangled their traffic in 'Gorbylock' and had all police leave cancelled as 6,000 policemen manned the streets to clear the way for the only news-media superstar with the power to blow New York off the face of the earth.

By contrast, the police department assigned a mere 400 to Princess Diana, and the 150 of them on duty in the East Side's slums yesterday were not happy at being taken off their real job: undercover work in the drugs squad.

It will take a lot of retouching and careful camera angles to make this visit anything like a success. But then the image is all. Mr. Rupert Murdoch's Channel Five television filled its screens with a cockney pearly king serenading the Princess at 7am, while the winner of Princess Diana lookalike contest handed out samples of shepherd's pie. It was a PR stunt that looks good on the television, even though the cockney was in the street and the Princess was out of hearing on the 17th floor of her hotel, and there were no crowds to watch.

Doubtless the visit to the opera and the billionaires' dinner party in her honour will fill British television screens with self-congratulatory images of glitz and glamour. But that is not how Princess Diana has been playing in reality, and high gloss of all that is less than fair to her.

Debrett's has illustrated perfectly how the Princess of Wales was packaged

Gosh, is it 9 years?

LET'S face it, the Princess of Wales looked a whole lot more appetising when she was plain old Lady Di – all rumpled cardigans and plump-cheeked teenage shyness. Nine years and a lot of hairspray later and we see her remodelled to the specifications of the royalist public and the tabloid press.

Here is the out-moded Sharon 'n' Kev hairdo (we don't like her changing the style), the nose thrown into hawkish relief by an overly gaunt face (we complain about her weight) and the lavish, constantly replenished wardrobe of slinky designer gear (we object to her wearing the same outfit twice). She is, as a result, a prisoner of her well-dressed image and in turn, the world's most photographed woman.

Debrett's Illustrated Fashion Guide to The Princess of Wales chronicles, in simpering, uncritical style, Diana's nine-year sartorial metamorphosis from shy kindergarten teacher to marginally less shy princess. How she learnt "fashion lessons" after the diaphanous skirt episode and the spot-the-nipple controversy which ensued after she wore a low-cut evening dress. Then came the punitive pussy-bow and frills period – the high necklines, calf-length skirts and strictly no cleavage. Eventually, under pressure from the press, public and the designers who clamoured to dress her, she lost an alarming amount of weight (Debrett's skirts around the issue of anorexia) and became the fashion world's most coveted clothes-horse.

The personality behind the Bruce Oldfield dresses, the Catherine Walker suits holds little interest for anyone, least of all the authors of the Debrett's guide. Most of what we know about her is based around the idea that she is a fairly empty-headed soul – kind to children and animals – with a penchant for pop music and TV and when she's not on public display, suffers from arrested sartorial development: "The Princess favours sweat-shirts embossed with cartoon characters – Mickey Mouse is a particular favourite." While Charles enjoys new, eco-friendly credibility, Diana goes on record as having said nothing more impassioned than Gosh or Hello in the last nine years.

But Debrett's doesn't want to dirty its hands with boring stuff like this – the book is strictly coffee-table dross which must hold a degree of fascination for almost everybody, if only through its detailed photographic illustration (chapters on the shoes, the tights, the hair etc) of how radically the princess has changed over the last nine years.

And then there's the delicious cock-ups when the press had a field day; the red and white striped Ronald McDonald outfit, the silly bow-tie, childish sweaters and the gruesome maternity wear. Bad camera angles, the gust of airport wind lifting a skirt and the off-guard goofy grin are cosy reminders that the Princess is only human after all, although it wouldn't do to see her like that too often. Jayne Fincher, one of the authors, squawks over the car phone on the way to Ascot that the public aren't unreasonable in their demands on Diana: "As long as she looks Princessy enough, they're happy." –
J. R.

● *Debrett's Illustrated Fashion Guide ; The Princess of Wales*. £14.95, published on June 29 by Michael Joseph.

The three questions you need to ask yourself are:
- 'Does your writing tend to lower the person in the eyes of society?'
- 'Does your writing tend to make the person hated, disliked or ridiculed?'
- 'Does your writing tend to make the person shunned by society?'

It is the adverse effect on a person's (or organisation's) reputation that matters.

It is not necessary to imply that someone is at fault in order to be defamatory. To say that someone has been raped or that

Planning and developing print material

4 HOME NEWS
Paper pays rape victim it 'labelled'

Clare Dyer
Legal Correspondent

A RAPE victim has won £10,000 damages from a paper which published the name of her street in what is believed to be the first case of its kind.

The 59-year-old divorcee accepted the payment – £1,000 more than the Criminal Injuries Compensation Board awarded her for the rape itself – in an out-of-court settlement from the freesheet publisher, Thomson Newspaper Group.

Now retired, she was working as a personal assistant when she was raped just before Christmas 1991 by a stranger who climbed through a window of her cottage during the night.

She told her next-door neighbour, who took her for hospital treatment for a broken ankle she got trying to escape, that she wanted the rape kept secret.

Her neighbour persuaded her to tell her three grown children and report the rape to the police, and helped her draw up a list of six close friends to be told.

But the Herald and Post, a Thomson Group paper circulated in Bedfordshire and Hertfordshire published the name of her road, which was a short street, identified her as "in her fifties", and implied she lived alone.

The information, added to the fact that she had a broken ankle, was enough for neighbours, friends and acquaintances to recognise her.

The Sexual Offences (Amendment) Act 1992 bans the media from publishing a rape complainant's name, address or picture, if likely to lead to her identification.

The woman's solicitor Louise Christian, believes her case is the first in which a rape victim has won damages from a newspaper in such circumstances.

The rape victim said she felt "labelled" by the newspaper story.

"I'm a private person. I can cope with things privately, but not for all the world to know.

"Someone who was just an acquaintance came up to me and asked if I would like to talk about it. I recoiled from that sort of offer.

"A chap followed me round a store and then followed me home and leapt out of his car and said "how are you?" He's a do-gooder, a kind man, but it was a horrendous incident."

So unwelcome was the attention that she resolved to sell her house, but was unable to find a buyer. "I loved my cottage. I bought it to retire in and there was no question of selling it after the incident. It was people trying to be kind.

"Some people would love that but I'm afraid it wasn't for me. When new people come in I think 'I wonder if they'll hear about it?' I'm not a cranky old person – I'm just very private."

Her story was featured on BBC TV's Crimewatch programme, but her attacker has not been caught.

Figure 3.9

▶ *The Writer's and Artist's Year Book*, A. & C. Black, London, revised annually

they are insane may not imply criticism, but both statements are defamatory. To show how careful you must be, look at 'Paper pays rape victim it "labelled"'. (from the *Guardian* 31.8.94), Figure 3.9.

For a thorough but readable treatment of the issue of libel consult the section on 'Copyright and libel' in *The Writers and Artists Year Book*, published by A. & C. Black. It is in most libraries.

Copyright

While you are free to copy and adapt someone else's ideas, you infringe the law if you use a substantial part of someone else's work. What 'substantial' means is not absolutely clear, but does not really apply to student journalism unless there is an unscrupulous plagiariser about.

Plagiarism is making very close copies of someone else's work. Facts and ideas cannot be copyrighted, but the treatment of them can be. To avoid plagiarising, always use more than one source of information and make the *treatment* of facts and ideas your own.

A safe guide to how much you can copy would be no more than fifty words, although more could be justified in a review of another publication. If you want to quote more you should contact the author via his/her publisher and ask for permission.

Sometimes you will have to pay for this, depending on the nature and circulation of your publication. It is important to get permission in writing.

It is always safest, even when quoting short extracts from published material, to acknowledge their source and that they are quotations.

As far as your own work is concerned, you hold the copyright of everything you write unless you are employed by, say, a newspaper, in which case the publisher holds the copyright.

Letters are the copyright of the writer and cannot be reprinted without permission.

If you are using publicity photographs to illustrate your work, make sure that there are no copyright restrictions on them. If there are, there will be a clear message on the print.

Ethics

A clear guide to the ethical conduct expected of a professional journalist is in the *Press Complaints Commission Code of Practice*.

Here is a summary of the guidelines which are relevant to individual writers:
- Don't write material which is inaccurate or misleading.
- Though you can be partisan, you should make sure you distinguish clearly between comment, conjecture and fact.
- Don't intrude into people's private lives.

- Don't pretend you are not a journalist in order to obtain sensitive information, unless it is in the public interest and the material can't be obtained any other way.
- Don't harass or intimidate people in order to gain information.
- Enquiries into stories where people are suffering from grief or shock should be made with sympathy and discretion.
- Children should not be interviewed or photographed at school without the permission of the school authorities.
- Don't interview children under 16 about their personal welfare unless a parent is present.
- Don't write anything pejorative about a person's race, colour, religion, sex or make prejudicial reference to physical or mental illness or handicap.

There are other recommendations about reporting sex and crime cases which do not apply to most student journalism.

Producing visual material

Photographs

Here are two photographs which are typical of work produced by students who can 'take a photo', but have had little or no photography training. Figure 3.10 below is meant to illustrate an article for a school magazine about a new careers library. How well does it do this job?

Figure 3.10 Picture from a school magazine

First it provides some appropriate information. We can see the library shelves, the students browsing for information and one student holds up a careers newspaper so that we can see the title. The image is clear and the lighting is suitable.

A Activity

Group discussion: try different ways of cropping (selecting just part of the picture) and scaling (enlarging or making it smaller) to produce a more effective image.

Discuss how different groupings of the students could improve the composition of the picture.

What are the relative merits of (a) having the subjects looking directly at the camera and (b) making them appear 'natural'?

Is an eye-level shot best for this subject or would you consider using different camera angles?

Try the same kind of analysis with Figure 3.11, another competent photo which could have been improved with a little more preparation and attention to detail. It was taken to illustrate an article about a school's new wild garden.

Figure 3.11

Here are some guidelines to help non-specialist photographers improve their pictures:
- Don't just look at the subject through the viewfinder, think about what else is in the picture, especially in the background and ask if you need it. Don't be timid about moving in close (see Figure 3.12).
- Encourage your subjects to do something which is relevant to the story (see Figure 3.13). Avoid 'firing squad' shots with groups of people facing the camera but doing nothing special. Here the sign, the paint brushes, the sweatshirts and the background all help the reader to understand the story. The low angle of the shot allows the photographer to include the cathedral in the background. Low angle shots tend to emphasise the importance or power of the subject, but that was probably not the purpose here.

Try to use details from your environment, or props, to emphasize the purpose of the picture. In Figure 3.14 the photographer has asked the subject to pose behind some railings (he was about to be imprisoned for failing to pay his Poll Tax). Notice too how the shot is not full face, but taken at a slight angle. Nor is the subject's face in the exact centre of the picture. If it were, the symmetry of the railings would be spoiled.
- Subjects taken dead centre often look static and dull. Take them slightly off-centre.
- When framing a picture through the viewfinder, divide it mentally into thirds and make the eyes just fit into the top third of the photo as in Figure 3.15.

Figure 3.12 A close-up photo

Planning and developing print material

Figure 3.13 Encourage your subjects to do something which tells the story

Figure 3.14 Use details from your environment

Figure 3.15 Frame the picture with the subject's eyes a third of the way down the image

Planning and developing print material

- For action shots, try to find a position from which you can take interesting or unusual angles and viewpoints.

  In Figure 3.16 the photographer has taken up a position just below a hill on a corner on a cross-country course. The manoeuvre that the athletes are making is a difficult one requiring much concentration. There is also a striking contrast between the expressions of the athletes and the spectators, which may well have been anticipated by the photographer. The picture is well composed, with the two groups seeming to lean into the centre.

Figure 3.16 Choose your position well

- You can create dramatic effects by going very close to your subject or by doing some really close cropping as in Figure 3.17.

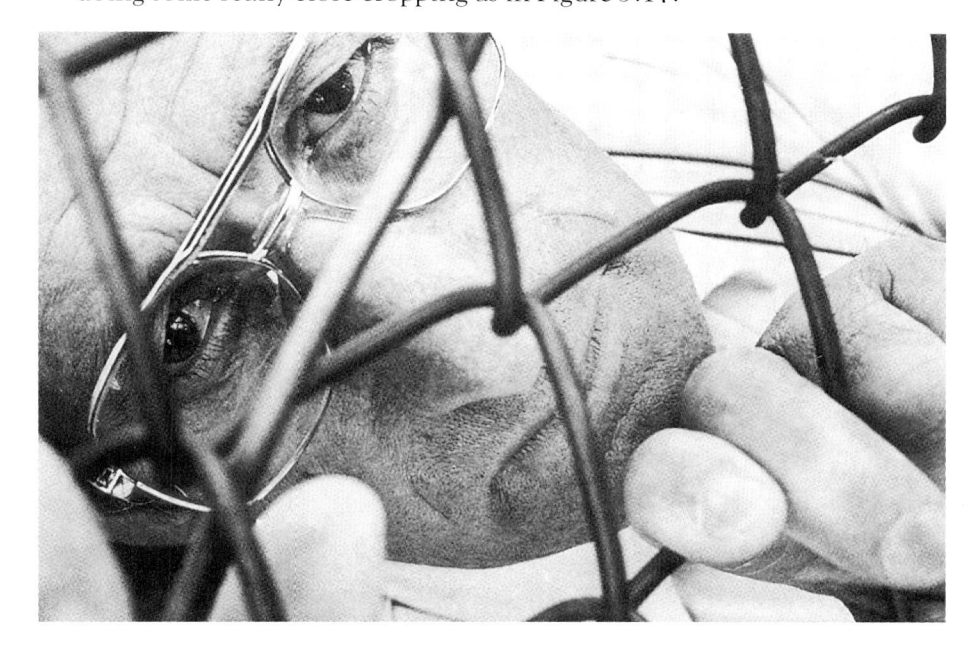

Figure 3.17 Going in very close can create dramatic effects

- Try to get your subjects to relax and be unaware of the camera if you want some natural shots. See Figure 3.18 which shows how effective this is when photographing young children.

Figure 3.18 Get your subjects to behave naturally

Graphics

The term *graphics* is taken to include all drawings and computer-generated artwork used to illustrate and explain parts of stories. Many graphic artists also use Adobe PhotoShop™ to modify photographs as parts of illustrations. The illustrations are used break up text and to provide visual information where words alone are less effective.

Graphics should be used if they help the reader to understand information. They should be avoided if they merely decorate something, unless your intention is to amuse rather than inform.

Figure 3.19 shows two sorts of information. First, the drawing explains clearly and strikingly how tornadoes happen.

Figure 3.19

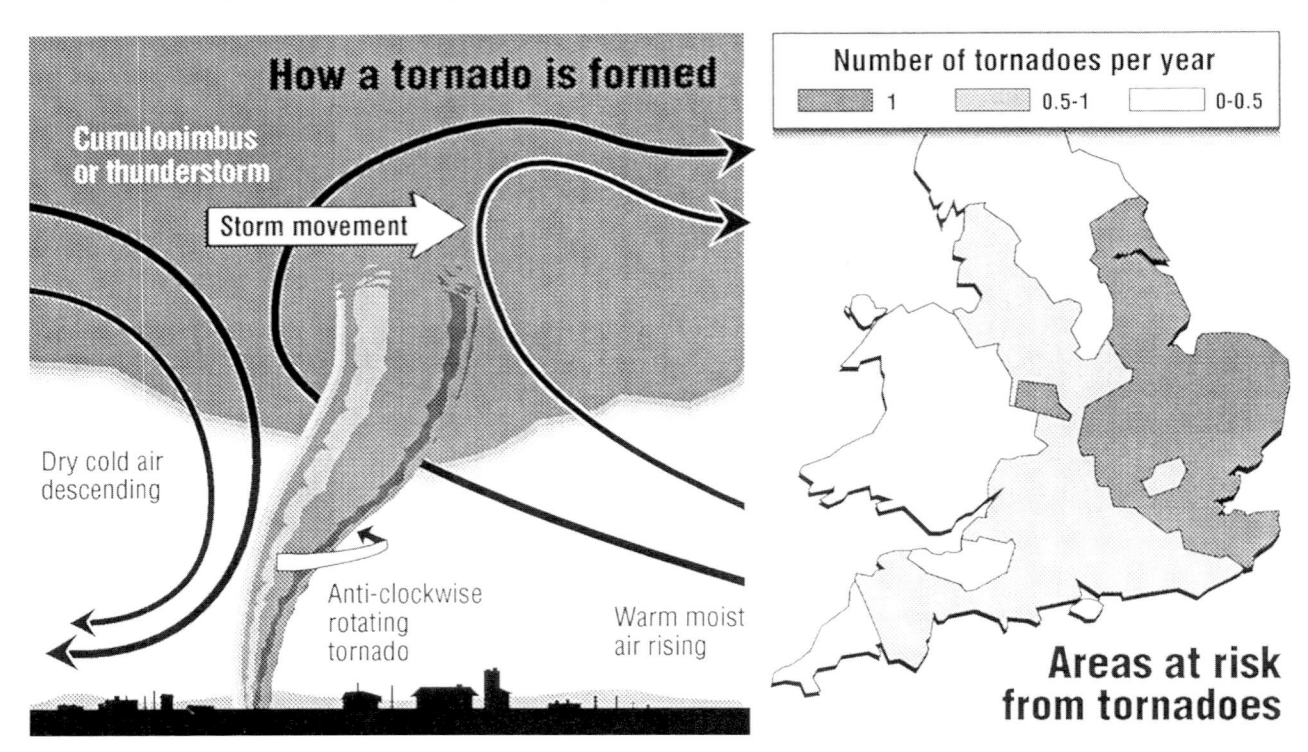

Does the image make the information more dramatic, easier to understand than a verbal description would? It depends on the quality of the verbal description. But it certainly helps quick communication of information.

Secondly the map, at a glance, tells readers, living in England and Wales anyway, what kind of risk they have of experiencing a tornado. It would be more difficult if the reader were simply given a list of counties and their tornado risk. The geographic distribution of tornadoes would be much less easy to understand without the map.

The information is kept simple. If there were need for more detail such as what levels of contrasting temperatures are needed to trigger a tornado, or why the Isle of Wight has a lower risk than Hampshire, this would be best explained in the text for the more curious reader.

Photographs are not always sufficient to help readers understand the story. The press carried many pictures of the crashed train in the Glanrhyd bridge accident, but it needed a drawing to show what was beneath the surface of the water. (see Figure 3.20). The artist has been able to include information about before and after the crash in the same picture.

Checklist of types of graphics

The amount of information and the type of information necessary or desirable should govern the choice of design. Where there is lots of information to give *a map, chart or graph* may be the only ways which will work (see Figures 3.21a and b).

The simplest graphic is a *photograph with symbols* added to highlight important details. It is possible to print photos with no mid-tones (i.e. with no greys) to give them more strength and impact. They can be combined with other techniques such as drawings or graphs.

Drawn images can be used to tell the reader about the location of a place or event, to present statistics or to explain something (see Figure 3.22).

There is ample scope for using graphics effectively in sports stories. They can *explain techniques* and tactics simply to the non-expert reader. (see Figure 3.23).

Sequential graphics (like comic strips) are useful for explaining processes in 'how to' articles such as gardening, DIY, car repairs or cookery.

Caricatures (see Figure 3.24) of famous people can be drawn and used instead of photos to add variety to a page.

Figure 3.20

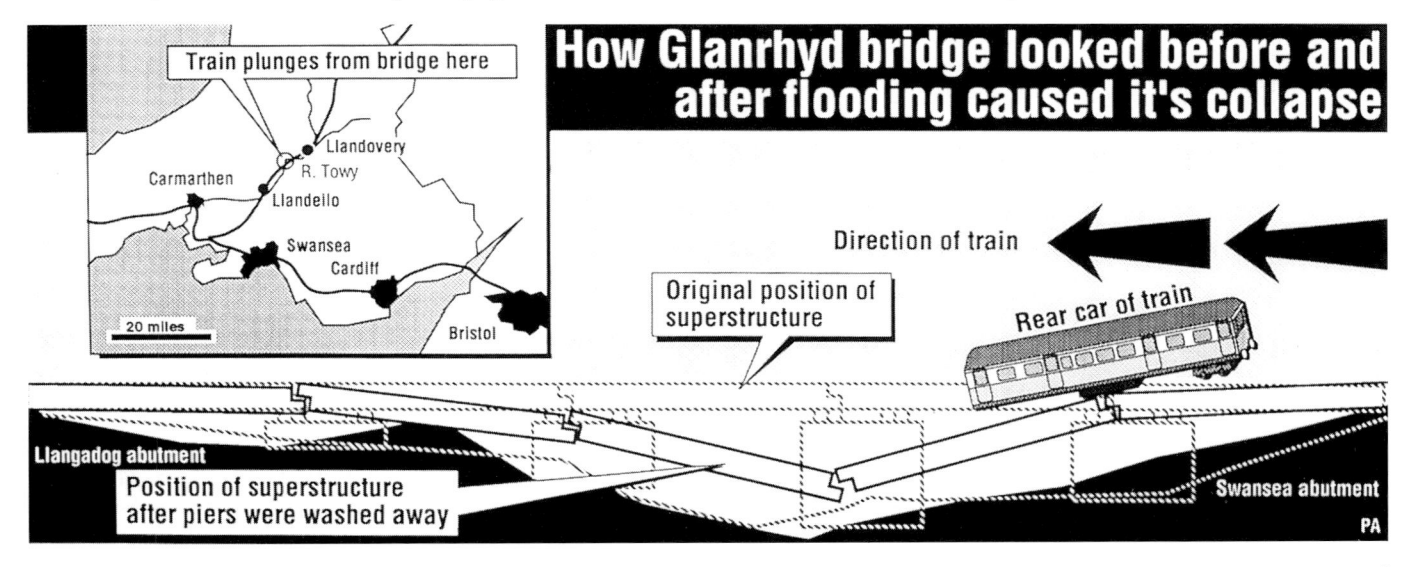

Planning and developing print material

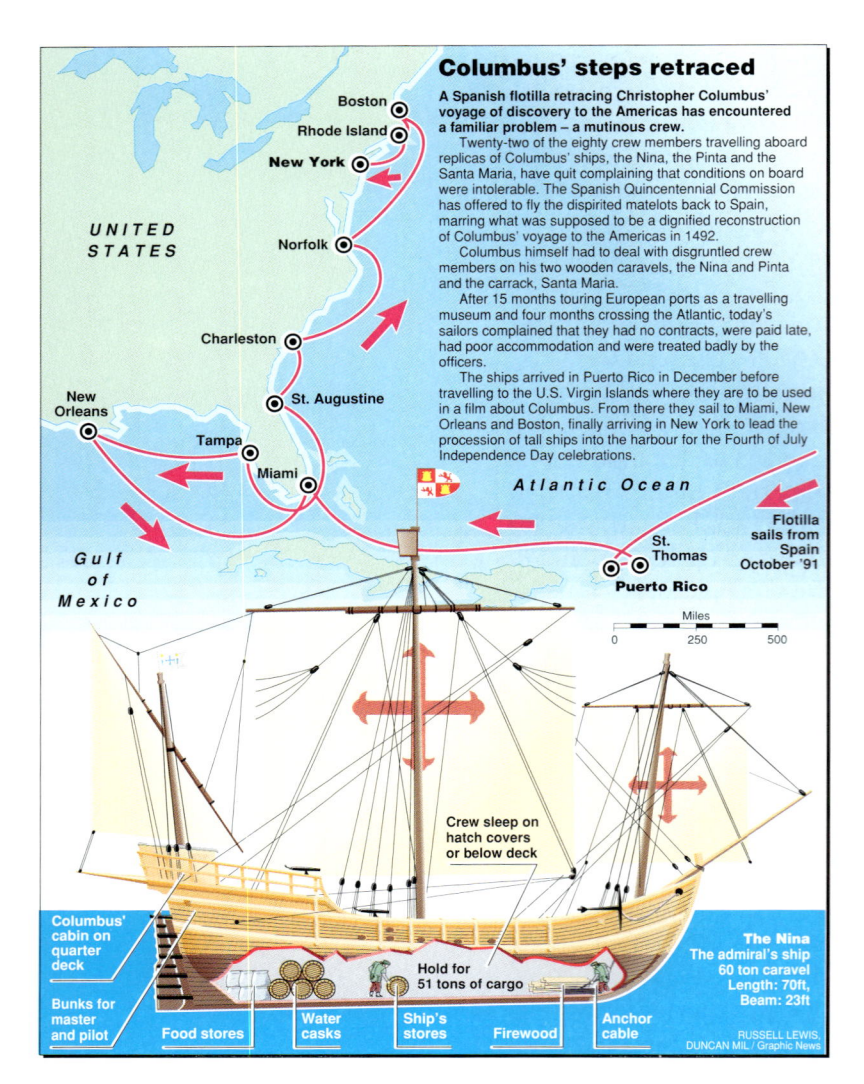

Figure 3.21 a

Figure 3.21 b

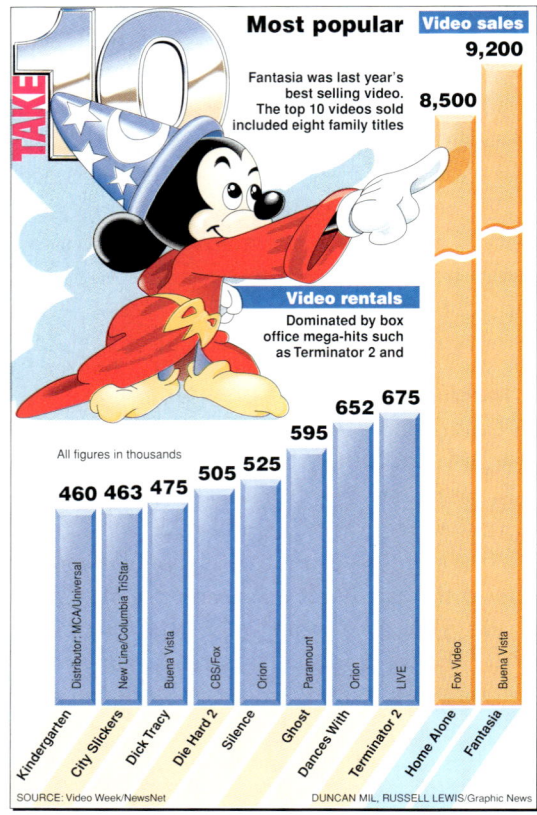

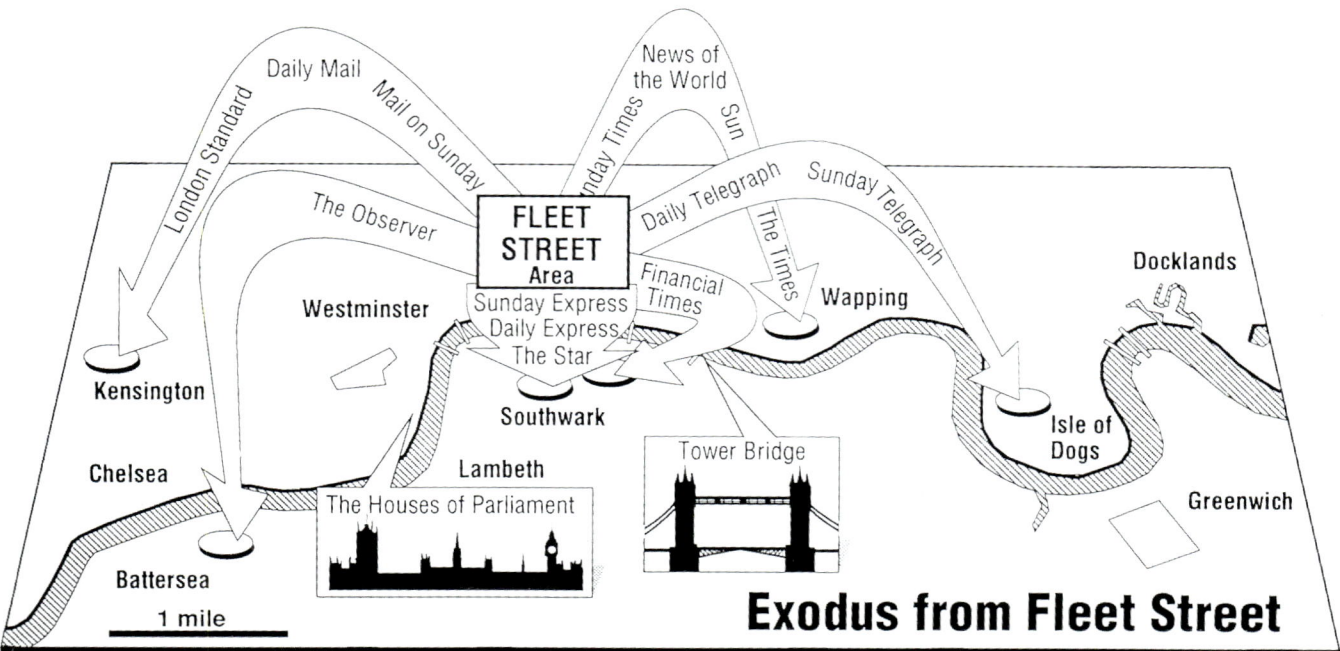

Figure 3.22

84

Planning and developing print material

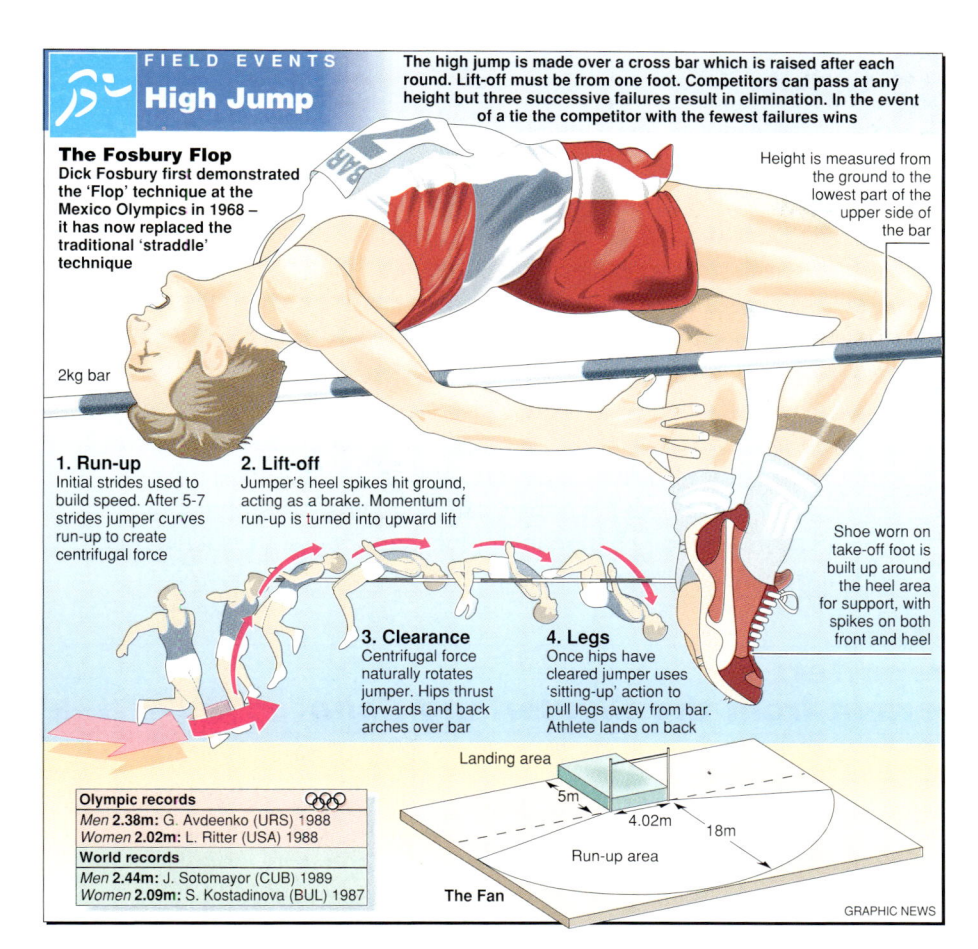

Figure 3.23

FIELD EVENTS
High Jump

The high jump is made over a cross bar which is raised after each round. Lift-off must be from one foot. Competitors can pass at any height but three successive failures result in elimination. In the event of a tie the competitor with the fewest failures wins

The Fosbury Flop
Dick Fosbury first demonstrated the 'Flop' technique at the Mexico Olympics in 1968 – it has now replaced the traditional 'straddle' technique

2kg bar

Height is measured from the ground to the lowest part of the upper side of the bar

1. Run-up
Initial strides used to build speed. After 5-7 strides jumper curves run-up to create centrifugal force

2. Lift-off
Jumper's heel spikes hit ground, acting as a brake. Momentum of run-up is turned into upward lift

3. Clearance
Centrifugal force naturally rotates jumper. Hips thrust forwards and back arches over bar

4. Legs
Once hips have cleared jumper uses 'sitting-up' action to pull legs away from bar. Athlete lands on back

Shoe worn on take-off foot is built up around the heel area for support, with spikes on both front and heel

Landing area
5m
4.02m
18m
Run-up area
The Fan

Olympic records
Men **2.38m**: G. Avdeenko (URS) 1988
Women **2.02m**: L. Ritter (USA) 1988
World records
Men **2.44m**: J. Sotomayor (CUB) 1989
Women **2.09m**: S. Kostadinova (BUL) 1987

GRAPHIC NEWS

Figure 3.24

▶ For a comprehensive guide to the subject see *Newspaper Graphics* by Peter Sullivan, IFRA, 1987.

Planning and developing print material

A Activity

- Draw a map and plan to guide people to an open day at a school or college. They must be accurate but not too detailed. They will be read quickly by people who will not be skilled map-readers. You should ask yourself what information your readers will need. Help people travelling from different directions by different means of transport. You should draw the plan and map much bigger than the eventual print size so that you can include fine detail. They can then be reduced in size by the printer.

- Devise an illustration to provide information about current best-selling records. You can obtain the information from specialist publications. Your information should include lists, opinion, details about record labels and notes about the movement of records in the charts. It should have illustrations that attract the reader's eye and let him/her know at a glance what your illustration is about.

PROFILE   Newspaper reporter: Graeme Anderson from the *Sunderland Echo*

As the *Echo*'s South Tyneside chief reporter I am always busy.

Because I am the only reporter covering the area full time, it is my job to make sure stories from South Tyneside are constantly coming in to the news desk. Every day is different, but there is a general structure to it.

I start work at 8 a.m., and work from Monday to Friday. I am supposed to finish work at 4 p.m., but like most reporters I am frequently at my desk well beyond 5 p.m.

When I arrive in the morning I check the local morning newspapers to see if there are any stories to follow up.

News desk tell me if there any stories they have picked up overnight or that they want me to do. Then I'm on my own.

I ring the emergency services on South Tyneside – the police, fire and ambulance, to pick up details of any major stories – and then follow them up.

Often I have to go out to the story, usually taking a photographer, to interview people involved.

I also regularly cover magistrates' courts and council meetings where many stories are found.

While I am out of the office, I meet many people in pubs, clubs, shops and churches who provide me with many stories.

These contacts also ring in to tip me off about stories I might be interested in.

If there is nothing much going on then I go out of the office and drive round South Tyneside looking for possible stories.

Assignment

Design a graphic

Here is some information about a plague threat in India. Use these details and information books from a library to design a graphic illustration which will make it easier for readers to understand the problem. Ideally you will need an atlas, biology books with illustrations of fleas and rats and a medical reference book with diagrams of the human body. You should re-draw the pictures rather than copy them.

- There is a ban on Indian food exports to the Middle East.
- Arab states have banned flights from India and send back ships coming from India.
- Europe imports over 30 000 tonnes of peanuts a year from Gujarat.
- Europe has postponed shipments of peanuts.
- Air India has grounded more than half its fleet.
- Europe has banned groundnuts.
- The Gulf States have banned chilled meat, Basmati rice, vegetables and fruit exports.
- Over 50 people have died from plague in India – two in New Delhi, one in Maharashtra and the rest in Surat, Gujarat.
- Of 1500 suspected cases of plague in India at least 250 have been confirmed.
- Plague is caused by the bacterium *Yersinia pestis* which lives among rodents and their fleas.
- A bite from an infected rat flea can lead to plague in humans.
- Bubonic plague causes headaches, fever and intensely painful swellings of the lymph nodes – especially in the groin area.
- Bubonic plague is spread by fleas who feed on rat blood before laying eggs. The eggs then fall to the ground developing in litter and dirt. The hatched larvae feed on the filth. After becoming adults they jump onto passing rats, renewing the cycle.
- Pneumonic plague is a complication affecting the lungs and causing severe coughing.
- Pneumonic plague is spread from person to person by drops of infected phlegm.
- Pneumonic plague is treatable with antibiotics.
- The Foreign Office are advising people not to travel to the affected area of Gujarat.
- In Britain in 1349 20% of the population including 50 000 in London were wiped out by plague – the Black Death – brought to Europe by traders and crusaders from the East.
- In Britain in 1664–65 a fifth – 100 000 – of London's population died from the Great Plague.

4 | Producing newspapers and magazines

This chapter will help you to organise the production of a print publication. The print publication unit in the GNVQ specifications assumes that you have already taken photographs, written rough drafts of stories and prepared graphic illustrations. You are now expected to work in a group to pool that work, select from it, edit it and publish a finished product which should look as professional as possible.

Introduction to print production

You will need to adopt some professional practices and attitudes during the production process. Teamwork is essential if you are not to waste your energy. This is easier to achieve in a professional setting because people's jobs depend on co-operation, but as students you still have the pressure of knowing that your individual assessment may depend on successful group interaction.

This chapter is organised into the following sections:
- Introduction to print production
- Evaluating product ideas
- Planning the production process
- Product design
- Case studies: *Babe* and *Manorisms*.

You do not need to assign formal roles in your team, though that is an option. It is better to work in a semi-formal way, using individual strengths where possible. If you are clear about what jobs need to be done in the end it does not matter too much who does them as long as they are done. You do not need an editor unless the group is wasting too much time arguing, but you do need editorial decisions to be made. This can be done through discussion. You do not need a chief sub-editor (i.e. someone whose role it is to check all the material for factual and typographical accuracy), but you do need to check the accuracy of everything you print. You do not need a pictures editor, but you do need to choose the best pictures to illustrate your publication.

From an educational point of view it is desirable that you should perform a variety of tasks, taking photographs as well as obtaining quotes from printers, helping to design pages as well as keying in text. Don't forget to keep a record of all that you do, as this may be needed for assessment.

Evaluating product ideas

When you evaluate the product ideas you should consider whether you have the *time* to produce the publication. If you are employing a printer, for instance, you need to find out how long before the print date s/he needs to have the completed proofs. If you then work backwards from this date, you can allocate time for proofreading, editorial selection, writing, research and page design. If you need to raise finance to pay for your production costs then that should be scheduled as well.

Make sure that you have access to the *technology* that you need to complete your publication and that it is capable of producing what you intend. If you are relying on a laser printer or inkjet printer, for instance, and want to produce tabloid size headlines for a newspaper, make sure that the printer can output the size you need.

Fitness for purpose would mean asking questions such as whether the readers will be able to understand the publication. If you are producing educational material for primary school children, for instance, you need to know what the reading ages of your target audience are. You need to know how to measure the reading age of your text and how to modify the text if it is unsuitable.

Evaluation in terms of *aesthetics* means considering what your publication will look like and whether its appearance will appeal to its readership. What sort of a front cover, for instance, will appeal to readers and give an idea of what the publication is about? You might also consider the relationship of text to visuals. Do particular stories need illustration? Do you need at least one illustration on each page? The evaluation is linked with questions of human resources. It is no good planning lots of graphic illustrations if you do not have a competent graphics designer.

You will need to make more specific aesthetic decisions when you come to designing your pages in detail at the sub-editing stage of production.

Before you begin to put your publication together you should have a *master plan*. This is sometimes referred to as a product specification. Here are some headings you can use with advice about what you need to consider.

Target audience

Who are you producing the publication for? You need to have a real audience, which, realistically, can be anything from your peer group to a school/college catchment area, although other possibilities can be considered such as publishing for a twinned organisation in a foreign country or using the Internet to disseminate your message.

Decisions you make about the *size of your audience* will affect all other decisions you make. Once you have determined the size of your audience you should investigate their needs and interests. What information do they need or want? What topics are they likely to be interested in? You can only find this information by conducting some audience research using face-to-face interviews or questionnaires.

Describe your audience in terms of age, gender, interests and geographical location. A paragraph is all you need – something like this:

'*Above the Rim* is a specialist basketball fanzine aimed at the 12–21 age group. It will appeal mainly to males who play basketball or support local teams in the Birmingham area.'

Figure 4.1 The number of 'fanzines' covering sport, music and other areas which have a significant following has grown enormously with the advent of 'desktop publishing'.

Objective

Apart from its educational value what is the main purpose of your publication? Is it to inform, educate, persuade, promote an event or a point of view, shock, titillate, amuse or a combination of some of these? To continue with the basketball example:

'The objective of *Above the Rim* is to inform and entertain basketball fans with a combination of profiles, information and pictures of American stars and to combine this with up-to-date information about local matches, leagues and fixtures.'

Production

You need to consider these questions:
- How many pages will your publication have?
- What size will the pages be?
- How many columns will you have?
- Who will print the publication?
- What methods will be used for typesetting?
- How will the illustrations be handled?
- Will any colour be used?
- What quality paper will be used?
- What will be the ratio of advertising (if any) to editorial?

Distribution

You need to consider these questions:
- How many copies will you print?
- When?
- Who will sell or deliver them?
- Will the publication be a one-off or part of a series?

Content
More questions to address:
- What information will you include?
- What sorts of feature articles will there be?
- Will there be any on-page involvement (e.g. crossword puzzles)?
- Will there be competitions and prizes?
- Will you include comment and opinion?
- Will there be specialist articles?
- Will there be anything to cut-out-and-keep?
- Will there be any 'how-to' articles (to encourage long term retention of the publication)?
- How many photos and illustrations will there be?
- Will there be any advertorials (i.e. text written to advertise something, but disguised as a newspaper/magazine feature and paid for by the advertiser)?
- What types of advertising, if any, will you try to attract?

You can relate your decisions to the parts of the target audience you are writing for.

Information sources
List the organisations and individuals who will be able to provide the information you need. Start with your own institution and work outwards with the help of a local directory and a reference book that lists pressure groups.

Thus you might produce a list that starts with your college/school marketing officer, mentions local libraries and recreation centres and goes on to organisations such as the RSPCA, Greenpeace and Life.

It is useful for a school/college to keep this list for use in subsequent years. It should be checked, updated and added to each year. A comprehensive and vital sources list is a prerequisite of lively journalism.

Finance
How will the publication be financed?

There are three methods of financing a publication:

a) Grant or sponsorship. Your school or college may be able to give you a budget to work from. A local business or grant funding body may finance your enterprise.

b) Cover price. You can sell your publication. This, however, is an unpredictable process and can lead to serious miscalculations of financing. Neither can you guarantee your sales to any advertisers.

c) Selling advertising space.

You can raise money for printing costs by selling advertising space in the paper.

This can be done by contacting businesses and organisations which need publicity either by letter, or telephone or by personal visit. It is a good idea to start with firms that already do business with the school/college, such as suppliers of furnishings and equipment.

It can be useful for different departments in a school/college to co-operate on a publishing project with the business studies students becoming involved in the financial organisation of the project.

Work out first how much you are going to charge for advertising. It is normal for a publication to have about 40% of its pages given over to adverts. Once you know the total cost of the printing, you can work out how much a page of advertising will cost. Advertisers are used to buying space in column centimetres so you will need to decide quite early how many columns your publication will have and how big the pages will be.

You need to design order forms which can be sent to potential customers. It is also useful to have a sample book of adverts with their costs.

Publishers are in the business of selling audiences to advertisers. This is the reason behind the fragmentation of Sunday newspapers with a number of separate sections appealing to specific groups of people. Magazines are also tending to become more specialist in order to offer advertisers specialist audiences. To put this in the context of your publication, if it is being distributed to every student in your institution then you should contact advertisers who need to appeal to that particular age group or that particular institution. You could decide to run a computer games review page in order to attract advertising from local computer games retailers. A feature on keeping fit could attract advertising from a number of local sources who want to attract teenagers, such as leisure centres, health clubs and leisure-wear retailers.

Production

You can produce small runs of a publication in-house by photocopying, but large print runs are better handled by a professional printer. The cost of printing a newspaper on newsprint can be relatively cheap. Some local newspapers have contract printing departments and will handle orders as small as 1000. You can keep the costs down by doing the type-setting yourself and by providing ready cropped and scaled photographs. Costs increase if you go for full colour, though even then it is considerably cheaper if you can provide a paste-up with coloured prints on the page. Using spot colour (i.e. one colour only) is not very expensive and can improve the look of a publication.

It is also worth being aware that some newspapers will print A4 magazines on newsprint, which for runs of 1 000 plus can be much cheaper than using a jobbing printer. It is good practice to obtain several quotations before making decisions.

In any case you need to consider the variables which include the number of pages, the quality of the newsprint, the use of colour, the number of photographs and illustrations and the typesetting costs.

Planning the production process

You should begin by making a list of all the procedures. Prepare an action plan as a list or as a flow chart or diagram. The list needs to include what needs to be done, by whom and when. It is worth getting into the habit of treating deadlines as sacrosanct, because they are so crucial in the publishing world.

Working backwards from the printing process, these are some of the questions you need to answer:
- Who will print the publication and how?
- What is the deadline for finished pages to go to printer?
- Have you checked the printer's requirements to make sure there are no last minute hitches? (Last minute scanning and scaling of visuals can be very time consuming and costly.)
- Who has to proofread the copy? (It is worth having at least two very reliable proofreaders who should each read the copy twice, once for meaning and once for literals (mis-prints).)

- Have you enough staff to typeset the copy? Are they able to work to the publication's format? For instance, can they set columns, select different fonts, highlight text, change font sizes, and work out techniques for fitting text to space?
- Will you have you enough material to fit the planned space?
- Who will write the material?
- Who will make editorial decisions if there is a choice of material and what criteria will be used?
- Have you arranged for someone to produce a flat plan or mock up of the publication which indicates what goes where on which pages?
- Have you arranged for photographs to be taken and developed?
- Who will design graphics and how closely will they work with the writers?
- Will the equipment you need for typesetting, developing photos and printing be available when it is needed?
- Who is responsible for the overall design strategy of the publication?

Figure 4.2 Planning is a crucial part of the production process.

Product design

'Planning is the key word in creating a graphic strategy for a [publication]. Imagine that you are taking a reader on a journey. Map your way from beginning to end. On the journey the reader will encounter a variety of ideas and paths that lead to surprises, knowledge and inspiration.' (Mario Garcia: *Contemporary Newspaper Design*)

Design is not about decoration. It is about helping readers to find their way around your publication.

Garcia, M., 1993, *Contemporary Newspaper Design,* Prentice Hall

Checklist of design features
- Help the reader with an entry and exit point on each page.
- Give each page one centre of visual impact.
- Make headlines big so that readers can find quickly what they want to read.
- Surprise the reader occasionally.

Readers' eyes are attracted into a page by a headline, photograph or illustration. Once they have been 'caught' it should be easy for them to know where to go next. Designers should chart the eye-flow through a page, to make sure there are no points where there is confusion and that there are no awkward eye-movements.

Typography

You should select a typeface for the body text of your publication and use it consistently throughout to give continuity. If you change it occasionally there should be a good reason to do with making things easier for the reader. You can choose a different font for headlines, but again aim for continuity. A standard and effective combination is Times for body text and Helvetica for headlines. Helvetica, Futura, Universe and Franklin Gothic are the most used headline fonts.

The size of the type is important. It should be between 9 point and 12 point for *body text* (i.e. the main bulk of the text, excluding such things as labels, captions and specially designed features). Try to avoid using different sizes of body text fonts in a publication. It is tempting when faced with the problem of cramming text into limited space to choose a smaller font, but this can give a messy look to a page. It is better to edit the text.

Checklist of legibility factors
Capitals and lower case
Capitals in large blocks of text and small fonts are difficult to read. They are effective in short headlines.

Figure 4.3 Serif and sans serif fonts

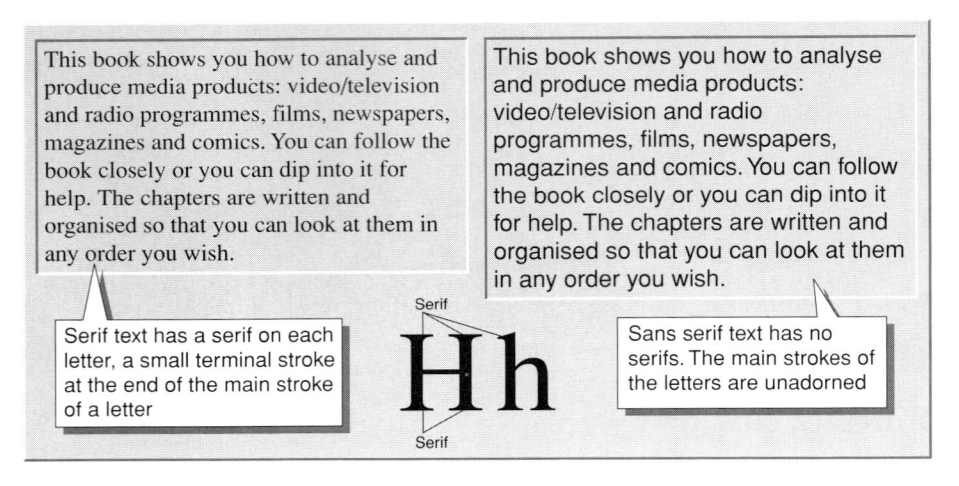

This book shows you how to analyse and produce media products: video/television and radio programmes, films, newspapers, magazines and comics. You can follow the book closely or you can dip into it for help. The chapters are written and organised so that you can look at them in any order you wish.

This book shows you how to analyse and produce media products: video/television and radio programmes, films, newspapers, magazines and comics. You can follow the book closely or you can dip into it for help. The chapters are written and organised so that you can look at them in any order you wish.

Serif text has a serif on each letter, a small terminal stroke at the end of the main stroke of a letter

Hh

Sans serif text has no serifs. The main strokes of the letters are unadorned

Serif and sans serif
Large blocks of sans serif type can be boring and most publications go for serif fonts in body text, believing they are easier on the eye. Sans serif fonts have greater clarity and are frequently used in headlines.

Kerning or letter spacing
This can be tightened or loosened – that is, the space between letters can be altered. This affects the reader's eye comfort.

Leading
This is the space between lines of print. Adjustments to leading can be useful in fitting text to space, but if leading is too tight it affects legibility. If it is too loose it can look sloppy.

Column width
This affects the number of words per line. You should make the column width match the size of the body text font. An average of six words per line makes for readable text.

Figure 4.4 Kerning (letter spacing): different densities

> This book shows you how to analyse and produce media products: video/television and radio programmes, films, newspapers, magazines and comics. You can follow the book closely or you can dip into it for help. The chapters are written and organised so that you can look at them in any order you wish.
>
> `condensed type`
>
> This book shows you how to analyse and produce media products: video/television and radio programmes, films, newspapers, magazines and comics. You can follow the book closely or you can dip into it for help. The chapters are written and organised so that you can look at them in any order you wish.
>
> `normal type`
>
> This book shows you how to analyse and produce media products: video/television and radio programmes, films, newspapers, magazines and comics. You can follow the book closely or you can dip into it for help. The chapters are written and organised so that you can look at them in any order you wish.
>
> `expanded type`

Figure 4.5 The effects of different leading on typefaces

> This book shows you how to analyse and produce media products: video/television and radio programmes, films, newspapers, magazines and comics. You can follow the book closely or you can dip into it for help. The chapters are written and organised so that you can look at them in any order you wish.
>
> This book shows you how to analyse and produce media products: video/television and radio programmes, films, newspapers, magazines and comics. You can follow the book closely or you can dip into it for help. The chapters are written and organised so that you can look at them in any order you wish.
>
> This book shows you how to analyse and produce media products: video/television and radio programmes, films, newspapers, magazines and comics. You can follow the book closely or you can dip into it for help. The chapters are written and organised so that you can look at them in any order you wish.
>
> Leading is the amount of space between lines of type. It can affect the amount of material which will fit on a page and how dense text appears

Figure 4.6 Different column widths

> This book shows you how to analyse and produce media products: video/television and radio programmes, films, newspapers, magazines and comics. You can follow the book closely or you can dip into it for help. The chapters are written and organised so that you can look at them in any order you wish.
>
> This book shows you how to analyse and produce media products: video/television and radio programmes, films, newspapers, magazines and comics. You can follow the book closely or you can dip into it for help. The chapters are written and organised so that you can look at them in any order you wish.
>
> This book shows you how to analyse and produce media products: video/television and radio programmes, films, newspapers, magazines and comics. You can follow the book closely or you can dip into it for help. The chapters are written and organised so that you can look at them in any order you wish.
>
> Different sizes of typeface require different column widths in order to accommodate the same amount of text

Alignment

There does not seem to be any agreement about how justification of text affects legibility. Unjustified text, with a ragged right edge, looks more relaxed, but a page of it can also seem disorganised.

Reverses and screens

Reverse print is white on a black background. It can have a dramatic effect but should be used sparingly. It is also more difficult to read, especially with a serif font, where the ink of the background merges with the letters.

Figure 4.7 Reverses and screens

Tint screens and 'reversed' text can be used to highlight material

There is a similar problem with screens or tints. However, if you need to attract a reader to something, then a screen, especially if it is coloured, will attract the eye instantly. Competing screens will lead to confusion.

More detailed guidance on typography can be found in *Newspaper Design* by Hutt and James and *Creative Typography* by March.

▶ Hutt and James, 1989, *Newspaper Design,* Lund Humphries

▶ *Creative Typography,* March

Using photographs

At the stage of preparing the material for your publication you should have a variety of photographs available for selection. There should be long shots, close ups, shots from different angles, individuals and groups.

Figure 4.8 Long shot

Figure 4.9 Close-up

96

Producing newspapers and magazines

Figure 4.10 a–c Try to get shots from different angles – they can add interest.

▶ Photographs, page 77

When it comes to selecting photographs, consider:
- Does the photograph enhance the story?
- Does the photograph have impact? That is, does it make the reader stop and look?
- Is the quality good enough? It must be in focus, and neither too light nor too dark.

You can create order on a page by the way you place your photographs. If you have only one picture for a page, then it is worth making it your centre of visual impact (see Figure 4.11).

Figure 4.11 (Left) Pictures used to draw attention to a page

Figure 4.12 (Right) Visually balanced pages

If you have more than one picture you should try to give balance to the page by distributing them so that both the top and bottom of the page have visual interest (see Figure 4.12).

It is worth making sure that you have different sizes and shapes of photographs. This can be done by scaling and cropping.

Do not try to use up all available space. White space around or next to a photo can lead to it having more impact.

It is useful to have a group of photos of different sizes, especially if you are producing a photo page.

Figure 4.13 Using photos of different sizes to good effect on a page.

The page should have a lead picture in the same way that a text page should have a lead story (see Figure 4.14).

Every photograph in your publication should have a caption (or at least a reference to it in the text). A caption should identify the people in the photo. It may describe what people are doing and/or give information about place and time. Good captions offer an insight into the story and an enticement to read it.

Producing newspapers and magazines

Figure 4.14 Using a lead photo

CASE STUDY   Babe

Figure 4.15 The front cover of Babe

Babe is a 24-page, black and white photocopied fanzine. It was produced by three 17-year-old students from St Robert of Newminster School in Washington, Tyne and Wear, as part of a media studies course.

The students, Lauren Cairns, Julie Watson and Joanne Hughes, were inspired to go into publishing when they met Slamm's manager George Krimpton-Howe, who explained that he started out in the music business by producing fanzines.

The target audience is teenagers, mainly girls, interested in pop music. 'We aim to give information about lesser known groups that you would not read about in mainstream magazines,' says Lauren.

The students get their information from the publicity departments of record companies and from informal interviews with bands that are visiting their area. The first edition had exclusive interviews with Slamm, Menergy and One World.

The magazine is typeset on Desktop Publishing equipment using Microsoft software and an inkjet printer. It is photocopied for 1p per page and then sold by the students themselves for 40p. They sell it at local gigs, at school and in local record shops and newsagents.

CASE STUDY   Manorisms

Manorisms is a 12-page newspaper which was produced by a class of 14-year-olds at Manor School in Hartlepool.

The publication was produced as part of an English course in school. One thousand copies of the paper were printed by the *Hartlepool Mail* for just over £300. The papers (free-sheets) were delivered to households in the catchment area of the school by a direct delivery firm. Pupils raised revenue by selling advertising space to local businesses. The advertisers were: a window manufacturer, a builder and decorator, a car sales firm, a childcare organisation, a shoe repairer, a printer, a men's outfitter's, a sewing centre, a hotel, a fashion shop and a mortgage and loan firm.

The students wanted to produce a community newspaper, so their lead story on the front page was about crime in the locality. They obtained three perspectives on the problem from the police, local shopkeepers and students from the school. Several of the stories were about the school – pupils being presented to Prince Andrew, visits from a poet and a dance expert and an ex-teacher who was sailing round the world, but they were written to appeal to the general reader who had no inside knowledge of the school.

There was a serious feature about drug abuse and a light-hearted one about local fish and chip shops. The pupils set up a Blind Date experience for two 13-year-old pupils and reported their reactions and experiences. There were fun items, reviews and some sports coverage.

Figure 4.16 *The front page of* Manorisms

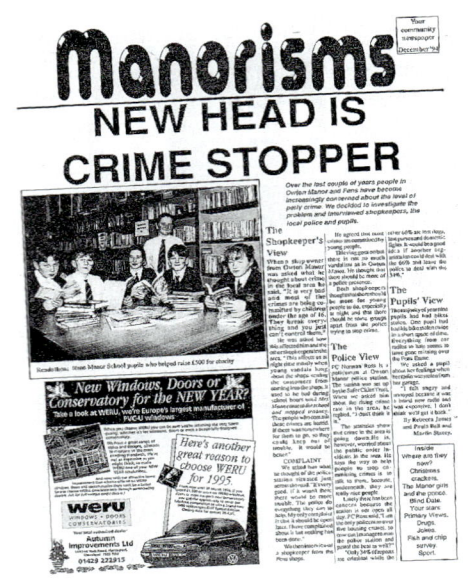

Assignment

Setting up communications

Set up a communications system which will provide a supply of information for a newspaper
- Make a list of all your contacts, i.e. people who may have some information which could form the basis of stories in a newspaper.
- Ask them to send you a press releases or news letters.
- Arrange to interview contacts if the story is important enough and you want more detail.
- Ask them to tell you what is new, different, important.
- Tell them when your paper is coming out and ask for any information they may like to have published. Make sure there is a contact person and phone number in case you want to check details. See if there are any photo opportunities, i.e. times when your photographer can take pictures of individuals or groups.
- Give them a contact person and a telephone number.
- Make clear what the deadline for information is.
- Say who your paper is for.
- Ring them up occasionally to jog their memories.
- Give them advance warning of anything of theirs which you are going to publish.
- Give them a copy of the paper.

5 | Analysing comics

> Analysing the media, page 10

This chapter considers another way of approaching Unit 1 of your GNVQ. It shows how to analyse a print product that relies on visual images more than words. It looks at the genre of juvenile comics, and uses the same analytical techniques as outlined in Chapter 0, 'The basic toolkit'.

The chapter is divided into the following sections:
- The *Beano*: production history and marketing context
- Introduction to analysing comics
- Analysis of comics by genre
- The narrative structure of 'The Bash Street Kids'
- Case study: 'Calamity James'.

Introduction to analysing comics

All criticism should be informed by a knowledge of how and why the publication has developed through time and how it is constructed to respond to the commercial pressures of the market-place. This is a reliable antidote to the wilder excesses of subjective analysis, where a critic's fanciful interpretation of images can lead to bizarre conclusions. Some of these interpretations are referred to in the section on the production history of the *Beano*.

> McCloud, S.,1994, *Understanding Comics*, HarperCollins
>
> Barker, M.,1989, *Comics – Ideology, Power and the Critics*, Manchester University Press
>
> *Comic Book Confidential,* 1994, The Voyager Company

If you are surprised to find comics subjected to academic analysis, you might like to read Scott McCloud's remarkable book *Understanding Comics – The Invisible Art*, while the more scholarly *Comics – Ideology, Power and the Critics*, by Martin Barker, shows how rigorous and rewarding close textual study of comics can be. There is an excellent CD-ROM called *Comic Book Confidential*, which has 120 comic pages showing the work of major American comic creators. It contains biographical details, interviews and a history of comics. It would be a useful starting point if you want to study a particular writer or sub-genre.

Comics make a good subject for analysis because they can be studied anywhere, unlike films, and they do not present the critic with large areas of text to plough through, as is the case with magazines and newspapers. They contain several kinds of visual images, from representational to symbolic, which can be used for image analysis, while the combination of image and text allows you to look at the concept of *anchorage* (the way in which text is used to limit or guide the reader's interpretation of the image), and there are several types of narrative structure to analyse.

The *Beano*: production history and marketing context

The *Beano* and its stablemate the *Dandy*, published by D. C. Thomson in Dundee, are the two most-read juvenile comics in Britain. Just over a quarter of the population aged 7 to 14 read one or the other or both. Their combined weekly sale is over 283 000, giving a readership of 1 214 000. Almost a third of the *Beano*'s readership are girls (see Figure 5.1). The highest readership by age is among 10-year-olds, but 15% of its readers are aged 14 or over. It seems to have an appeal across social classes too, with almost half of its readership belonging to the ABC1 social groups. The *Beano*'s advertising sales department proclaim that *Beano/Dandy* readers have 'potentially over £2 million to spend each week'. They also entice potential advertisers with information about *Beano* readers' lifestyle patterns – 94% of its readers aged 7 to 10 visit burger bars or pizza restaurants, for instance (see Figure 5.2).

▶ Audience, page 16

Figure 5.1 *The readership breakdown of the* Beano

> HOWDY FOLKS! I'M DESPERATE TO TELL YOU WE'VE GOT A STRONG GRIP ON THE 11-14 AGE GROUP READERSHIP TOO!

> WOW, THESE TABLES ARE WORTH MAKING MAKING A SONG AND DANCE ABOUT!

Albert Square, Dundee DD1 9QJ
Tel: 0382 23131. Fax: 0382 25511.   ADVERTISEMENT MANAGER: J. I. FOGGIE.

The Beano and the Dandy – Britain's all-time favourite comics with a weekly sale of 283,880* and an estimated four readers per copy!
These magazines are seen by a very wide age range. The Beano for example commands an enormous 91%[†] of the total readership in the 7-14 age group. It also tops the high social grade category ABC1 in the 7-10 age group and comes a desirable fourth in the 11-14 age group.
The Beano and the Dandy readership is extremely strong in the 11-14 age group. In the past advertisers may have underestimated this and not realised their considerable potential.

THE BEANO
READERSHIP PROFILES

TOTAL READERSHIP	1,118,000[†]	AGE 7-19
BOYS	769,000	69%
GIRLS	349,000	31%
ABC1	508,000	45%
C2	286,000	26%
DE	325,000	29%

AGE	No. of READERS	%
7	103,000	9
8	124,000	11
9	130,000	12
10	174,000	16
11	148,000	13
12	161,000	14
13	114,000	10
14+	165,000	15

* Publisher's Independent Audit July-Dec. 1993
[†] Age 7-19 Youth T.G.I. 1993.

Figure 5.2 *Readership lifestyle breakdown*

The *Beano*'s first issue was on 30th July 1938, a little later than the *Dandy* which began on 4th December 1937. 'Big Eggo', an omnivorous ostrich, was on the first cover of the *Beano*, which cost 2d and offered a free 'Whoopee Mask' as an inducement to buy. The early stories were a mixture of the familiar (school, gangs, families), the surreal (a character who lives on the sea bed and fish that act like highwaymen) and the western (stories like 'Whoopee Hank – the Slap-Dash Sheriff'). Several of the early stories seem to have taken their inspiration from popular films of the time.

Not long after the launch of the two comics, the Second World War began. Paper shortages were a major problem, but the comics continued to be published on alternate weeks through the war years. They became patriotic and included several stories involving stock characters such as Lord Snooty and his gang with real people such as Hitler and Goering. Figure 5.3 shows an example of a propaganda piece from 7th September 1940. The publishers claim that the *Beano* and *Dandy* 'were recognised as having done a lot to keep up the morale of young folks in the anxious days of evacuation and bombing raids and the lack of other relaxations and pleasures' (D. C. Thomson Media Pack).

In its early years *Beano* included text stories without illustrations, in keeping with juvenile magazines of the time such as *Adventure*, *Wizard* and *Hotspur*. But the arrival of television made readers want a more visual style in their reading matter. Nevertheless the *Beano* did not go all comic until 1975.

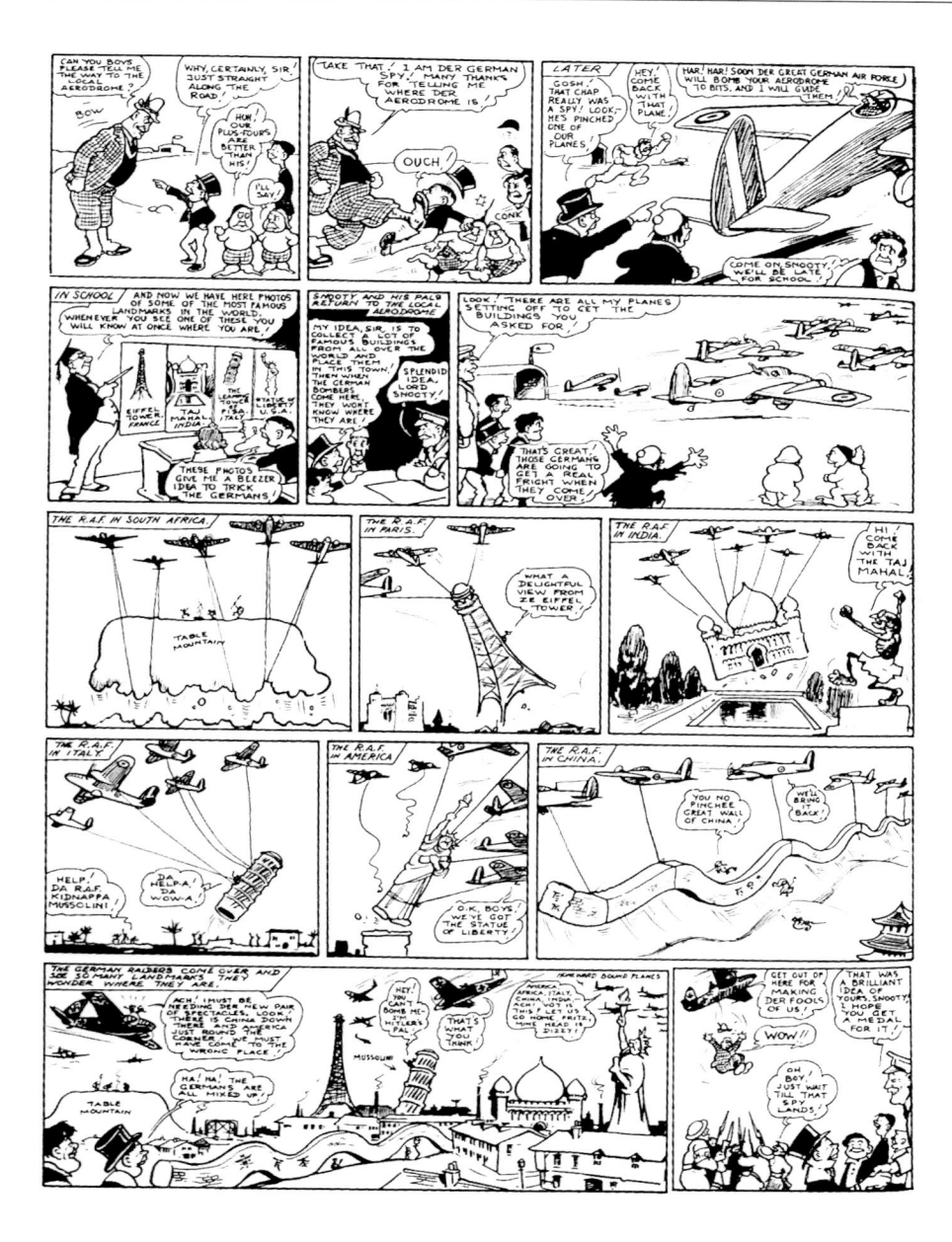

Figure 5.3 'Lord Snooty' from 7th September 1940

The *Beano* has sought to appeal to children's sense of knockabout fun, often achieved at the expense of teachers and parents. Characters have been dropped through the years as their popularity has waned, or survived because of their continuing appeal.

Publishers' view

This is how the publishers describe the early appeal of both the *Dandy* and the *Beano*:

'The humour in both comics was basic. The fun stemmed from the characters ... a wide selection of different cartoon types ... in well-formed stories. ...Both the *Dandy* and the *Beano* created fantasy worlds in which children might question the probability of the exploits, but not the attitudes or the standards of behaviour. There was a moral code. A code of ethics. Parental and school authority might be challenged but there was inevitably a punishment to suit the "crime".'

Critics' views

It is interesting to compare the publishers' view of their product with the view of a critic, George Gale, who was thinking of The *Beano* among others when in a debate on comics he said:

> 'While violence is the main feature of these children's comics, the systematic destruction of the English language runs it a close second. The blows, falls, shrieks, crunches etc. are accompanied by a proliferation of non-words ... A regular survey of these and similar comics would show that each week children are invited to laugh at people who are fat, deformed, handicapped or ugly, especially when pain is being inflicted. This is accompanied throughout by crude, ugly language. Such a regular diet can do nothing but harm to children.'
> (Quoted in *Comics–Ideology, Power and The Critics* by Martin Barker).

Another to express dislike of what comics are supposed to be doing to children is Bob Dixon, who says:

> 'The main aim of the creators of these comics ... is to give rise to fun and humour. This is of a knockabout farcical type though verbal humour in the form of puns, is also important. The humour nearly always arises through someone getting hurt though this isn't peculiar to these comics. It's the most common form of humour and it's a sobering thought.'
> (Quoted in *Comics – Ideology, Power and The Critics* by Martin Barker).

▶ Barker, M.,1989, *Ideology, Power and the Critics,* Manchester University Press

Artist's view

The creator of the *Beano*'s 'Bash Street Kids', Leo Baxendale, explains how his characters were created and what his intentions were in *On Comedy – 'The Beano' and Ideology* (Reaper Books, 1989). He tells of a struggle between himself and the *Beano*'s editor of the time, George Moonie, which took a year to resolve. In 1953 Baxendale had applied to do freelance work for the *Beano* and was told to supply material similar to what was already in the comic and the *Dandy*. Baxendale was not comfortable with the 'Lord Snooty' story and its public school setting, nor with the comic's 'persistent element of magic'. (It contained stories such as 'Jimmy and his Magic Patch', for instance.) 'My childhood peers had scoffed at any belief in magic as soft,' claimed Baxendale. Moonie, however, was convinced that 'the power of magic' was an important ingredient of comic strips.

Baxendale was influenced by the zany Warner Brothers film animations and Giles' uninhibited cartoons. He was influenced too by the ratty dialogue of comedian Tony Hancock, the double meanings of character actor Kenneth Williams and the characters in the radio programme *The Goon Show*. What particularly appealed to Baxendale was Giles' 'uninhibited portrayal of the stampeding inhabitants of large urban schools'. He used this as an inspiration and sent several sketches to Moonie. Moonie was unimpressed and instead asked Baxendale to draw a 'magic' set called 'Jock the Giant Killer'.

Baxendale says there was a basic difference of opinion between Moonie and himself over the matter of retribution. Moonie believed that 'those who receive a poke in the eye should have done something to deserve it'. Baxendale believed that a 'deserved' disaster had no meaning in a comic world.

After Baxendale had been producing another story, 'Minnie the Minx', for a few months, Moonie wrote to him and asked him to produce a set featuring 'a bashing, thumping crowd of children pouring out of school'. He had found Baxendale's original proposals and reconsidered them. Baxendale produced a winter's scene with about 50 children in it:

> 'I didn't sketch the characters separately beforehand – I created them individually in the course of the drawing – and drew two leaders, a girl and a boy.'

He describes the girl, Toots, as a variant of Minnie the Minx, but 'I made Toots a Boadicea, being a leader. (Minnie was the leader of no one – she acted alone.)'

At first Baxendale modelled his boy leader on the hero of Richmal Crompton's 'Just William' stories, but then added a skull and crossbones motif on his jersey to draw attention to him. The awful cook is supposed to be based on the *Beano*'s office tea lady and the teacher looks remarkably like the first editor of the *Beano*.

Pressure was put on Baxendale to include a posse of police to keep the kids in order. He included police in one of his early scripts, but, in his robust way, armed them. Moonie complained about arming the police and asked Baxendale to tone this down. Baxendale complied, but resolved to banish the police from the strip henceforth, which he did.

The Bash Street Kids first appeared in the *Beano* in February 1954. It was then called 'When The Bell Rings'. It was still going strong in 1995. Baxendale's attitude to morality gradually prevailed. He felt that if the feature was to develop, the kids had to 'burst out into the world and marmalize it under their trampling hooves'.

He is particularly proud of an early 'Army Display' story where some kids inflict a resounding defeat on the army in the foreground while in the background others are shelling Bash Street School and machine-gunning fleeing teachers, and he remarks that 'This was quite some years before Lindsay Anderson's film *If...*, where rebelling students in a public school attack the staff with weapons.'

Before Bash Street, the dominant presentation of schoolchildren had been as characters from public school. (See George Orwell's essay 'Boys' Weeklies' in *The Collected Essays, Journalism and Letters of George Orwell, Volume 1*.)

▶ Orwell, G., 1968, *The Collected Essays, Journalism and Letters of George Orwell, Volume 1*, Secker and Warburg

Baxendale intended something very different:

> 'to present "ordinary" secondary school children (though comedy demanded that they should at the same time be extraordinary) so that Bash Street would appear near to the everyday life of the greater number of children in the country.'

In representing the teachers, Baxendale did not hesitate to use 'archaic symbols'. In his own grammar school, teachers had worn gowns throughout the year and mortar boards on speech days, but Baxendale says there were two purposes behind using this image of teachers:

> 'On pages printed by letterpress, those patches of solid black gave weight to the page and drew the reader's eye to Teacher ... secondly, the presence of mortar board and gown made the status of Bash Street school ambiguous. To seize the widest readership I deliberately blurred the status of Bash Street. Mortar board and gown suggested grammar school; yet I carefully excluded Latin and Greek from the Bash Street Kids' homework ... grammar school kids wore blazers; the Bash Street Kids did not. Though this blurring of status was deliberately done, for

the market, it caused me unease whenever I did it, since I believed that art, and in particular comedy, should be specific.'

Baxendale gives some useful insights into the characters of Bash Street and how they emerged. Of the permanent group of kids, only three appeared in the first set: Danny, Toots and Fatty. The antecedents of Fatty (Hungry Horace and Billy Bunter) were depicted as greedy and the butt of jokes. Baxendale says:

> 'This would not do for me. I did not intend to portray Fatty as greedy, or a butt. It would be alien to me; and there would be no source of comedy in it for me. Fatty's purpose was visual. In a group of characters who were mainly even and stocky his circular shape was a visual contrast. The tall and gangling Plug and the dwarfish Wilfrid were created for the same reason – visual variety.'

Plug came into Baxendale's mind as a child version of Eccles from the radio programme *The Goon Show*. He thought that Spike Milligan had modelled the voice of Eccles on that of Walt Disney's Goofy, and that is how Plug (name inspired by the American phrase 'plug ugly') came to be gangling and goofy.

Teacher, based on George Moonie, the *Beano*'s editor, is portrayed as an ineffectual character. Though he is twice as tall as the kids, 'his cane, vainly flailing' was the symbol of his ineffectuality.

Baxendale takes issue with a number of assumptions about Bash Street made by academic and journalistic commentators. He was annoyed by an arts programme, *Arena*, claiming that his characters are often rewarded with food and that the stories are preoccupied by physical punishment. Baxendale denies both claims and for his book *On Comedy* lists all the examples of feeds and whacking in the Bash Street sets which he drew before leaving the *Beano* in 1962. He concludes that feeds were never used as rewards and that, of his 424 Bash Street sets, 351 had no whacks and in the rest 'where Bash Street Kids got whacked it was not judiciously applied punishment, but the result of frenzied revenge, or of the flailings of a soul in torment – Teacher'. He goes on: 'Looking anew at the 424 weekly Bash Streets I drew, it is hard to say exactly what they are, taken together, "about". The most constant observable factor (apart from *joie de vivre*) is that each week was unlike the next.'

Analysis of comics by genre

If you are studying comics as a *genre*—as distinct from magazines, cartoons and short stories, say then these are some characteristics that you might observe:

- Comics are sequential. A cartoon is a single frame which does not show progression, but a comic shows one thing happening after another. All genre definitions are, in the end, subjective, and you will need to consider whether you agree with Scott McCloud that strip cartoons, simple 'how-to' diagrams and even those strips of photo-booth portraits count as comics.
- Comics use frames to to create the illusion of time and movement.
- They use motion lines to create the illusion of movement.
- They use bubbles to show speech, clouds to show thought.
- Sound effects are introduced with special typography.

Analysing comics

Figure 5.4 Spread from 'The Bash Street Kids', 1st April 1995

- Symbols are used to represent the invisible (e.g. hearts above someone's head to show they are in love).

If you are studying *juvenile comics* as a sub-genre of comics, here is a checklist of some of their characteristics, but note that genres can change and can be challenged; you should check these and modify them in the light of your own reading.

- Characters are uncomplicated, with one significant characteristic.
- Drawings are iconic (simplified) rather than representational (lifelike).
- Protagonists (characters who make things happen) are children or else behave like children.
- Plots are simple and involve people playing tricks on each other.
- Characters do impossible things without explanation.
- When characters suffer they recover and are unchanged, ready to start the next 'episode'.
- Characters who are rational, cissy, pleasant or a teacher's pet suffer.
- Most natural laws can be broken.
- Stories are full of action.

A Activity

Look closely at the stories in three different juvenile comics, for example the *Beano* or *Dandy*, *Buster* and the *Beezer-Topper*. Test the genre criteria outlined above to see how accurately they can be applied to the comics you study. Modify them in the light of your findings.

The narrative structure of 'The Bash Street Kids'

The stories analysed below come from the following issues:
1 24th Aug 1991
2 17th Sept 1994
3 1st April 1995 (see Figure 5.4)
4 20th May 1995.

The opening frames of these four stories establish a basic situation:
1 Teacher wants one of his pupils to participate in the World Athletic Championships.
2 Teacher starts a handicraft lesson.
3 Teacher has a treat for the kids (a visiting outdoor education lecturer).
4 Kids decide to pay a visit to Teacher, who is in hospital.

Though presumably drawn by different staff artists over the years, Teacher's dress and appearance are unchanging. He is a middle-aged man whose balding head is usually covered by a black mortar board. He wears round rimmed glasses and has a rather weedy Hitler-style moustache. Over his blue pullover his red jacket looks a little tight-fitting and seems to have patches in the elbows. There is no sign of a cane in any of these stories. If Teacher appears in establishing frames he seems to be earnest, friendly, anxious to help the Kids, but perhaps a little naive. The Kids, who vary in number, are always cheerful, keen to join in any action or else amusing themselves with childish pastimes such as throwing paper darts.

By the fourth frame something unexpected and usually painful, though the pain is not emphasised, has happened to Teacher (usually) or another character. In 1 Fatty has fallen through the ground as he tries to putt the shot; in 2 Teacher has found himself nailed to his chair; in 3 the outdoor education tutor has made his entrance by bursting through the floor of the classroom, propelling Teacher into the corridor; in 4 Teacher, lying in bed in hospital, has been stung on the nose by a bee which has flown from a bunch of flowers.

In each story, action is crammed into a short space. Each story has about 18 frames, which gives about 12 for the middle of the narrative. This allows for three or four incidents (or jokes). In 1, apart from Fatty's misfortune, the relay team use their batons in a swordfight, Plug throws a hammer through the school wall to land on the Head's head and the Kids force Teacher to jump over the high jump by bombarding him with peas from a pea-shooter. In 2 Smiffy makes a teapot without a spout (because his mother doesn't drink tea), Plug's metal mirror curls up when he looks into it, Toots destroys the CD player Cuthbert has just made by trying to play a CD on it and when Teacher throws away Sidney's 'bread basket' he is chased by the snake that was hiding inside it. In 3 (see Figure 5.4), after the teacher recovers, the Kids try out the instructor's climbing shoes by walking up the walls and along the ceiling. The Head chases off Olive the cook because she fancies the instructor. The Kids trick the instructor and their teacher by tying them together, as the instructor demonstrates his climbing prowess, and by giving them one of Olive's very heavy sponge cakes. This makes them plummet to earth where they make a mighty crater in the school playground. In 4 Toots pulls Teacher's nose, the kids take him to the operating theatre where they give him giggle gas, threaten to cut off his toe, remove a tap from his toe, but leave a grease gun stuck to it.

There seem to be no barriers to where the Kids can go, whether it be a world athletics championships or an operating theatre, and nothing which they cannot do, such as walking on ceilings or instantly making CD players. There is no problem either with finding and using the most bizarre props for the story. A pet python can suddenly materialise, or the Kids can be instantly kitted out in medical clothing and have access to an operating theatre.

Endings sometimes show the Kids suffering, as in 1, where they end up with a professional athletics coach replacing Teacher and forcing them to compete. In 4 they are chased from the hospital by Teacher. In 2 and 3, however, it is Teacher who is suffering, first concussed at the bottom of a crater and then escaping from a snake by climbing up a home-made ladder.

The settings of the stories can be anywhere, but, as with the school, they are always drawn simply with very little background detail. This minimal approach helps to give the story its timeless appeal and presumably has practical advantages, as the *Beano*'s production team has to come up with a new story each week.

CASE STUDY   Calamity James

Here is an analysis of the 'Calamity James' story from the *Beano* of 16th January 1993, looking especially at the codes and conventions used by the artist.

The first picture introduces the two main characters. James's fear of the world is shown and regular readers will know that that is because wherever he goes terrible calamities happen to him. Everything that happens to him, however, is reversible. He is always restored to normal so that another sequence of disasters can occur. This is a convention of juvenile comics – no physical distortion or suffering has lasting consequences.

James's friend is an animal, but like most animals in juvenile comics he behaves with human

Analysing comics

Figure 5.5 'Calamity James'

112

characteristics (anthropomorphism). The technique used by this particular artist to give information is to attach a label to Alexander, explaining to new readers who he is. Much of the fun in 'Calamity James' comes from the bizarre labels and signs which the artist inserts often with no relevance to the story. You will notice that James lives opposite the Bum Scratchers and Nose Pickers Social Club, for instance. And look at the creature who is not there in frame 3.

Comics are visual and static which means that techniques have to be used to show movement, sound and smell and mental states. The stork dragging the title has movement lines near its wings. There are movement lines to show the lemming's throwing action and the trajectory of the brick. Sound is shown by words – 'Friendly thunk'. The wavy lines over the bin suggest smell which is reinforced with verbal explanations beside and on the bin itself. The picture has elements of realism such as the television aerial and the window frame combined with the surreal – a brick that bounces off a window pane and a talking lemming. Alexander's confusion is shown in the second last frame by a question mark over his head and James's dizziness is shown by a series of stars.

The drawings are not representational and rely on significant details to create atmosphere. The poverty of James's environment is shown in the second frame by the hole in his shoe, the taped split in the hot water bottle, the broken plaster on the wall, the stitched curtain and the patched pillow. His sloppy lifestyle is hinted at by the underpants hanging on the lightshade and the nibbled hamburger which he is keeping for a midnight scoff (the label tells us).

In a comic world the rules of logic and nature can be defied. In 'Calamity James' the humour lies in the extremes of absurdity which are possible after something as mundane as standing on a filled hot-water bottle. After being propelled around his bedroom, hitting bed, ceiling and floor, James falls through to the ground floor of his house where some random and seemingly innocuous ingredients fall into his trousers (which often become enormous containers) and create a nuclear explosion which propels James's house into space. Meanwhile, back on Earth, James's mother goes on watching a soap opera on the television, oblivious to what has happened.

While this absurd main event has taken place, other impossible things have happened. The writing on the bottom of James's bed has changed and the social club has turned into a factory which makes plastic false teeth.

In non-representational comic art the body can take on any shape the artist wants to imagine. A tongue can become longer than an arm, a bump on a head can be bigger than a nose, an ear can be wide enough for a sausage to lodge in it.

The exuberant vitality of the artist's creation leads him into breaking some of the 'rules' of comic strips. The drawings seem to burst out of their frames with energy and there is a profusion of sound words.

The artist is able to take any point of view from anywhere and is not constrained by the practicalities and realities of non-animated film, for instance. Here he can switch from a view from space showing an explosion on a distant Earth to a close up of a perplexed lemming.

Assignment

Analysing a comic

Analyse a comic. (It is better to read Chapter 6, 'Making a comic' before doing this assignment.)

Find out from its publisher something of the publication's history and its commercial circumstances, such as circulation figures, target market and competition.

Read several issues of the publication, preferably from different times. Describe the genre characteristics of the publication either as a comic or as a type of comic (e.g. girls' comic, science-fiction comic).

Examine several examples of a particular story to establish underlying patterns of story construction and characterisation.

Examine the same story or another one from the point of view of its use of comic codes and conventions such as framing, ways of representing sound, including speech, movement, ways of showing time and place changes, ways of showing thoughts, feelings and ideas, use of symbols and simplification of images.

6 | Making a comic

The production of a comic allows you to satisfy the GNVQ requirement to write a proposal for a print product which is predominantly image-based. It also gives you the opportunity to produce a fiction product.

Unit 3 asks you to prepare two proposals and to take one of these forward to the editing and production stage. This chapter shows you how to prepare a proposal and how you can then go on to produce a comic should you wish to make this your final print product.

This chapter shows you how to produce a comic by explaining how a low-budget educational comic was produced, giving you a model to learn from.

The chapter is organised into the following sections:
- Introduction to making a comic
- Case study: *Lasses' Night Out*
- Finding a client and an audience
- Research
- Production
- Comic conventions.

Introduction to making a comic

You do not have to be brilliant at drawing to become a comic artist. It is possible to use very simple drawings to make effective comic stories (see Annie Lawson's work in Figure 6.33). You can improve your drawing skills by practising and using some of the techniques illustrated in this chapter. If you are working in a group, each member of the group can prepare draft drawings at the pre-production stage. If you decide to produce a finished version of the comic, you can appoint the best artist to draw the characters while others in the group can do backgrounds, speech bubbles, lettering and sound and movement effects.

CASE STUDY   Lasses' Night Out

The main aim of the comic *Lasses' Night Out* (see Figure 6.1) was to take a light-hearted look at the issue of contraception. It was produced by a group of women from the Meadow Well Estate in North Tyneside for a teenage audience. Its intention was to provide information about contraception in a form that was easily understandable and down to earth.

The idea of a comic came from discussions among the young women's group in Meadow Well who thought there was a lack of information about contraception which was both appealing and comfortable.

Once the idea of a comic was decided on, the group identified areas of research. They decided to find out:

1 What methods of contraception were available to women?
2 What were young women's experiences of using different methods (both good and bad)?
3 Where can young women get advice and supplies?
4 How do young people feel when asking for advice and supplies?
5 Was there anything else that young women needed to know, such as information about side effects and what could be done if they are not happy with the way they have been treated?

Figure 6.1 Lasses' Night Out

At this stage the group set up a series of workshops with the professional illustrator, Suzy Varty. The workshops looked at the practicalities of layout, design and funding. The funding was in fact met by North Tyneside's youth service.

It became clear that the information which the group had found during their research was more than they needed. It was also sometimes very technical and not very memorable. So they decided to concentrate on young women's real life experiences and on what seemed most important for young people to know.

The group decided to make the comic humorous as the best way to get information across to its audience. They also tried to correct some of the common misunderstandings about the subject. It was decided not to include too many details but to leave a space on the back page where details of local family planning services could be included.

The comic was produced in A5 format in black and white. After an introductory frame on the cover there are 6 frames to a page.

The basic idea is uncomplicated, with one naive girl, Sally, asking her friends for contraceptive advice on a girls' night out. There is only one setting, a pub (or club) with two very minor male characters – a feller the girls fancy and an eavesdropping barman. The information given about contraceptive devices includes the names of the devices, how they work and how effective they are. Their availability is also mentioned. The humour comes from the naive images Sally has of the devices as she interprets the names literally.

The faces are simply drawn, with the changing expressions indicated by different shaped mouths and eyes. They are meant to be iconic (simplified image) faces rather than realistic, representational faces. Speech is placed, conventionally, in speech bubbles, while thoughts, which are often expressed in visual images, are in clouds. One unusual technique used by the artist as a variation on a convention is to turn Sally's hair into an expressive device. It curves into a heart shape to show she is 'in love', a question mark when she is perplexed and an exclamation mark when she is surprised.

If you aim to produce a comic similar to *Lasses' Night Out* you need to work out a schedule and methodology similar to that used by professionals.

Finding a client and an audience

Ideally you should try to find someone who has a need to communicate a message to a real audience in the way that *Lasses Night Out* was a response to a particular need. There would also have to be a good reason for using a comic format rather than another kind of publication.

Here are some possible contacts which might need such a publication:
- local community groups
- schools with young children which need topical, local interest reading materials
- local businesses which have links with the education system. Some may be interested in publications explaining their training or recruitment policies. Some could have their own staff publications and they might well be interested in a comic format as a variation on what they already do or as a supplement in their publication.
- local pressure groups who may have funding to publish material which informs and educates on issues that concern young people, such as drugs or car crime.

It is useful if your school or college can build up a list of contacts who might need publications annually, so that you do not have to start from scratch looking for clients and audiences.

Research

You need to identify the sources of information you will need to consult before you start writing your story.

This will probably involve doing some background reading – in *Lasses' Night Out*, for instance, the writer would have consulted pamphlets and books about contraceptive methods – and some interviewing of people with expert knowledge.

Production

Write a script which should be set out like this:

Frame 1 Picture. Cover shows four young women getting ready to go out. In the foreground is an open handbag which reveals a packet of condoms. The four characters are inset (head and shoulders) and named.

   Sharon – 'Can I borrow your lipstick?'
   Shelley – 'Wey, man, get it out me bag.'
   Suzy – 'Well lasses, we look so gorgeous, we're bound to score.'
   Caption – '... and we all know where that might lead.'

Frame 2 Picture. The four girls are at a bar. They see a handsome young man go past. Part of his face is in foreground.

   Suzy (thinks) – 'Mmmm'.
   Shelley (thinks) – 'Cor!'
   Sharon – 'Yeah!'
   Sally – 'Cor!'

Frame 3 Picture. The man winks at Sally, who smiles. Background pattern suggests burst of excitement. No dialogue.

And so on.

Draw the pictures. If the comic is to be printed it is a good idea to make the pictures twice the size of the eventual printed size so that small details can be more easily drawn. Colour can be added at this stage if it is required.

Figure 6.2 Frame 1

Figure 6.3 Frame 2

Figure 6.4 Frame 3

Add *speech bubbles* which can be prepared separately with either handwritten or typeset lettering. These are then pasted onto the drawings. Alternatively the speech bubbles can be drawn straight onto the artwork, in which case it is better to draw the bubbles round the words rather than fitting the words into the bubbles. See Figure 6.5.

Add *sound effects and movement lines.* See Figure 6.6.

Figure 6.5 Using speech bubbles

Figure 6.6 Movement lines and sound effects

The finished artwork can then be either photocopied or sent to a professional printer. If your comic is to be printed in full colour the printer will make four separate printing plates, each one using a different colour – cyan, magenta, yellow and black. When these are printed together they combine to produce any colour required. This process is very expensive, however, and you may have to settle for monochrome printing or spot colour. Spot colour involves adding one colour, in different tones if you wish, to a black-and-white drawing.

Equipment

You will need good quality drawing equipment, as follows:
- a choice of hard (H grade) and soft (B grade) pencils
- a choice of pens
  - dip pens for flexibility where you need to vary pressure and direction
  - technical pen for fine, consistent lines and stippling effects
- a choice of brushes
  - a drawing brush (good quality for keeping a clean point)
  - round hair sable colouring brushes or cotton buds
- self-adhesive tint sheets
- watercolour paints and coloured inks
- thin, flexible card which can be used on a revolving drum for scanning (if you are having your comic printed in colour)
- tracing paper for roughs so you can build up your own store of images with overlays and semi-transparent layout paper
- plastic erasers
- transparent ruler with bevelled edge and a steel rule
- set square and a drawing board
- process white for covering up mistakes
- ellipse and circle templates
- scalpel and a cutting mat
- light box.

Figure 6.7 Drawing equipment

Figure 6.8 *A selection of comic icons*

Comic conventions

The use of icons

Icons are images which are used to represent a person, place, thing or idea. These can be divided into non-pictorial icons, such as words, numbers, a CND symbol, a Christian cross or musical notation and pictorial icons which in some way resemble their subjects.

Comics make use of both types but are especially concerned with pictorial icons. These can vary in how closely they resemble 'real life'.

The style you as a creator of comics decide to adopt will depend on your subject matter and your audience. However realistic you make your drawings, though, the art of comic-making relies very much on *simplification*. Because the cartoon artist misses out details, the image becomes simpler. What is intriguing, though, is how the simplification works by focusing on essentials. This in turn leads to greater universality of meaning; so in the faces in Figures 6.10 – 6.13, the further you move away from realism the more representative the image becomes. The picture in Figure 6.9 represents one person, the image in Figure 6.13 represents all people.

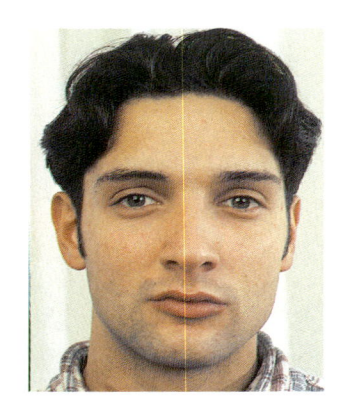

Figure 6.9 *A face as seen photographically*

Figure 6.10

Figure 6.11

Figure 6.12

Figure 6.13

Framing

Comics have frames or panels. These are usually divided by gutters or spaces and they have an important function. A series of frames contains different still images that represent different moments in a sequence. The space between these is important because, through experience, the reader

Making a comic

learns to supply the missing information to connect the different images in the sequence. In Figure 6.15 we do not need pictures of the house travelling through the earth's atmosphere to tell us what has happened. The reader supplies that information.

Scott McCloud, in his book *Understanding Comics – The Invisible Art*, distinguishes six different categories of *transition between frames* in comics.

The first is *moment to moment*, which requires very little information input from the reader (see Figure 6.16). The others require an increasing amount of input from the reader.

Figure 6.15 'Calamity James' cartoon frame showing an explosion followed by a view of the house travelling through space.

Second, there is movement from *one action to another* by a single subject (see Figure 6.17).

Third, there is transition from one *subject to another subject* within the same scene (see Figure 6.18).

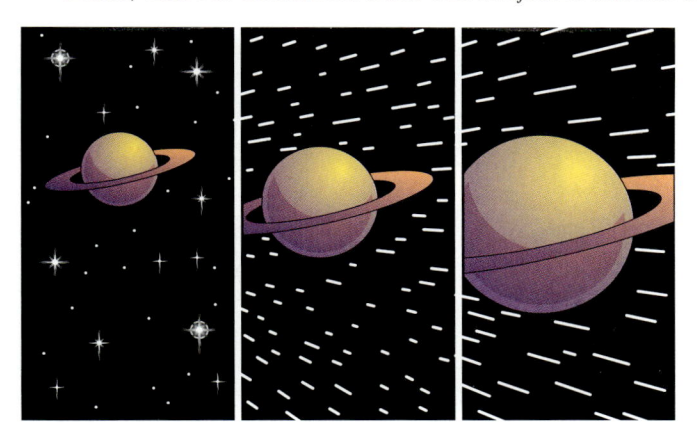

Figure 6.16 Moment-to-moment transition between frames

Figure 6.17 Movement from one action to another

Figure 6.18 Transition from one subject to another

Figure 6.19 Transition from one scene to another

Fourth, there is transition from *one scene to another* (see Figure 6.19) often linked by time words such as 'Meanwhile'.

Fifth is transition between two different *aspects* of the same subject, idea or mood where time is not relevant (see Figure 6.20) and the sixth is the **non sequitur** where there is no relationship between the frames at all (see Figure 6.21).

Though it is helpful for the comic artist to be aware of these techniques, it is important to select the ones that are most appropriate to the demands of the storyline and the expectations and abilities of the audience. If your story is to be a series of connected events then types 2, 3 and 4 will predominate.

121

Making a comic

Figure 6.20 Different aspects of the same subject

Figure 6.21 Non sequitur transition

Selection
The choice of what to put into a story and what to leave out is important as demonstrated in the following activity.

Passage of time
Though the *passage of time* in a comic can be indicated by the gutter between frames, it can also be shown by the inclusion of words within a panel (see Figure 6.22). In this frame several seconds must elapse for the frame's action to be completed, starting with the photographer's 'Smile' and going through to the chess player's gentle reprimand after his opponent's move.

Figure 6.22 Showing the passage of time by including words in a text panel

The size of a frame can influence the reader's perception of the passage of time. In the sequences in Figure 6.24, page 124, the second one gives a feeling of a greater passage of time.

Movement
Movement in comic art can be depicted by the sequence of frames but it can also be depicted in single frames by the use of *movement lines, multiple images and streaking*. An example of the liberal but effective use of movement lines is the 'Bash Street Kids' image from the *Beano* Calendar (May 1995) shown on page 124 (see Figure 6.25). It is worth analysing this in detail by trying to describe in words what is happening to each character and each object.

Streaking can be of the object itself (see Figure 6.26) or of the background (Figure 6.27). Multiple images are sometimes used to show repeated movements (see Figure 6.28).

A Activity

Look at the story reprinted from Scott McCloud's book (see Figure 6.23) Edit the story down to 15 frames, then 10 frames and then 4 frames. Discuss with others the most effective version. Are there any extra images which you would like the artist to have included?

Making a comic

Figure 6.23

Making a comic

Figure 6.24 *Showing passage of time by different frame size*

Figure 6.25 *The use of movement lines*

If you look again at 'Calamity James' you will see many more comic conventions to do with lines. In the fourth frame (Figure 6.29) lines are used to depict something visual – the water exploding from the hot water bottle. If you look at frame one (Figure 6.30) you will see wavy lines above the dustbin. These show something which is not visible – smell. The reader

124

Figure 6.26 *Streaking of the object*

Figure 6.27 *Streaking of the background*

Figure 6.28 *Multiple images used to show repeated movements*

Figure 6.29 *Lines used to show explosion and its consequences*

Figure 6.30 *Lines above dustbin indicate smell*

who is not familiar with this convention is given the extra verbal information 'Steaming, cheesy hum'. Even the flies in this frame have a meaning as indicators of smell.

There is a whole *vocabulary of images* that have come to represent certain invisible ideas or feelings. Each one must have been dreamed up by an individual artist, but because they have been appropriate they have been imitated by other artists and have been accepted and understood by readers. In 'Calamity James' there is the question mark above Lemming's head showing he is puzzled; the antenna on the housewife, marking her as an alien being; the stars around James's head showing he is dazed.

Making a comic

A Activity

Use comic conventions to illustrate the following:
- someone in love
- the fast curved path of someone running away in terror
- a bawling baby
- someone 'looking daggers' at something
- someone with a bright idea
- someone who is drunk
- someone who is dreaming of food.

Backgrounds in comics can vary from minimal to highly detailed. The style you choose will depend on the kind of story you want to tell. In 'The Bash Street Kids' (see page 109) the backgrounds are simple, almost symbolic, and this makes the story timeless and more universal. In 'Calamity James' the details in the backgrounds are themselves a source of humour as in the sudden appearance in James' bed of an aerosol can containing 'garlic anti-vampire spray'.

Figure 6.31 Building up a background

126

The illustrations in Figure 6.31 show you how a background can be built up if necessary to add to the atmosphere of your story. The first image shows a character who is meant to be standing on a surface. All that is needed is a horizontal line. The addition of a vertical line in the second picture suggests a building. The third frame adds detail to make the place more specific and to suggest (roughly) time, while the fourth frame adds drama to the scene by giving weight and depth to the image mainly through the use of shading.

Stock characters or stereotypical characters are useful in comics where instant recognition is needed in constrained space. So readers will know immediately that they are looking at a prisoner if he is in a suit covered with arrows even though such suits are no longer worn, or at a burglar if he is in a stripey jersey and a mask.

Props can be stereotyped for quick recognition too, so that female teachers are often depicted as primly dressed and bespectacled standing next to a blackboard with a piece of chalk in their hand. There are stock settings too, such as desert islands with a single palm tree.

Lettering adds the final touch to a comic and is best done on patch paper and stuck directly on to the inked page. The style of lettering should reflect the type and volume of the sound being described, which gives marvellous scope for invention and originality (see Figure 6.32).

If this is all sounding too daunting to novice comic artists, here is an effective comic story told in a very simple style (see Figure 6.33).

Figure 6.32 Lettering conventions for comics

Assignment

Make an educational comic

You need to find a school that would be interested in co-operating on a project like this. It is very important that you find a head teacher and a class teacher who will be helpful and constructive.

First discuss possible ideas for storylines of the comic with you group. Identify the purpose of your ideas: is it to make the children aware of road safety, is it to make them more aware of the need to care for the environment, or does it have some other purpose? Make a short list of the most promising ideas and send these to the school before you organise a planning meeting with the class teacher.

In the planning meeting, discuss with the teacher what teaching materials are needed or desired and which, if any, of your ideas he or she thinks are worth developing.

Find out the levels of reading ability of the children the comic is aimed at. Ask the teacher to give you examples of publications which he or she values and which are popular with the children.

Analyse these publications as part of your research.

Ask to work with or observe the children so that you develop a feel for your audience. Draft two or three possible treatments and test these on a sample audience (both teachers and children).

When you have decided your topic, conduct research into it. If it is road safety, for instance, it might be worth interviewing the road safety officer responsible for the school you are working with.

Draw up and follow a production schedule as suggested in this chapter.

Figure 6.33 Sample of the work of Annie Lawson.

7 | Analysing film fiction

In this chapter you will learn how to analyse feature films.
The chapter is divided into the following sections:
- Introduction to analysing film fiction
- Looking at film genre and production context
- Analysis of film images
- Analysing film as narrative
- Case Study: *Four Weddings and a Funeral*.
- Assignment: Analysing film fiction

Introduction to analysing film fiction

You do not have to know the films which are referred to here as main examples in order to understand the analyses, although it helps to have viewed them. The films which are given as the main examples are:

Title (and where made)	Year	Studio/Production Company	Director
On the Waterfront (US)	1954	Columbia/Horizon	Elia Kazan
The Curse of Frankenstein (UK)	1957	Hammer	Terence Fisher
The Birds (US)	1963	Universal/Alfred Hitchcock	Alfred Hitchcock
Bhaji on the Beach (UK)	1993	Film Four/Umbi Films	Gurinder Chadha
Four Weddings and a Funeral (UK)	1994	PolyGram/Working Title	Mike Newell

Looking at film genre and production context

▶ Genre analysis, page 13

When you use the word *genre* in analysing a film you are referring to the idea that films fall into known types. This idea comes from fiction feature films with certain common characteristics such as 'the western', 'the musical', 'the horror film', 'the science fiction film'. Genres are not fixed, or ready-made. Genres develop and change. Films in the '90s tend to mix elements from different genres.

When you describe how a film came to be made and seen – the history, the studio etc. – you are referring to the *production context*.

Introduction: how film genres developed

The 'classic' time and place for the development of film genres was Los Angeles, USA, in the 1930s. At this time the 'big five' Hollywood studios

(20th Century Fox, Paramount, MGM, RKO, Warner) became dominant. They were the major owners of resources in the US film world, controlling not only the means of production, but also the distributors of films and the exhibitors, i.e. the cinema chains. The other studios, 'the little three' (Columbia, United Artists, and Universal), were not 'vertically integrated' in this way. This meant that anyone who wanted to make it in the film business, including the little three, had to work with the big five in order to get their films onto the screen. In business terms the big five dominated as a result of controlling all the different stages of production, distribution and exchange. The studios organised themselves to follow a form of production which resembled an assembly line in order to keep a constant flow of films in production and on release.

The marketing of films as genre products was also linked with the Hollywood 'star system', which used the predictable talent and appeal of famous actors to market films. The studios attempted, and largely succeeded, in making these 'stars' their property through labour contracts which tied actors to work with one studio.

The studios wanted to be able to predict and repeat the types of films to be made in order to simplify production. They also wanted the films they selected to fit into the product types which they knew audiences would recognise and buy tickets for. In addition, different audiences could be identified and catered for through different genres, such as the melodramatic 'weepies' targeted at female audiences. Film genres with predictable elements and appeal were needed in order to sustain a factory system where films were made on an assembly line, rolling through the different stages of writing, casting, filming, editing, marketing etc.

In summary, reasons for the development of Hollywood film genres in the 1930s included:
- predictability
- industrial reasons, i.e. production planning
- the need to target films at identifiable audiences
- the need to make and market films as products
- the need to be able to predict returns on investment.

The process which cultivates genres can still be seen today in the tendency of American producers to repeat the formula of a successful film.

How to analyse a film genre
A film genre has certain elements which are characteristic and repeated in films from that genre. These elements include characters, use of space and setting, iconography or 'key signs', storyline, a certain relationship with an audience and characteristics of style. The example analysis here will be drawn from 'the horror film'.

Analysis of the horror film genre
Characters
There are usually predictable heroes, villains and stock characters, in a story belonging to a traditional film genre. In horror films the heroes are normally representatives of 'normality' and remarkable only for their innocence and tendency to blunder into danger with a conspicuous lack of caution. Villains tend to be deviants from normality, distorted beings, such as scientists with unhealthy curiosity and strange ideas, and/or monstrous characters from somewhere beyond or 'outside' human society. Often in horror films monstrous beings become sympathetic, and they may even become a kind of

alternative hero. The monster in Frankenstein is a good example of how this can happen. Stock characters include weird assistants to the villainous scientist or monstrous character. Victims are essential characters in horror films. Sympathetic victims tend to have strong relationships with the heroes; less sympathetic victims may relate to the villains.

Figure 7.1 The poster for the 1957 film The Curse of Frankenstein

Figure 7.2 The poster for the 1995 film Interview with the Vampire

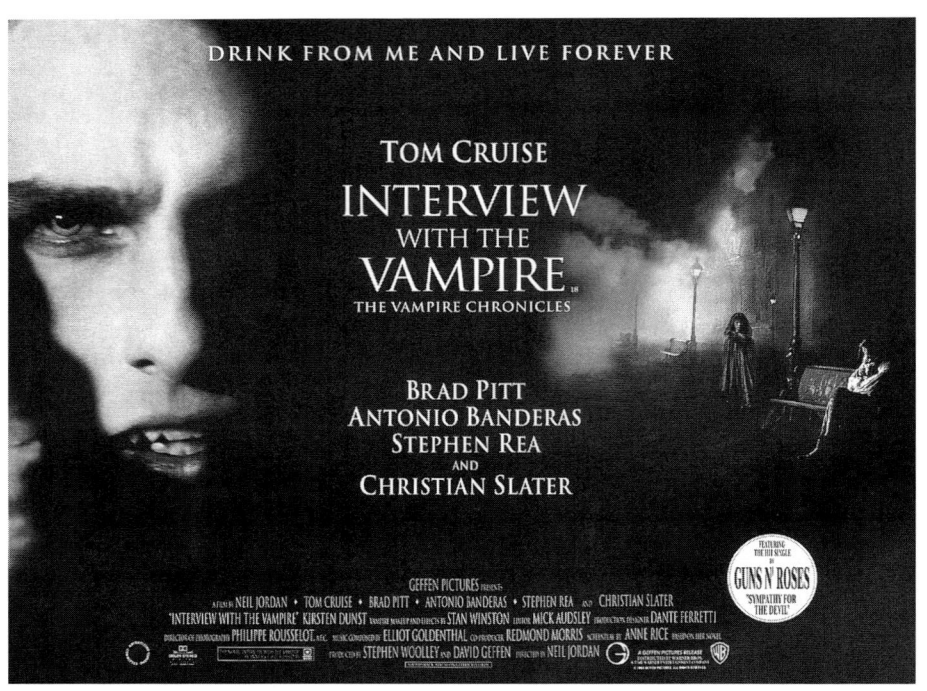

Space and setting

The opposition between normality and the irrational continues into settings. The idea of normal human society may be represented by 'human spaces'. These might be a small town or car, or even a space ship. The irrational, deviant element may be represented by remote places and

Gothic architecture such as castles or ruins. Horrific threats will emerge from anywhere surrounding the safe space of normal human habitation: from underground, from outside, from the roof space.

Key signs

We have learnt to recognise certain signs as having horrific meaning. Many of these have originated from folk tales and the *Gothic* literature of the eighteenth and nineteenth centuries: thunderstorms, the moon, fierce animals particularly wolves, and human features with strongly animal characteristics such as abundant hair and sharp teeth. Eerie music, and the exaggeration of sound effects such as footsteps or doors opening, are also key signs for the horror genre.

Storyline

In the simplest terms, the opening to a horror film will establish the hero and introduce at least a suggestion of the threat to normality. The middle section will reveal more and more of the monster. It will build encounters between the hero and the threat to a climactic confrontation. The ending will resolve the narrative with victory or defeat by one of the parties. Horror films are more often resolved with the defeat of the threat, but they are unusual in that the defeat of the hero is a real option. There are, too, horror films whose main purpose is to shock without resolution (*The Evil Dead*, for instance); these often have no identifiable hero at all.

The storyline of the Hitchcock film *The Birds* uses the horror genre in order to turn part of the natural world, the bird species, into a monster which threatens a relatively remote seaside community. The abandonment of Bodega Bay by the human community, including the heroes of the narrative, represents a substantial victory for the horrific birds.

Figure 7.3 *Film poster for Alfred Hitchcock's* The Birds

Audience

The audiences for horror films experience powerful emotions, and measurable physical effects of arousal such as increased heartbeat. Effects such as fear, shock, suspense and horror are made out to be pleasures which

Analysing film fiction

in order to attract and build audiences. The traditional view of the horror audience is biased towards young adult males. However, horror films can have a very wide appeal and a bias to any particular audience will depend upon the way in which the genre is used. Stephen Spielberg's *Jurassic Park*, for example, uses aspects of the horror genre and is aimed at family audiences.

Style

The styles of horror films can be analysed from different aspects. There are styles associated with different periods of time, such as '50s science fiction monster films. There are the influences of movements in film and art, such as German expressionism. There are styles associated with studios, such as Hollywood's Universal or Britain's Hammer. There are also personal styles, such as those of directors like Hitchcock and Roger Corman. In *The Birds*, for example, Hitchcock's influence can be seen in his personal interest in mixing genres, his typical use of violence against women, and his characteristic use of the camera to build suspense through point-of-view and low-angled shots.

Some generalisations about horror film style are possible. Negative ingredients, such as fear, violence and repulsive representations are exploited to an extreme, or to *excess*. Also, horror alternates to varying degrees between leaving the horrific to the imagination of the audience, through hint and suggestion, and showing the worst.

Messages

Horror films exploit material which goes beyond the borders of the everyday, rational world. They allow the representation of unusual or repressed sexual possibilities, as in vampire films, for example. The effects of horror films and their sexual and violent content have attracted attention not only from film critics but also from a wider audience.
A recent example is the debate about the effects of the *Child's Play* films, including an alleged link with the murder of Jamie Bulger. Further back in the 1950s there was concern verging on panic regarding the success of the X-rated Hammer horror films.

Critics with an interest in *gender* or feminism have put forward arguments around the role of the woman as the victim of violence, the differences between horror monsters and 'normal' ideas of what is male, and the role of the female viewer, in particular her place in looking at the monster. There are horror films, such as the *Alien* series, which have a female hero and other aspects with a feminist bias.

Horror films have attracted attention and criticism from groups with interests in the representation of people with disabilities in the media. They have presented research findings which show that representations of the disabled as normal people are rare in the media. Monstrous or evil characters who deviate from normal humanity into the areas of the subhuman and the ill are important in horror, and raise questions about the representation of normality and disability.

▶ Representation, pages 27 and 148

A Activity

Make notes on the ingredients of the main film genres (western, musical, gangster, crime thriller etc) under the headings above. Write an analysis of a mainstream film genre using the same headings and methods as above.

Production context

When you analyse a film you should also take into account who made it, how it came to be made, and how it was marketed. This is the 'production context'. The manner and setting in which a film was made will have an effect on the final product.

Certain studios are sometimes associated with particular genres. The MGM of the 1930s is often associated with musicals, Warner Brothers in the 1930s are associated with gangster films such as *The Public Enemy* (1931). Universal in the early 1930s was well known for horror films such as *Frankenstein* and *Dracula* (1931).

Let's take film versions of *Frankenstein* as an example of how some understanding of the production context helps the explanation and analysis of a film. In 1931, the American studio, Universal, made a version directed by James Whale. In 1957, the British studio Hammer made a version, *The Curse of Frankenstein*, directed by Terence Fisher. Many of the differences between the two films can be explained by reference to the production context. The Universal film was intended as a piece of escapism and the monster is like an animal, whose death is predictable. The scientist who creates him is forgiven. Hammer studios were compelled to ensure the their version of the story was very different from that of the Universal film by the prospect of copyright difficulties and expensive legal action. The Hammer version also may reflect fears about the Cold War and the control of technology at the time. The monster commits a series of hideous murders and the scientist who creates him is executed. The Hammer film is in colour, which is significant because Hammer believed that there was an audience for a new version of *Frankenstein* using the still relatively novel colour technology.

Analysis of film images

Films affect us, the audience, through various things – the story, the editing, our understanding of the genre. First and foremost, however, film affects us through the images which it presents on the screen. One technique for the analysis of film is to look at, and describe, the various aspects or components of significant images from the film chosen in detail. This kind of analysis is sometimes called *mise en scene* analysis. *Mise en scene* means 'brought to the stage', or 'production' in French. In film it thus refers to the selection of lighting, colour, actors, movement, objects, setting, and composition, within the film image. *Mise en scene* analysis is not confined to single images and may range over how any aspect of the image is used throughout a film.

The instruction for the first step in image analysis of film images is to describe exactly what you see. This appears to be a simple task, but if you try it you will find judgements and interpretations beyond the literal representation creeping into your description. When you simply describe exactly literally what you see, you are giving the 'denotation'. As soon as you move on to interpretation and judgements about what you see, beyond the literal content, you are giving the 'connotation'. Denotation and connotation are not simple opposites, rather they are at the opposite ends of a line representing the processes by which images are 'read'.

▶ Image analysis using a semiotic approach, pages 10 and 11

Sample analysis of a film image

This is an analysis of an image from the film, *The Curse of Frankenstein*. The film is actually in colour, but this image reproduced here is in black and white, and is taken from a still held in the British Film Institute stills library.

Figure 7.4 Still from The Curse of Frankenstein

Denotation

The image shows a figure dressed in black carrying a woman dressed in white through an open doorway. The shadow from the figure's head cast on the ceiling of the passageway behind indicates lighting from below, or 'underlighting'. There are shadows on the floor and to the rear of the passageway.

The setting is that of a building with brick walls and metal supports across the ceiling and around the door. The ceiling supports are in the shape of a cross. The scene is barren of furniture.

The face of the black clothed figure is made up to distort the features, as if he has undergone crude surgery. He is looking up slightly to his left. He is holding the body of the female in front of him with his right arm outstretched to lift her torso, and his right hand cupping the woman's body under her right shoulder. A manacle and broken chain is dangling from his wrist. The woman's body is prostrate, her eyes are closed and her head, right arm and legs are hanging down. She is wearing a dress cut off at the shoulder and the knee, gloves and high-heeled shoes.

The camera position has a slight low angle, so that the viewer is looking up at the figures and the doorway. The image is framed so that the top of the doorway is at an angle off the horizontal, and the sides off the vertical. These lines, and the figures, create strong diagonals within the composition of the shot.

Connotation and genre

The body language of the monster figure gives the impression of a simple strength, but with the threat of the unknown as to his intentions. The figure has connotations of maleness in dress and appearance, but whether the figure is a male monster or something else, a 'he' or an 'it', is open to interpretation. The figure appears powerful, a connotation emphasised by the low angle shot. His clothing is sombre. With his crude facial features, he appears subhuman. The sophisticated dress and attractive facial features of the woman are in strong contrast to this. The body language of the woman is of complete submission as if she is asleep, like a child being carried. The lighting extends the oppositions between the two: the monster comes from the shadows, whilst the woman is brightly lit connoting 'innocence' or moral goodness. We can build these oppositions into a list which reveals a structure of contrasts in the image:

Oppositions
(Between the woman and the Frankenstein figure in the still from *Curse of Frankenstein*):

    human being . . . . monster
    female . . . . male (?)
    captured . . . . escaped
    powerless . . . . powerful
    passive . . . . active
    light . . . . shade
    beauty . . . . ugliness
    normality . . . . abnormality

The building has the appearance of a cellar and a warehouse. It creates the impression of a stark, industrial setting. The half cut-off 'NOTICE BEWARE ... DROP' suggests an institutional setting, such as a warehouse, and underscores the danger.

Within the horror genre an image such as this gives certain signs which indicate a predictable storyline and connotations of sex and danger. The image of a male monster carrying the vulnerable figure of an unconscious, and beautiful woman in a bleak and inhospitable building is an *icon* (i.e. a characteristic and representative image) of the genre. The monster is played by Christopher Lee, the star of many horror films. The importance of the ceiling as part of the decor, and its contribution to a certain claustrophobia, is typical of Hammer horror.

▶ The use of icons, page 120

Analysing film as narrative

▶ Analysis of narrative structure, page 14

Narrative in film analysis refers to everything to do with the story. Here, the emphasis is upon 'narrative structure', broken down into openings, middles and endings. *Openings* will be considered first, then *endings*, before looking at how the *middle* of a film can be described. An alternative approach to narrative structure will be introduced through the analysis of film narrative as 'fairy tale'.

Film openings

The opening to a film may be analysed in terms of three main ingredients: a title sequence which credits the players, the director, the producer etc; an opening sequence or opening sequences which introduce the story; the first shot the audience sees, the so-called establishing shot.

Analysis of an establishing shot (On the Waterfront)

The importance of the establishing shot is based entirely on its position in the film as the first shot. A 'normal' establishing shot, if such a thing exists, is a long shot of an important and recognisable setting, such as a building.

Thus, a film set around a hospital or a hospital doctor as 'hero' will most likely begin with an exterior long shot of a hospital building. However, an establishing shot does not have to conform to any 'normal' rule. It could be any kind of shot, providing that it engages the audience and performs some introductory function. Even a shot of the back of a someone's head may engage the audience's attention.

Figure 7.5 Still from the opening sequence of On the Waterfront

The first example of an opening comes from *On the Waterfront*, an American crime film with strong gangster elements first released in 1954. The story concerns ex-boxer Terry Malone (Marlon Brando) and his struggle with his conscience about whether to inform the authorities about corruption in a dock union. The opening shows the gangland-style killing of Joey Doyle, a dock worker who has spoken out against the corruption in the union. It establishes the main characters: the criminal gang led by Johnny Friendly, which crookedly runs the dock union, Terry, who is troubled by guilt at his part in luring Joey Doyle to death at the hands of the gang, and Edie, Joey's sister, who wants to expose her brother's killers. The analysis here will concentrate upon the establishing shot and the manner in which it sets up the opening sequence.

The first shot is preceded by the *On the Waterfront* title sequence, which credits the main personnel. This has fairly mournful background music of flutes and horns connoting a *drama*.

The first shot the audience sees is a long shot in black and white. The scene of the establishing shot very clearly denotes the waterfront and the workplace of the docks. In the background is a huge ocean-going liner. In the foreground there is a small hut down beside the water. The camera is positioned slightly above this on an embankment above the shore. A group of men come out of the hut and ascend a stair to the shore in single file.

The ocean liner fills the frame of the shot, dwarfing the hut and the men who come out. It seems to connote society, and contextualises the world of the docks within a much bigger world of wealth and power. The men are at the level of the hull, and the superstructure of the liner is over their heads.

The soundtrack is of loud drums beating out a jazz beat which signifies a primitive, male environment. It is very dramatic. It gives the purpose of the gang who are setting off power and menace.

This shot clearly establishes the setting. It introduces a gang of men from whom characters will later be differentiated. It sets up an atmosphere of drama and the threat of violence. The audience is also drawn into the question of the mission indicated by the departure of the gang.

A Activity

View the opening sequence of a feature film, and go back and analyse the first establishing shot. What further information of importance can you see and read into the establishing shot, in the context of having seen the opening (or even the whole film)?

If you wish you can use *On the Waterfront* (available on video under the Cinema Club label).

Analysis of a film opening (Bhaji on the Beach)

Figure 7.6 Bhaji on the Beach: *the coach trip*

Bhaji on the Beach is a British film made by Umbi Films for Film Four International (backed by Channel Four) and released in 1993. Its director, Gurinder Chadha, is the first Asian woman to direct a commercial British feature film.

Bhaji on the Beach is a very different film from *On the Waterfront*. However, the openings to the two films are similar in that they both introduce settings, characters and problems from which their stories can proceed. *Bhaji on the Beach* concerns a day's outing to Blackpool for a group of Asian women of different ages, organised by the Saheli Women's Centre.

Bhaji on the Beach opens with the following:

Title sequence
The title and cast in alphabetical order are shown in a credit sequence of four frames against a yellow background. An animation resembling blue waves makes the transition as if the credits are washed away by the waves.

Analysing film fiction

Opening Sequences (1–7)

1. The camera tracks past the shops of an urban street in middle England: butchers, supermarket, empty premises with posters, shutters with National Front graffiti, Asian grocers, newsagent with Hindi video rentals.
2. In a parody of the conventions of popular Indian cinema, a blue lit Hindu temple figure of a god confronts a middle-aged Asian woman in a yellow sari (Asha). There are images of her demanding family. She flees through huge representations of shop goods: giant packs of cigarettes, videos etc. A voice over calls out 'duty, honour and sacrifice'. The sequence has connotations of dreaming and may indicate a religious vision.
3. The film cuts to the setting of a newsagent's shop. On the soundtrack a radio broadcast for the Asian community in the Midlands establishes a more everyday reality. Asha is beset by husband and family demanding breakfast.
4. In the women's centre, Ginder reads a letter on the stairs. Cut to boy (Amrik) in mask playing. Ginder talks to and comforts her son, Amrik, who wants his father. She promises him candy floss at the beach.
5. Ranjit, her husband, lies on his bed in the extended family home. He is apparently troubled by a similar letter.
6. Two giggling Asian teenage sisters, Madhu and Ladhu, sneer to each other about the boy next door. 'The guys in this town.'/ 'Tell me about it.'/ 'Blackpool here we come.'
7. In Ranjit's home, his mother objects to the letter and its demand for an 'English' divorce. The parents despatch the three brothers, Balbir, Ranjit and Manjit to bring 'only grandson' Amrik, and possibly Ginder, home again.

With similar 'mini-narratives' the opening continues up until the departure of the minibus for Blackpool. These continue to introduce further characters and issues, such as Oliver and Hashida and her 'problem' pregancy, and Rekha, a sophisticated visitor from Bombay.

A Activity

View the opening to *Bhaji on the Beach* on video.

Complete the list of sequences above, in summary form, up to the departure of the minibus.

The opening to the film introduces a large number of female characters and the various problems or dilemmas which their journey to the seaside will influence and possibly resolve. Asha, one of the older women who spends her life behind the shop counter, has a chance to escape from this everyday drudgery for a while. Ginder is isolated from the other women by her decision to leave her husband, Ranjit. Ranjit and his brothers are determined to challenge Ginder's decision and are in pursuit of her. Madhu and Ladhu, teenage sisters, are on the look out for boys with more style than back home. Hashida has a place at medical school, but her reputation and her future is to be changed by the discovery that she is pregnant by her West Indian boyfriend, Oliver.

Figure 7.7 Hashida (Sarita Khajuria) and boyfriend Oliver (Mo Sesay).

Bhaji on the Beach is an *ensemble piece* with at least 14 principal characters. It is marketed as a seaside comedy, but it is a mixture of elements from a number of genres often overlaid with irony as much as comedy. The opening refers to real life social issues such as racial prejudice, mixed relationships and the taboos around separation and divorce in Asian communities, which are to be important in the storyline of the film. This interest in issues is in the tradition of British social realism going back to *Saturday Night and Sunday Morning* (1960). The stress upon strong female characters whose lives are problematised by men puts the film into a category of female-orientated melodramas, or women's films, with a long history. Like the British musical film *Summer Holiday*, to which it ironically refers, the film also works out a plot based on a journey. The opening sets up the first set of action on a journey: preparations. It also sets up the essential ingredients of any *road movie*, namely escape, and characters in pursuit.

Endings

What are the particular relationships which the endings of narratives can have to the rest of the story? Also, what functions can the endings of narratives perform?

Activity

Make a list of your own ideas in answer to the question of how endings work in relation to the overall narrative of a film. Here are some prompt questions to get you started.

- What kind of dramatic events often come towards the end of a narrative?
- What kind of ending most easily 'satisfies' the curiosity of the reader?
- What distinguishes the ending of a sad story from other kinds?
- What kind of ending ensures that the audience looks forward to a further episode or sequel?
- What kind of ending shows that a story is complete in itself, rather than looking forward to further developments?

Analysing film fiction

'And they all lived together happily ever after' (Or did they?)

Endings may supply climaxes, revelations, rewards, punishments, implied moral lessons and other means of completing a narrative. Each stage of a story represents a choice from a range of possible choices. However, the ending of a story usually narrows down the range of options for further development, action and interpretation. You will have your own ideas about the most satisfactory story endings, and, of course, they depend upon what kind of narrative you're talking about. In the simplest terms, there are two kinds of endings: *closed* and *open*.

Closed endings finish off stories by answering the questions the narrative has thrown up. They may end happily, looking forward to a rosy future, for example. Alternatively, they may end sadly, as in separation or death. However they end, they will tie up the threads of the story. To use the jargon of Media Studies, such endings have *closure*.

Open endings leave the story unfinished with more questions than answers. They leave the audience wondering what will happen next. They offer the audience the chance to second guess the authors of the narrative by predicting what is more likely to ensue. To use the jargon, such endings 'lack closure'. However, it is still arguable that such endings narrow down the range of options for the progress of the narrative by making clear the questions the audience must ponder.

Analysis of a film ending

The Birds is a film directed by Alfred Hitchcock and adapted from a short story by the English writer Daphne du Maurier. In the film version a young woman, Melanie, pursues Mitch to his home town, where his mother and sister live. This might be a conventional love story. However, there is a parallel science fiction narrative of military attacks upon the human community of the town by crows, gulls and other birds.

The events

a) Mitch boards up the family home. His mother, Lydia, becomes hysterical with fear. Melanie looks after Mitch's sister Cathy, but as soon as the birds attack she runs to her mother. Mitch manages to prevent the birds from breaking in. The family falls asleep in the lull after the attack.

b) Melanie goes up to the attic to investigate a noise. She finds the attic full of birds which broke in during the attack and they descend upon her. Mitch manages to rescue her from certain death, and he and his mother tend her wounds.

c) The birds surrounding the house fall into a calm. Mitch decides that they must flee the house and take Melanie to hospital in San Francisco. They drive off, leaving the birds in possession of their home and the area.

The visual narrative of the film

a) The visual narrative of the boarding up of the family home and the subsequent attack of the birds on the windows and doors builds up an atmosphere of siege and fear. The frame of the house is like the frame of the camera. To begin with the birds are mainly a threat *outside the frame*, but during the attack they begin to invade the house and the camera frame. The ceiling and walls of the small house give a strong sense of being shut in, as if the human characters are almost shut in a protective cage.

b) There is a tremendous build-up as Melanie approaches the door of the attic which uses the technique of 'reverse shot'. We cut from shots of

Melanie to shots of the stairs and door from her *point of view*. This *montage* has various effects, one of which is to cause the audience unease and the sense that she is approaching danger. During the attack inside the attic, some of the shots of Melanie and parts of her body appear to be from the *point of view* of the birds (see Figure 7.8), so that it is as if the camera takes part in the attack.

▶ Shot/reverse shot, page 180

Figure 7.8 *Melanie from the point of view of the birds*

c) In the final sequence there are many shots with many birds, sometimes hundreds, crammed into the frame. This emphasises the message that the birds have taken over possession of the local area in which most of the narrative is set. In the final shot the foreground is full of birds, and the car dissappears down the road into the distance.

The role of the ending of *The Birds*
a) The first part of the attack by the birds is a build up to the attack upon Melanie. It may be seen as a false climax, which, because it has no resolution, simply keys up the audience for the second part of the birds attack.
b) The attack upon Melanie is the climax of the narrative. Throughout the narrative, the birds have played the role of the villain (although like many good villains they can seem more interesting than any of the heroic characters). Now, as in any classic Hollywood narrative, there is a showdown.
c) The scene where Mitch leads his family and Melanie to escape is the part of the film which carries the audience from the climax to the *fadeout*. It allows the audience to take in the impact of the ending. The atmosphere is relatively low key, although tense at times. This kind of winding down of the narrative is often called the *denouement*.

In the entire ending sequence there is a resolution of the different strands of the story. The bird attacks culminate in a victory; the birds have taken over the town. In terms of the love story, Mitch has regained the initiative of the male hero figure in rescuing Melanie and taking care of her and his family during the final escape.

Activity

The last few comments here emphasise those aspects of the final sequence to *The Birds* which achieve closure. Make a list of those aspects of the ending to *The Birds* which achieve, and those aspects which lack, closure. For example:

Achieving closure:

- The victory of the birds represents a new order or a new kind of stability.

Lacking closure:

- It is not really clear at the end of the film who will win. The question as to whether the birds will continue to defeat humanity, or whether human society will be able to mount a successful backlash is left open.

Complete the list of points for and against with your own findings.

The middle section of a narrative

Middles are the major segment of any narrative. The classic ratio is that the middle is at least half of a narrative. What are middles? Well, let that be your first task.

Activity

Take a piece of paper and jot down some notes on what you expect in the middle of a story, after the opening has been established, and before the ending winds things up. You should give your answers with reference to stories in film, television, print etc. you know well.

Analysis

What roles does the middle, or *body*, of a narrative play? If the opening sets up and establishes, and the ending gives a climax, an answer or a new stability, what does the middle do?

The middle of the narrative consists of the main body of the story. It builds on the foundations of the opening in order to reach some kind of climax and/or resolution in the ending. This building up intensifies the main area of interest in the foreground of the story, and fills in the background. It will include ingredients such as obstacles, conflicts, suspense and character development. Other ingredients may include funny or sad moments, an increasing pace, false trails which deceive the audience or the characters, revelations about character and other surprises. Also, the middle will look forward to the ending so that the audience will find it credible.

In the film *On the Waterfront*, the opening shows the gangland-style killing of Joey Doyle, a dock worker who has spoken out against corruption in the union. The opening establishes the main characters: the criminal gang led by Johnny Friendly, which crookedly runs the dock union, Terry Malone, the ex-boxer who is troubled by guilt at his part in luring Joey Doyle to death at the hands of the gang, and Edie, Joey's sister, who wants to expose her brother's killers. At the end of the film, Terry himself testifies to the commission investigating the dock union, fights with the gang and leads the workers back into the docks, having broken the authority of Friendly.

The middle of the narrative is essentially concerned with the following:
- Revealing Terry's character.
- Building the relationships between Terry and the opponents of Friendly's gang: that is, the dockland priest, Father Barry, and Edie.
- Putting Terry into conflict with his past allegiances with Friendly's gang.
- The attempts of Friendly's gang to silence any dissent increases the tension. For example, they send the mob to attack a meeting in Father Barry's church; they arrange an 'accident' to silence Kayo Duggan, who is prepared to testify; they murder Charley when he fails to bring Terry back to the gang.
- The ending of the narrative is foreshadowed in Terry's previous experience as a boxer. He explains the determination which kept him going as a boxer when he talks about himself with Edie in the scene near the opening where they meet in a bar. He recalls 'taking a dive' in the scene in the taxi cab later on in the narrative, where he refuses Charley's request to take on a job to prove his loyalty to Friendly.

Figure 7.9 The taxicab scene from On the Waterfront

A Activity

Choose a feature film for narrative analysis. Write a sample analysis of the narrative structure of the film in terms of the three parts. You may find it easier to write out a summary of the story of the film as a first draft, before organising this into an analysis of the three-part structure for your final draft. You may use these prompts to remind you of how to go about such an analysis.

1 What does the opening establish?
2 How does the middle section build character, obstacles, conflict, tension etc?
3 What does the ending resolve?

> Propp, V., 1968, *The Morphology of the Folk Tale,* University of Texas Press.

Films as fairy tales

Another way of looking at film narrative is to compare the story which a particular film tells with the old and familiar storylines which are favourites in many cultures and countries. *Cinderella*, for example, is an old storyline which has been used and adapted in many film narratives. *Pretty Woman* is a *Cinderella* story.

There is a description of character behaviour and story events in folk stories and fairy tales, originally put together by a Russian called Vladimir Propp, which has been used by a number of writers when they analyse film narrative. Propp isolated a number of character roles and *functions* which events could play in a story. The character roles include *hero* and *villain*, unsurprisingly. They also include a *false hero*, a *princess* and her father, a *helper* and a *donor* (who gives the hero some kind of magical gift).

The complete and original version of Propp's story functions is cast in a set order which must be followed chronologically. The simplified version below is intended to be more flexible. You should be able to use it to show that character and the structure of the story are related. This list is therefore easier to use than the original, but if you wish you can consult the original for your own analyses.

Here is a simplified version of Propp's functions (this is not a complete list).

a) A group of people (family, community etc) and/or the hero are introduced.
b) A rule is broken, or a warning ignored.
c) The villain seeks information about the hero or victim.
d) The villain attempts to deceive.
e) The hero or other victim is deceived.
f) The villain harms a member of the family.
g) The hero is given a mission to find or accomplish something.
h) The hero is tested, attacked or questioned.
i) The hero receives a magical gift or a helper.
j) The hero uses the magical agent.
k) The hero and the villain fight.
l) The hero is injured, or 'branded'.
m) A false hero makes false claims.
n) The hero is recognised.
o) The villain is exposed.
p) The villain is punished.
q) The hero is rewarded: for example, he marries and/or ascends the throne.

The best way to demonstrate how this kind of analysis works is to apply it to an example narrative. The example used here is the story told in *On the Waterfront*.

Joey Doyle is thrown off the roof by the gangsters because he is planning to give evidence against the union. Terry Malone had called Joey up to the roof at the request of the gangsters, even though he did not realise that they would go as far as murder. Terry Malone is an amateur boxer and obviously plays the role of the hero. Edie Doyle, the sister of Joey with whom Terry falls in love, is the heroine or *princess*. Charley Malone, Terry's brother, fails to persuade him to do some more work for the gangsters, and is killed by the gang as a warning to Terry. Father Barry, the dock worker's priest who supports Terry when he gives evidence against the gangsters, plays the role of *donor*, and possibly helper as well. At the end of the film, Terry fights it out with Johnny Friendly, the main villain and leader of the gangsters.

We have identified character *roles*. What about *functions*? Here is a possible list.

1 The hero breaks a rule. (This happens both when Terry lures Joey onto the roof and when he gives evidence to the authorities.)
2 The hero is given a mission. (This happens early in the film when Edie meets Terry in a bar and asks him to help her find out about who killed her brother.)
3 The villain harms a member of the family. (The gangsters kill Joey from Edie's family, then Charley, Terry's brother.)
4 The hero is tested/The hero receives a magical gift. (Father Terry acts as 'donor' when he persuades Terry that it is right to give evidence to the authorities and wrong to gun Friendly down.)
5 The hero fights the villain.
6 The hero is injured, or 'branded'. (When Friendly is losing, the gangsters beat Terry up.)
7 The hero is recognised/the villain is exposed. (This is the end of the film where Terry leads the dock workers back to work, and they all turn their backs on Johnny Friendly.)

Propp's analysis draws attention to the bare bones under the flesh of stories. What we can learn from this is that there are patterns under the surface of all stories, and that films and folk tales have similar deep narrative patterns. This is not to say that Propp-type analysis is easy, or that it always works well. In *On the Waterfront*, for example, who plays the role of *false hero*? There are arguments to place a number of the characters in this role. Arguably, Terry is a false hero, until he makes his decision to fight back and avenge Joey's murder. Terry's brother, Charley, who is killed when he lets Terry escape, is a kind of false hero. It is a feature of the Propp analysis that more than one character can play a role, and that a character can play more than one role.

CASE STUDY Four Weddings and a Funeral

This case study will carry out an analysis of the British-made film *Four Weddings and a Funeral* under the following headings:
- Introduction
- Genre
- Narrative
- Use of film images
- Representation
- Conclusions.

The introduction will deal with the production context of the film. In addition to covering the areas indicated by the headings, the case study will attempt to answer the following questions:
- How does the film build an audience?
- Why is this such a popular film?
- What are the strengths and weaknesses of this product, especially as a British film?

Introduction

In terms of ticket sales worldwide, *Four Weddings and a Funeral* is the most popular British film ever made. *Four Weddings and a Funeral* was made by Working Title Productions, backed by PolyGram, who distributed the film and put up 70% of the investment, and Channel Four. Working Title was set up in the 1980s and their previous successes include *My Beautiful Laundrette* and *Wish You Were Here*. The script was written by Richard Curtis, who has previously written the filmscript for *The Tall Guy* and the television comedy *Blackadder*. *Four Weddings* is aimed at adult audiences. Although romantic rather than sexually explicit, the sex scenes and the use of strong language probably explain the 15 certificate given by the BBFC in Britain.

Figure 7.10 Charles and Carrie, Four Weddings and a Funeral

Four Weddings is a representative product of the British film industry in the 1990s in many ways, one of which is the 'synergy' by which the film is tied up with a hit single, 'Love is All Around' by Wet Wet Wet, and a soundtrack album with other songs from Elton John and Swing Out Sister.

The story concerns a group of friends, including a gay couple, Matthew and Gareth, and their attendance at weddings. This outline will concentrate on the story of 'the hero', Charles. This means ignoring a number of parallel plots and stories for now. Charles, with his flatmate Scarlet, always manages to arrive late at weddings. Charles is a 'serial monogamist', who has had many admirers but still at 32 runs away from 'commitment'. At the first wedding, he is best man and, despite his many comic mistakes and difficulties, has a one night stand with American beauty, Carrie (Andie McDowell). He meets her again at the second wedding and discovers that she is now engaged to a rich Scotsman, Hamish. It is now that he asks himself, 'Why am I always at weddings and not getting married?' They make love again, but the third wedding with Carrie marrying an older man goes ahead. At Carrie's wedding, Gareth has a heart attack. The funeral which follows includes a speech by Matthew, during which he reads the poem, *Funeral Blues*, by W. H. Auden. The last wedding is between Charles and one of his former 'admirers', Henrietta. To cut a long story short, Charles discovers Carrie is now separated, and when he has to admit that he cannot marry Henrietta during the wedding service, she gives him a knock out punch. Everything ends 'happily', with Henrietta and all Charles's group of friends finding partners, and he and Carrie unmarried, but together.

Country	Release date	Number of first-run screens still playing	Total box office to date
US	9 March	–	52,584,880
France	27 April	83	34,529,345
Switzerland	29 April	14	4,947,472
Australia	5 May	–	15,663,969
UK	13 May	30	44,663,362
New Zealand	10 June	4	2,273,562
Singapore	16 June	–	839,508
Belgium	22 June	10	3,481,090
Brazil	6 July	–	3,416,455
South Korea	16 July	–	1,690,515
Taiwan	16 July	–	928,604
Austria	4 August	9	2,798,529
Germany	4 August	171	28,496,193
Denmark	5 August	18	2,456,116
Iceland	5 August	1	318276
Norway	5 August	8	2,587,278
Hong Kong	25 August	2	1,448,490
Argentina	26 August	–	1,021,955
Spain	26 August	50	8,326,708
Israel	27 August	10	1,141,760
Poland	2 September	15	584,044
South Africa	2 September	25	1,499,416
Sweden	9 September	58	5,373,915
Turkey	16 September	2	163,899
Finland	30 September	8	491,695
Czech Republic	7 October	8	17,515
Japan	8 October	40	3,292,768
Italy	13 October	76	3,592,361
Slovenia/Croatia	20 October	7	172,040
Greece	4 November	8	293,988
Mexico	4 November	36	401,209
TOTAL			234,389,467

All figures $US. Source: PolyGram Film International. Compiled on 15 November 1994
*'Four Weddings' opened in French-speaking Switzerland on 29 April and in German-speaking Switzerland on 10 June. The total is for both markets.

Figure 7.11 Four Weddings and a Funeral, *box office gross in $US by country in order of opening date (source PolyGram Film International, table used in Nick Roddick 'Four Weddings and a Final Reckoning',* Sight and Sound *January 1995)*

Genre

Four Weddings and a Funeral is a romantic comedy. The comedy is foregrounded in characters like the trainee priest Gerald (Rowan Atkinson) who gets his marriage service words wrong and the flamboyant middle-aged gay man Gareth (Simon Callow) who enjoys dancing extravagantly during parties. The romantic characters are the young men and women looking for (or in the case of the central character Charles avoiding) potential mates. Four weddings seem the ideal setting for a romantic comedy, and the funeral simply allows the gay couple a ceremony which allows them to celebrate their true love for one another in a dignified manner, albeit after one of them has died. The key signs of romance as given for the hero and his 'princess' are in the *mise en scene*, the music soundtrack and the telling of the story. The lovers look at one another across the crowd, they kiss, they go to bed together, they go shopping, they try to marry other people, they make it up in the rain. The key signs of comedy are in the jokes, the 'sight gags', the verbal and visual banana skins. *Four Weddings* is able to pitch itself at a very broad audience, since it covers love and romance between Britons and Americans, heterosexual couples, a gay male couple, and a disabled man and the woman who learns sign language in order to chat him up.

Narrative

The opening sequence shows the group of friends getting ready to go to the first wedding, and Charles and Scarlet, who oversleep, in a frantic dash up and down the motorway to get there in time. The first wedding establishes the range of characters and the central 'star-crossed' relationship between Charles and Carrie. The agent of change upon which the 'main story' depends is Charles falling in love with Carrie. This is in conflict with the 'established situation', which is that Charles fears any long-term romantic or sexual commitment. This shows when he is panicked by Carrie's half-serious quip about getting engaged after their first night together.

Weddings two and three, and the funeral, function as the 'middle' of the film during which the main plot, about Charles and Carrie's love affair, and the sub plots, about the group of friends, develop.

The wedding between Charles and Henrietta brings the action to a climax. What will Charles do? The audience is kept in some suspense until he finds a way to pull out. The denouement is a romantic conversation between Charles and Carrie in the rain, when he finally manages to find the right words for the occasion and avoid making a fool of himself. The 'end sequence' shows shots of the other friends with their marriage partners.

Propp's analysis is used here in a way which will tend to foreground Charles's role and push out the sub plots. However, in the terms of Propp's analysis the group of friends is like the 'family' which he describes:

- Hero: Charles.
- 'Princess': Carrie.
- Donor: David (Charles's brother performs something 'magical' when he interrupts the final wedding in sign language to force Charles to pull out).
- False hero: Hamish (Hamish is not a villain, since he has nothing for Charles but indifference, and Charles does not 'fight' against his false claim. Henrietta, whom Charles finally attempts to marry, is a 'false princess', or 'false heroine' since she puts one final obstacle between him and Carrie).
- Helper: the group of friends (Scarlett, Tom etc), who also appear like Propp's 'family'.

The plot functions in Propp's terms as follows:

1. The 'family' of friends is introduced.
2. The hero breaks a rule. (Charles breaks rules by leading women on without being able to 'commit himself'. This is underlined when he reacts to Carrie's half serious suggestion that they get engaged with panic.)
3. The hero is given a mission to find or accomplish something. (Charles's quest is to find Carrie again and 'marry' her.)
4. A false hero makes false claims. (Carrie is 'claimed' by Hamish.)
5. The hero is pursued. (At least two of Charles's former lovers continue to make their feelings a 'claim' upon him.)
6. A false hero makes false claims. (Charles is 'claimed' by Henrietta.)
7. The false hero is exposed. (Carrie tells Charles that Hamish was unsuitable, Charles tells the vicar that he cannot marry Henrietta.)
8. The hero receives his final reward. (The hero, Charles, has his 'princess', Carrie.)

This interpretation stretches Propp's roles and functions to fit in *Four Weddings* but nevertheless it does seem to tell us something about how the story works. There are no villains in this story. If there are any, then Charles and Carrie are their own villains. If they were not so indecisive about one another, then there would be no story. Arguably, Propp's function 'the hero is tested' applies to the final two weddings since Carrie and Charles's weddings each 'test' the feelings of the other lover.

Use of film images

The typical images in *Four Weddings and a Funeral* mostly concern people at weddings and a sombre funeral. The 'wedding sequences' are set either around the parties in wealthy settings or the churches where the ceremonies are enacted. These settings allow for a rich spectacle of activity, decor, costume and human interest. Close ups on Charles (Hugh Grant) and his girlfriends, particularly Carrie (Andie McDowell), allow the audience to identify with the central characters and establish the romantic nature of the narrative. The main exceptions to this summary are the sequences where we see Charles and others preparing to leave their homes for the ceremonies, and meetings between Charles and Carrie, as when she takes him shopping for her wedding dress.

The shot which is given close analysis here occurs during the fourth wedding ceremony. The service is interrupted by David, and Charles reveals that he loves another woman. Henrietta delivers a knock-out punch and this shot follows.

The shot is a 'crane shot' so that we, the audience, have a 'bird's eye view' of the scene. At the centre of the image Hugh Grant (Charles) is spreadeagled. He lies flat on his back on an engraved memorial stone set into the tiled floor. His arms are stretched out and his eyes are closed. Another figure is bending over him from the left side (David). In the left of the picture the bride in her wedding dress is being restrained by two male figures on either side of her. All the men are dressed in the same formal dark morning dress and Charles is further distinguished by his light brown waistcoat.

Figure 7.12 Poster for Four Weddings and a Funeral

The shot is set in a church, with the wedding ceremony signified by the dress of the figures. This, and the importance of Hugh Grant at the centre, is quite typical of the *mise en scene* of *Four Weddings and a Funeral*. The angle of the shot is not typical. The extreme high angle (90 degrees) of the shot signifies drama and reflects the fact that this is effectively the climax of the film. Charles has finally 'gone too far', and is symbolically laid flat as a result of his final blunder.

There is an element of cartoon violence in the way in which Charles is apparently thrown flat on his back by the preceding 'punch'. The two previous shots have shown Henrietta draw back her fist followed by a shot of Charles's face being struck. We then see Charles lying flat on the floor. We, the audience, 'fill in' the gaps between these three shots to make a narrative in which Henrietta flattens Charles with her punch. This filling in is called 'closure', and the same term may be used to describe the 'filling in' of the story that the audience makes at the end of a narrative.

The comedy of the scene is pointed up by the narrative detail that the two men are restraining the furious bride from having another crack at the groom. The memorial stone and Charles's pose have connotations of death, and so this shot refers back to the funeral which preceded it.

Representation

Issues of the representation of gender, disability and nation are all interesting topics for debate in looking at *Four Weddings and a Funeral*. Charles and the other males in the film represent some of the uncertainties and changes in views of masculinity which have taken root in Britain in the 1980s and 1990s. The positive inclusion of David, a man whose hearing is impaired, and of British sign language is of some merit given the widespread absence of people with disabilities as 'ordinary' characters in commercial features like *Four Weddings*.

Four Weddings and a Funeral gives a distorted view of Britain which plays to the national stereotype of Britain overseas. Although the Britain portrayed is not entirely white, all the important characters are white with the exception of Matthew. *Four Weddings and a Funeral* gives an idealised representation of a Britain in which 'problems' are a significant absence. The images of Scotland at the third wedding, for example, are like those from a tourist brochure. Britain is represented as a Utopia of happiness and plenty, at a time when the country actually suffers from serious economic problems such as poverty and unemployment. After the second wedding Charles meets Carrie on London's South Bank, the site of the

Museum of the Moving Image and the Festival Theatre. One of the features of this area at this time is the presence of homeless people and beggars, but any such images are carefully excluded. The group of friends to whom Charles belongs are a strangely unrealistic mixture which includes Tom, one of the richest men in England, at one end and characters like Scarlet and Matthew, who appear to have working- or lower-middle-class origins, at the other. The dominant representations in the film are of wealthy people who move in an upper-class and upper-middle-class circle. However, the way that social class creates divisions and barriers between people in Britain is absent from the film.

A Activity

What, in your view, are the arguments for and against the kind of representation of Britain given in *Four Weddings and a Funeral*? For example, are such 'positive' and stereotypical representations necessary in order to build international audiences for British films?

Conclusions

Four Weddings and a Funeral is a film with many positives. Its success has been important to the morale and the finances of the British film industry. It has turned Hugh Grant into an international star. The film has been widely described as a 'feel good' film, and this seems to have found international appeal for cinema going audiences around the world. The film is successful in its own terms. As a romance and a comedy, it provides images and a narrative which arouse romantic sentiment and laughter. The world it shows is not meant to be representative of society as a whole, but it does include positive images of a gay couple, and of Charles's hearing impaired brother.

On the other hand, *Four Weddings and a Funeral* is a slight film which offers entertainment but not any messages of great significance about life and its problems. Its representation of Britain verges on that of a tourist brochure, and Hugh Grant's character, Charles, agrees with American stereotypes of the twittish, ineffectual upper-middle-class Englishman. Such representations are shrewd from the point of view of international marketing, but do they sell Britain short?

Assignment

Analysing film fiction

For this assignment you will produce a case study of a film of your choice. This can be carried out as an individual piece of work, or in groups with individuals taking on certain tasks. Your case study should include the areas covered under the main headings in this chapter.
- Looking at the film genre and production context
- Analysis of images from the film
- Analysis of the film as a narrative with a beginning, a middle and an ending.

Your case study should have a sense of purpose. This means that you need to set out on the analysis with some questions to answer. When you write up the final report you should have a theme and/or argument to follow. This will help you to write a conclusion with something to say.

In order to do this you will need to follow some kind of action plan. Here is an example:

Action plan:
1. Decide which film you want to analyse. Take into account your own interests and abilities, what information is available, the genre of the film and what you need to cover from the course Units and Elements. You may decide to choose a film mentioned in this chapter: there is plenty more to be analysed in each.
2. Plan your research and the likely shape of the final report. You need to prepare an outline of your introduction, setting out what you will cover and what questions you will answer.

3 The model case study above was organised under these headings:
- Introduction
- Genre
- Narrative
- Use of images
- Representation/Messages
- Conclusion

There were also questions to be answered through the study, such as the questions about the building of the audience and the strengths and weaknesses of the film.

4 Allocate a certain amount of time for viewing and research, with a clear deadline for completion.

You will need to view the film a number of times, picking out particular scenes and shots for analysis. You should also carry out some library research. This is important for finding out how the film was made and its production context.

If there is a University Library nearby, this may be worth visiting. The British Film Institute in London has a library which you can use if you purchase a day pass.

5 Make the final plan of how you will write up the case study, and organise your notes under the various headings.

6 Write up the case study. Produce a draft which you can change, and put through a check on spelling, punctuation, accuracy of expression etc. Then produce the final product by the deadline set.

You can use the case study of *Four Weddings and a Funeral* as a model if you wish, or you can change the structure to suit your own findings. The case study does not have to be in written form: if you and your teachers wish to produce a report in another medium, such as film or tape, than that is acceptable on GNVQ courses.

8 Analysing and producing quiz shows

This chapter refers to the GNVQ unit on investigating the content of media products by looking at quiz shows as a television genre. It goes on to relate this to Unit 5 on producing a moving image product in terms of planning and producing a quiz show. It also includes material which is useful in terms of Unit 2 on originating media products.

This chapter is organised into the following sections:
- Introduction to analysing and producing quiz shows
- Analysing quiz shows
- Studio production of a television quiz show
- Planning for production
- Production.

Introduction to analysing and producing quiz shows

In this chapter you will be shown how to analyse a non-fiction radio or television studio production. You will learn about how to make an example of such a product for television or video. The example taken of a studio production here is a quiz show, although much of the production process can be applied to other studio products, such as talk shows and game shows. If you do not have access to a studio you may be able to adapt a room for the purpose.

Quiz shows are *non-fiction* in the sense that they show actual events with real people appearing as themselves. In addition, the questions are factual and relate to the real world rather than imaginary items. They may be produced on radio or on television. They may also be staged as public performances, and their radio and television versions nearly always include an element of public performance with a live audience who often also participate in the programme.

We will begin by looking at ways of analysing quiz shows, and go on to examine how they can be produced on video.

Analysing quiz shows

The quiz show as a phenomenon is a classic example of most, and probably all, definitions of *popular culture*. Quiz shows are often looked down on, even though everybody views or listens to them. They attract large audiences of ordinary people. They follow a game plan or formula which is easy to understand. They stimulate the mind, the emotions and the senses. They also overlap with major activities of everyday life, such as education.

The concept of genre is very useful in understanding and analysing popular mass media products such as quiz shows. A *genre* refers to a type of media product in which certain things are repeated, so that these elements of the genre are predictable to some degree. A *genre product* has stock roles or characters, common action sequences or situations, characteristic images or decor, and other predictable elements. Quiz shows have predictable elements and are genre products. The essential roles are those of the *contestants*, the *host* and the spectating *audience*. The action centres on the answering of questions and the separation of winners and losers. Popular quiz shows usually have a glitzy decor using bright lights and colours. Others, such as *Mastermind,* use light and shadow to dramatic effect.

▶ Genre analysis, page 13

Figure 8.1 *The* Mastermind *set*

Putting quiz shows into a box as a single genre poses some questions. What is a quiz show? What is not a quiz show? Are quiz shows and game shows part of the same genre? There is also a big difference between quiz shows which feature ordinary people as contestants, and those which feature stars as contestants. For the purposes of this chapter we will put *quiz shows* which *test* the contestants through questions to which there are right and wrong answers into one genre category, and *game shows* which set up other kinds of tasks, games and performances into another category. We will put both *celebrity* quiz shows and *participation* quiz shows which offer ordinary people their moments of celebrity into the same genre of *quiz show*, which is the genre we will examine here.

In the quiz show genre the host occupies the position of authority and may have an assistant (stereotypically, this is an attractive female whose physical qualities are emphasised). The audience may be divided into a studio audience and the audience at home. The typical action sequence is a game *round* in which different contestants are set against one another. The organisation of the show, and the set, into spaces which are occupied by, or limited to, audience and contestants is usually very rigid. For example, the contestants are usually limited to a small space behind some kind of desk.

Fiske, J., 1987, *Television Culture*, Routledge, p.265.

The activity of quiz shows can be divided into two basic elements: *rituals* and *games*. The purpose of the rituals are to bring people together and celebrate their status. Rituals include the introductions to the contestants, and the celebration ritual at the end which puts the winner on an equal foooting with the star host. The purpose of the game, or games, is to separate out the winner from the rest. The content of the 'game' section of a quiz show includes the rules of the competition, the kinds of knowledge which are tested and the role which luck plays. The rituals and games which quiz shows follow, and ways that people participate, reflect and overlap with the real world. Some people think that quiz shows represent the values of competition which drive people in the 'rat race' of the capitalist world we inhabit. This is sometimes more evident in the participation quiz show, where ordinary people compete. For example, the contestants in participation quiz shows are usually selected out into *winners* and *losers* through elimination and *prizes*. Critics have also pointed out that the fact that most quiz show hosts are male, and the often sexist presentation of female *assistants*, reflect male dominance or *patriarchy*. When you analyse a quiz show in terms of *representation*, you should consider not only how representative of the population at large the contestants and studio audience are, but also how concepts such as gender and competition are represented.

The stories which quiz shows tell follow a sequence of *establishing*, *contesting* and *celebrating*. The establishing stage is a ritual in which the contestants are introduced and something about their characters revealed. The contest is the set of questions and the game which separates out winners and losers. The celebration consists of the ritual(s) which give the contestant who has been separated out from the rest the changed status of winner. In participation quiz shows, the celebration stage is often more important than it is in celebrity quiz shows. Why do you think this is so?

Quiz shows overlap not only with everyday activities but also with other programmes and mass media products. We have already mentioned game shows, and there are also other *panel* programmes which feature celebrities, which are different from quiz shows. If the quiz show is scheduled on commercial television, the advertisements which break up the show will often tell you something about the target audience. Quiz shows are similar to soaps in the ways in which the audience participates in the action and tries to predict what will happen. The ways in which different media products influence and make reference to one another is referred to as *intertextuality*. For example, the formal tone of the quiz show *Mastermind* and its use of high status settings such as University and civic halls make it intertextual with serious discussion and panel programmes such as *Question Time*.

The appeal of quiz shows is very wide, but they are aimed at particular groups of people which will make up their *target audience*. The target audience for a quiz show will be evident from things such as the scheduling, the nature of the questions, the types of contestant and the studio audience (if there is one). The stereotype of quiz shows that they are watched by 'couch potatoes' is wrong. There are many different ways in which the audience at home can follow and participate in the progress of the show. Are the uses and pleasures of a 'participation' quiz show significantly different from those of the 'celebrity' quiz show?

Audience, page 16

> **A** **Activity**
>
> Make your own list of the different types of use and enjoyment which the audience can gain from watching or listening to a quiz show.

Textual analyses of quiz shows

A radio celebrity quiz show: the News Quiz

The first broadcast quiz shows were radio quiz shows. Most audience participation quizzes on radio are not complete 'shows', but are short competitions as part of other programmes such as disc jockeys' music shows. The BBC offers a number of radio quiz shows, but most of these are celebrity shows. The celebrity shows on Radio 4 include the *News Quiz*, which is analysed here.

Figure 8.2 The regulars on the News Quiz: Jeremy Hardy, Francis Wheen, Barry Took (chairman), Alan Coren and Andy Hamilton

The *News Quiz* is broadcast on Radio 4 on Saturdays at 12.30 and repeated on Mondays at 6.30 for limited runs. It lasts for half an hour and consists of a humorous, jokey examination of the previous week's news. The most important ingredient is the set of questions about the previous week's news items, mainly from the newspapers, which are addressed to the celebrity contestants.

The questions are often puzzles which are more like witty crossword clues. The contestant not only has to know about the news item, but also has to be able to match it with the clues given. For example, a contestant guessed wildly that the following question was about a nudist when in fact it was about burglars.

'Whose cheek took the biscuit after stealing everyone else's?' (13/5/95)

The correct answer referred to a story about some burglars who phoned up the victims of their theft in order to sell them their goods back. There are very few sound effects on the *News Quiz*, but music is used as a lead in before the question is given. For example, in the edition broadcast 11/3/95, the chorus from 'Another One Bites the Dust' by the pop group Queen was played in order to introduce a question about the resignation of a government minister. In another edition, Cliff Richard singing 'Summer Holiday' introduced the following question.

'Whose summer holiday will be a big family affair?' (13/5/95)

The correct answer to this referred to a newspaper story about an extended family with 103 members who had all booked onto the same package holiday in Spain.

The presenter of the *News Quiz*, Barry Took, has a script which he works from. This allows him to follow up the celebrities' answers with his version of the correct answer, including some scripted jokes about the news item in question. As an extra ingredient, news items which are humorous, intentionally or unintentionally on the part of the source, are read out by an announcer. These are often sent in by listeners to the programme, who are then given a credit. At the end of the show, the contestants read out similarly humorous 'cuttings' from the newspaper which they have chosen themselves.

The laughter of the studio audience, the contestants and the presenter are the main sound effects of any significance. The audience also sometimes applauds to show its approval.

The *News Quiz* dramatises the humorous aspects of news stories. It reflects the fact that news stories are selected and perceived as significant, not only for serious reasons such as importance and scale, but also for more humorous aspects such as their surprise value or oddity. The *News Quiz* will select news stories according to their joke value, so that stories which involve stereotypes of people, sexual subject matter, toilet humour etc frequently occur.

The *News Quiz* is a male-dominated programme, as all the participants are usually male. It gives a representation of the world as a funny and bizarre place in which odd things happen. Human beings are full of faults, which the show draws attention to and mocks. The show tends to have a view of the world which is not 'politically correct', and it often reinforces conventional ideas and stereotypes of people, especially 'marginal' groups such as women and 'foreigners'. In this way, the *News Quiz* is close to the values of the tabloid press.

The *News Quiz* is intertextual with the satirical magazine *Private Eye* (see Figures 8.3 and 8.4). The show uses celebrities who write for this magazine. The selection of the humorous aspects of news stories is also a feature of *Private Eye*, and both these media products share a similar sense of humour and a habit of laughing at the failures of the rich and powerful. A very successful television version of the *News Quiz*, called *Have I Got News For You*, is broadcast on BBC Television.

An audience participation quiz show: Fifteen to One

At any one time there are hundreds, perhaps thousands, of quiz shows being shown on television around the world. Quiz shows are popular with television channels and companies because they are relatively cheap to make and attract large audiences if they are any good. The most reliable and successful formulae for television quiz shows come mainly from the United States, although quiz shows are adapted to the culture of the country in which they are made and to their target audience. Why do quiz shows attract such large audiences? One answer is that they allow their

Analysing and producing quiz shows

Figure 8.3 Private Eye *front cover*

Figure 8.4 *A typical page from* Private Eye

audiences to participate and measure their own performance against that of the contestants.

Fifteen to One is a quiz show which has been made to a British formula. It was originally invented by a British Telecom engineer, John M. Lewis. The show is produced and presented by William G. Stewart and made by Regent Productions for broadcasting on Channel 4. When it is being broadcast, the show is shown daily Monday to Friday on Channel 4. The show is based on the elimination of contestants, from the fifteen who start each show down to a single winner per programme. The winners vie for a position on a scoreboard running from programme to programme.

▶ Audience, page 16

Figure 8.5 Fifteen to One *set*

157

The contestants on *Fifteen to One* have three lives, and are penalised if they are unable to answer a question correctly in a short time by losing a life. Contestants who lose all their lives are eliminated. In the first round every contestant is able to compete by answering questions. In the second round contestants who answer a question correctly may choose to answer another question themselves or nominate another contestant. If the person nominated answers wrongly, then the candidate who nominated them may nominate another contestant, and so on. In this way, the contestants are knocked down to the three survivors who carry on to a further contest after the commercial break. After the break, the three survivors compete to be the first to answer questions worth ten points each. They begin with three lives and a point for each life they had remaining from the contest before the break. If they answer a question correctly, they gain ten points. If they answer a question incorrectly, they lose a life and ten points. In the second round of this part of the game, the first to answer a question correctly may again choose to answer another question or nominate another contestant. In the final round, the winning contestant who remains after all the others have been eliminated answers questions to increase his or her score. The winner of each programme is in competition with the winners of previous programmes on the basis of the score each achieves. The winner's score is rated against the others according to whether it qualifies to appear on a running scoreboard and at what position it appears. The highest scoring winners compete in finals.

Fifteen to One resembles the quiz shows organised in local communities which allow many people to compete. It is intertextual with the pub quiz, for example. There is a certain amount of luck in whether the kind of question the contestant is asked is in their field of knowledge. The kinds of knowledge tested fall within the area of general knowledge, but are often biased towards traditional, even old fashioned, 'school' topics such as geography, mathematics, geometry, Greek mythology and the Bible.

Fifteen to One has a simple set which consists of a set of tall desks, at which contestants stand, around a central floor with a circular design painted on it, and a row of arches in the background. The tall desks resemble pulpits in that the contestants stand behind them. Each desk has three green vertical strip lights representing the lives which that contestant will lose for incorrect answers. Correct answers are followed by a high-pitched electronic bell; wrong answers are identified by a lower-pitched buzzer. After the commercial break the survivors move to three desks set up on the circle in the centre of the floor. The main colour of the set is blue, with some grey or green. The arches are blue and resemble windows. The lighting sets up dramatic contrasts of light and shadow; for example, the host is lit so that, in the first contest with the contestants in the large circle, he casts a long shadow behind him.

The show has various rituals. There is a ritual introduction to the contestants at the beginning of the show. The survivors are introduced in more detail after the break. William G. Stewart congratulates the final winner, coming round behind the winner's booth to celebrate that person's *star* status at the end of the show. There is no public prize other than this star status for winning through a single programme.

Fifteen to One includes a wide audience from all over Britain and Ireland, but there is a tendency for white males to dominate. The male presenter and the emphasis upon factual topics, competition and speed of response makes the show more masculine, although there are always some female contestants. *Fifteen to One* has been criticised for its use of elimination by failure and said to have its roots in 'that most competitive of models of education, the Victorian classroom' (Garry Whannel in Goodwin and Whannel, 1990, p.107). On the other hand it could be argued that the speed and competitiveness of the show allows a large number of people to participate, up to 75 per week. The viewer is able to give a lot of attention to the participants. The elimination techniques as they develop give the contestants the power to choose who should answer the next question, which increases the sense of the 'empowerment' of ordinary people.

▶ Goodwin, A., and Whannel, G. 1990, *Understanding Television*, Routledge

Figure 8.6 *Three booths from the* Fifteen to One *contest following the commercial break*

Fifteen to One has five characteristics of popular culture – abundance, energy, intensity, ease of understanding, and community participation. Firstly, it celebrates the abundance of knowledge which 'ordinary' people possess. Secondly, it has energy in the fast pace it moves at. Thirdly, it has intensity in the way that the contestants try so hard and struggle to win. Fourthly, it is easy to understand and enjoy for almost any viewer. Finally, the competitive nature of the game is balanced by the number of people who participate and the good manners with which they compete.

Assignment

Analyse a quiz show
The assignment is broken down into four tasks and a questionnaire which will help you to perform your own viewing and analysis.

Task 1
a) Decide why you want to analyse a quiz show.
b) Choose the programme which is to be the subject of your analysis. Answering question (a) should help you to make your choice in (b). You

might simply decide to analyse a very popular quiz show in order to find out why it is so popular. Alternatively, if you decided you wanted to look at the links with education in a quiz show, you might choose a show such as *Mastermind*, in which the representation of education is an important theme. Of course, analysing a quiz show and how it works is an essential first step towards making one yourself.

Task 2
Hold a meeting to decide how you will report your research, and review the purpose of the report which will record your analysis.

How will you present your report and in what medium? Will it be a written report? Will it be presented in a talk for other students, an exhibition, a video tape, or a combination of these?

Which format will you use for your research? Here is an example format to help you:

Introduction
What are the aims of your analysis?

Method
How did you go about analysing the programme? (For example, how did you use and adapt the questionnaire given below?)

Results
What did you find? You might use the questionnaire headings to organise your findings.

Conclusion
What is your interpretation of your results? Evaluate your own research.

Task 3
View a recording of at least one episode of the quiz show, making notes in answer to the various questions raised in the questionnaire. You will need to view the episode a number of times. There are various ways of concentrating upon different aspects of the show. You can use the video controls to help you do this, listening to the opening music without vision, viewing without the sound, using the freeze-frame facility, slowing down certain sequences for close analysis, etc.

Task 4
Write up your report and present it through the medium and format you have chosen.

Quiz Shows: textual analysis questionnaire
Communication factors
1 What is the title of the show?
2 Is this a radio or a television quiz show?
3 What channel is it shown on?
4 What is the production company?
5 When is it scheduled?

Genre and narrative
1 Are the contestants ordinary people participating in the show, or celebrities?

2 What are the rules of the game?
3 Describe the set or, in the case of radio, any music or sound effects.
4 How are the roles of the host and the contestants characterised or developed?
5 How are the contestants introduced?
6 How is the status of the winner 'celebrated'?
7 How is the appearance of 'live' transmission achieved?

Representation
1 How representative of the population at large, or otherwise, are the contestants?
2 What is the effect of the professional roles in the show? (For example, is there a male host and a female assistant?)
3 How are key themes such as competition, participation and/or education shown?
4 Does this show link with or express any other aspects of everyday life?

Popular culture and intertextuality
1 How does this show reflect popular culture?
2 Are there any reasons for giving the show low status as a media product?
3 (If a commercial product) what relationships are there between this show and the advertisements which interject in the breaks?
4 In what ways is this show similar to, or comparable with, other genres such as soaps?

Audience
1 What are the target audiences for this show, and how can you tell?
2 How is the audience at home involved?
3 If there is a studio audience, describe its contribution.

Conclusion
1 What would you criticise about this show?
2 What would you 'applaud' or celebrate?

Studio production of a television quiz show

This second part will be set out under the following headings:
- writing a formula and script
- planning and preparing for production
- production.

Writing the formula and script

The formula
Your design for a quiz show and its format should relate to a needs analysis. You need to develop a brief which shows that your idea fulfils a need. Your brief should be set out under headings and answer the following questions.

Why make this product?
The first purpose of quiz shows is to entertain an audience. What are the *particular* purposes of your show?

Who is the target audience?
In quiz shows, the nature of the questions asked and the types of contestant will reflect the age, gender and social background of your target audience.

What will be the subject matter of the show?
Quiz shows do not have to restrict themselves to questions about 'facts'. Quiz shows like *Blankety Blank* and *Family Fortunes*, for example, ask questions which require the contestants to predict the reactions of groups of other people.

What will be the format of the show?
At its most basic the quiz show offers the spectacle of a knowledge contest. The format of the contest varies according to the rules of the game.

As we have seen, *Fifteen to One* works through the elimination of individual competitors. Will you have individual competitors or teams, or a combination of the two? In addition to the nomination option used in *Fifteen to One*, there are other techniques, such as the offering of wrongly answered questions to another competitor, 'bonus' questions with higher points, 'tie breaker' questions which immediately identify a winner etc. Your format should reflect the purpose of the show.

How will the show use or break genre conventions?
Your formula and design will have to follow some, if not most, of the generic characteristics of a quiz show in order to make sense as such. On the other hand, you have the freedom also to break with the expectations of the audience. You can break some of the normal rules or conventions and offer something new, or even *alternative*.

Blankety Blank was a quiz show which parodied the genre. Contestants were literally wheeled on and, if they lost, wheeled off. The prizes were cheap and part of the joke.

Fifteen to One uses elements of the genre such as sound effects for right and wrong answers and a score board. It is a fairly conventional product within the genre. However, it does not use a glamorous female, or any assistant to the host.

You might wish to experiment and introduce an alternative element in your use of the genre.

How will the product be used and marketed?
Since you are probably making your show on video, you might like to consider the potential for a quiz show on video. For example, if your contestants are school or college students, the video might be marketed to other students and students' parents. You might also wish to consider sponsorship, or a charitable purpose and link. You will want to organise the exhibition of the product and will need to publicise this.

In addition to the more obvious aspects, such as where and how the product will be found, you need to consider how your audience will perceive your quiz show. A good way of thinking about this is to consider your programme in relation to other, similar products. For example, *Fifteen to One* is a more popular, *downmarket* version of *Mastermind*. Like Mastermind it relies heavily on the *educational* for its version of general knowledge. Interestingly, its use of lighting is similar to *Mastermind* in its use of strong light and shadow. On the other hand, the packaging in terms of the use of music, colour, set and the title sequence is much more *pop*. The range of contestants on *Fifteen to One* is much broader.

The script
The script for a quiz show will include the following:
- a slogan or introduction to the show

- introductions to the contestants – these may take the form of personal questions
- an introduction to the rules of the show for the television or video audience
- the questions (and the answers) for the host
- *signposting* of the progression of the game – rounds, scores, losers/winners etc.
- a conclusion which signs the programme off.

You will need to think about how you want to use your studio audience and write this into your script. You will need to research your questions and answers, checking their accuracy and effectiveness. You will want to write in information about the shots to be used as the planning of the production develops. You may have to make some last-minute changes to the script after rehearsals.

Planning for production

Although we will be talking here about a studio production you do not necessarily have to use a studio in order to make a video of a quiz show. If you do not have the use of a studio you can adapt a large room, build your set, and film your show using portable cameras. You can use editing as an alternative to vision mixing in the studio, although you should make a storyboard or shot list to simplify the final editing. If you do have the use of a studio book it well in advance. Plan and rehearse as much as you can outside the studio, and budget your time in the studio very carefully.

▶ The edit, page 196

▶ Story board, page 181

The basics of planning studio production for a quiz show are similar to most other studio productions. You will need to do the following:

- decide on the roles for the team
- allocate roles
- design the set and draw up a floor plan
- hold planning meetings
- finalise the script and prepare a shooting script
- run through the complete programme
- film the final production.

We will now consider each of these steps in detail.

Figure 8.7 Planning the production of a video is a team effort

Roles

The roles for a studio production may be broken down into three smaller teams: the production team who direct the planning and organisation of the show; the technical team who make the programme in the hands-on technician sense; and the artistes who provide the *talent* on camera. The production team is headed by the director which may also include a floor manager or production assistant and a designer. The technical team includes camera operators, a supervisor in charge of sound, and a vision mixer. In a quiz show production the team of *artistes* include the host, the contestants and the possibility of assistants to the host. After everyone has been allocated a role, or a combination of roles, the individual members of the team should either be given or write out themselves a description of their roles. For example, the designer will consult with the director and the rest of the team, in order to produce designs for the set and a floor plan.

Set design and floor plans

This entails various decisions. First of all you need to make a survey of the studio, or room, that you will be using, measuring the length and width. You will need to make note of the position of any fittings, the lighting and cameras. How will the studio be laid out? The layout of the set must take into account the shots to be used and the positions of the cameras. It must take into account the positioning of the 'talent' and any movement. The host should have some freedom of movement. Which studio wall will be used as the main backing wall? What will be used as the backdrop for the set? Where will the title of the show be displayed? What will be the dominant colours on the set? Will a graphic design or logo be used? How will the sides of the set be screened off? How will the set be furnished? What props will be used? Avoid clutter or distractions from the action. Keep the set simple.

Figure 8.8 Example of a set design

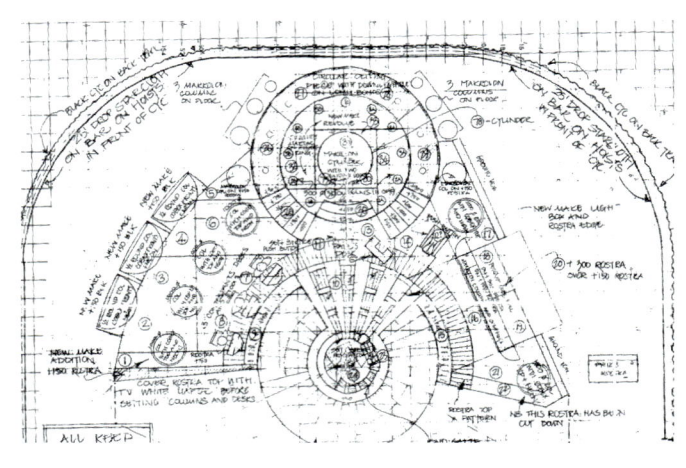

Figure 8.9 Example of a floor plan

The floor plan is drawn up from the set design and should be to scale with the measurements of the studio. It should be used to plot the movements of the host, and the movements of any other artistes. The camera positions should also be plotted. The floor plan and the set design may evolve together, as either may throw up problems or the necessity for changes. From a safety point of view you should ensure that exits are clearly marked and fire exits not obstructed.

Figure 8.10 A camera in use

We need to add in a note about sound and lighting. The simplest sound pickup arrangement is a single hand-held microphone which the host points at each contestant in turn. Other possibilities include operators pointing directional microphones, boom microphones or radio microphones. The action should be at the centre of the main key light. You may also have backlighting, and some directional lighting to create soft light or shadows. The needs of lighting and sound make an argument for having as few different areas as possible where action takes place on the set. You will need to try out the studio and the set for lighting and sound, looking for and avoiding problems such as shiny surfaces, reflections, distracting shadows from people and equipment etc. Indicate the arrangements for lighting and sound on the floor plan.

▶ Microphones, page 227

Figure 8.11 Hand-held microphone

Figure 8.12 Basic lighting set up for a studio production

Planning meetings

You can hold as many or as few planning meetings as you wish, as long as the whole team are quite clear at the end of the process how they will go about making the show. It is the responsibility of the director to make sure that the paperwork is brought to the meeting, including the floor plan with the positions of the cameras and the positions and movements of all the performers. The meeting will normally be chaired and run by the director.

The planning meeting before the production should begin with an outline of the programme. The director should then run through the action, explaining who will be when and what shots will be required. There should be a question phase where the technicians and the artistes can ask any questions they want about their roles in the production.

The floor manager or another suitable person should be designated to look after the studio audience if you have one. This person can give the audience encouragement or prompts to applaud, by holding up applause signs if necessary. Be aware of and try to avoid the problem of the studio audience slowing down the action, not only through long applause, but also through long laughter.

Finalise the script and prepare a shooting script

Your final script will include speech: the introduction of the artistes and the contestants, the description of the game and the rules, the 'signposting' of the stages of the game, the declaration of winners and credit given to the losers, and the final farewell to the audience. You may also wish to write in some jokes or 'patter' for the host. You will wish to leave some of the programme unscripted. The host will have the questions written on cards and, obviously, the contestant's answers are unscripted.

Once you have your final script, you need to add in the 'camera logic' or the allocation of shots to sequences. The shots you will have will depend upon the number of cameras and their positions. Your shot allocation will include a wide *cover shot* of the entire action, shots of the host and shots of the contestants. If you have teams of contestants, you will have the choice between close ups of individuals and group shots. If you decide to include studio audience participation and have response shots or cutaways to the audience, these will also need to be written into the shooting script where possible. When planning shot sequences and actually filming, you will have to take into account the *flow* of the shots and make sure that there is a logic to the cutting, so that you are not cutting to the same size of shot showing similar things.

▶ Cutaways, page 191

If you have only one camera, then you can devise a camera logic which includes camera movement to follow the action, but this is not conventional and will require a storyboard. The convention of studio quiz shows is that camera movement as shots are changed is not seen. If mistakes are made they can be edited out; this is where careful recording of cutaway shots is important.

You will have to make a number of copies of the shooting script. Each member of the technical team should have one. You may wish to develop special versions for the camera operators and vision mixer. These are sometimes called 'camera cards' and include the shot number from the shooting script, the type of shot, the content of the shot, and cues in and out from the script and the action.

Run through the complete programme

The time and place to check over all this planning is in rehearsal or run through. This gives the director the opportunity to go through the complete programme shot by shot. The director will take each shot and either confirm or change it. Every change should be noted down on the shooting script.

At the end of the run through all the changes will be read back, and the technical team should change their shooting scripts (or camera cards) accordingly.

Figure 8.13 Shooting using a shooting script. In the studio, the producers will watch from the gallery, and will usually follow and direct the action on monitors.

Production

Here are some final tips for production, technical and otherwise.
1. Always be ahead of the action. You need to anticipate what will happen next. If you are the host you need to be ready to 'improvise', to relax the contestants if they are tense and respond to any unscripted humorous opportunities which crop up. If you are the camera person you need to have the next shot ready as soon as your camera is free to move. If you are the director you will need to give your instructions to the vision mixer a second or two before you want them carried out.
2. If you have the use of a studio, you will find that there are all kinds of fancy effects with picture in picture, fancy wipes, echo, computer graphics, etc. By all means make yourself familiar with these effects, but do not use them for the sake of it. Keep things simple and relevant to the needs of the show.
3. If you have only one or two cameras to work with, you can work in some more complicated material by pre-recording part of the programme and playing it in from video tape at the time or in later editing. This is useful for the opening sequence and the titles at the beginning and end.
4. At the beginning of the programme, bring up the sound before you bring in the picture. It appears better if sound leads in to the picture rather than the other way around.
5. Remember the rules of composition. Make sure that important information is not lost at the edge of the screen.
6. Make a note of time lost, especially if it is not your fault but due to technical breakdowns or other external causes. This is not only important if you have to write up a log or report of the production; you may need to argue for extra studio time owed to your production if this happens.

7 If there is a serious disruption to the progress of the show or the action of the contest, simply go back to a convenient point and start the show again. The problem, whatever it is, can be edited out during post-production. When you have finished recording the show, everyone should wait while the recording is checked. If any further retakes are necessary, these can be re-recorded with the studio time remaining or scheduled for a future booking.

Assignment

Producing and filming a quiz show

In this assignment you must go through the various stages of planning, writing and producing a quiz show of your own devising.

- Task 1: Find a client who will commission a quiz show.

You will need to consider such factors as access to audiences and the need for the product. You then need to go around to agencies in your school, college or locality who might be interested in publicising themselves through a quiz show. For example, a teacher or a careers officer may be interested in becoming your client for a quiz show about careers.

- Task 2: Write a planning brief for the quiz show.

Your brief will 'sell' your ideas to a client. However, it will reflect research you carry out into the client's needs and the intended audience. You may need to negotiate some of your ideas with the client before, during and after writing the planning brief.

The brief will put forward the subject of the quiz show and the justification for commissioning such a project. It will address details such as the title of the show, and more general points such as the nature of the audience.

- Task 3: Produce scripts for the quiz show.

The preparation for scripting the show should begin with writing the rules which will control the game. It is possible to divide the script up into parts: the introduction; the script for the host; the questions and answers; links; the conclusion to the show. The questions and the acceptable answers will have to be researched, and carefully written.

- Task 4: Allocate roles.
- Task 5: Design and make up the set.
- Task 6: Run through the show.

This cannot be an exact run through of the final show for obvious reasons. The questions will have to be different from those used in the final filmed programme. However, the introduction, the conclusion and even the jokes can be rehearsed.

- Task 7: Film the show.

This has to be performed from start to finish. Where mistakes occur, that section of the show can be repeated. Such mistakes can be edited out in post-production.

9 | Planning a video production

This chapter provides help in planning the production of a video film. This refers to GNVQ Units 2 and 5, which require you to develop skills in planning and setting up production of moving image products. The chapter will also bring in skills which come up in the units referring to research, and marketing what you finally produce.

The chapter is organised into the following sections:
- Introduction to planning a video production
- Generating and developing ideas
- Product specification
- Case study: Video assignment report
- Carrying out research
- Contract issues
- Case study: Video assignment
- Developing production scripts
- Planning the production process.

Introduction to planning a video production

The production process of a video film falls into four phases: pre-production; production; post-production; and distribution. This chapter is concerned with pre-production, which involves all the preparation which goes on before actual filming. This ranges from the initial specifications for the product, the generation of scripts and budget and the agreement of a contract, to actual planning of the production process and the allocation of roles in the production team.

It is a grave mistake to be impatient to get on with production and rush through the planning stage. The more time spent on research and planning, the more economical will be your use of production time, and the more professional will be the standard of the final product.

Generating and developing ideas

This is what you have to do:
- Think up and list a number of ideas for a video product.
- In a production team work out which are the best ideas.
- Make up a list of what you need to find out. This will include health and safety issues, any background research for the content of the film, research about the audience and other research required.

Compile a list of what you will need in the way of resources, such as budget, equipment, props etc.

Finally, write up a plan and specification of what you will produce in the form of a 'brief'. This document which will show that you have thought through the process above. It will also set out what your product will do, how it will do it and to whom it is addressed.

Before we look at ways of generating ideas for a film, we need to make a checklist of the points to consider in answer to the question, 'Why make a video film?'. Before you look at the list of answers here, jot down on a piece of paper your own ideas about why a film would be the best answer to a communication need.

1 There is an audience who will want to watch the end product. If your film idea has not got a clear and defined target audience, with a reason to watch, then you have to rethink or choose another idea.
2 The purpose of your idea or message is best served by a video. It is a good idea, when you evaluate ideas, to ask whether your idea could be put across any better in another medium. What is it about the idea that is best served by moving images? For example, an exercise video would seem to have advantages over a book. However, a set of exercise instructions about how to exercise on the train, or at work, might be best put over through the print medium.
3 There must be a need for the visual aspect of the video film. Films are not very good for putting over detailed information full of facts and statistics which the audience needs to remember, for example.
4 The idea or message can be filmed with the resources, locations and talent available. This does not have to be a limiting requirement. There used to be a theatre company of two men called 'The National Theatre of Brent' whose speciality was the staging of historical epics with very, very few resources. They got round this in various amusing ways, putting over important events in scenes with few characters.

Figure 9.1 The National Theatre of Brent performing

You will be given an assignment by your teachers for this production. Part of this will be information about the kind of product they want you to make for your video or film. This kind of information is usually called 'a creative brief'. In other words, some things are decided for you, but within the limits of those decisions you have room to be 'creative' and bring in your own ideas. Here is a sample assignment in the form of a 'creative brief'.

Assignment

'Teenagers now and then'

Your task is to make a programme, for your age group primarily, about what it means to be a teenager. You will either include some historical background about the origin of the concept of the teenager or a background study of teenagers in a previous decade, or both.

Target audience
The primary target audience is in the 15–19 age range. You may further segment the audience if you wish. For example, you could concentrate on one sex.

The secondary target audience is an older age group who will be interested in the historical background you bring in.

Message
You have freedom to decide the bias of your message. For example, you might decide to seek historical similarities in the experiences of 'teenagers' over the decades.

Style
You have creative freedom here also. However, your product must have a style which copies something in existence, or experiments with it.

Criteria for success
We are looking for something short and snappy, which shows evidence of research, planning, careful filming and post-production in some form.

The next step
We are expecting from your group a treatment which will sell your ideas and set them out in answer to the following headings:
1. What is the product and its title?
2. Who is the target audience?
3. What media are to be used?
4. What is the purpose of the product?
5. What is the content of the product?
6. How will the message be put across?
7. How will the product be made?

We will now look at ways of generating ideas, and means of evaluating ideas.

Generating ideas: 'Brainstorming'

Brainstorming is a way of getting people to contribute a large number of ideas without allowing any evaluation to interfere with the list which is first put together. Here is a structure which shows how a brainstorming meeting can be run.

1. Draw up a briefing document which gives:
- who is in the group and their roles
- where the group will meet, date, start time, finish time
- a definition of the end product; for example, 'ideas for a video about the school/college'

- any useful background material which is not too long or difficult to read.
2 Appoint a *facilitator* who will run the meeting with the aims of allowing everyone to participate equally, contribute ideas and listen to the ideas of others.
3 Appoint a *scribe* who will write down a list of all the ideas generated.
4 The brainstormers should number between three and six.
5 The meeting should be devoted to producing quantity of ideas, regardless of quality. No idea can be rejected or evaluated during the brainstorming meeting.
6 At the end of the meeting the scribe or the facilitator will run through all the ideas recorded, and ensure that all the ideas generated have been recorded, before ending the brainstorm session.

Figure 9.2 A brainstorming session

Evaluating ideas

In the next session, a meeting will be needed to evaluate these ideas. The brief for this meeting will be to measure the value and feasibility of the ideas. Here are some ways in which this can be done.
- Can any of the ideas be combined in order to make an even better one? For example, an idea to make a drama about a school or college might be combined with a promotional idea, to make a promotional video in the form of a dramatic narrative with fictional characters.
- Get everyone to rank or give the ideas scores to see if there is a strong consensus on which are the 'best'.
- Once you have a manageable number of ideas to evaluate look at the arguments for and against each.
- Try out the front running ideas on some people who are from the target audiences.
- Be a devil's advocate for the idea and look at the potential for it all to go wrong.

There were a lot of ideas at the beginning of this section on how to evaluate an idea as an idea for a film. Here are some further, more general questions to be thinking about when evaluating prospective projects. How original, or new, is the idea? Has it been done before? Does the idea make good use of the talents and strengths of the production group? How difficult will it be to promote the final product?

Product specification

When you have come to a decision you will carry out research and write a planning document, under headings, which gives your interpretation of the final specification of the product to be produced. You will write the *treatment* (sometimes called a *promotional brief*).

The treatment makes sure that everyone agrees and understands the product, and can be used to persuade anyone who must approve your work that you know what you are doing and have a worthwhile product in view.

Carrying out research

Time and effort put into research is never wasted. If you want to make a really good video product then you have carry out the following research:
- find out information about your subject
- find out about the resources you will need to make the product

Figure 9.3 Interviewing with tape recorder

- visit any locations you will use and gain permission in writing to film at specific places and times
- interview people (this is called a primary source)
- carry out research using books, articles, audio tapes, and/or video tapes (this is called a secondary source)
- keep lists or logs with precise details of any sources you use – certain of these will have to be credited at the end of your film
- hold meetings with the rest of the production team in order to plan the research and keep to the deadlines for this stage.

Here is an example of a record of some research. Read the following account by a student about a video film that his production team made about the different languages used in the London college where he was studying.

CASE STUDY Video assignment report

'We had decided to make a film about the many different languages used by the students in my college. About half this particular class are bilingual. We found that the students who spoke mainly English only were interested in the other languages and the culture too. In our meetings we decided that the film was going to show that these languages reflected the area. It was going to use location shots of different languages on some of the signs in the streets around the area, including some interesting English ones. There were going to be interviews with students who were interested and involved in the different languages spoken in the community. We had allocated about a week for the research stage. We shared out some of the jobs. One student liked using libraries so she looked up information in books and magazines about some of the main languages we knew were used in the community. Someone else visited some local video shops which had a lot of Indian films, and got a lot of help from them. We used mainly portable video with a hand-held mike. A small team went around the college interviewing different students and finding out about different attitudes to English and the other community languages. Some students agreed to be interviewed on film. There was a group of boys who, well, they wouldn't admit it very clearly, but they talked about Creole and Black English. As the work went on they talked about it more. And they were certainly able, in terms of the film, to go out to their friends in the college, and get them to speak sort of Creole in front of the camera.

I worked with a friend of mine talking to people in local shops, businesses and restaurants. We got a lot of information. After we had talked to them no-one refused us permission to film their signs. We tape-recorded music like Reggae, Bhangra and Rai. We wrote to local radio stations broadcasting in languages other than English, and they agreed to let us edit in some of their material on the soundtrack. One of the teachers put us on to a lecturer who had done a survey on community languages, and we interviewed him in the college studio.

I think it was useful to learn more about the different languages and cultures we put in the film. In the end, I think I enjoyed the research even more than making the film!' (see Nicholas, J., 1994, *Language Diversity Surveys as Agents of Change*, Multilingual Matters)

A Activity

Read through the account above and make notes on the following points:
1. What were the objectives of the research?
2. What material was actually collected?
3. Make a list of the primary sources.
4. Make a list of all secondary sources.
5. What other resources were used?

Now, what about *your* research? You will need to say what your objectives are. You will need to find out the sources you will use, and record some useful information. Finally, you will keep a list of the resources used. We recommend you use the Harvard system, i.e. the author (surname first), the year, the title and the publisher, for example:

Nicholas J., 1994, *Language Diversity Surveys as Agents of Change*, Multilingual Matters.

Finally, you put your details of resources into a list; the authors should be in alphabetical order.

Contract issues

Making a visual product such as a video film involves various issues. There are issues about the resources and budget available to make the product. There are issues about the law and people's rights. There is, for example, the issue about who owns the product. This is known as copyright. There are issues about what it is right and what it is wrong to say and do on film. For example, in recording information about people's personal lives for exhibition in a film, permission and consent needs to be asked for and given, often in writing. There are issues about what happens if disaster strikes and unforeseen changes have to be made. There are important issues about health and safety, especially when using electrical equipment.

You should take these factors into account when writing your treatment and scripts. One way to explore these issues is to negotiate a contract between you as the production team and those with whom, and for whom, you are making the product. You can obtain specimen contracts from organisations which advise film makers. You can use one of these as a framework or 'pro forma', or produce a simpler version as your own working contract.

A contract should include the following:
1 Who made the agreement and when.
2 The deadlines for completion of the various production stages.
3 Who has the ownership and rights over the product.
4 Whether and how changes can be made to the agreement.
5 A let out clause in the event of *force majeure*, or 'acts of God', such as fire, earthquake, natural catastrophe etc.
6 What will be included in the credits and any other copyright notices.
7 A notice, or clause, about any confidential information (or any other 'sensitive subjects' you wish to include).
8 A notice, or clause, referring to the laws of the land which govern the product and the agreement.
9 Issues about health, safety and safe working practices not covered above.

The treatment and any other important information may be attached to the contract as additional items or 'appendices'.

Before you start scripting, your treatment should be agreed and approved. The approval of your treatment as the basis of the visual product to be made, and the signing of an agreement based upon it, should be completed before you move on to the next stage.

Developing production scripts

We now get down to writing the ideas and language for the visual material we intend to produce. Writing for visual material has some characteristics and some forms which may be different from those you are used to. Writing for visual material is different from, but not more difficult than, other forms of writing.

Writing is usually put with the pre-production process; however, at this stage it overlaps with the production process. When you are writing down your ideas, you must imagine what it is you are going to produce. Here are some writing tasks which it is useful to go through in producing a script:

1. Write down a summary of how you will fulfil your instructions, or *brief*. This is called a *treatment*.
2. Write down summaries, or 'synopses', of the individual stages, or scenes, in your video film.
3. Develop script material for each stage or scene from the synopses.

Fiction and non-fiction differ sometimes in that parts of non-fiction may be unscripted. Commentary, questions, introductions and other prompts for non-fiction material are written in advance. Answers and other responses which are recorded for non-fiction material are 'edited in' and written out, or 'transcribed' into the final 'post-production' script. By contrast, fiction material will be entirely scripted in advance.

Treatments

Let's start with treatments. A treatment is very close to a brief. We will make a distinction between a brief and a treatment (they are not always separated in this way in the media industry). A brief is a set of specifications from which a more detailed narrative or structure of events is developed. By contrast, a treatment sets out your approach to the brief and tells you something about what happens in the video/film.

There are many possible ways of laying out a treatment. Here are some headings under which treatments can be written:

- audience
- characters
- content
- emotional appeal
- genre
- intellectual appeal
- media/medium
- message or premise
- product specification (also known as the Requirement)
- purpose
- resources
- setting
- storyline
- story detail
- title.

These headings can be changed or added to. You can make up your own headings. The sub headings above are in alphabetical order. In a treatment they would follow a more logical order, and might be written in another form. Questions, for example, are often used as sub headings. Here is a sample treatment based upon the Brief set out at the beginning of the chapter. You may care to tick off those headings above which are covered in answering the question headings given.

Planning a video production

CASE STUDY Treatment: Video Assignment

Note that this case study is an example of a piece of work referring back to the assignment on page 172.

1 What is the product and its title?
The product is an 'oral history' of the 1960s compiled from a series of interviews with people who were teenagers during the 1960s. It will be titled 'What was it like in the 60s, Grandad?'

2 Who is the target audience?
The primary target audience is teenagers who have an interest in 1960s music and culture. These are likely to be the same teenagers as those who follow old-fashioned rock and roll.

The secondary target audience is middle-aged people 45–55 who remember the 1960s with some nostalgia.

3 What media are to be used?
The product will be in the medium of video film. The reason for using video is to show the teenage interviewers and the middle-aged interviewees. The audience will relate to these people more closely if they can see them. It also means that images and film clips from the 1960s can be inserted.

Short excerpts from 1960s music and other soundbites will be recorded on audio tape for dubbing on. Still images from news photographs and interviewees' souvenirs will also be used.

4 What is the purpose of the product?
The primary purpose of the video is to inform the target audience about people's experience of what it was like to be a teenager in the 1960s. They will compare it with their own experiences of being a teenager.

The secondary purpose is entertainment. The comparison or clash between teenagers now, interviewing in the 1990s youth television style, and the middle-aged person talking about their own youth will be entertaining.

5 What is the content of the product?
The video will open with a 'piece to camera' by a teenage presenter who will introduce each interview.

Each interview will have a theme. The themes will be parents, the generation gap, friends, sex, rock and roll, pop festivals, television, cinema, Vietnam and hippies. The interviews will be presented in a collage of 'edited highlights' rather than complete interviews.

The video will conclude with a collage of images from the 1960s, including memorabilia loaned by the interviewees.

6 How will the message be put across?
The visual appeal of the video will be the images from the 1960s. The images from the interviews will use the 1990s conventions of youth television, with bright colours. Close-ups during the interviews will convey drama. There will also be aesthetic appeal in the images and music clips chosen.

7 How will the product be made?
The production will use the following methods, schedule and resources:

- The method of production will be studio based, using two cameras.
- The schedule will be broken down into pre-production, production and post-production. During pre-production the budget, interview questions, introductory and linking script and action plan will be established and agreed. There will be a series of studio bookings, to be used during the production period. The post-production will consist of editing, promotion and the launch. The editing period will be completed to an agreed deadline. Promotional material will be produced before the final launch date.
- The resources will be as follows: 10 hours of studio time, 20 hours of editing time. Human resources will be students, 10 hours of technician support and 20 hours of teacher support. The interviewees will be drawn from students' relatives and personal contacts.

Synopses and scripts

A synopsis is simply a summary. You might use a synopsis of the whole product or story you are going to make. You might break down the product into sections, or scenes, and produce synopses of these.

Here is a synopsis of a scene which dramatises an incident.

Planning a video production

SYNOPSIS

A girl comes to the door of a flat in a wealthy neighbourhood. When the male occupant opens the door, she asks if 'Valerie' lives there. The occupant says that he does not know such a person. The girl is upset and asks for a glass of water. The occupant asks her inside.

He returns with the glass of water. She drinks. She asks the man if he will 'lend' her £5. He refuses. She becomes very upset and threatens to set fire to the flat. The man goes off to call the police. When he comes back she is trying to set fire to the curtains. He tries to restrain her.

A policeman arrives. He asks to talk to the girl alone. They talk and she leaves the flat. The occupant of the flat returns and the policeman reveals that he told the girl off for her behaviour and gave her the £5 she had asked for. The occupant of the flat is indignant.

Your task now is to script the second scene, and any further scenes, in the synopsis above. The first scene, outside the door, is done for you. Your script should put all the dialogue in lower case, and all headings and names in the instructions in capitals. Lay out your script as follows.

Scene 1

EXTERIOR, PASSAGEWAY OUTSIDE WEALTHY MAN'S FLAT.

GIRL COMES TO THE DOOR AND RINGS BELL. SHE IS WELL DRESSED, BUT HER CLOTHES APPEAR CRUMPLED AS IF SHE HAS SLEPT IN THEM OVERNIGHT. SHE LOOKS TIRED AND UNKEMPT.

MAN IN PINSTRIPE SUIT OPENS DOOR.

MAN   Hello?

GIRL   Is Valerie in?

MAN   There's no Valerie living here.

GIRL   No Valerie?

MAN   No. I think you must have the wrong flat.

GIRL   Oh no, I was sure she would be here. Look, I'm sorry to trouble you, but ... could I please have a drink of water? (PAUSE, MAN LOOKS UNCERTAIN) ... Please?

MAN   Ermm. (PAUSE) OK. Come in for a minute while I get it.

GIRL   You're kind.

GIRL GOES INTO THE FLAT. THE MAN CLOSES THE DOOR.

Planning the shots

Moving images for visual products, such as video film, have a language of their own. In fact, you know a lot about this language already, since you have 'read' so many visual products.

The most important terms in this language of film are the three shots: LS (Long Shot), MS (Medium Shot) and CU (Close Up). The easiest way to introduce and explain these three shots is in relation to a shot of

Figure 9.4 Close-up

Figure 9.5 Medium shot

Figure 9.6 Long shot of figure from head to toe

Figure 9.7 Long shot showing distant object

someone facing the camera. Anything including the head and shoulders or less is a close up. A medium shot may extend to the waist or the knees. Anything from the full figure to infinity is a long shot.

Here are some more terms which are very useful.

The establishing shot
An establishing shot is the first shot the viewer sees. It can tell the audience where they are and introduce them to the 'story'. A typical establishing shot is a long shot of a building which is the scene of the action.

Master shot
The master shot is the shot which includes all, or most, of the actors in the scene. It could be used as the only shot for that scene, since it covers the entire scene of the main action.

Shot/reverse shot
Typically, this shows someone looking at something, and then the something they are looking at. It is used to describe the pattern of alternating close ups of people talking to one another, as used in soap operas.

Shot plan
Planning the shots for a visual product may come before or after the script. You can visualise the story, the scenes and the characters before you start to write the script. The more traditional approach is to write down the words and the dialogue before you start to plan the images, as in the example script narrative above.

It would be perfectly possible to visualise and plan the images to be used for the film in the case study on page 178 before writing down script material in words. Here is a suggested shot plan for two scenes from the film:
1. Medium shot of middle-aged woman looking at vinyl album cover.
2. Close up of album cover: The Beatles, *Revolver*.
3. Fade to photograph of woman taken in 1966, when she was 15.
4. Cut to long shot of studio interview: woman facing teenage interviewer.
5. Close up of woman talking.
6. Fade to close up of album cover: Bob Dylan, *Blonde on Blonde*.
7. Cut to medium shot of middle-aged man looking at *Blonde on Blonde* album cover.
8. Cut to close up of man talking.
9. Fade to photograph of man taken in 1965, when he was 19.
10. Zoom out to long shot of studio interview: man facing teenage interviewer.

A Activity

Can you identify any master shots, or shot/reverse shot patterns? If you were to insert an establishing shot before shot (1), what would you use and what would be included in the establishing shot?

The scripting for such a shot plan would have to include the questions which the teenage interviewer would ask.

- What kinds of question should she or he ask?
- How could the questions be researched beforehand?
- What else could be scripted in advance before the interview material was recorded?

The visualisation and shooting of a treatment or script can be planned in many ways. The director David Byrne describes planning his film *True Stories* by covering a wall with drawings, and applying the characters and stories to the drawings afterwards. This is not the conventional way of doing things! In addition to the shot plan as above, the traditional tools of shot planning are the shot list and the storyboard.

Shot list
This can be written under headings, and consists of the action and/or dialogue down one side and a description of the shots to be used side by side with the action and dialogue they contain. An example of a set of headings for a shot list would be duration (in seconds), action, dialogue or voice over, music and other sound effects, plus camera instructions.

Storyboard
At its simplest, a storyboard consists of a set of frames representing the shots, drawn in, with words about the corresponding action, dialogue and technical instructions either under or beside each frame. It can be compared to the way a comic strip can relate to an animated film of the same story.

You do not have to possess skills in drawing to produce a good storyboard, although obviously it can help the storyboard to look impressive on the surface. What is most important in a storyboard are your ideas and your ability to use the conventions of editing and genre to produce an interesting and effective visual narrative. Here is some advice about storyboarding.

Planning a video production

Storyboarding tips

1. Don't 'write' a storyboard in the way you would write a story, beginning with the first frame and then going through the storyboard, frame by frame, until you get to the end. Start by brainstorming ideas for interesting shots out of order. What would make an interesting close up? Medium shot? Long shot? Jot down ideas in a 'spider's web diagram' branching out from the central title.
2. Remember that the storyboard frame is not a piece of paper. Your 'drawing' in that frame is an instruction to the camera operator on how to set up that shot. Draw the illustration so that it fills the frame right to the edge. Always name the shot at the very least as a close up, medium shot or long shot.
3. Follow the basic rules of shot composition. Only leave white space for a purpose. For example, it is conventional to leave more space in the direction of people's gaze or movement than behind them.
4. Frame the shot. Beware of empty space above the heads of figures and faces. There should be a reason, as in (3), for any empty space.
5. Use the position, angle or movement of the camera to say something and interest the audience. For example, low-angle (camera tilting up) shots are used to show powerful people.

Figure 9.8 A blank storyboard

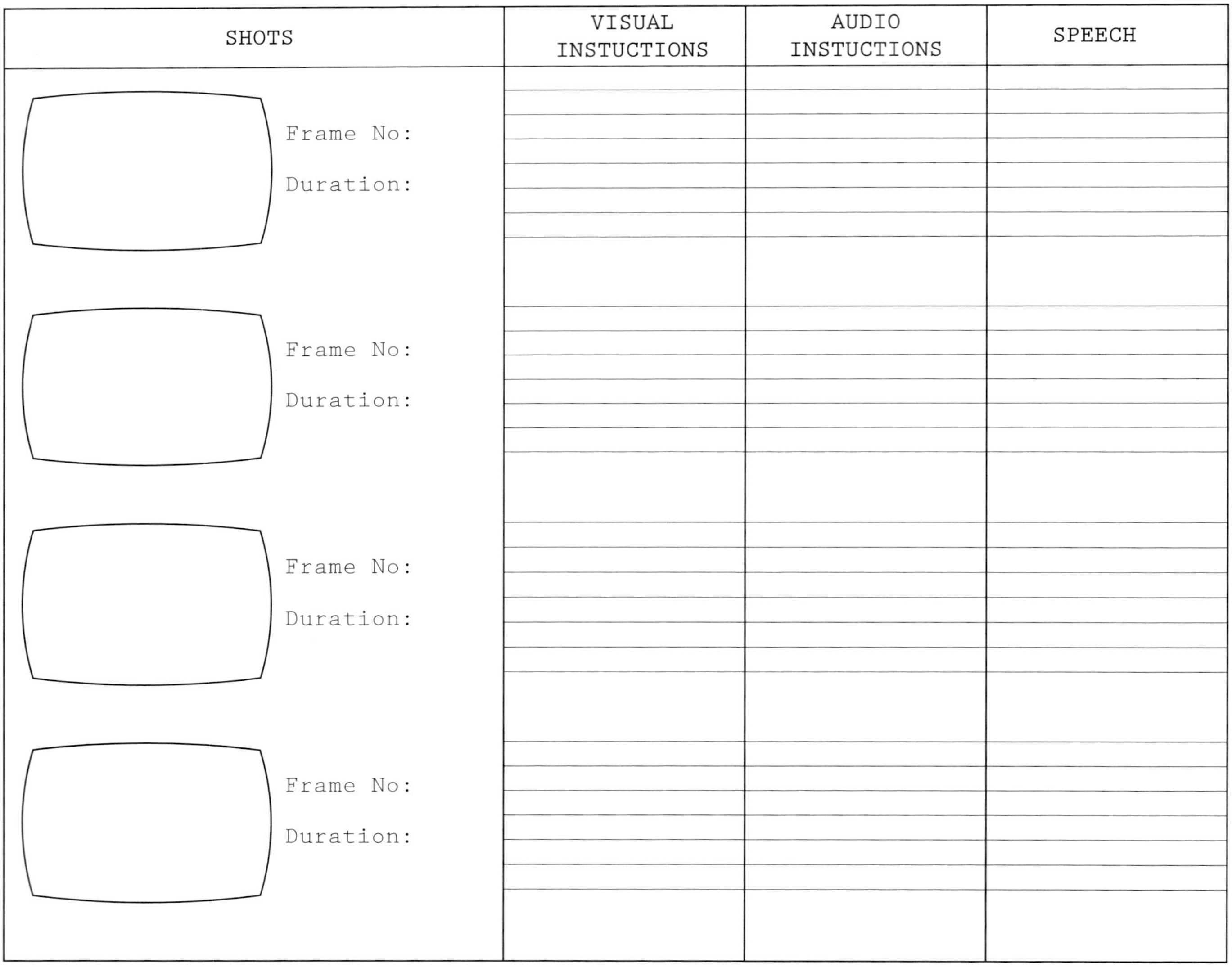

SHOTS	VISUAL INSTUCTIONS	AUDIO INSTUCTIONS	SPEECH
Frame No: Duration:			
Frame No: Duration:			
Frame No: Duration:			
Frame No: Duration:			

Planning a video production

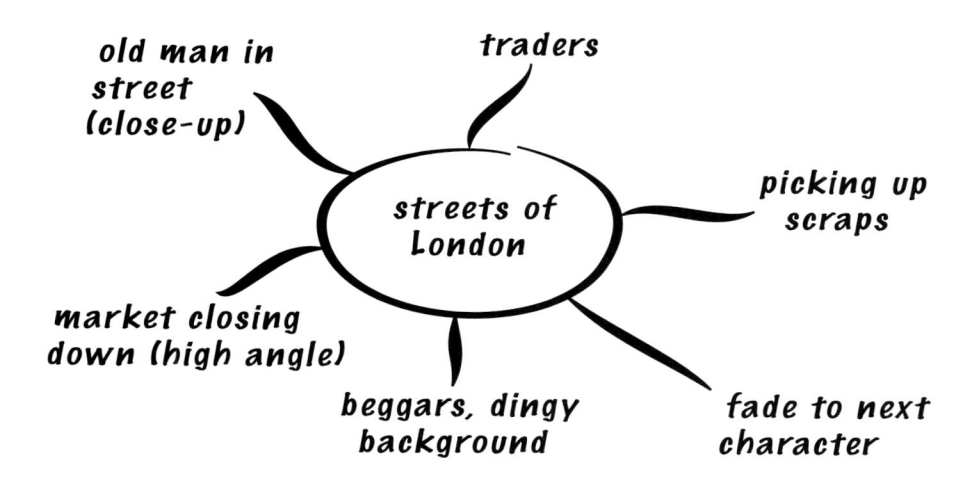

Figure 9.9 Spider's web diagram developed from a brainstorming session

[Spider's web diagram with "streets of London" at center, connected to: old man in street (close-up), traders, picking up scraps, fade to next character, beggars, dingy background, market closing down (high angle)]

6 Remember that the other components of the storyboard, such as the sound and other effects, are important.
7 You only need to give indications of the dialogue or voice over which corresponds to the beginning of the shot.
8 Follow the conventions of editing. For example, do not break the 180 degree rule which says that you should not cut from a shot of someone looking or moving left to another shot of them looking or moving right. Try it out yourself on camera to see what happens, and to see why it is avoided.

Figure 9.10 is an example of a student's storyboard for *The Streets of London*.

Figure 9.10 Storyboard showing the opening five frames to The Streets of London

SHOTS	VISUAL INSTUCTIONS	AUDIO INSTUCTIONS	SPEECH
Frame No: 1 Duration: 10 secs	High angle long shot in black and white (b/w) Slow zoom into awning of one stall	1 sec silence then music intro 'Streets of London'	
Frame No: 2 Duration: 4 secs	Medium shot (b/w)	Music continues: Lyrics begin	Have you seen the old
Frame No: 3 Duration: 4 secs	Close up (b/w)	Close up (b/w)	man / in the closed down market?
Frame No: 4 Duration: 4 secs	Long shot (b/w)	Long shot (b/w)	kicking up the papers
Frame No: 5 Duration: 4 secs	Close up (b/w)	Close up (b/w)	with his worn out shoes

Planning a video production

> ### A Activity
>
> Compile a shot list and/or storyboard for part of 'the curtains and the policeman' synopsis on page 179.
>
> Alternatively, take a pop song of your choice, and compile a shot list or storyboard for an extract from the song and its lyrics. Use some of the conventions of the pop video such as repeat shots, lip synchronised shots of the star 'singing', broken or 'confused' narrative etc.

Planning the production process

The three phases of production preceding distribution of the finished product are: pre-production, that is writing and researching; production, that is shooting the video; and post-production, that is editing film. The next chapter will deal with production and post-production in practice. We will end this chapter by looking at the final planning required for production itself in terms of three aspects:
- production and post-production roles
- action planning and the shooting schedule
- making a reconnaissance.

Production and post-production roles

Each phase of production has a number of roles. You might like to review the pre-production roles in the pre-production phase described in the previous sections. Here is a breakdown of the roles involved in the production and post-production phases which follow. These are roles, not necessarily people, and more than one role may be taken on by one person. Any of these roles may be combined or shared, and equally any one may have an assistant, except perhaps the last three roles listed.

You should draw up a list of responsibilities and the names of those responsible. You should draw out a diagram of how the team will work, either in the pyramid shape of a hierarchy or in some other organisational chart.

Producer
You are responsible for ensuring that the product gets made. You run pre-production meetings and brief the Director about what is needed. You supervise any contracts or budgets, and take the final responsibility for ensuring that decisions are made and deadlines are met. You are responsible for ensuring that health and safety issues are identified and safe working practices followed.

Director
The Director is responsible for managing the actual making of the film in creative and technical terms. The Director is in charge of any casting, the script materials, the research and the shooting of the script. You will provide information about the script and how it is to be shot. You will work closely with everyone, but especially the producer and the design/art director.

Design/Art director
You provide information on locations and organise all matters to do with the set, props and any other objects which are needed.

Camera operators
You make sure that the shot is set up when it is needed.

Sound recordist
You make sure that sound is recorded accurately and sound recording is logged.

Editor
During filming you supervise any mixing of shots or control room work. You also ensure that all recordings are logged. You are in charge of the cutting and editing during post-production.

Figure 9.11 Sound recordist at work

Figure 9.12 Editors at work in video suite

Production assistant
You are the general dogsbody who makes sure that everything and everyone is available and ready when needed. You also act as 'secretary', recording and writing up minutes from meetings.

Talent
This is anyone who appears on camera: presenters, interviewers, actors etc.

Script editor
The writers may be 'everybody', but one person in particular should be in charge of the script materials. This person will be the Script Editor responsible directly to the Director for the script.

Action planning and the shooting schedule
You should also compile an action plan for each stage of production. The action plan for production is called a shooting schedule and will cover the following.

Resources and limitations
The availability of people, equipment and accommodation for shooting:
- appointments with key people
- booking of equipment and accommodation

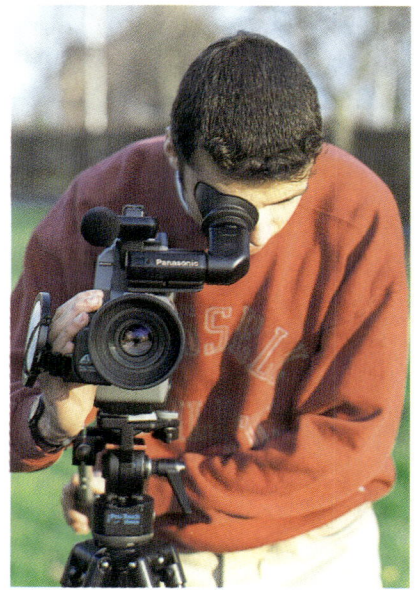

Figure 9.13 Video camera operator at work

Planning a video production

Figure 9.14 A video production team at work on a production

- Dates and locations of any events or interviews that are to be filmed or recorded.

Setting up the shoot
- The selection and briefing of the 'talent', including any interviewees, any actors and any other participants outside the production team
- Selecting locations and making any special arrangements concerning them
- Reconnaissances (see below)
- Setting up any permissions needed, including police permission if public places are to be used
- Arranging access to any organisations or special places, and informing the crew about any limitations or special etiquette to be observed
- Dates, personnel and locations for shooting
- Keeping to and meeting deadlines.

Here are examples of a Planning schedule and a Production schedule to help you.

Health and safety
- Arrangements for the safety, return and storage of equipment and film
- Safe working practices e.g. loose cables are taped down
- Any insurance conditions, and the implications of not having insurance for such things as bad weather, loss or damage, third party liability etc.

The reconnaissance

Part of your pre-production work may well involve a reconnaissance if you are planning any shots on location. If you take the example of the video about people's reminiscences of the sixties, you will probably need to shoot several interviews in people's houses. Representatives from the production team should visit locations to familiarise themselves with each one.

Decide whether or not you are going to take establishing shots of the exterior of each house. If you are, you need to work out which angle would give you the best shot. Note any health and safety problems, such as the proximity of a busy road.

Talk to the person you are going to interview and ask to be shown around the house so that you can choose the best situation for the interview. If you establish a rapport while you are doing this, you are more likely to get a confident interview.

Make a note of the location of electricity points for your equipment, and of areas that might be noisy, too dark, cramped or even dangerous.

This is a good time to be on the lookout for cutaway shots. These are shots that could be useful when you are editing your final tape. You will probably need to edit the interviews, and it helps to avoid awkward-looking cuts if you can insert a picture of something other than the person talking for a few seconds. You can then cut back to the speaker at the beginning of a new sentence. If your topic is the sixties, look for images or objects from that time (LP covers or platform sole shoes, for instance) around the house which you could film for these cutaway inserts. Alternatively, you might notice certain characteristics of the interviewee. These might include gestures such as the nervous tapping of fingers on a chair arm, or details of appearance such as earrings, hairstyling or a badge. One or two of these could be used as cutaways showing character or personal style.

(See assignment at end of Chapter 10, 'Producing a video')

10 | Producing a video

This chapter guides you through the process of producing a video after the pre-production phase. Before you look at this chapter, you should have done the preparation and have a treatment and a storyboard or shot list completed. You should have done a reconnaissance and allocated roles, such as camera operator and sound recordist, in the production process.

Pre-production is covered in GNVQ Unit 2 and in part of Unit 5. The rest of Unit 5 is about shooting a video (or film), editing it and evaluating it.

This chapter gives you advice about the kinds of shots you should try to take, so that the task of editing is not too daunting, and some tips on the editing process. It also has advice about making CD-ROMs.

The chapter is organised into the following sections:
- Preparation
- The shoot
- The edit.

Preparation

Equipment

For GNVQ you need to use the following equipment:
- a video camera
- a tripod
- portable lights
- portable microphones.

Even if you use a camcorder, which has a microphone built into it, it is still worth taking additional recording equipment so that you can capture additional sounds which you can add to your video when you edit it. You can use it to record a *buzz track*, which could be of street or room noises, for instance. Make sure you make a list of all the sound recordings you take, so that you can find them easily should you want to use them.

You need a tripod to give you a steady shot. Try to use the biggest and heaviest you can get. It is also useful to have a built-in spirit level and smooth pan and tilt movement.

If possible, connect your camera to a television monitor so that you can see more clearly than through a viewfinder what your pictures look like.

It is useful having lighting equipment in certain situations, but you should be careful how you use it. It is best not to mix artificial light with natural light, for instance, as you can produce some odd colours. Try experimenting with lighting and looking at the effects on a television monitor.

It is worth bouncing light off a ceiling or reflective white cards so that you increase the lighting without producing deep shadows.

Practice shoot

It is usually worth having a practice shoot, especially if you are making a video on location. In this way you can become familiar with using the equipment and become aware of unforeseen difficulties. You can decide the best positions for placing your camera and what lighting you will need. You could try out different gels (coloured transparent film) with your lights to find the most suitable effects.

The practice shoot also helps you to decide who does what in a team and make sure that everyone has enough work to keep them involved. It is time to check for any possible health and safety problems.

The shoot

Shooting for editing

It is important to take notes when you are shooting and even more important to label your video cassettes. Many directors like to give a visual indication of the 'take'. Some use a clapperboard which indicates the cassette, the shot and the take (e.g. 1:1:2 indicates cassette one, shot one, take two) but a clapperboard is used in film to synchronise sound and picture. With video, because you are recording synchronised sound, you only need a visual reference, so a piece of paper with the required information on will do. A wipe-clean board is more convenient, however. This will save you considerable time at the editing stage.

Remember that your programme is going to be edited, so shoot long. Make each shot at least five seconds longer than you think you will need at both ends. This will ensure that you give your editor as many options as possible.

Crews are getting smaller and smaller all the time. A typical news crew comprises three people – a director, a lighting cameraman/woman and a sound recordist. However many people there are in the crew, it is worth spending time to make sure they all know what you are trying to do in the programme overall, what you are hoping to achieve on this particular shoot and finally what you are looking for in each particular shot. You will also need to brief those appearing in front of the camera. They do not always need to know the technical details, but they will need to know what you are trying to do in each shot.

The establishing shot

It is a wise idea to shoot a general shot to show the location and its surroundings. This applies to outside locations particularly but also to interiors and even to interviews. A wide angle shot of the interviewee chatting to the interviewer but too far away to see precise lip movements, for example, could be a very useful cutaway (see Shooting Interviews). For exterior locations it is very often worthwhile taking long shots as well as panning slowly across the terrain, possibly more than once at different speeds.

Figure 10.1a Wipe-clean board being used in a video shoot

Figure 10.1b Clapperboard

Producing a video

Shooting for continuity

Continuity of action on television is a carefully constructed illusion. In most cases characters' actions are interrupted continually and in dramas scenes are often shot out of sequence.

The master shot

Most directors choose to shoot a short scene from start to finish in a long shot. This serves as a master shot to which editors can cut when they do not have a more interesting close-up to use. It follows, then, that many close ups are repeats of actions already taken. Imagine you are filming a student choosing a book in the library. You film the action in long shot, then you ask her to repeat the action so you can film it in close up. You should do the whole thing, even if you are only after a shot of her reading the book. If you just ask her to repeat the bit you're after, she may change the way she did it the first time and you may regret not having more options in the editing room.

Cutting on action

In order to ensure smooth continuity, it is normal to cut on action. A man buys an ice cream from an ice cream van and begins to eat it. Shoot the whole scene in long shot, showing the ice cream van. Then shoot the scene again in close-up, focusing on the man. You will find that the most 'natural' place to cut will be as he raises the ice cream to his mouth.

If you are filming somebody walking along a corridor in long shot and opening a door in close up, then you should cut as the hand reaches forward to grasp the door handle. This can be followed by a medium shot from the other side of the door as it opens. If you ensure that the shots overlap, you will give your editor more options in the cutting room. A further tip is that if you cut out some of the action, the eye will accept it, but if you repeat some of the action it will look like a mistake.

Another important tip that gives you more options is to start and finish with the person out of shot. This allows you to move more freely between locations (man walks out of shot in railway station and into shot in the park even though they may be miles apart) as well as allowing you to compress time. Pay attention to the speed of his exit in order to match it with the speed of his arrival in shot.

Crossing the line

In order to maintain the illusion of continuity there are a number of other rules which should be followed. The most important of these is known as not 'crossing the line'.

If you are filming a character setting out on a journey, or a chase sequence, the direction of movement across the screen should be consistent. This means ensuring that the camera is always on the same side in relation to the action. There is an imaginary line as in Figure 10.2 which should not be crossed, or else the viewer will be confused.

This rule can be broken. In his famous film *Stagecoach*, director John Ford 'crosses the line' several times in a sequence where the Indians chase the stagecoach across Monument Valley. Audiences appeared not to notice or care. Where there are several characters moving in a chaotic fashion, keeping to this principle is difficult and clearly not essential. For more straightforward scenes, though, you ought to have a good reason to break the rule.

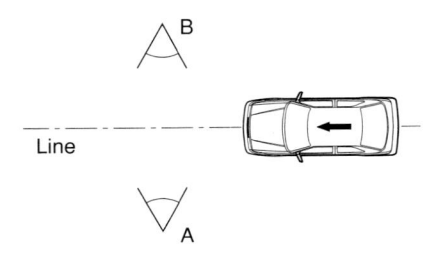

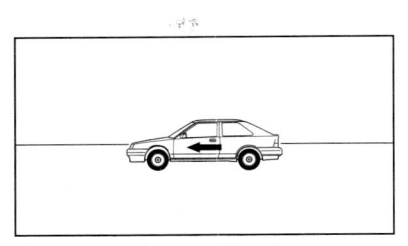

Car as seen from position A

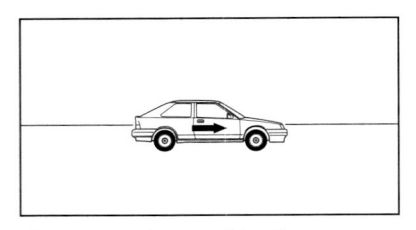

Car as seen from position B

Figure 10.2 Crossing the line

If a cyclist travels from left to right in the first shot, she should continue to do so in subsequent shots. In this case it would be acceptable to cross the line if you are more interested in the scenery than in the journey. The viewer will accept that the cyclist has not changed direction.

Continuity of direction is also important for things that don't travel. Imagine an interview in which the camera is positioned on either side of the line (see Figure 10.3). If you cross this line the viewer will feel that the interviewer is moving around or that there is more than one of them. Here the imaginary line runs between interviewer and interviewee. This confusion often arises when the director uses the terms right and left. But does she mean the interviewer's right or the interviewee's right? In professional practice the answer is that she means to the camera's right from a position behind the camera.

Jump cuts

If you are trying to create a smoothly flowing narrative or you are filming an interview and want to create the illusion of continuity, then your enemy is the jump cut. A jump cut is quite literally when the picture appears to suddenly jump on the screen. This usually occurs when the subject moves slightly in the frame from one shot to the next (e.g. when you want to edit an interview). Some directors prefer to leave jump cuts alone or even draw attention to them with the use of a special effect and so make it quite clear that the programme has been constructed.

In order to lessen the impact of a jump cut and to achieve continuity at the editing stage, the camera should be moved by at least twenty degrees after every shot. The eye finds it easier to accept a cut from full face to profile, for example, than a slight change in the subject's position in front of the camera.

Another way of avoiding the awkward effect of jump cuts is paradoxically to exaggerate them. If you cannot change the angle of shot, then change the size of shot. To go from a long shot of a cow in a field to a close up will look better than a slight change in shot size.

Cutaways

More usually, however, these jump cuts are eliminated by using cutaways. The most commonly used is the much derided noddy shot, where the interviewer looks interested in what the interviewee is apparently saying even though the person may have gone home! Though cutaways are usually used to shorten the text, the best cutaways add something new to the story or illustrate the speaker's point.

A farmer reminisces about hard times in the past; you cut away to fields of golden wheat swaying in late evening sunshine. An old soldier talks about returning home from the war; you cut away to photographs from his album, his wedding photograph, a picture of him in uniform. Typical cutaways used on television include shots of the crowd during the edited highlights of a football match (to shorten the game) or a shot of a manager nervously watching his team during a live game.

Cutting to 'parallel action' is an effective device. Parallel action simply means actions which occur at the same time as the main action. The player scores, the fans celebrate, the parade goes by, the crowds wave. These shots will be collected at a different time to the filming of the main action, though in the case of live sports broadcasts a number of cameras will be used, so genuine parallel action is possible.

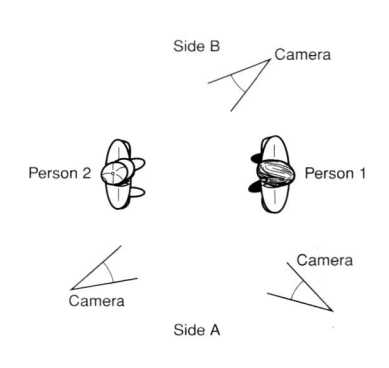

Figure 10.3 Maintaining continuity of direction

Using the zoom

Overuse of the zoom facility is a common fault with student films. Too often, a director attempts to make a dull scene more interesting by zooming in on a subject or out to show the subject in its setting. Zooming can cause problems at the editing stage because it is difficult to cut during a zoom. It looks ugly and grabbed. If you do choose to use the zoom, then make sure you know why and hold the zoom for a few seconds at either end so you have a close up and a long shot to play with as well at the edit stage.

The zoom is an excellent tool for framing. When the camera zooms in, the background is foreshortened. A cow in a field may be standing twenty metres away from a tree; in a close up it may appear only five metres away, and in a long shot it may appear forty metres away. Experiment with your framing using the zoom. Zooms can sometimes add a legitimate sense of drama to a shot. Think of *Mastermind* on television. The camera zooms in on the contestants towards the end of their questioning to increase tension.

Panning

Like zooming, panning is often overdone, and like zooming it is a difficult shot to use well in the final edit.

The best pans have a reason and they usually follow the action. In this case the speed of the pan is determined by the speed of the action. There are sometimes good reasons to ignore these conventions. Imagine a scene between a middle-aged husband and wife in which she tells her husband that she has been having an affair for years without his knowledge. The camera pans slowly from the wife across the 'dead space' of the room before alighting on the stricken figure of the husband. The slow speed of the pan adds considerably to the drama of the incident.

A 'whip pan' is a pan shot that moves so quickly the picture is blurred. There are occasions when this unusual shot can be used very effectively. To capture the experience of travelling on a fun fair ride might be one such example, or to indicate a dramatic change of time or place in a science fiction film (a character moves through a time warp or travels from one side of the world to another).

All of this advice can of course be freely ignored if you want to be experimental, but remember: you might know what you are doing, but does your audience?

Shooting close ups

Television is an intimate medium and close-ups emphasise this (see Figures 10.4 to 10.7). Actors in the theatre have to make grand gestures for the people at the back of the auditorium; on television an actor may merely have to raise an eyebrow to achieve the same effect. On a television screen close-ups are approximately life-size and viewers can relate comfortably to people at this distance from their armchairs.

Close-ups also ensure, if they are well framed, that the whole of the frame is being used to interest the viewer. If you use too many long shots in your video the viewer may feel that the subject is remote from them, and if you use too many big close-ups you risk intimidating your viewers, but they can be used for dramatic effect in fiction productions. Indeed extreme close-ups and big close-ups are not allowed in documentary work.

Producing a video

Figure 10.4 Extreme close up

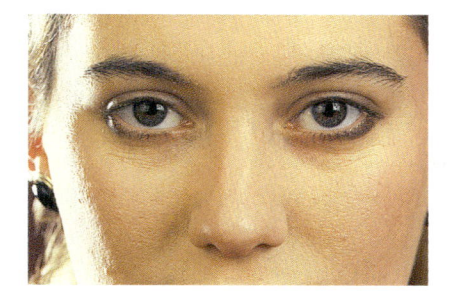

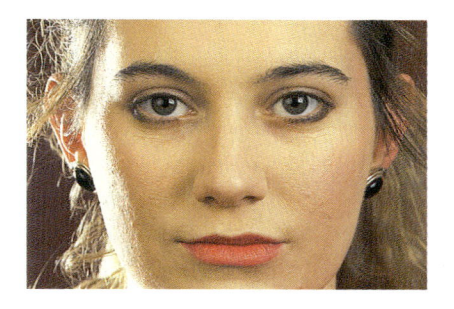

Figure 10.5 Big close up

Figure 10.6 Close up

For these reasons, then, close ups are important. However, the closer your picture, the more likely you are to have camera shake, and if you are filming for any length of time the camera operator can get tired and may not be able to keep perfectly still. Generally, when you are filming close ups you should use a tripod. Often this can seem like a hassle, particularly if you are pressed for time, but the quality of the pictures you shoot using a tripod is well worth it.

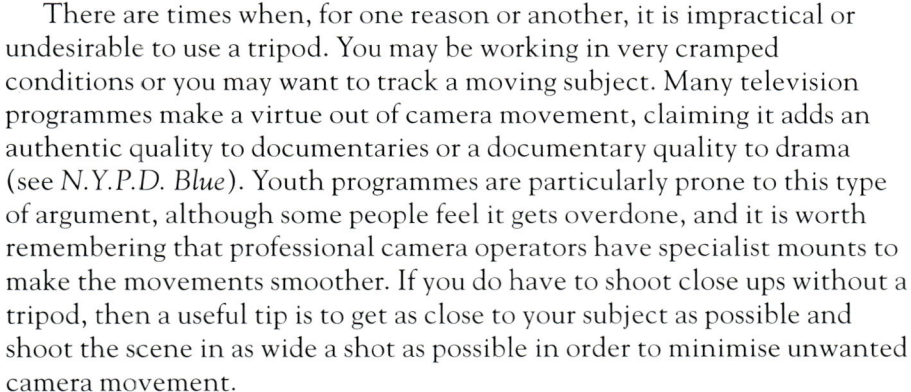

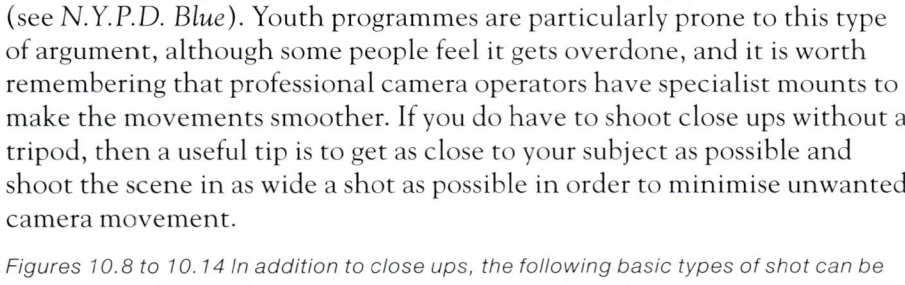

There are times when, for one reason or another, it is impractical or undesirable to use a tripod. You may be working in very cramped conditions or you may want to track a moving subject. Many television programmes make a virtue out of camera movement, claiming it adds an authentic quality to documentaries or a documentary quality to drama (see *N.Y.P.D. Blue*). Youth programmes are particularly prone to this type of argument, although some people feel it gets overdone, and it is worth remembering that professional camera operators have specialist mounts to make the movements smoother. If you do have to shoot close ups without a tripod, then a useful tip is to get as close to your subject as possible and shoot the scene in as wide a shot as possible in order to minimise unwanted camera movement.

Figure 10.7 Medium close up

Figures 10.8 to 10.14 In addition to close ups, the following basic types of shot can be used: Figure 10.8, medium shot; Figure 10.9, medium long shot; Figure 10.10, long shot; Figure 10.11, very long shot; Figure 10.12, extremely long shot.

Figure 10.8 Medium shot

Figure 10.9 Medium long shot

Figure 10.10 Long shot

193

Producing a video

Figure 10.11 Very long shot

Figure 10.12 Extremely long shot

Framing

When you look down a viewfinder or at a monitor, you have a tendency to look at the centre of the screen or at movement within the picture. This often means you don't pay sufficient attention to the outside edges of the frame. It is important to ensure that your picture is well framed, that you have given your subject head room and looking room (see Figures 10.13, 10.14 and 10.15) and that you have included everything you want to see and excluded everything else.

Figure 10.13 Shot with adequate head room.

Figure 10.14 Shot without adequate head room.

Figure 10.15 Shot showing the benefit of giving a subject adequate looking room so that he or she is not looking straight into the side of the frame as if up against a wall.

194

Beware, however, because the two centimetres around the outside of a monitor do not appear on the television screen. You need to remember this particularly if you are filming notices. Don't get too tight.

Shooting an interview

Conventionally there is almost a set procedure for shooting an interview. Start with a two-shot of interviewer and interviewee, cut to a medium shot of interviewee, cutaway shot of interviewer followed by a close up of interviewee or even in particular circumstances a big close up. This pattern has evolved because it allows for flexibility and variety.

An interview which lasts for only three minutes on screen may well have lasted fifteen or twenty minutes originally. It pays to shoot the interviewee in a variety of shot sizes, as these will be easier to edit. Changing the shot size should be done while the interviewer is asking questions (these can be repeated later) so that variety is ensured and editing will be more straightforward. Big close ups are not usually used in interviews, for ethical reasons. They are invasive. As you have read earlier, the usual shot is a close up. If you decide to hold a medium shot for too long, viewers will start to lose interest.

It is important to match eyelines when shooting interviews. This basically means that the subject of the interview should appear to be looking towards the interviewer in a fairly frontal shot. Indeed, the closer the shot – convention dictates – the more frontal the subject should be. A profile shot of of the subject will leave the viewer feeling excluded and a direct address to camera, it is felt, is just too direct. It is interesting to note who does get to address the viewers directly. Generally, only reporters and presenters clearly identified as station employees are afforded this privilege. Another convention normally applied in interviews is to shoot the interviewer slightly smaller in the frame than the interviewee.

The conventional two-shot is now an over-the-shoulder shot, where we see part of the back of the head of the interviewer and at least a mid-shot of the subject (see Figures 10.16 and 10.17). This conforms to the important rule for shooting interviews, that is to keep the camera close to the interviewer. This is where the subject will look, and you will find it much easier to match eyelines with this as your basic shot. However, it is worth pulling back further than this at some point, possibly at the end of the interview, and asking the interviewer to talk and the subject to listen, so that you will be able to drop in any question you like over this shot.

Figure 10.16 Standard over-the-shoulder shot

Figure 10.17 Over-the-shoulder shot with very large foreground

Another convention for shooting interviews is that the height of the camera should be that of the subject. When the interviewer is being shot, the camera should be adjusted to the height of the questioner. This means that a tall reporter will still be looking down on a short politician, but the camera will be looking straight across at both of them.

Sound

Of course, the most important element in any interview is the sound quality. Make sure you choose somewhere relatively quiet. Take a sound check (ask the subject what they had for breakfast) and listen to the playback. If the sound is poor then you may need to rearrange the whole thing. Viewers will tolerate poor pictures much more readily than poor sound.

A useful tip is to have your questions written on cards so that you can read them to camera after the interview is over. More important than this, though, is to listen carefully. Many an interview is damaged by a question which the subject has already answered.

It is very important to make your subject feel at ease, and a useful way of doing this is the false start. In this case, after an initial 'fluff' by the interviewer or by the subject, the cameras are 'kept rolling' and the interview is started again. There is often an almost tangible release of tension. Whenever possible, interviews should be shot without lights, as they will almost certainly affect the spontaneity of the 'performance'. Video cameras are getting better all the time at dealing with low light conditions and, although lighting will add warmth and depth to the colours, the cost may be high.

Shoot synchronised sound and keep quiet is the golden rule for video. Minimise background noise and shoot a 'wildtrack', that is, location sound that you may use later in the editing process. You can identify this section on the tape by de-focusing the camera.

One of the great advantages of video is that it can be instantly reviewed. This facility should be used judiciously. Too much playback will quickly tire batteries and it will waste time. There are times, though, when it is almost essential.

Whenever you move to a new location or use a new cassette you will need to check the first shot for colour balance and particularly sound.

The edit

List and view all your material and decide on a rough cutting order. You will probably want to work very closely with your editor if it is not yourself! Without viewing all the material you will be working in the dark, laying bricks without an architect's plan.

Your list should include the number of the shot, the time of the shot and its duration, the type of shot, the sound you want for each shot and the opening and closing action or remarks. Give your editor a copy of this list with what you consider to be the best shots clearly marked. This is known as a paper edit.
From this you can then produce an assembly script with your selected material, duration of shot after the edit and instructions for sound.

A videotape has four tracks. One for picture, two for sound and a control track. This last track is rather like the sprocket holes in film.

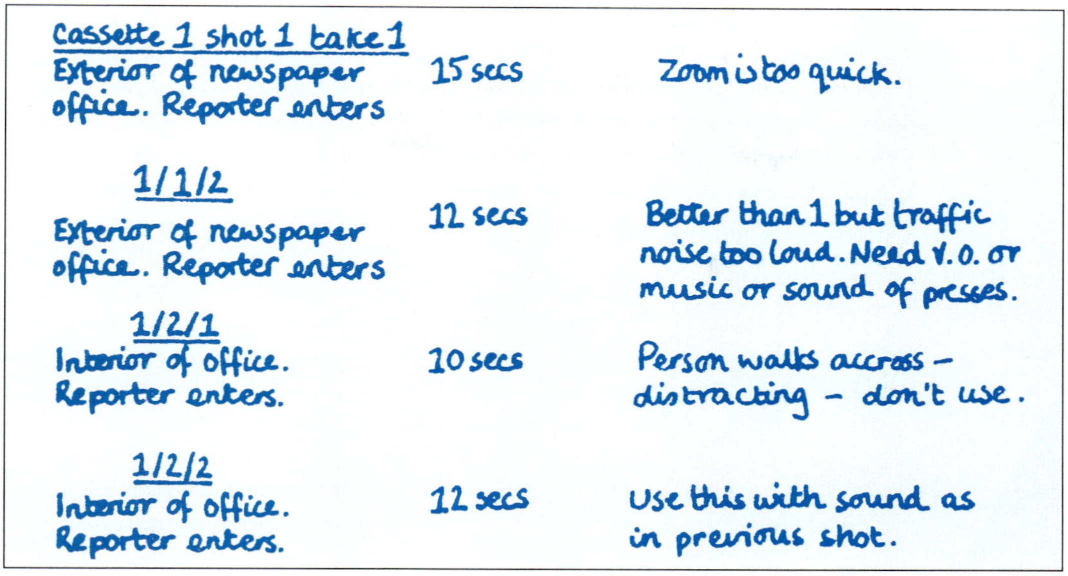

Figure 10.21 Paper edit

> Cassette 1 shot 1 take 1
> Exterior of newspaper office. Reporter enters.   15 secs   Zoom is too quick.
>
> 1/1/2
> Exterior of newspaper office. Reporter enters.   12 secs   Better than 1 but traffic noise too loud. Need V.O. or music or sound of presses.
>
> 1/2/1
> Interior of office. Reporter enters.   10 secs   Person walks across – distracting – don't use.
>
> 1/2/2
> Interior of office. Reporter enters.   12 secs   Use this with sound as in previous shot.

Editors like to have an unbroken control track in order to minimise *glitches* (slight jumps in picture at the point of the edit). To this end the master tape is often recorded black over its whole length. (You can record over the whole tape with the lens cap on.) This is known as black bursting. Some cameras have a facility for recording colour bars on a tape and this is equally effective in producing a control track. The purpose of this will become clearer when we come to discussing the two different modes of editing (Assembly and Insert editing).

The editing process gives your film shape, rhythm and pace. In the stillness of an edit room it can be quite difficult to judge these qualities. Video tape plays at twenty-four 'frames' a second. When you are shuttling tape backwards and forwards at slow speeds in order to line up your edits, it is very easy to lose track of real time. Remember to view all your edited material in real time if you are unsure.

All the attention in an edit suite tends to focus on the visual, but it is important not to forget sound. Whether you are using narration, music, effects, sync sound, wildtrack or interview as voice over, ensure that there is variety in your sound track. You should also give your video room to breathe and allow pictures to 'speak for themselves'. There is sometimes a tendency to overdo narration and a desire to cover the images with explanatory remarks. Narration does not always have to precede the images it relates to. Very often it is more effective to see an event and then hear some words of explanation afterwards. It makes sense, then, to write your commentary as late as possible.

There are two basic types of editing, known as *assembly editing* and *insert editing* respectively. *Assembly editing* involves copying chunks of sound and picture fom one cassette to another. This method disrupts the control track and apart from making your edited tape more susceptible to glitches it means that you have to work forwards all the time. If you feel you want to change a shot near the beginning of your programme you will have to start rebuilding from that point.

Insert editing allows you to drop pictures and sound onto a control track either separately or together without disrupting the control track. This allows you to replace either the sound or the picture at any point in your programme.

If you are unfamiliar with editing equipment it is best to practise with some material that you will not use in your final video. Copy some material from the playback machine to the record machine and then view it to check that everything is connected properly. Then try a simple sound and picture edit, making sure that the record machine has precisely the material you select.

Get to know the equipment you are using and what it can do. Are you able to mix sound tracks? Can you control the levels of sound reaching track 1 of the record machine? Can you send sound only from one track and then add commentary to track 2 of the record machine?

Try editing a cutaway onto the material you have edited. Check that the start and finish of the cutaway is exactly as you want it and that there is no 'drift'. If there is, it could be that you are not being precise with your selection of in and out points, or it could be that the machinery is not accurate.

Editing tips

A distinctive sound often makes a good place to edit. Viewers will be distracted by the sound and the louder the sound, the easier it will be to make the cut unnoticed.

- Overlap sound and pictures. Edits always look and 'feel' better if the sound precedes the picture slightly. Imagine an exterior long shot of a school followed by a cut to children having a P.E. lesson. The cut will be much more effective if we hear the sound of the lesson taking place before we see the new shot. Occasionally it will work equally well if the sound cut comes after the picture change. Imagine an interview finishing and as the speaker says her last sentence we cut to a new scene.
- Professionals generally advise newcomers to err on the side of brevity. Keep each shot short.
- As mentioned before, cutting on movement will make for smoother editing, and cutting down action will be more acceptable than any overlapping action.
- Don't cut during camera moves. It is usually better to wait until the camera has completed the move before you make the edit. Occasionally a cut to another pan or zoom at the same speed will work.
- Each new shot should be on a different camera angle from the preceding shot.
- Shots should vary in length and type if your programme is not going to feel predictable.
- Don't cut unless it's necessary. A thirty-second shot can be fine as long as it advances the programme.
- Finally many cameras have special effects built into them and editing suites now have special effects machines hooked up to them. Beware – they can be great fun but they are very seductive. Use effects sparingly. Mixes, dissolves, wipes, freeze frames, strobing, mosaic patterning are widely available but they distract from the substance of a film. Mixes, fades and wipes also slow down a film. You should use them only when you can make a strong case for them.

Making multimedia

There is still no accepted definition of what multimedia actually consists of. A good working guideline is that multimedia should include at least three of the following:
- text, numerical or statistical data
- still images including photographs, maps, drawings, film stills
- computer graphics
- animation
- audio, including words, music or sounds from both the computer and the natural world
- moving images captured from video or film.

Slideshows

If you plan to start using slideshows as a way into multimedia, your equipment requirements can be quite minimal. Basically you need a software package which allows you to add and link text, graphics and sound. Many of the new authoring tools allow you to do so with great ease.

Painting packages enable you to create pictures, add text and sound and then link the pictures or frames together in a simple slideshow. There are different transitions from frame to frame, wipes, fades etc. and you can control the time each frame spends on the screen. At this level the only add-on to your computer would be a microphone.

In the main, slideshows are single pages linked in a linear fashion which do not allow interaction; even so, they do allow a good way into the production of multimedia.

Hyperstudio

Using an authoring program called Hyperstudio^{TM}, available on all hardware platforms, you can move a stage further with your multimedia productions. While still being easy to use, Hyperstudio^{TM} offers dynamic links between pages. You can create buttons which take the user to a specific page. Buttons can also be created which play a movie or audio clip.

Hyperstudio is like an electronic book which allows you to bring your ideas to life. These 'books' are usually referred to as stacks, each page being a part of the stack. Hyperstudio^{TM} comes with sound clips, ready-made computer movies and clip art, and as such allows the building of multimedia without additional hardware, although a microphone to add your own sound is important. The facility to add painting and text is included within the authoring package, which means you can create from start to finish in the one software program.

Adding movies

With additional equipment you can incorporate your own movies into Hyperstudio^{TM} along with digitised still images. These can then be shown within your project; however, any alterations to your stills or video must be done outside the Hyperstudio^{TM} environment.

Hyperstudio^{TM} comes with its own scripting language, which can be used to develop aspects of control and programming, enabling you to extend your work beyond the electronic book format. While you can import other resources into Hyperstudio^{TM}, its main attraction is that it allows the creation of a multimedia presentation, from start to finish, without leaving the program. As an inexpensive introduction to multimedia, Hyperstudio^{TM} offers everything necessary to start production.

If you add your own movies, animation and still images to Hyperstudio™, there are implications for add-ons and computer power. Once you start to add movies or large digitised images two things happen: first, you start to run out of hard disk space very quickly, and second, you start to run out of RAM even more quickly. Full colour, full screen video comprises twenty-five individual images per second, amounting to 1 500 frames per minute and a total of 90 000 for a full hour of non-stop moving footage. A compact disc which is capable of holding 250 000 pages of text would be hard pressed to hold more than a few minutes of broadcast quality video. To get around this problem, video on computer tends to be smaller, slower and restricted in its colour range.

Before you can add a movie to your multimedia presentation, you must first be able to get it from video tape into your computer. One way to do this is to use a video-in board which allows you to plug a camcorder or video player into your computer. The video footage is then converted to digital images, and software, usually supplied with the board, allows you, via the computer, to view and perform simple editing of your footage.

With the video-in facility you can use video from any source, providing you have permission and are not breaking copyright law.

▶ Copyright, page 76

A new camera has come onto the market that does not require a video-in board. It interfaces directly with the computer and passes 'video' already digitised. The drawbacks of this system are that the camera must be plugged into the computer while it takes the pictures, hence no outside shots, and the pictures are a little jagged-edged, but the camera is inexpensive and you do not require any additional hardware. A colour version of the camera is available and as compression techniques improve, so will the camera's performance.

Still images

Getting still images into your computer is generally less of a problem than video, but you have more options to consider.

If your computer has a CD-ROM player attached you could make use of some of the hundreds of picture CDs now available. These CDs cover an immense range from full screen, full colour images to grey-scale images to simple line art. These images can be copied from the CD onto your computer, where they can be enhanced, cropped or enlarged.

Artwork which has not been previously digitised needs to be scanned into the computer using either a hand-held scanner or a flatbed scanner. Like most computer equipment these too have come down in price, and like video-in boards they normally come with their own software.

Scanning an image is usually straightforward, but a word of warning: it always takes longer than you think to get a good image from the scanning process. You will invariably find that the contrast needs adjusting, and some clean-up of the image is usually necessary. Scanning line artwork is more straightforward than grey-scale or full colour images. Once in the computer, your image can be taken into image processing software and manipulated to obtain the desired effect. Scanning from books is prohibited unless you get permission from the copyright holder.

Digital still cameras store pictures on disk rather than on film. As long as you have a video-in board, you can plug your camera into the back of your computer and view the images taken by the camera. They are generally more expensive than a 35 mm camera but you do not incur any developing cost. The disk in the camera holds about fifty images and can be used again and again.

Graphics

Graphics can be created within a single package or ported across to other programs to create special effects. These might include *morphing* one image into another or rendering shade or texture onto a three-dimensional image. Much of what you can achieve is related to how much you spend. Some graphics software now costs more than the hardware to run it! However, even with low-level programs some stunning effects can be achieved.

With few exceptions multimedia authoring programs give the user limited control over text. Most will let you alter size, font, style and colour but not much more. Software is available which allows you to mould text into different shapes, run text along a given path or add a shadow effect from any given light angle. Some software is cheap and cheerful, with a limited number of effects, but is very easy to use. Other programs allow greater flexibility, but these tend to be more expensive and considerably more difficult to master.

Sound

There are many ways to get sound into your computer. The most straightforward way is to plug a microphone into your computer. All machines purchased for multimedia creation should have this facility. With Hyperstudio you can record sounds from within the program. With an additional lead to the computer you can record straight from radio or cassette, but do remember copyright! To edit your sounds you will require some sound editing software, which in the main is very easy to use. Sounds are displayed as waves and the bits you don't want can simply be highlighted and deleted. Most sound editing software will also allow echo creation and other special effects. CDs full of sounds intended for use in multimedia are also available. Most contain a mixture of music, the spoken word and sound effects, and most are copyright free. The sounds on CD should be in a format that allows them to be easily read into your authoring program; sounds which can only be read by the software which created them can pose a problem. Composing your own music through a midi keyboard linked to the computer is yet another alternative, as is composing through a music notation program.

Some tips

- Keep it simple.
- Try to achieve a consistent look throughout the project.
- Don't clutter the screen with too much information.
- Write concisely and plan thoroughly before you start.
- Look at commercial multimedia CDs and learn from the good and bad alike.
- Don't be put off by the technology: seek out an easy to use authoring package which will allow as many actions as possible, linking, adding sound or incorporating video at the click of a button.
- Only attempt multimedia creation on hardware that is powerful enough for the job.
- Don't feel you have to include every of possible type of resource.
- Set a realistic timescale.

Producing a video

Assignment

Produce a video

Scenario

You have been approached by a client (e.g. the local cable distributor) requiring a low-budget short video with fictional content, shot to a tight schedule and deadline.

The client company have asked you to participate in a project in which local people with an interest in video will be given opportunities to contribute to some fictional material shot in the local community. They have asked participating groups to produce a brief, treatment, storyboard and final filmed production of a short sequence entitled 'Murder in ...' (you have to complete the title yourselves). As one of the aims of the project is to offer training opportunities in video production, you have also been asked to submit an individual log recording the process and what you learned.

The content of the sequence is up to you, but it should include some clues as to the identity of the murderer, the weapon and the motive. These clues should not be too obvious, so that the audience has something to work out. You have been advised to create as much suspense as possible.

You have been asked to limit yourselves to areas which are within a short walking distance of where you are working.

The quality of your planning materials and video for this short production will be assessed in order to decide whether to award you with a commission of further work.

Brief

1 Set up a time, place and agenda for your first production planning meeting. The purpose of the meeting is to agree the promotional brief which you will send to the cable company, convincing them that

your approach is well thought out. The agenda will include discussions on the aims, audience, settings and title of the short film. You will also plan a schedule of meetings to get you through the following tasks.
2 Open a log which you will use to write up what you learn during the planning and production schedule.
3 Perform a reconnaissance of the locations you will use. Organise any permissions you may need to get, with written evidence that they have been obtained.
4 Write out your brief 'selling' your approach to the film.
5 Write the story of the sequence in the form of a video treatment. Make reference to the visual aspects and the effects of the soundtrack.
6 You have to include a long shot, a medium shot, a close up and a pan in your sequence. You must also set up at least one creative lighting effect. Brainstorm different visual ideas for the shots.
7 Select the shots you will use. Sequence them for the storyboard. Check that the sequence will read or edit together to good effect.
8 Produce a storyboard with appropriate technical instructions.
9 Organise a 'dry run', not only rehearsing but setting up shots with the camera. Decide how titles and credits will be set up. This may be a good opportunity to set up the titles and the opening shot.
10 Film the sequence. This may be for later editing, or use the technique of 'editing in the camera' by shooting exactly what you want the audience to see.
11 Use studio dubbing to record a soundtrack for the sequence. Complete the edit.
12 Show the film to your client or a group of local people for their comments. Decide how you will elicit and record their feedback.
13 Complete your log with a record of not only your audience's evaluation of the film, but also your evaluation of the whole process.
14 Submit your work as a package in a box with a contents list.

11 | Analysing radio programmes

Unit 1 of GNVQ Media is an analysis unit and requires you to analyse, among other things, radio programmes. The analysis should be of the sound images (in jingles, adverts and programme extracts, for instance), the different formats of radio broadcasting such as phone-ins, news and drama, and the different ways stories are told. This chapter introduces you to the critical techniques you need to develop to perform this analysis and is divided into the following sections:
- Introduction to analysing radio programmes
- Critical listening
- The nature of radio
- The listeners
- Format radio
- Radio presenters
- Radio genres.

Introduction to analysing radio programmes

▶ Audience, page 16

▶ Why analyse?, page 10

The main purpose of analysing professionally produced radio programmes is to become more aware of the techniques which are used so that you can learn from them for your own production. Analysis also makes you a more independent consumer of the media, and if you share your perceptions and interpretations of radio programmes with others you will understand more fully how audiences make sense and use of what they hear. The activities that follow are designed to encourage critical listening. You should refer to the sections in the introduction on audiences and analysis before working through this chapter.

Figure 11.1 Inside a radio studio

Critical listening

To produce radio programmes you must understand how they are structured and become familiar with a range of radio stations.

First you must get to know the airwaves and begin to distinguish different stations, different types of programmes and their audience appeal. You will also need to 'tune in' to the boundaries and markers of a purely aural medium and become aware of the building blocks of acoustic construction.

Let's take a straightforward example. Think of a radio broadcast of a football match. This is a classic form of factual radio. A commentator has to describe the action taking place in front of him or her to an audience who are not there to witness it themselves.

A number of conventions have developed which are now taken for granted so that they have almost become invisible. The BBC generally use no fewer than four voices for an important football match. There is the studio anchorman who will tend to pose questions to the others and by implication to the listening audience about the state of football generally, perhaps related in some way to the game in progress.

There are two professional commentators who divide the game between them and an expert summariser at the game who will make observations about the tactics being employed. This person will normally be drawn from the world of football, either a player, former player or manager. Almost inevitably all the voices will be male. Importantly there is the background sound of the crowd without which the commentary on the game would lack any colour.

The commentary team may appear to be having a normal conversation but who gets to speak to the listener is a carefully managed process which is at least partly predictable and pre-determined. The expert summariser is called upon when there is a break in play or to comment upon a particularly exciting piece of action immediately after the incident.

The whole unified experience of listening to a football match on the radio is clearly presented to us in what the station hopes is reliable, perceptive, intelligent and attractive conversation, designed to appear natural and spontaneous; in reality it is carefully constructed.

This chapter aims to help you unearth some of the production 'rules' across a range of programmes and to use the conventions of popular radio with a clear sense of purpose.

The nature of radio

According to Wilby and Conroy in *The Radio Handbook* (Routledge 1994) radio has six essential features, some of which are to do with the nature of the medium itself and some of which are the result of the particular ways in which people use the radio:

1. it is immediate
2. it is about people
3. it is simple
4. it is targeted at specific audiences
5. it needs an endless supply of features
6. it engages the imagination.

A Activity

Discuss in a group how suitable the following sports are for the radio:
- snooker
- golf
- cricket
- tennis
- football
- athletics
- swimming.

Does radio have any advantages over television as a medium for covering live sports?

The development of radio has been determined by technological change. Some people feel that the most significant development in the history of radio was the invention of the transistor. This led in the 1960s to portable radios which were cheap to buy and could be listened to in the bath! By the 1970s radio had become commonplace in cars. Radio became a solitary and individual experience. It meant that young people could listen to pop music stations with minimum disruption to family life. The arrival of the Sony Walkman® in the 1980s intensified this trend.

Figure 11.2 *1930s style valve radios*

The listeners

Figures for radio listening are compiled by Radio Joint Audience Research (or RAJAR). This data is based on averages and gives rise to a generalised analysis which is useful to present to potential advertisers, but its scope is limited. More detailed surveys of radio listening reveal a complicated pattern of radio usage. So how does radio fit into people's lives?

Jeremy Tunstall (*The Media in Britain*, Constable 1983) identifies three different levels of attention which can be paid to media. He defines these as *primary* (close attention), *secondary* (the medium is relegated to the background) and *tertiary* (although the medium is present, no conscious monitoring of it is taking place).

Since the rise of television, radio has become almost wholly a secondary or background medium. Indeed many people say that this is one of the most attractive features of the medium. You can listen with your eyes closed!

▶ Tunstall, J., 1983, *The Media in Britain*, Constable

A Activity

Conduct a survey on how radio is used in your household. Ask your family or fellow householders either to keep a diary for a limited period or prepare a complete a questionnaire (see the one in Chapter 14, page 000). Think carefully about the information you will need to collect in order to assess the importance of radio in people's lives. For example, when do they listen on their own, when as part of a group?

Advertisers, like professional broadcasters, need to know their audience. To this end a great deal of market research and a number of listener surveys are undertaken. Even so, a broadcaster needs to appreciate how the radio fits into the day-to-day lives of the audience, and they need to be tuned in to their listeners as much as the other way round.

▶ Wilby and Conroy, 1994, *The Radio Handbook*, Routledge,

This awareness of the rhythm of ordinary lives has led to *streamed* programming where the output is of one predictable type organised into strips or sequences which may last several hours, according to Andrew Crisell in his book *Understanding Radio* (Routledge, 1994). The pattern usually includes a breakfast show, a morning show, a lunch time show possibly with extended news coverage, an afternoon show, a drive-time show and early and late evening shows each with their own distinctive features. This allows listeners to 'dip into' the programmes and still make sense of them, though it makes sweeping assumptions about the normal behaviour of a typical listener.

Format radio

Although there are some all-news or all-talk shows, music radio is by far the most common format. Music is ideally suited to radio because the listener is not disadvantaged by the lack of any visual references. Music radio, however, is never continuous. It is always punctuated by speech. Radio is predominantly a live and personal medium and appears to require a presenter even on so-called serious music stations like Radio Three or music stations that play predominantly dance music.

Music radio is certainly the most successful and repeated format on air and this has led some critics to dismiss it as an impoverishment of the medium and to complain about the narrow range of music played and the lack of genuine diversity and choice, despite the number of new stations.

Radio 1 operates with two main playlists. The twenty tracks selected for playlist A are guaranteed fifteen plays per week and the B list ten plays.

There is also an album list where six new album tracks will be played at least four times a week. Playlisted records account for half of Radio 1's daytime output. Many music stations use a computer to select the music played. Information held on computer includes *start pace* and *end pace* as well as *start density* and *end density*. This refers to the fullness of sound – a quiet solo instrument would be level one while a heavy metal thrash would be level five. The computer also stores information about *image*. Image A tracks are played most frequently. Images B and C are tracks whose repeated broadcast would prove tiresome.

Some commentators have argued that these are sinister developments but the use of computers to select the music played ensures a smooth musical flow of new songs and old songs which vary in tempo and mood and remain consistent enough not to alienate the target audience.

Most music stations, however, include a wide range of different items such as news summaries, travel reports, competitions, jingles, trailers, adverts, and despite the possibilities of fully automated programming, the personalities of the presenters themselves.

A Activity

Draw up a playlist of twenty records for an imaginary radio station broadcasting specifically for 16 – 20 year olds. Which records would be more likely to be played at breakfast time? Which records might be played immediately after the news? Which would be better played late at night? Compare your list with that of your fellow students. See if you can reach agreement on your lists. (You may like to draw up an A-list and a B-list.)

Radio presenters

A presenter must represent the interests of the listeners, the identity of the station and must provide a continuous flow of output. The style of the radio presenters is related to the type of music they play, the time of day they are on air, the nature of the audience and the personality of the presenter themselves.

Although there are many different types of presenter, they all share certain skills. They are able to read scripts so that they sound like natural speech. 'The Chairman of the Education Committee' may be changed to 'education chief', and 'pupils' may be changed to 'schoolkids'. Reports that may read perfectly well in a newspaper may need to be changed significantly for radio. Take this report from the *Guardian* for example,

'The Government's rail privatisation programme suffered an embarrassing set-back yesterday when British Rail's planned closure of the heavily loss-making sleeper and Motorail services between London and the West Highlands was blocked by a Scottish judge.'

The people who are affected by this news are only identified towards the end of the sentence. The tone is formal. The report is written in one long sentence and uses a passive verb 'was blocked'. If the statement were read out on air like this as an introduction to a mini news package for example it would sound dull. A livelier version would be:

'The people of the West Highlands are celebrating the news today that
    trains will be running between London and Fort William for a little

longer yet. A Scottish judge has blocked British Rail's plans to shut down the service which has been losing money.'

Although radio needs to make speech sound natural, in reality all speech on the radio is much more formal and artificial than everyday conversation. It is rare for people to interrupt or talk over one another and even fairly commonplace slang expressions tend to be avoided.

At one extreme presenters minimise their personalities in order to focus attention on the content of the programme. This type of presenter has been described as *referential*. On music stations they rarely, if ever, talk over the music. This type of presenter is commonplace on classical music stations.

At the other end of the spectrum there is the presenter who emphasises his or her personality in order to make a more personal relationship with the listener. This expressive type of presenter has been described as *emotive*.

The BBC offers new or celebrity presenters voice training. This consists of lots of practice on inflection and intonation, confidence building and listening. It is a common reaction for people to feel negatively about the sound of their own voice. A broadcaster has to learn to accept the sound of his or her own voice and to work on developing its expressive qualities.

A Activity

Place your favourite presenters on a referential – emotive scale, starting with the most referential

Consider styles of radio presentation. How do presenters tell you something about the style of their station?

How do they represent the interests or values of listeners?

What professional techniques do they employ to maintain a constant flow of output (timechecks, traffic reports, weather, special features, phone-ins)?

Do they strike a balance between the familiar and predictable on the one hand and the spontaneous and novel on the other?

An increasingly popular style of presentation, especially for youth programming, is *zoo format* radio. This usually involves several presenters talking to each other with the listener invited to 'eavesdrop' on the conversation. This anarchic and chaotic form of multi-voice presentation was popularised in this country by Radio One DJ Steve Wright and has even been adapted by Ned Sherrin for Radio Four's *Loose Ends*.

Unless you are intending to establish your own radio station we need to move away from format radio and streamed programming to more individual programmes or what is known as mixed programming. But format radio is important to understand in order to become aware of what slots are available for speech-based programming. It is important to listen to a wide range of speech-based programmes in order to categorise them into different types or genres and to familiarise yourself with their dominant codes and conventions.

Wilby and Conroy, 1994, *The Radio Handbook*, Routledge

Radio genres

Wilby and Conroy argue that we identify factual programmes by recognising a wide range of conventions that enable us to instantly categorise items such as reviews, news, and personality interviews, to distinguish between announcers, presenters and newsreaders.

A Activity

Consult the *Radio Times* or another listings magazine and make a list of as many different *types* of radio programmes as you can. Write a short definition of each type.

We can tell the difference between scripted and unscripted dialogue, between informal chat and formal interview and can interpret the use of sound effects, music and background or *ambient* noise. They describe the codes used to present the real world as *journalistic*. Typical features include the absence of strong regional accents, the use of a formal mode of address to introduce interviewees or studio guests, serious subject matter and a clear, deliberate and steady delivery. Conventionally, news items are introduced by a presenter, described by people involved in the story, followed up by a reporter and passed back to the newsreader to *wrap it up* and move on to the next item. In other words there is a hierarchy of voices all controlled at the top by the presenter.

Figure 11.3 Knowing me, knowing you, *with Steve Coogan* which started as a radio show

Some comedy programmes, like Steve Coogan's spoof chat show *Knowing Me, Knowing You* deliberately set out to subvert these generic conventions. The strained conversation between the chat show host and bandleader, and the embarrassingly personal questioning of his 'guests' break the rules of normal chat show behaviour. These programmes depend upon our understanding of the dominant genre conventions in order to be funny.

Alternatively the codes and conventions of fictional radio may be identifiable through the type of speech produced, the use of faders and silence and the use of music or studio laughter. Music in drama, for example, can be used in at least three ways. First as background music heard by the protagonists, second as a marker to start or end the programme or as a bridge between scenes and third, and more rarely, to emphasise dramatic action within a scene.

Phone-ins

In recent times phone-ins have become among the most common type of radio programme. They capitalise on the essential qualities of the medium. They are immediate, interactive, simple and about people. Crisell identifies three different types of phone-in, *the expressive* where callers air their views on some issue or topic, *the exhibitionist* where the caller aims to project his or her personality as in a game show or quiz programme where members of the public call in to participate, and *the confessional* where the caller's primary aim is to express his or her individual needs or problems and get advice.

▶ Crisell, A., 1994, *Understanding Radio*, Routledge,

A Activity

Record examples of different types of phone-ins and identify the characteristics of the callers who get put on air. Why do you think they have been chosen?

How does the presenter deal with them? How does this reflect upon the station's image?

Radio drama

Radio drama is talk radio at its most creative. Before we look at the specifics of radio drama, we must make a few observations about drama generally.

What makes good drama?

Steve Chambers, the writer of *Victoria Station*, makes the following observations:

▶ *Victoria Station* extract, pages 214–222

'Drama is essentially about conflict and good drama is about unresolved conflict. Drama should leave you with questions not answers.

A good play should undermine audience expectations and be full of reversals. Characters should move from happy to sad and from sad to happy. This can be done over and over again.

A story can never be too dramatic. Betrayal, death, love, divorce and coincidence are all the stuff of good drama.

A rule of thumb is to get to the heart of a story straight away. If a conflict is going to end in a fight then have one character hit another and find out why later. Plays will often begin therefore with a dramatic incident or crisis.

Drama is also about simplification and opposites. If a man in a story is married and has a mistress then the women should be very different from each other to realise their full dramatic potential. If one is middle class then the other should be working class. If one is quiet then the other should be loud. If one is glamorous then the other should be dowdy. An audience might expect a man to choose a mistress who is loud, glamorous and working class so it may make for a more interesting story if the mistress was quiet, middle-class and dowdy.

Characters should be easy to recognise. It is a good idea to make them obsessed. Look at the characters in the American television comedy *Cheers*. Cliff is obsessed with the postal service, Norm is obsessed with drinking, Rebecca is obsessed with finding a man and Sam is obsessed with philandering. The more extreme the characters the more dramatic the possibilities, although it is dangerous to make their obsessions so bizarre that the audience is switched off. Successful writers write about their own obsessions which are shared by their audience.'

Radio drama offers unique opportunities for writers. It is much cheaper than drama on television. Although there are few outlets for radio drama (Radio 4 is the only station which broadcasts full-length plays) radio can afford to try out relatively unknown writers (of the 500 original plays broadcast each year between 70 and 80 are by new writers). The pre-requisite of any drama is that it fits into an existing slot and that the narrative structure fits the format required.

Each episode of *The Archers* lasts fifteen minutes. It contains five scenes, each approximately three minutes long. Generally these comprise two scenes indoors and three outdoors. *The Archers* has a rule that you can't re-visit a location until you have been to two others. Usually no more than seven characters appear in each episode with generally no more than three characters in each scene and it is rare for the stories in any one episode to run longer than a single day. There is one episode broadcast every week day and an omnibus edition which lasts an hour broadcast on Sunday. Indeed *The Archers* is so tightly structured that often writers are asked simply to write the dialogue to storylines already produced. (Some of these elements have become standard in other forms of radio drama too. It is now commonplace for all scenes in all radio dramas to last three minutes.) One scene from each episode is dropped for the omnibus programme. Because radio is blind it can afford to be more ambitious in terms of character numbers (one actor can play more than one part), sets and settings. If radio offers imaginative opportunities for dramatists, however, it also is constrained in certain ways. Because the listeners do not have the sense of sight to get their bearings it is confusing to write scenes for too many characters and a character cannot be passive in a scene, that is, merely listening. How would you know they were there?

Radio drama is also constrained by the basic need to be clearly audible. Noisy locations which are often essential to provide a drama with colour must often be suggested and then faded out entirely in order to hear what the characters are saying.

Even before Steve Chambers wrote the six episodes of *Victoria Station* he had a lot of research to do.

'Having decided to set the play in a railway station one hundred years ago there were all sorts of things that I needed to find out. In one episode I had a group of football fans singing songs. I needed to know what songs were being sung at the time. I found a book called *Association Football and English Society 1863 – 1915* which provided the words but not the tune. In the end we chose *Bread of Heaven*. There were lots of questions like that. What did passengers eat on trains in 1895? Were bananas and cucumber sandwiches available to all social classes? I consulted with an expert on social history – Dr Janet Blackman.'

Analysing radio programmes

Having made these key decisions the writer produced a sample scene for episode one and a storyline for each episode. After consultation with the producer, the storylines in episodes two and three were combined.

'It made sense,' said Steve, 'There wasn't really enough material for two episodes when I looked at it again. Each episode is supposed to last 45 minutes. That's fifteen three-minute scenes. I produced a scene-by-scene breakdown and then wrote the dialogue. I found myself having to write extra scenes at the rehearsal stage and even then the radio station had to resort to back announcing and previewing to make it fit the slot. Each episode ran to sixty-five pages.'

'In general each episode has a major plot and two or even three minor sub-plots. In episode two, the major plot which runs through the whole episode concerns 'The Curse of The Tunnel'. There are two minor plots. First, there is the protest by the women at the arrival of the notorious actress Miss Ellen Davison. Second, there is the sub-plot of the relationship between Porter Robson and Miss Josie Braddock. There are also actions like the suicide whose importance will not be revealed until the last episode.'

Writing the script, however, is only a part of the process. At the studio the producer or director (the titles are interchangeable in radio drama) is responsible for casting and recording the play. The production assistant is responsible for arranging the schedules and looking after the cast.

'The scenes were recorded out of sequence,' recalls Steve, 'to take account of the availability of actors.'

At the studio there are three studio managers, one in charge of the mixing desk (*panel*), one responsible for recorded sound effects (*grams*), and the third responsible for sound effects recorded on the studio floor (*spot*).

The producer is also responsible for selecting the signature tune although the writer can make suggestions.

'It took ten days to record the five episodes,' Steve remembers. 'Little things stick in your mind. Actors theatrically turning away from the mike to turn the pages of their script and not missing a beat. The sound of the lift was achieved by running a roller skate over a metal rail.'

Figure 11.4 Actors in studio performing in a radio drama

Analysing radio programmes

> **A** **Activity**
>
> With a group read the extracts from episode two *Tunnel Vision* and, using the information and advice above, produce some of it for radio.

Characters

JOE BRADDOCK	43 STATION MASTER. Working class made good. Has a habit of sniffing sharply when he thinks he's made a point.
MR TIDMARSH	43 CHIEF CLERK. A fussy bureaucrat who insists on calling Joe 'Station Master'; he enjoys the rules of Station existence while being frightened of life.
JACKSON	21 JUNIOR CLERK. Tidmarsh's trainee in both work and personality. A tentative young man who says 'I mean to say' when he's nervous.
JOSIE BRADDOCK	19 TEA-ROOM WAITRESS. Joe's daughter, who is like her father: stubborn, red-blooded, idealistic and honest.
PHOEBE SCULLION	42 TEA-ROOM SUPERVISOR. No-nonsense, down-to-earth, practical.
ADA BIGGS	68 JOE'S AUNT. Working class, self-reliant, tough, works as cleaner.
PORTER ROBSON	30 PORTER.
LYDIA CARRINGTON	34 LEADER OF BRIDGFORD WOMEN'S PURITY LEAGUE.
PROFESSOR GAIDAR	55 EMINENT HUNGARIAN DOCTOR. RENOWNED EXPERT ON DIPHTHERIA.
ELLEN DAVISON	25 FAMOUS ACTRESS.
GED MORAN	36 PLATE-LAYERS' GANGER.
TOMMY MCCARTHY	28 PLATE-LAYER.

Scene Six

SFX	LADIES TEA-ROOM ATMOS. SOUNDS OF CROCKERY AND ECHOING. ADA WITH MOP AND BUCKET TALKING TO PHOEBE
ADA	I know I'm a bit late, ducks. I'll just clean round everyone today

PHOEBE	That's all right Ada...it's your first week
ADA	I'll do you earlier tomorrow. (SOUND OF MOP AND BUCKET) On your own this morning?
PHOEBE	Might as well be
ADA	Where's Josie?
PHOEBE	At the window...discussing station business with Porter Robson
SFX	WINDOW ATMOS. THE SOUNDS OF THE PLATFORM MINGLE WITH THOSE OF THE TEA ROOM.
ROBSON	So Josie Braddock, are you coming dancing with me tonight?
JOSIE	(PLAYFUL) What makes you think I'd want to go dancing with you Jack Robson?
ROBSON	Your father thinks you would
JOSIE	How do you know?
ROBSON	He made me Goods Porter to keep me away from you
JOSIE	You shouldn't be hanging about the platform then
ROBSON	I had some urgent business to attend to...it couldn't wait
JOSIE	Really?
SFX	SOUND OF FOOTSTEPS ALONG PLATFORM. DOOR OPENING TEA-ROOM BELL.
JOSIE	Look at her
ROBSON	It's one of them purity women. Look at what she's wearing. Lunies if you ask me
PHOEBE	(HEARD FROM JOSIE'S POINT OF VIEW) Josie!
JOSIE	I'd better go
ROBSON	Don't I get a kiss? (JOSIE GOES. AFTER HER, FROM WINDOW) You can give me your answer later
SFX	TEA-ROOM COUNTER. TEA-ROOM ATMOS.
LYDIA	Two pots of tea, ten cups and assorted sandwiches please

PHOEBE	I can't let you take them onto the platform...things go missing you know
LYDIA	Will you not support your sisters in their struggle against lechery and vice?
PHOEBE	They're not my sisters besides, I have responsibilities...I am in charge
LYDIA	My ladies are chained up I hardly think they are going to run off with a few cups
JOSIE	It can't do any harm, Phoebe, and it is a cold day. I'll collect the pots up
LYDIA	Thank you...(SOUNDS OF CROCKERY FROM NOW UNTIL LYDIA LEAVES)
ADA	Chaining yourselves up in this weather...no good'll come of it
LYDIA	We may prevent Miss Davison giving her salacious performances in Bridgford
PHOEBE	Stuff and nonsense. The poor woman's had a terrible time ever since she started the role...They say her husband won't let her out of his sight now
LYDIA	That is beside the point. We must fight to prevent women from being corrupted and used as the playthings of men
PHOEBE	At least she knows how to look pretty...I wouldn't be seen dead in 'bloomers'
LYDIA	That's what the prostitutes say...but then you know what they say about prostitutes and actresses. Thank you for the tea...good morning...(EXITS)
PHOEBE	(ANGRY) It's all right for Miss Hoity-toity...she doesn't have to cook and clean after a day's work
ADA	That's right Phoebe ducks...things don't change for the likes of you and me
JOSIE	But surely they are struggling for all women. Women are more than men's playthings...
ADA	(LAUGHING) Been a while since I was a plaything eh Phoebe?

PHOEBE	Anyway, I didn't notice you objecting when Porter Robson was at the window
ADA	Couldn't take their eyes off each other...(CHUCKLING)
JOSIE	That's not true
PHOEBE	She's got independent means and you're the Station-Master's daughter
JOSIE	What do you mean by that?
PHOEBE	Protest's all right for them that can afford it
ADA	Very true duck
JOSIE	I'll show you both. You see if I don't!

Scene Thirteen

SFX	OUTDOOR ATMOS. SHOES CRUNCHING ON GRAVEL. SOUNDS OF THE GOODS YARD IS EVER PRESENT.
GAIDAR	The young man who killed himself...may I see the body?
JOE	I'm afraid the police have taken it away...but I don't think it is connected
GAIDAR	So these men...the er?
JOE	The plate-layers
GAIDAR	Yes...they work in the tunnel and each time one is afflicted, the man cry out and collapse
JOE	Correct
GAIDAR	Always in the tunnel?
JOE	So far. This is the banana warehouse
SFX	SOUND OF THEM ENTERING. INDOOR ATMOS. QUIET BUT MILD ECHO.
GAIDAR	Ah...so many bananas...and they are green...(CHUCKLES) I expect yellow
JOE	We take shipments most weeks. They ripen in here and then we move them on
GAIDAR	Magnificent

JOE	Here we are...this is McCarthy...(QUIETLY) How are you feeling?
MCCARTHY	Not too good sir. Who's this?
GAIDAR	I am a doctor...tell me what happened
MCCARTHY	I was working by the tunnel wall...and I felt this stinging pain in my hand all of a sudden like
GAIDAR	Show me your hand
MCCARTHY	It's swollen now
GAIDAR	Ah yes...does it hurt there? (MCCARTHY CRIES OUT) and there? (CRIES AGAIN)
JOE	What do you think?
GAIDAR	Interesting. The swelling is very localised...The others, they too had swollen hands?
JOE	One had a pain in his shoulder
GAIDAR	Where are they?
JOE	Recovering at home
GAIDAR	They get better? They do not die?
JOE	No, they get better. Look, this is very good of you Professor, but you've been inconvenienced enough
GAIDAR	My luggage has been located. It will be back in Bridgford in two hours...what better way to pass the time than with a mystery to solve. Now, your bananas...where do they come from?
JOE	Africa, the Far east...all over the Empire
GAIDAR	The Americas?
JOE	We had a shipment from the West Indies...last week
GAIDAR	Mmm...I wish to see the place where the men fall
JOE	That's in the tunnel
GAIDAR	We will need a powerful lantern
JOE	All right
MCCARTHY	Doctor?

GAIDAR	Yes
MCCARTHY	Do you believe in curses?
GAIDAR	I am Hungarian; I could hardly do otherwise
MCCARTHY	Have I been cursed then?
GAIDAR	If you have, I do not think it has caused your illness

Scene Fourteen

SFX	SHERWOOD TUNNEL ATMOS. DISTANT SOUND OF THE STATION. A TRAIN PASSES NOISILY, THE SCREECHING OF THE WAGONS DIMINISHING AS THE TRAIN MOVES AWAY. THE TUNNEL IS QUIET WITH THE SOUND OF WATER DRIPPING. SOUND OF JOE AND GAIDAR WALKING.
GAIDAR	This is the place?
JOE	Yes...Maybe they're right...maybe the tunnel is haunted
GAIDAR	You disappoint me Mr Braddock...you are a Station Master, a man of the railways, of science. There are no ghosts...only facts to be determined
JOE	You think you know the answer?
GAIDAR	Yes...I think I do
JOE	It isn't diphtheria?
GAIDAR	Hardly...shine the lantern on this wall here
JOE	There?
GAIDAR	Thank you...it is very warm in here
JOE	The lads have been complaining about that. It's because of the engines waiting in the tunnel
GAIDAR	So this temperature is unusual?
JOE	Yes. What do you think it is Professor?
GAIDAR	I have seen something like it before, I think
JOE	Where?
GAIDAR	When I was a young man, I spent some time in the jungles of Panama

JOE	Panama?
GAIDAR	Lower the lantern. Ah yes, just as I thought
JOE	What?
GAIDAR	In the tunnel wall look there are your ghosts
JOE	All I can see is a few spiders
GAIDAR	A few spiders, no. Tarantulas, Mr Braddock. That is what you can see
JOE	What are they doing in the Sherwood Tunnel?
GAIDAR	I imagine they travelled with some of your bananas from the West Indies
JOE	McCarthy and the others were bitten by tarantulas. But how?
GAIDAR	Like many strange events. A series of coincidences...they escape the week your tunnel is being repaired...the locomotives have to wait. Their heat keeps the creatures alive. The men do not see them in the dark. This way are superstitions made
JOE	I see...(SNIFFS)
GAIDAR	Facts to be determined. No ghosts

Scene Fifteen

SFX	UP PLATFORM. A CROWD HAS GATHERED TO WAIT FOR ELLEN DAVISON. PHOEBE AND ADA ARE WAITING IN THE CROWD.
PHOEBE	I don't know why I'm waiting. My Jamie will wonder where I am
ADA	He'll survive. I want to see what all the fuss is about
PHOEBE	Much ado about nothing
ADA	It were enough to get them women worked up...and Josie, eh duck?
PHOEBE	She's only got herself to blame...he should never have let her work here
ADA	She acts on her principles like Joe...that's why they clash so much

PHOEBE	I'd respect her principles if she suffered a bit more of them
ADA	Ayup...there's a train coming
SFX	SOUND OF TRAIN APPROACHING. IN ANOTHER PART OF THE CROWD.
JOE	Your wait is nearly over Miss Carrington
LYDIA	The struggle for purity is without end Mr Braddock
JOE	How exactly do you intend purifying Miss Davison?
LYDIA	We trust that the force of our argument will persuade her
JOE	And if doesn't?
LYDIA	We shall picket the theatre
SFX	TRAIN COMES TO A HALT. DOORS OPENING, SOUND OF PEOPLE DISEMBARKING. PART OF THE CROWD CHEERS, ANOTHER PART BOOS.
GUARD	Victoria! Bridgford Victoria!
LYDIA	Let me through...Miss Davison?
MR DAVISON	Stay back madam! Miss Davison is in my protection
LYDIA	Protection or custody? Men frequently confuse them don't you find?
MR DAVISON	How dare you!
MISS DAVISON	Let her through
LYDIA	Miss Davison...on behalf of the Bridgford Women's Purity league. May I present you with this petition?
MISS DAVISON	Thank you
LYDIA	We urge you to reclaim your body and spirit and renounce your role
MR DAVISON	(INTERRUPTING) That's enough! I am Miss Davison's husband
LYDIA	She has my sympathy
MISS DAVISON	(LOUD) I would like to make a statement
SFX	CHEERS AND BOOS.

9	MISS DAVISON	Ladies and gentlemen, since undertaking the role which has become notorious, I have been overwhelmed by the great mass of letters I have received...some have been supportive but most have been critical and these I found hard to bear
	SFX	LOUD CHEERS.
1	MISS DAVISON	I enjoy acting and I would have continued were it not for the love and esteem in which I hold my dear husband. He has forbidden me to continue and as I do not feel able to countenance his displeasure, I shall perform the role no longer
2	LYDIA	No!
	SFX	CHEERS, BOOS.
3	JOE	Congratulations Miss Carrington. You have got what you wanted.
4	LYDIA	Out of fear instead of enlightenment...A woman should no more be owned by one man than by the financial power of all men. I shall write to her
	SFX	ATMOS TO BACKGROUND, THEN FOREGROUND AGAIN SIGNIFYING A MOVE TO A DIFFERENT PART OF THE PLATFORM.
1	ADA	I feel right done...I was thinking of going to the play
2	PHOEBE	Well, it stands to reason. I mean what man is going to put up with his wife behaving like that?
	SFX	FADE ATMOS TO THEME MUSIC, CREDITS. BOOKINGS HALL ATMOS TO FOREGROUND.
3	JOE	I'm leaving you in charge Mr Tidmarsh
4	TIDMARSH	I think I can manage Station Master
5	JOE	A word of advice, if it isn't broken, don't fix it
6	TIDMARSH	(SOTTO VOCE) I'll show you how the station should be run

Assignment

Analysing a radio format

Choose a broadcast format to examine from:
- talk show
- phone-in
- news
- magazine
- quiz
- serial
- single drama
- situation comedy.

Listen to three different programmes for whichever format you have chosen. Describe the overt and implied meanings of single images taken from these programmes. It might be useful to listen to the opening twenty seconds of each programme and examine the meanings you and other members of the group make of introductory music, sound effects, background sound and speech (including tone of voice and style of language).

Try to work out with other members of your group the characteristics of the format. If you were studying radio sitcoms, for instance, you might consider, as well as the introduction:
- whether there is an audience or whether laughter is canned
- whether the actors respond to the audience
- whether there are the same characters in each episode
- how far these characters change and develop
- how far the characters are flat and predictable and how far they behave unexpectedly
- how far humour depends on the characters being put into unusual or incongruous situations
- the use of sound effects for laughs
- the use of catch-phrases
- how the programmes end (for example, is everything neatly resolved or left open-ended?)

After collecting and discussing the evidence write about the formal characteristics and narrative structure of your chosen format.

12 Producing radio programmes

GNVQ Unit 4 requires you to produce scripts for two radio programmes, one fiction (such as a play) and the other factual, such as a magazine type of programme. You then have to record the programmes, edit them, present them to an audience and evaluate them.

This chapter is organised into the following sections:
- Introduction to producing radio programmes
- Setting up a radio station
- Planning audio productions
- Factual programming
- Equipment.

Introduction to producing radio programmes

There are many reasons why radio is an excellent medium in which media students can demonstrate their skills. The technology is simpler than video. It is less complicated to realise your ideas in sound alone than to do the same with sound and pictures, and because radio is 'blind' it makes a direct appeal to the imagination. With radio it is possible to be much more ambitious in terms of locations for drama productions, for example, simply because they are suggested rather than presented to an audience. Radio is certainly the fastest growing sector of the media with new stations proliferating across the airwaves almost weekly. In comparison with television, radio is cheap to produce. This means that radio can be more experimental, using new creative talent and innovative programme forms.

Students interested in a career in radio are well advised to investigate the local media scene and should not forget community radio and hospital radio, which have both provided starts for many people working in broadcasting.

Setting up a radio station

If you want to set up a radio station in your school or college you will need permission from the Radio Authority, Holbrook House, 14 Great Queen Street, London, WC2B 5DG.

The most basic and cheapest system to install is a studio linked by cables to loudspeakers. If more funds are available it is possible to broadcast on airwaves rather than through cable. You need to broadcast on AM (amplitude modulation) frequency to a restricted area (such as a school) so as not to interfere with other radio services. This system is called *induction loop* AM. You need to pay a licence fee to the Radio Authority, have a call sign to show the station's identity and keep a tape recording of everything you broadcast, in case there are any complaints about programme content.

It is possible for educational establishments to broadcast more widely, using an FM transmitter and having a temporary licence for a day or a week.

Figure 12.1 A college radio station

Planning audio productions

There is a considerable range of forms of audio production to choose from. The forms include:
- a quiz show
- a game show
- a documentary
- a discussion programme or chat show
- commentary on a live performance
- an extended interview
- a magazine programme
- a short story
- a drama
- or even an entirely new hybrid form of your own devising!

Each form has its own codes and conventions and before you start you will need to research similar programmes and identify the conventions commonly employed. You should not, of course, merely copy these. You may decide deliberately to adopt a radical approach but you should be able to justify your decisions.

Factual programming

Most factual programmes consist of news and news features. There are relatively few opportunities for longer documentaries except on Radio 4 and occasionally Radio 5. Most reporters on local radio are working at great speed to produce *packages* which last five minutes at most. A basic package consists of a cue or introduction from the studio presenter, a couple of short interviews and the reporter's own words used as links between the interviews and at the end of the package. In this way the reporter is the storyteller or guide through the story.

Producing radio programmes

This is how a package might be put together:

CUE	Students at St Olaf's College were devastated today when they opened their A-level English papers and found they had been studying the wrong set texts.
LINK	Alice Spring was one of the people who realised that she couldn't answer any of the questions.
INTERVIEWEE 1	'I just could not believe my eyes. I'd never heard of some of the texts. I couldn't answer a single question. We all just got up and walked out and went to see the lecturer but he wasn't even in college. It's two years' work up the spout and I'm absolutely furious.'
LINK	The lecturer in charge of the A-level English course was not available for comment but the college principal, Dr Alan Jones, had this to say:
INTERVIEWEE 2	'I have contacted the examination board and explained the circumstances and they have told me that it is possible to have a special exam set on the set texts which the students have studied. I need to make a full report on what has happened and why. In the meantime I can only offer my apologies to the students concerned who must be very distressed. I am doing everything in my power to remedy the situation.'
LINK	Twenty of the students have other examinations tomorrow morning and they will be keeping their fingers crossed that this time they've studied the right course. This is Harry Porter at St Olaf's College.

▶ Generating, developing and evaluating ideas, pages 63 – 64

When you are deciding on your programme, think about the length of time it will last and the slot it could occupy in the schedules. It is quite a useful discipline to have a fixed time slot in mind. Aim for between five and fifteen minutes. The process of originating ideas is the same as that described on pages 63 – 64.

You will need to identify a number of key people to interview and select appropriate music. You will also need to strike a balance between the music and voices and decide when you will need to link up different speeches with comments from a narrator. You may have to see what material you get before you can make final decisions about this.

A narrator can be an impersonal voice of authority with a neutral delivery style, but you could use the first person for a more informal style. Other options are to use more than one narrator, which enables you to select contrasting voices, or to use one of the main characters from your programme.

Equipment

You will need access to a good quality portable tape recorder using quarter-inch tape, microphones, a mixing desk with an editing facility, and a soundproofed or quiet room.

Portable tape recorder

This is the most commonly used piece of equipment and is likely to be the first piece of equipment that trainee reporters will learn to use. The Uher tape recorder is still the industry standard. It is simple to operate and robust. It records directly onto 1/4 inch tape which can be transferred on to a studio tape machine and edited immediately. Uhers are fitted with rechargeable batteries which can provide enough power to record four 5-inch reels of tape at 7.5 inches per second (approximately one hour's worth of recording).

Occasionally radio stations use high quality portable cassette players for longer projects where the size of the equipment is a consideration. Andy Kershaw certainly used one to record music and document his travels around Africa for a series of programmes for Radio 1.

Microphones

There are several types of microphones used in professional radio. Decisions about which microphones to use are made by balancing creative and technical considerations. The amount of background noise or *atmosphere* desired and the practicalities of using radio microphones, for example, might determine the selection of equipment.

The basic microphone types are as follows.

Cardioid or unidirectional microphones

Studio presenters often speak into a unidirectional or cardioid microphone. The unidirectional mike picks up sound from directly in front, while the cardioid mike responds to sound from a heart-shaped area (see Figure 12.3). Both microphones pick up the minimum of background sound. Studio mikes which are mounted on an angle-poise arm, are moved before the faders are opened as they are highly susceptible to handling noise.

Ribbon microphone

Studio interviews and music are often recorded with a ribbon mike. These can be unidirectional or bi-directional. Bi-directional microphones pick up sound from in front and behind. They have a figure of eight pick up pattern (see Figure 12.4). They provide a rich tone to the voice as they are particularly responsive to bass frequencies. Their sensitivity to sound makes them unsuitable for outside locations, but they are good for conducting interviews in the studio with people either side of the microphone. The lip mike is a ribbon mike which can be used outdoors. It is less responsive to wind noise and has a very limited field in which it can pick up sound. Presenters speak into the mike with their lips pressed into a special casing.

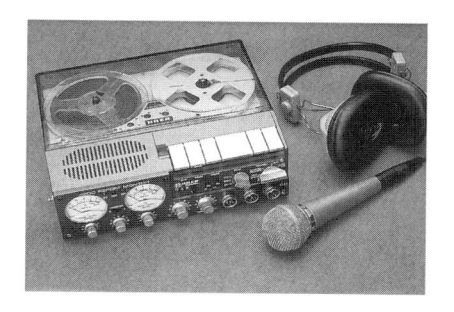

Figure 12.2 Uher portable tape recorder

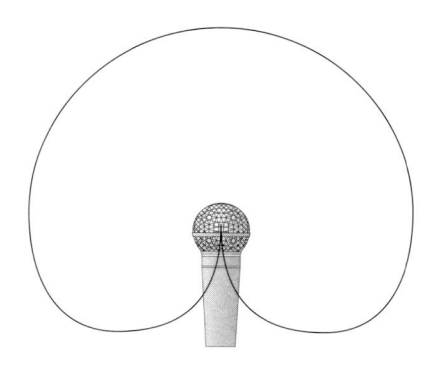

Figure 12.3 Pick-up area of cardioid microphone

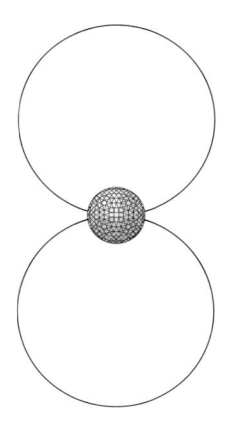

Figure 12.4 Pick-up area of ribbon microphone

Omni-directional microphone

This microphone is used most frequently by reporters and correspondents on outside locations to add colour to their reports. It is equally sensitive to sound picked up from all around (see Figure 12.5) and produces a different quality of 'actuality' sound in contrast to the quieter cleaner sound of the studio. It is the least susceptible to handling noise but is not used in the studio because of the problems it can cause with feedback.

Figure 12.5 Pick-up area of omni-directional microphone

Radio microphone

When reporters cannot for practical reasons be linked to a transmitter or recorder by a lead, they will use a radio microphone with its own built-in transmitter and a nearby receiving unit. These microphones are susceptible to interference from electrical sources or physical obstruction.

Lavalier (cord) or clip microphones

Though these are more commonly used in television studios they can sometimes be useful for interviews or documentary features where the presence of a microphone is likely to affect the performance of the participants.

Mixing desk

Live radio requires a mixing desk with faders to control a variety of sound sources. The desk or control panel is used to mix pre-recorded material, trailers, jingles and live speech. It can also be used to prepare material for future programmes by mixing sound effects or music with interviews and voice reports.

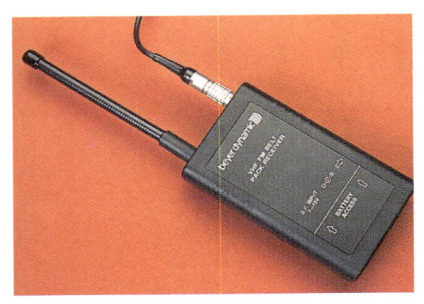

Figure 12.6 Radio microphone

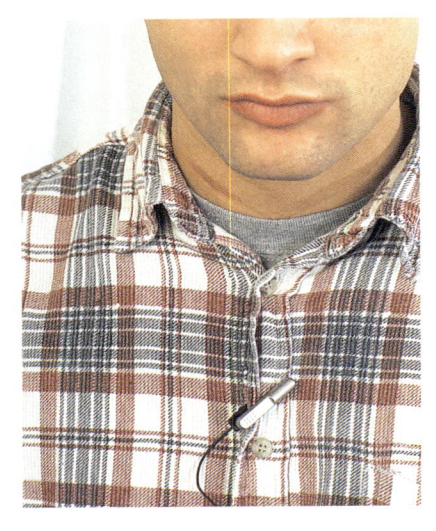

Figure 12.7 A clip microphone in use

Figure 12.8 Mixing desk in a radio station

Editing equipment

In order to edit radio broadcast material accurately, you will need the following basic equipment:
- chinagraph pencil
- scalpel or razor blade
- splicing tape
- coloured leader tape
- an EMI editing block.

By listening through headphones as the tape passes backwards and forwards over the playback head, you can locate the editing points which you then mark with a chinagraph pencil. You will probably have to remove the cover of the recorder to reach the replay head. Place the tape on the splicing block, cut diagonally (45 degrees) the first mark. Leave the end which you want to keep in the channel on the splicing block. Bring the other end of the tape, lay it on the block and cut that at the same angle. (You should save and label the tape you have removed as you might need it again if you change your mind about the edit). Lay the two bits you want to keep end-to-end in the channel on the block. Cut a small piece of splicing tape and lay it over the join, pressing it down firmly. Play the edited tape to check for accuracy. Put a length of green leader tape on your edited tape and red tape at the end.

When you edit you should be trying to fit the material to the required time, which means reducing and discarding material. You will also probably have to alter the sequence of what you have recorded. If you have mixing equipment you can also add some creative touches by including music, sound effects and using fading techniques.

Fading up and down makes a smooth transition from one item to another as can a *crossfade*, which involves fading one sound in as another is faded out. The crossfade is often used to mix music or sound effects with speech. A *pot cut* is where the fader is closed rapidly after an item and must be done at a natural pause in the speech. Gradual fading in and out is done when music or sound effects are added to a recorded item of speech. The audience should not be aware of either the start or the finish of the fade.

To achieve smooth editing you should be very careful with selecting the right split second in a pause to make your cut. There should be breathing space in the edited version. It is helpful to cut after the intake of breath before a speaker continues with a new sentence. It is important when editing tape to listen to the background noise as well as the foreground speech. The sudden chiming of a clock or the sound of a passing ambulance can spoil an interview.

Editors should also be aware of the ethics of editing. You should not distort what someone is saying by missing out significant parts of an interview. It is very easy, for instance, to make people sound more extreme than they meant to be if you miss out qualifying statements. You might make a more powerful story this way, but you are not being fair to the interviewee.

Microphone technique

Basic microphone technique using a portable tape recorder involves choosing the precise location for recording a commentary or interview that will add atmosphere to the piece. The reporter will then record upwards of ten seconds of *wildtrack* sound which may be useful in the final edited piece. The sound of a heavy downpour or the noise of a police helicopter might be used to introduce the item for example.

The experienced reporter judges how far away from the speaker to hold the microphone to achieve the right balance between background noise and speech. If the microphone is held close to the mouth and the recording level is set correspondingly low then there will be less background noise recorded.

More creative microphone techniques can be heard in radio drama. Characters are sometimes heard off-mike or behind an obstacle or receding into the distance.

Producing radio programmes

> **PROFILE**   Vickie Thompson: Radio Journalist in her first job

'I work for a new local radio station called Sun City, 103.4. I prepare and read a three minute news bulletin every hour.

We're a bit short staffed so in a way I'm doing two jobs. If I'm on the 9–5 shift I have to be a reporter and go out on stories, which usually involves recording interviews. Then in the studio I either write the story I've just collected or work on stories from other sources.

We get the news from agencies such as the Press Association, from press releases, letters and the emergency services.

I have to select and prioritise the news from the available stories, so I'm an editor as well.

We have a target audience of mainly 24–45 year-old housewives in the local area. There is no particular social bias.

I have to have a mix of stories with an emphasis on human interest and local interest topics.

The language I use to tell the stories is the kind you would use if you were talking to someone in a pub but toned down slightly. You have to be authoritative but conversational.

I practise reading the stories out before I broadcast and I get used to judging that, say, three paragraphs take twenty seconds.

Before I got this job I trained on a postgraduate broadcast journalism course for one year. I already had an HND in Music and Entertainment Management.

The journalism course involved learning about law, local and national government, shorthand, voice training, and how to handle recording and editing equipment.

I have to do shift work which means giving up nights out if I'm doing a 6 a.m. broadcast. Listeners can soon tell if you're hung over. You have to be responsible. The good thing is that you have afternoons off sometimes. I quite like the variety that irregular hours give you.

The job can be tense sometimes as you have to meet strict deadlines, but I love the excitement. You have to be brassy and pushy sometimes if you want information for a story and some stories can be emotionally difficult.

You have to be able to work on your own and have initiative, but you also need to work in a team. You have to learn to be tolerant and make life easy for other people. You have a common goal so you need to get rid of you personal baggage.

I want to be in the media forever.'

A Activity

Design a recruitment advertisement for a job similar to Vickie's, described above. Say briefly what the job entails and what skills and personal qualities you expect from applicants.

A Activity

Which microphone would you choose to record the following?

- a rock band playing at your school or college
- an interview with the owner of a ten-pin bowling alley
- a programme about a helicopter pilot
- a local marathon event
- a discussion with schoolchildren in a classroom.

A Activity

Write a two minute extract from a play based around two friends coming home from a night out. Set one scene on a bus.

You might begin by deciding what will happen and then improvising the dialogue or you may prefer to improvise the whole thing. Eventually you will need to produce scripted dialogue.

Once you have produced your script, discuss it with a fellow student who will act as producer. Number the speeches so that if you have to re-record sections because of mistakes you and the rest of the cast will know where to pick it up again. Mark the script for special effects (SFX).

Assignment

Producing a radio programme

Your task is to produce a short magazine programme about drug abuse in your local community. Describe the target audience for your final programme.

- You need to include two case histories of people for whom drug-taking is having or has had a major influence on their life. These will be presented as monologues with the questions edited out. You might have to consider whether the people involved should be named or identified. Do some desk research into drugs and their effects and write a brief, informative script about your findings.
- Interview officials from the police and the local authority to obtain their views about the problem of drug abuse and what can be done to solve it.
- Conduct a vox pop where you interview members of the public in a busy shopping arcade about a simple proposition (e.g. that all convicted drug dealers should be given life imprisonment).
- Select or compose music which can be used to open and close your programme. If you use recorded music you should obtain permission from the copyright holder. Contact the record company to ask advice about this.
- Write a linking script which joins the various sections of your programme to give it continuity.
- Write a production schedule to say who in the group is responsible for what part of the production and by what deadline. As well as recorded items this should include making sure that equipment is available and that permission to use certain locations has been secured.
- When you have recorded all the material, you need to edit it so that it has a logical narrative flow and is clearly audible. You should try to use fading and mixing effects.
- Play your final programme to a small sample audience – a class of eleven-year-olds, for instance – and obtain feedback, either written or spoken.
- Make your own evaluation of the programme, explaining what you considered effective and what should be improved and how.

13 | The purposes and methods of media research

Unit 6 of GNVQ requires you to understand how and why media organisations conduct market research and then to conduct some research of your own on your own media product and on a professionally-produced text.

This chapter is organised into the following sections:
- Introduction to the purposes and methods of media research
- Who needs research?
- Industry research organisations
- Academic research
- How to conduct research
- Case study: Focus groups

Introduction to the purposes and methods of media research

It shows you how to locate examples of research findings and interpret them. It mentions academic investigations into how audiences interpret media texts in different ways. This will lead you into considering debates about the influence of the media on audience behaviour.

The section on how to conduct research introduces you to techniques which you can use to enquire into the reception of your own media product as well as audience reaction to a commercial product.

Who needs research?

Figure 13.1 Students carrying out research

Commercial media organisations are interested in dependable research findings because they often serve two audiences. The products they make and sell have to appeal to the public and the audiences they attract have to appeal to advertisers. The television companies which broadcast *Coronation Street*, for instance, are interested to know the size of the audience it attracts because the rates they charge for advertising during the commercial breaks depend on audience size. They get their information from the Broadcasters Audience Research Board (BARB) which is jointly owned by the BBC and ITV Association. Its findings are published weekly in *Broadcast*, the weekly newspaper of the television and radio industry. These show that (in 1995) *Coronation Street* took the top three positions in the audience size table with around 18 million viewers per episode, figures which include the viewing of the omnibus edition. Advertising slots just before, during and at the end of the programme are therefore the biggest revenue earners for the broadcasting station.

The producers of *Coronation Street* will also be interested in the numbers of people watching the programme and how they compare with the previous week's figures and the previous year's because they want to maintain the popularity of the programme. But they also need in-depth study of audience reaction to the programme so that they know what precisely keeps viewers' attention. They employ researchers to investigate audience responses and attitudes and use their findings to influence storylines and production values.

Academic research is done by universities and, though it may be of interest to commercial organisations, its main purpose is not usually commercial. This kind of research has a number of different objectives but looks at, among other things, the nature of popular culture, the ways audiences interpret and use media products, and the powers and influence of media organisations. A number of centres for academic research of this kind have developed in universities such as Birmingham, Glasgow, Leeds and Leicester.

Industry research organisations

BARB (Broadcasters' Audience Research Board)

The organisation provides information about audiences to both broadcasters and advertisers. This information is collected from meters installed in television sets in a sample of homes throughout the United Kingdom. The sample is selected to give a representative picture in terms of viewing habits, television equipment owned and family composition etc.

The meter registers when a television is switched on and what channel is selected. In addition, each individual in the house has a remote control with numbered buttons on it which they press to show when they are watching television. The system even provides for guest viewers who watch television. All the information is stored and then transmitted automatically each night by a computer linked to a telephone.

BARB can also measure those programmes which are recorded and played back through a video recorder. The recording itself is not measured, but the playback is. This kind of viewing, called *timeshift viewing*, can be reported separately or added to live viewing. Playback of pre-recorded videos cannot be measured.

BARB issues information regularly to show the numbers and percentages of viewers watching particular programmes or adverts. It issues weekly press releases which are reported in the *Media Guardian* and the magazine *Broadcast*.

Another service provided by BARB is the confidential Audience Appreciation service. This is available to organisations who subscribe to BARB and can ask specific questions about programmes and personalities. The information provided is confidential.

There are selected panels of people – 3 000 adults in one panel, 1 000 children aged 4–15 in another and several smaller regional panels. Individuals in a panel keep a viewing diary and mark each programme they watch on a scale of 0–11 according to how much they like it. The programmes can then be given an appreciation index which is shown as a mark out of 100. Subscribers can ask the panels any specific questions about any aspect of any programme. Broadcasters can use this system to check on the popularity of a particular presenter, for instance, or on attitudes and responses to a series of programmes.

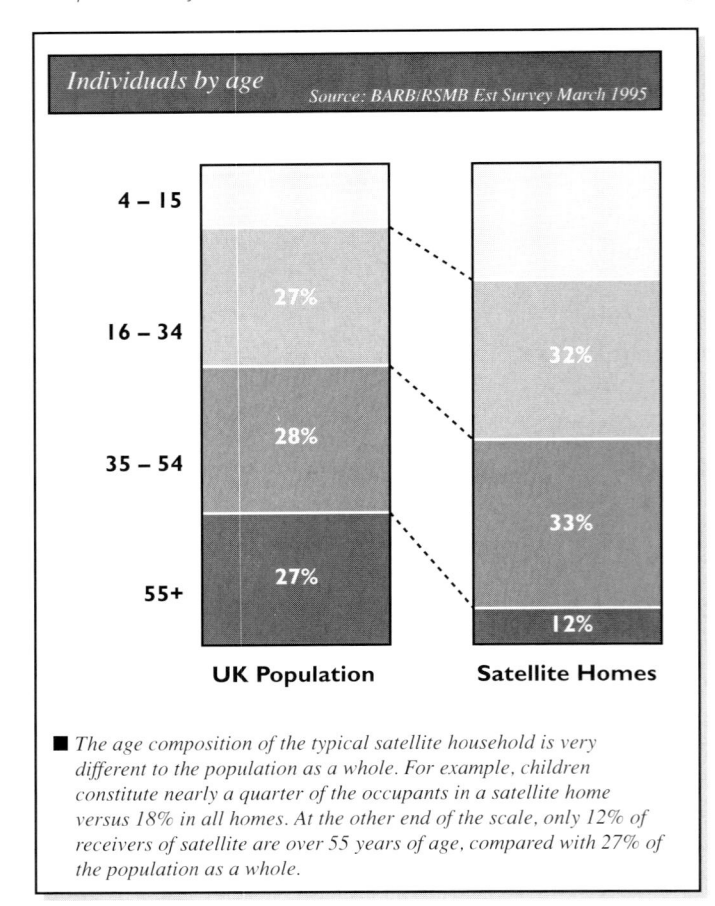

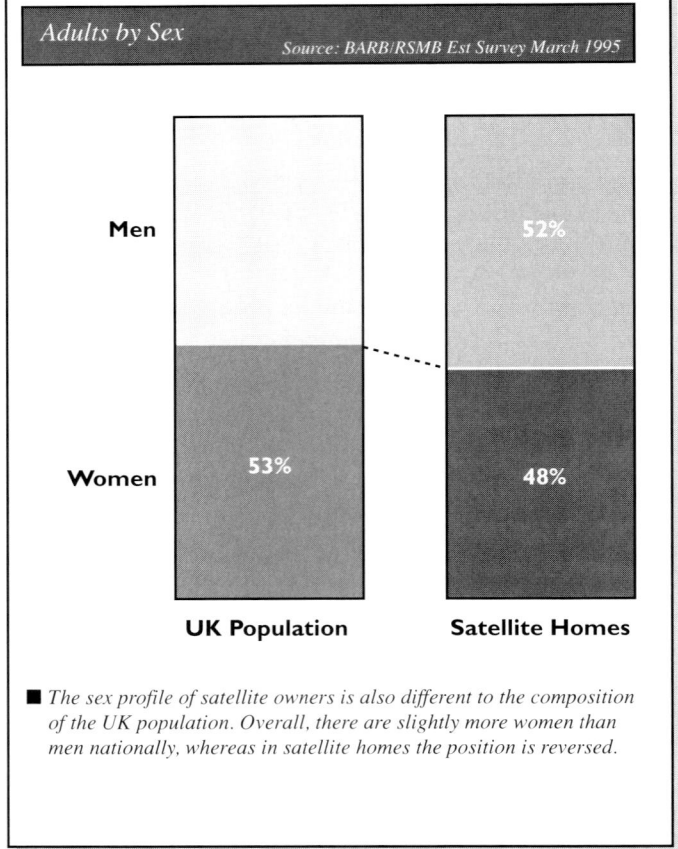

▶ Further information can be obtained from BARB, Glenthorne House, Hammersmith Grove, London W6 0ND, Tel: 0181-741 9110 Fax 0181-741 1943.

Figure 13.2 Satellite ownership – a breakdown. An example of information provided by the BARB.

Individuals by age *Source: BARB/RSMB Est Survey March 1995*

Age	UK Population	Satellite Homes
4 – 15	18%	23%
16 – 34	27%	32%
35 – 54	28%	33%
55+	27%	12%

■ The age composition of the typical satellite household is very different to the population as a whole. For example, children constitute nearly a quarter of the occupants in a satellite home versus 18% in all homes. At the other end of the scale, only 12% of receivers of satellite are over 55 years of age, compared with 27% of the population as a whole.

Adults by Sex *Source: BARB/RSMB Est Survey March 1995*

	UK Population	Satellite Homes
Men	47%	52%
Women	53%	48%

■ The sex profile of satellite owners is also different to the composition of the UK population. Overall, there are slightly more women than men nationally, whereas in satellite homes the position is reversed.

The National Readership Survey (NRS)

▶ Further information about NRS can be obtained from National Readership Surveys Ltd, Garden Studios, 11-15 Betterton Street, Covent Garden, London WC2H 9BP.

This is a private research company which was formed in 1991. It provides information on the readership of newspapers and magazines for both publishers and advertisers. Figure 13.3 shows an example of the research findings on the readership of newspapers.

The organisation interviews a sample of 40 000 people about their reading. The sample needs to be large to obtain accurate figures. Small

Average Issue Readership All Adults

	TOTAL		SEX MALE		FEMALE		AGE 15-44		45+		SOCIAL GRADE ABC1		C2DE		MAIN SHOPPER	
UNWEIGHTED SAMPLE	19625		8586		11039		9424		10201		9816		9809		13432	
ESTIMATED POP, (000s)	44722		21737		22986		23424		21298		21562		23160		28227	
	000	%	000	%	000	%	000	%	000	%	000	%	100	%	000	%

Daily Morning Newspapers – 6 Days

The Sun	10001	22	5637	26	4364	19	6162	26	3839	18	3020	14	6981	30	5728	20
Daily Mirror	6876	15	3741	17	3135	14	3485	15	3391	16	2146	10	4730	20	4088	14
Daily Record	1959	4	1044	5	915	4	1169	5	790	4	584	3	1375	6	1141	4
Daily Mail	4544	10	2294	11	2250	10	2043	9	2501	12	2940	14	1604	7	2814	10
Daily Express	3328	7	1738	8	1590	7	1414	6	1914	9	1970	9	1358	6	1984	7
The Daily Telegragh	2554	6	1434	7	1120	5	1001	4	1554	7	2197	10	358	2	1578	6
Daily Star	2063	5	1409	6	654	3	1431	6	632	3	532	2	1531	7	1085	4
Today	1710	4	914	4	795	3	994	4	716	3	780	4	930	4	1021	4
The Times	1391	3	799	4	593	3	750	3	642	3	1215	6	176	1	892	3
The Guardian	1314	3	726	3	588	3	857	4	457	2	1108	5	206	1	851	3
The Independent	1003	2	624	3	379	2	679	3	324	2	848	4	155	1	618	2
Financial Times	743	2	572	3	171	1	447	2	296	1	673	3	70	*	433	2

Daily Morning Newspapers – Saturday Issues

The Sun	10136	23	5469	25	4667	20	6052	26	4084	19	2906	13	7230	31	6069	21
Daily Mirror	7274	16	3834	18	3441	15	3654	16	3620	17	2354	11	4920	21	4347	15
Daily Record	1988	4	1058	5	929	4	1170	5	818	4	583	3	1405	6	1152	4
Daily Mail	4876	11	2402	11	2474	11	2156	9	2720	13	3091	14	1785	8	3145	11
Daily Express	3418	8	1732	8	1686	7	1392	6	2026	10	1986	9	1432	6	2058	7
The Daily Telegraph	3267	7	1751	8	1517	7	1267	5	2001	9	2766	13	501	2	2063	7
Daily Star	2005	4	1261	6	743	3	1387	6	617	3	496	2	1509	7	1091	4
Today	1640	4	850	4	790	3	872	4	768	4	722	3	918	4	1001	4
The Times	1360	3	733	3	626	3	678	3	681	3	1203	6	157	1	875	3
The Guardian	1546	3	802	4	744	3	1014	4	532	2	1256	6	290	1	1055	4
The Independent	1177	3	664	3	512	2	765	3	412	2	996	5	181	1	750	3
Financial Times	569	1	403	2	166	1	266	1	303	1	497	2	72	*	337	1

NOTE: The standard Average Issue Readership question and the Saturday Issue Readership question are different in kind. It is incorrect to draw a direct, numerical comparison between the Saturday issue readership estimate for a given title and the standard six-day AIR figure.

Figure 13.3 Average issue readership all adults

samples can produce very distorted information. Samples are selected to provide a representative cross-section of society in terms of sex, age, region and social class. Fieldworkers call at homes to interview each person in the sample. The fieldworkers (or interviewers) show booklets of mastheads from publications and ask which publications the interviewee has looked at for a least two minutes in the last year. They also ask how often people read individual titles and when they last read particular ones.

There is a problem of people being interviewed tending to overestimate the amount of reading of titles mentioned early in the interview, so the order of mastheads being shown has to be rotated.

Once the sample has been interviewed the results are weighted to produce estimates of the number of readers in a total population of 45 million adults.

The information available to publishers and advertisers can be broken down into particular target groups: by age, social status, lifestyles, shopping behaviour, employment status, income and marital status, for instance. There are different lifestyle categories. Some such as Sagacity are based on a combination of income, social grade and stage of life, with classifications such as 'better-off white collar worker with a family'.

Others, such as Super Profiles, are based on a mixture of attitudes, age, wealth and geographical location as in the classifications:
- affluent achievers
- thriving greys
- settled suburbanites
- nest builders
- urban venturers
- country life
- senior citizens
- producers
- hard-pressed family
- have nots.

Information is also available on what readers own or use. This kind of information can be important to an advertiser who may want to sell a product to a very specific group such as unmarried males in the 18–25 age group who use electric razors and shop mainly in supermarkets. The advertiser would be able to find out from the survey the most read magazine or newspaper among such a target group.

Research into audiences for radio programmes is organised by Radio Joint Research Limited (RAJAR), which is owned jointly by the Association of Independent Radio Companies and the BBC. The information is collected and analysed for RAJAR by Research Services Ltd, an independent research company which specialises in large surveys. Audience figures are produced each week and show the total number of people who listen to each programme for at least five minutes in a week. This is called 'reach'. Figures which show 'share' of audience are also produced. The share of audience is calculated by multiplying the number of listeners by the number of hours they are tuned into a particular station. This figure is then compared with other radio stations in covering the same area and expressed as a percentage. These figures can show how popular a station is in relation to its competitors.

The information provided by RAJAR also covers total numbers and percentages of audiences measured in segments based on gender, age and social class. Such information is important for advertisers on commercial radio. It is also possible to know how audience figures change for every half hour through the day and programme planners can use this information to pinpoint the parts of their programming which are less successful.

Figure 13.4 An example of Rajar's research findings into radio listening

QUARTERLY SUMMARY OF RADIO LISTENING

QUARTER 1/95 — 2 January 1995 - 26 March 1995

Rajar — Radio Joint Audience Research Limited

PART 1 - UNITED KINGDOM
Adults aged 15 and over: population 46,958,000

	Weekly Reach '000	%	Average Hours per head	Average Hours per listener	Total Hours '000	Share of Listening %
ALL RADIO	40284	86	18.1	21.0	847750	100.0
ALL BBC	27798	59	8.8	14.9	413107	48.7
All BBC Network Radio	23897	51	6.9	13.5	322295	38.0
BBC Radio 1	10514	22	1.9	8.7	91236	10.8
BBC Radio 2	8713	19	2.4	13.1	113999	13.4
BBC Radio 3	2401	5	0.2	3.2	7791	0.9
BBC Radio 4	8256	18	1.8	10.1	83411	9.8
BBC Radio 5 Live	5126	11	0.6	5.0	25858	3.1
BBC Local/Regional	9779	21	1.9	9.3	90812	10.7
ALL COMMERCIAL	27745	59	8.7	14.8	410175	48.4
All National Commercial	11135	24	1.8	7.6	84093	9.9
Atlantic 252 *	4419	9	0.6	6.4	28080	3.3
Classic FM	4467	10	0.6	5.8	25952	3.1
Talk Radio UKø	-	-	-	-	-	-
Virgin Radio	3825	8	0.6	7.9	30061	3.5
All Local Commercial	22783	49	6.9	14.3	326081	38.5
Other Listening	3863	8	0.5	6.3	24468	2.9

ø Talk Radio UK launched on Tuesday 14th February. Listening to the station is included in 'other listening' in the table above, which is a report of the audiences for a 12 week period. The following results are based on the first full five weeks, 20th February - 26th March, of Talk Radio UK's operation:-

	Weekly Reach '000	%	Average Hours per head	Average Hours per listener	Total Hours '000	Share of Listening %
Talk Radio UK	1553	3	0.2	5.1	7981	0.9

Figure 13.5 A newspaper article based on RAJAR/RSL findings

600,000 rise in listeners halts decline of Radio 1

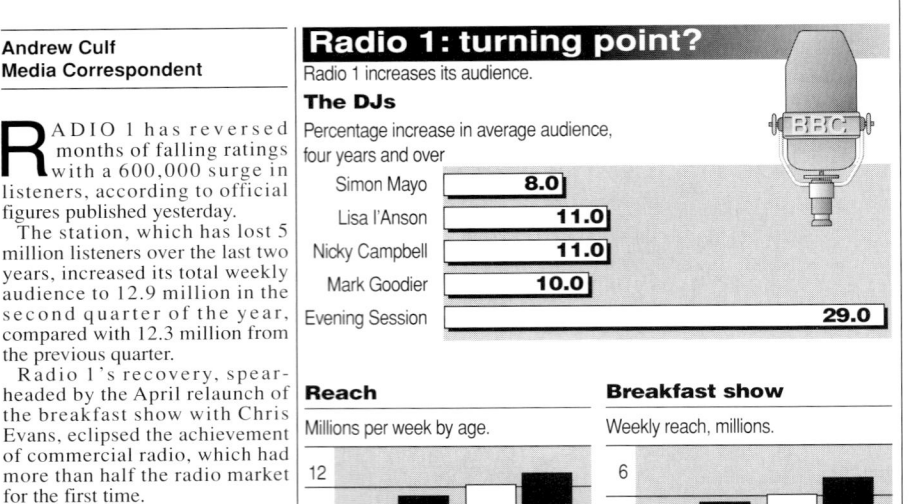

Andrew Culf
Media Correspondent

RADIO 1 has reversed months of falling ratings with a 600,000 surge in listeners, according to official figures published yesterday.

The station, which has lost 5 million listeners over the last two years, increased its total weekly audience to 12.9 million in the second quarter of the year, compared with 12.3 million from the previous quarter.

Radio 1's recovery, spearheaded by the April relaunch of the breakfast show with Chris Evans, eclipsed the achievement of commercial radio, which had more than half the radio market for the first time.

Matthew Bannister, controller of Radio 1, said "Chris Evans has been a major success but our daytime shows and our distinctive evening output have shown significant increases."

He saw the figures as vindication of the repositioning of Radio 1, aiming it at younger listeners.

Radio 1's audience in the 15-plus age group was 11.1 million in the second quarter of 1995, according to figures from Rajar (Radio Joint Audience Research Limited), compared to 12.3 million for the same period last year.

But there was a 600,000 increase in the total audience between the first and second quarter of 1995. Excluding under-15s, the rise between the two quarters was from 10.5 million to 11.1 million, and including children from 12.3 million to 12.9 million.

Sue Farr, BBC Radio's head of marketing and publicity, denied suggestions Radio 1 had spent nearly £5 a head in marketing campaigns, although she said the network had received priority treatment. A £2 million poster and press campaign was launched earlier this year and a trailer about the station is being screened in cinemas.

The total audience for the breakfast show has increased from 6.2 million to 6.8 million since the arrival of Chris Evans, who recently signed a new contract to stay with Radio 1 until the end of 1996.

The station's daytime presenters, including Simon Mayo, Lisa l'Anson, Nicky Campbell and Mark Goodier all recorded increases of between 8 and 11 per cent in the second quarter.

The BBC's other success story was Radio 5 Live, with a 700,000 increase year-on-year.

Commercial radio, with 28.6 million listeners a week, attracted an extra 895,000 over the past three months. The sector, which had 38.9 per cent of the radio cake two years ago, passed the 50 per cent audience share barrier for the first time.

Radio 1: turning point?
Radio 1 increases its audience.

The DJs
Percentage increase in average audience, four years and over

DJ	%
Simon Mayo	8.0
Lisa l'Anson	11.0
Nicky Campbell	11.0
Mark Goodier	10.0
Evening Session	29.0

Reach
Millions per week by age.
Over 15 years / Over 4 years
□ Q1 ■ Q2
Source: RAJAR/RSL

Breakfast show
Weekly reach, millions.
Over 15 years / Over 4 years
□ Q1 (before Chris Evans)
■ Q2 (after Chris Evans)

▶ If you want information about radio audience measurement you should contact the Radio Joint Audience Research Ltd (RAJAR), Collier House, 163-169 Brompton Road, London SW3 1PY.

Academic research

Universities conduct academic research. They are not researching for commercial purposes (though some research may be commissioned or supported by organisations such as UNESCO or the Broadcast Standards Council) but to explore an idea for its own sake or because it helps people's understanding.

In 1976 the Glasgow University Media Group published their first findings following their analysis of television news. The group were interested in how conflicts between unions and employers were reported. They recorded and analysed thousands of hours of television reporting of industrial conflict and demonstrated that the coverage was biased against workers and in favour of management. There seemed to be underlying assumptions made by the people who made the news programme that strikes were harmful and that management exercising power was legitimate, but workers exercising power was wrong.

The group also analysed the coverage of the 1984–85 miners' strike and concluded that successful manipulation of the news by the Coal Board and the government helped to defeat the miners. They showed that the news agenda was dominated by a support for those miners who were returning to work, called 'drift back' by the Coal Board (a term accepted by the media) and a criticism of picket-line violence. Issues such as the plans to close pits by the Coal Board and police provocation of the strikers were largely ignored by the media.

Academic research is conducted at places such as The Centre for Mass Communication at Leicester University. The Centre opened in 1966. Among its research interests in 1995 were:
- how pop music figures are constructed into 'stars'
- the production and reception of science programmes in the mass media
- the effects of satellite and cable television on viewers
- the role of television in food choice
- the gendering of public knowledge in television programmes
- the media use and preferences of ethnic minorities.

▶ More information about current academic research at the Centre can be obtained from The Centre for Mass Communication Research, University of Leicester, 104 Regent Road, Leicester, LE1 7LT.

How to conduct research
- Observe carefully. You need to know what it is you are looking for, what to study and what to ignore.
- Record accurately what you observe.
- Define your terms precisely. If you are studying the effects of television violence on children, you need to say what you mean by violence. Do you mean just physical violence or would you include verbal violence?
- Distinguish between cause and correlation. If you discover in your research that people who are more disposed to violent behaviour also watch more crime programmes on television, you cannot say that therefore the television watching caused the behaviour. You have simply established a correlation.
- Don't let your personal feelings affect your research or your findings.
- Choose representative samples.
- Be honest with your conclusions.

Pitfalls
When you are researching be prepared for:
- people telling you lies
- people not being well-informed but having lots to say
- people having different perspectives on the same event
- people just saying things to get away from you.

Research techniques

Surveys
Surveys can be done by asking people questions and filling out a form or they can be questionnaires which are sent to people to fill in and return.

Conducting a survey is a good way of *quantifying* something, such as how many 12–13 year-olds read comics or how often students listen to the radio, when and in what circumstances. It is also a relatively cheap method of research.

You need to be careful about the kinds of people you are surveying. You must select a relevant sample which is a cross-section of the group you are investigating (*representative sampling*). If, for instance, you want to find out about comic readership in a particular age group you would need to survey boys and girls, children from different geographical areas, of different ethnic origin and from different social backgrounds, otherwise you could end up making a false generalisation based on an atypical group.

Surveys must have a clear *focus*. In other words you must know exactly what it is you are investigating. Your results will be more reliable if you limit the focus of your investigation.

It is always worth *pre-testing* your survey with a small sample group so that you will be able to spot problems such as ambiguous questions.

Questions need to be constructed carefully. Too *open* a question – 'What do you think about Australian soap operas?' – gives you so many varied answers that you cannot quantify them. Too *closed* a question – 'Do you think that Australian soap operas are a) very interesting, b) quite interesting, c) neither interesting nor boring, d) pretty boring or e) very boring?' – is likely to prevent respondents giving their real opinions because the responses are oversimplified. A loaded question – 'Why do you think so many people watch trashy Australian soap operas?' may force people into agreeing with your point of view rather than stating their own.

You also need to make sure that questions are understandable, that they are in a logical order, that there are not too many (so that respondents do not give up) and that their intention is clear.

Content analysis

Here is an example of the results of content analysis conducted by the Broadcasting Standards Council (1990) to investigate sexual stereotyping in advertising.

- 64% of women as opposed to 22% of men were considered 'attractive'. (Defined as the type of person who might appear in a fashion magazine.)
- 50% of women and only 30% of men fell into the 21–30 age group.
- 75% of the over-30s characters were men.
- Women were twice as likely as men to be seen doing housework.
- Women were twice as likely as men to be married.
- Men outnumbered women in adverts by two to one.
- 89% of advertisements had a male voice over.
- 38% of men were represented as being in some sort of paid employment, while only 16% of women were.

To provide information like this requires a close and regular viewing of television advertising and a careful recording of observations. The terms being used in the survey have to be understood by those conducting it. Here it would be easy enough to decide whether characters were male or female, but some definition of 'housework' would have to be agreed.

Content analysis can be fairly easy to organise and inexpensive to conduct, especially if you are analysing print media. A good library should be able to provide you with a wide selection of contemporary newspapers and magazines so that you can investigate current trends and social movements. It should also have collections of newspapers on microfilm or CD Rom.

This kind of analysis also lessens the problem of the researcher getting in the way of the research as there is no human interaction with its problems of people acting abnormally if they are being observed.

A disadvantage of the method is that large samples have to be taken so that they are representative.

Focus groups

Focus groups are small discussion groups which talk fairly freely about the topic being investigated. They are often used by media organisations to find out people's attitudes to and opinions of a product or service.

If you are organising such a group, your role should be to encourage people to talk as freely and honestly as possible. The aim is not to reach agreement but to explore individual differences and shades of opinion. The results of such investigations are used by media producers to modify their products.

If you are organising a focus group to evaluate, for instance, a teenage magazine, you should aim to gather between four and twelve readers, most of whom are regular readers of the magazine. Your task is then to set a mood where people feel free to contribute to the discussion and are not intimidated, but you must also be able to keep the conversation to the point. You should aim to accept all opinions without judgement. If you agree with a point of view this might prevent someone else from expressing a divergent view. Rejection can also keep people quiet when you need them to talk.

Professional researchers have found that it is better not to have a focus group with very different social classes – for instance it is said that 'If you mix Ds and Es with As and Bs the Ds and Es will keep quiet.' Single sex groups work better than mixed groups, and it is better not to have too much divergence of opinion as this can lead to conflict rather than insight.

▶ Audience segments, page 16

Unobtrusive audio or video taping of the discussion can help you to analyse the evidence more thoroughly.

CASE STUDY   Focus groups

Here is an extract from a verbatim report of a focus group being asked questions about a local newspaper's content. The group consisted of female readers aged 45+. (Other groups interviewed were male readers aged 45+, female non-readers under 45 and male non-readers under 45.)

Interviewer: What about the supplements? Do you read those?
A: Well, it depends what's in it.
B: There's a big one tonight and there was last night.
C: Last night's was about word processors or something.
Int: Was that an ad?
B: Well I don't know why it was in. To be honest the average person wouldn't know what a word processor was. It was all about the new technology, how the paper is now produced and I wouldn't think most people are interested in seeing people at a word processor and how the journalist writes something up and then the editor calls it up on a VDU and takes things out and puts things in. I mean I understand it because I've done it, but most people wouldn't know what they are talking about.
A: They are not interested, the average person really.
B: I don't know if it was an ad or not.
C: I think a lot of people would be interested to find out how it works.
A: I mean I'm not interested in computers. A lot of kids are but I bet they didn't read it.
Int: What about other supplements that you get with the local paper? Can you tell me about some of those?

A: Pop artists – well that's for the kids isn't it?
B: There's supplements about houses and cars. And football supplements.
C: There's a lot on pop isn't there?
A: There's generally a few pages on pop and this and that and the other and groups that I've never heard of. The kids would go for that part. But I don't mind that.
B: You see if they do supplements on local shopping areas, it's like an advertising supplement. You know, you ask the local baker and the butcher to put an advert in, probably cheaply, and that's how you get a small supplement. I suppose that's why you don't get too much news. And so on....

Figure 13.6 A focus group discussing a local newspaper

From these often very long transcripts the researcher then has to draw conclusions like this:

Sections and features of the paper liked

Individuals expressed their own personal preferences, but the following lists those (apart from news content) which were frequently mentioned with approval:

- classified adverts
- deaths births and marriages
- sport
- court round up
- 25 years ago
- problem page
- letters
- crosswords
- bingo
- Stars (horoscopes).

Overall the deaths column appeared to have the widest readership:

- 'See what's happening. See who's dead.' (Male reader)
- 'In fact it's the first thing you read really, isn't it? Death's births and marriages.'(Female reader)

▶ Scannell, Schlesinger and Sparks, 1992, *Culture and Power*, Sage Publications

Depth interviews

These are conducted on a one-to-one basis and can take a long time because they are extended conversations aimed at finding reasons for people's behaviour or opinions which may at first be hidden. The longer people talk the more they are likely to reveal.

Depth interviewing is used by commercial companies to discover hidden reasons why people buy a commodity or choose a particular brand. A typical use in media would be in audience research to find out why people are regular viewers of a particular soap opera. Or it could be used to find out how different people interpret a controversial documentary.

An interesting application of the technique can be found in an essay in *Culture and Power* (Sage Publications edited by Scannell, Schlesinger and Sparks). It is called 'Reading reception: mediation and transparency in viewers' reception of a television programme' and is by Kay Richardson and John Corner. They were interested in finding out how people made sense of a documentary called *A Fair Day's Fiddle* from the *Brass Tacks* series, and in particular, how far viewers took what they saw at face value and how far they believed they were being manipulated by the programme makers.

The researchers were careful in their selection of interviewees to choose a variety of people (a mix of gender, class and occupation) so that their accounts of the programme would be *significantly different*. They also decided not to use group discussion because of the problems of having dominant personalities in groups who could inhibit individual interpretations, the difficulty in using follow-up questions and the pressure towards agreement caused by the group.

> 'The interviews were one-to-one sessions of about one hour's duration conducted immediately after each viewing. We chose this method because of our interest in the interpretive process, and our sequencing and manner of questioning often varied from one interview to the next in our attempt to avoid the kinds of answers that are elicited in questionnaire based audience research. We wished to explore the subtleties of viewer understandings even if this had to be at the expense of direct comparability of different accounts.' 'Reading reception' (Richardson and Corner) in *Culture and Power*, page 162.

If you are interested in depth interviewing you could attempt to repeat Richardson and Corner's investigation with five or six viewers giving their interpretations of a documentary which studies a controversial subject.

A Activity

Interpreting research findings

Look at the circulation figures for newspapers printed in Chapter 1 on page 23.

- Prepare a graph which relates the cost of full page advertising with readership figures.
- Prepare a bar chart ranking daily newspapers according to their readership figures.
- Prepare pie charts for three different newspaper titles to show the percentage of readers from different age groups.

Which popular tabloid daily newspaper would you choose to advertise each of the following products in and why?

- inexpensive holidays for the over-50s living in the north-west of England
- inexpensive sporty cars
- top of the range cosmetics for females.

Prepare a graph to show the relative changes in circulation of five different newspapers.

Assignment

Conducting your own research

Content analysis

In ten episodes of a soap opera count the number of times characters apologise. Write about the importance of the apology in the narrative structure of the programme.

Depth analysis

Interview several young children who are keen on either *Neighbours* or *Home and Away* about their knowledge and awareness of moral dilemmas in the programmes and report on how effective the programmes are in helping young people to develop their own moral codes.

Conduct a focus group meeting with young people who are regular listeners about the content of radio programmes aimed at the teenage market. Summarise your findings and send copies to the radio stations whose programmes are mentioned.

14 Marketing

Advanced GNVQ Media requires that you should 'market' your own products. This means having to design a marketing plan and produce draft advertising material for your products. You should then present these to an audience. As you do this you are expected to learn about the principles and methods of marketing media products.

This chapter helps you to understand media marketing. First, it shows you how to investigate the marketing activities of a media organisation, in this case a local newspaper. Second, it gives a case study of a marketing activity which is based on the improvement of an existing product. There follows a detailed case study of an advertising campaign produced by an advertising agency for an electric company. Before the chapter ends with advice on how to market your own media product, there is an explanation of how a film is marketed. The chapter is organised into the following sections:
- Marketing activities of a regional newspaper
- Case study: the *Herts Herald*
- How to prepare a marketing plan
- Case study: Northern Electric Super Tariff Campaign
- Marketing a film
- Marketing your own product.

Introduction to marketing

Marketing is about the promotion and distribution of a commodity for sale. You can think of media marketing by describing your own consumption of the media. What newspapers or magazines do you read? What films, television and videos do you pay to see or choose to watch? Which radio programmes do you listen to? Make a list of those things that you pay for directly and those that you do not pay for directly. Those that you do not pay for directly will have been paid for (bought) by someone else. A few media products are financed by the producer – promotional magazines for instance. BBC programmes are paid for by a licence fee, while a large number of products are financed by advertisers (Channel 4 television programmes for instance).

Marketing activities of a regional newspaper

If you have to investigate the marketing activities of a media producer and assess their effectiveness it would be best to approach an organisation for up-to-date information. It should be possible for a marketing specialist from a local media company to visit your college or school and give you this information.

Some information can be obtained from company documents. The most accessible are those which are produced for advertisers, but these will only give you part of the picture. It is far better for schools and colleges to nurture a close working relationship with a local media company so that you can arrange access to people as well as recorded information.

Once you have established that link, however, it pays to know something in general terms about how marketing departments are organised so that you can ask pertinent questions. Here is a rough guide to the marketing operations of a regional newspaper.

Marketing in media terms usually involves selling the product to an audience (e.g. a newspaper to its readers) and then selling that audience to advertisers. That is to say the advertisers will buy space in the paper in order to get a message to the readers.

All newspapers have a *sales and promotions department* (sometimes divided into two departments). This department will be responsible for trying to maintain or improve sales, but it may also earn revenue for the company.

A key to effective sales is to have an efficient *distribution* system. Newspapers must be on sale in the right place at the right time or sales will be lost. A newspaper has no shelf life. People do not buy yesterday's dailies or last week's weeklies. This means the company has to organise a network of outlets which will include newsagents, street sellers and home delivery people. It also means having a reliable transport system with carefully worked out routes.

You can find out about many *promotional* activities by looking at the newspaper itself.

Figure 14.1 An example of a reader offer

FREE! New shampoo for you

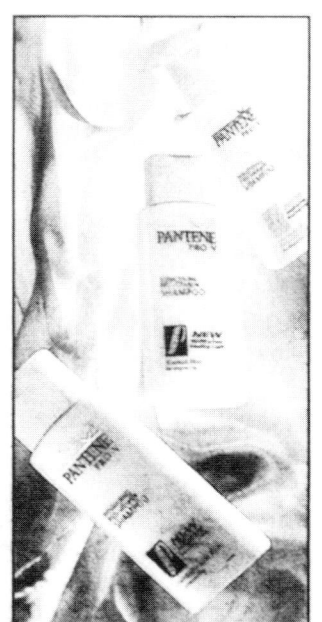

OUT with the old, in with the new with a FREE bottle of new Pantene Pro-V shampoo!

We've teamed up with Pantene Pro-V to give every *Mirror Woman* reader the chance to sample the new improved Pantene Pro-V shampoo without paying a penny. With your free bottle of Pantene Pro-V your hair will feel as good as it looks.

New Pantene Pro-V shampoos are the latest development in haircare technology.

They have been technically proven to improve the texture of hair, leaving it super silky, shiny and looking and feeling healthier than ever before.

The patented protective ingredients in the new Pro-Vitamin shampoo formula help protect and strengthen hair. Tests show that hair will now be more resistant and therefore more able to cope with the damage and torture it faces every day.

To claim a coupon for a FREE bottle of new Pantene Pro-V shampoo simply send in a full-size empty bottle of ANY shampoo complete with two tokens and a special voucher from the *Daily Mirror*. Token One is printed today and Token Two along with the voucher will be printed tomorrow.

Fill in your name and address and send the voucher, two tokens and your empty bottle of shampoo to: "In With The New Pantene Pro-V", Freepost (TK2), PO Box 6, Hampton, Middlesex, TW12 2BR.

Only complete, legible and original applications (2 tokens plus voucher), received with the bottle in a strong envelope will be valid.

Applications must be received by February 16, 1996. This offer is available in the UK and Republic of Ireland only. Only one entry per household. Allow 28 days for delivery of your coupon.

Coupon is only redeemable against 200ml 2 in 1 shampoos or 250ml shampoos at all leading stores.

Daily Mirror
PANTENE PRO-V
TOKEN 1

You may find *reader offers*. These are meant to give added value to the newspaper and a reason to buy for some people. They are also revenue earners. The newspaper negotiates a deal with a wholesale company to offer a particular item for sale exclusively through the newspaper. Usually a purchaser will have to send a reply slip from the paper to the wholesale firm. The newspaper takes a percentage of sales. The offers are often linked with seasons with, for instance, sunglasses on sale in the summer.

Reader *travel schemes* are negotiated with travel firms who offer a package such as travel, accommodation and tickets for shows and concerts. The schemes are seen as a service to readers and therefore an inducement to buy the paper. They are also a revenue earner as the newspaper receives a comission for sales.

Regular *competitions* such as *Spot the Ball* and *Bingo* are an inducement to buy the paper as people need material found in the paper in order to take part. Such competitions are organised and administered in-house as they earn revenue. Other competitions are provided by firms wishing to introduce a new product. The firms provide the competition, usually offering a choice of activities at different levels, and prizes. They pay the newspaper for the space taken by the competition, usually at standard advertising rates. The competitions are easy to do to encourage maximum participation and therefore product awareness.

Shopping discount cards are offered to loyal readers – seen as people who have regular home delivery of the newspaper. These are publicised to convert casual readers into regular readers. The newspaper negotiates special offers with local retailers and organisations. Shops will sometimes offer goods at a loss in order to attract customers into the store to buy other items. A theatre with an undersold show may offer two seats for the price of one.

External promotional *events* are often linked with fairs and shows. Usually bulk sales of the paper are negotiated with the event organisers who will buy large numbers of copies of the newspaper at a reduced price to give away to those who attend the event, in exchange for in-paper publicity.

A newspaper may also have a *media communications* or advertising department. This deals with public relations, prepares news releases for other media and advertises the paper through in-house advertising, radio and television commercials, posters and so on. It is concerned with developing a positive corporate image of the organisation and might organise special events and corporate hospitality.

Another major type of marketing activity is *marketing intelligence and research*. This involves, among other things, *tracking the progress* of competitors, their sales and marketing strategies. For instance, many paid-for newspapers are in competition for advertising revenue with free sheets. Tracking here would mean looking at the adverts the free sheet is running and finding out what they cost. Advertising departments will show the results of the tracking as 'market share', that is the newspaper's share of the total amount of advertising money which has been spent.

Marketing is concerned with product development, that is changing the content and style of the publication in the light of research into readers' reactions. Newspapers often conduct their own readership surveys based on in-depth questioning of a random but representative sample of readers. The purpose of such surveys is to provide information for both advertisers and the newspaper's editorial department.

Marketing

A Activity

Here are some typical questions from a newspaper's readership survey. What use would the paper make of the information gained from the responses to these questions? Use the questions to design a questionnaire which has spaces for answers. You can then use this for your own research.

1. I am now going to ask you about those papers you said you had read or looked at most recently. For each one I'd like you to tell me how long you spent reading the most recent issue. (The titles are then read out.)

2. Approximately how long do you spend reading the following sections of the paper? (There follows a list including property adverts, job adverts, television page, motoring section and so on.)

3. In a local newspaper how interested are you in reading a) local news, b) national news, and c) international news? (The possible responses range from 'very interested' to 'not interested at all'.)

4. I am going to read some statements about local paid-for newspapers and I'd like you to tell me how much you agree or disagree with them:
   - It looks after the interests of people like me.
   - It is well laid out and easy to read.
   - I can believe what I read in my local paper.
   - It provides good value for money.
   - It is modern and up to date.
   - It is entertaining to read.

5. How likely is it that you will buy a new or used car in the next twelve months?

6. Do you use any of these outlets for servicing your car? (Followed by a comprehensive list of local garages.)

7. Which store do you use for your major food shopping? (Followed by a list of stores.)

8. Which towns or shopping centres do you consider when you want to buy
   - clothes
   - electrical goods
   - furniture, DIY equipment
   - food and groceries? (A separate response for each one.)

9. Which football team do you support?

Marketing departments sometimes *investigate new markets* for products. They could give advice and information about a proposed extension of a circulation area or an attempt to attract younger readers. They monitor test marketing of a new product or venture. They could, for instance, check on a small sample of people what the effects of a 20% reduction in the cover price of a paper would be.

249

Marketing

CASE STUDY The *Herts Herald*

Here is an extract from marketing strategy for a local newspaper based on a real business but with a fictional name. It sought not to design and sell a new product but to improve the quality of an existing one, a local paper, to halt a decline in its sales. In order to do this it had to identify accurately the reasons for the decline of sales, to devise ways of solving the problems and to plan the resources needed to do this.

Marketing strategy overview

The paper has had a declining circulation over the last year, with an annual drop in sales of 3%. The *Herald* is seen as offering poor value for money compared with its rivals. This is especially true when on some days it drops to 24 pages.

In order to hold sales at last year's levels the *Herald* needs to be seen as good value for money by its readers.

It is our intention to introduce two supplements – one on Sport on Mondays and another on Lifestyles on Wednesdays.

We intend to introduce full colour pictures on front and back pages and in the supplements.

Increasing paging for the *Herald*

The Henley Centre's report on the *Herald* and its competitors pointed out that papers with long-term success are thicker than those that are long-term under-performers.

Pagination of the Herts Herald *and its competitors*

	Monday	Tuesday	Wednesday	Thursday	Friday	Saturday
Herald	24	24	24	52	44	24
Welwyn Star	40	40	44	52	76	40
Shire Express	48	40	56	80	80	44

Proposal

Over the next financial year the *Herald* will aim to address the problem of providing value for money by:

1. Mondays – introducing an eight-page sports supplement with full colour pictures covering Saturday's sports fixtures.
2. Wednesdays – introducing an eight-page supplement on contemporary lifestyles aimed at young married couples beginning families.
3. Currently the *Herald* produces four pages of sport on a Monday. This will be expanded to eight pages and moved to the centre of the paper. Sport is an area of major interest and there is scope for improvement in quantity and quality of coverage. An essential element in this is the inclusion of full colour pictures and a colour mini-lab will have to be purchased to speed the developing of film. An extra writer will be recruited to join the sports team.

Costs

1 writer for full year plus £2 000 on costs.	£18 000
Purchase of mini-lab	£62 000
Materials for extra pages (e.g. newsprint)	£17 000
Total £99 000	

New lifestyle supplement

There are many lifestyle topics which the *Herald* fails to cover in depth and in some cases at all. The new full colour supplement will address the following topics:

- Health – how to stay fit and advice on illness.
- Consumer Advice – what to buy and where to get it. New products on the market and warnings about dangerous goods.
- Family Finance – mortgages, tax, insurance, investment.
- Eating out guide.
- Comprehensive out and about guide.
- Food and drink – recipes and a wine column.
- Women's issues.
- Childcare.
- Travel – what's a good deal, holiday tips.
- Fashion and beauty – aimed at the average woman, not the supermodel.

Costs for new financial year

Materials	£32 000
Editorial material bought in	£12 000
Total	£44 000

Revenue

To cover part of the costs the cover price of the *Herald* will be increased by 1p, generating additional revenue in one year of £52 000. Advertising revenue for new supplements is estimated at £10 000. A sales increase of 1% because of added value will produce £13 900 in one year.

A Activity

Prepare a proposal for a teenage supplement for the *Herald* as an alternative to the lifestyle proposal. Describe its contents and and argue that it makes better commercial sense to attract a younger audience, especially as your competitors do not have much editorial content aimed at this segment of the market. Devise a half page press advert and a point-of-sale poster to inform the public of this new 'value-for-money' content.

PROFILE Keith Metcalfe: Newspaper Sales Director for North East Press

'A newspaper lives or dies by its circulation figures. It needs the revenue from the cover price, but its advertising rates depend on the 'audience' (readers) it can sell to customers. The higher the circulation figures, the more a newspaper can charge for its advertising space.

A newspaper's readership is higher than its circulation, as more than one person, normally, will read a single copy of the paper.

The main sales outlets are newsagents who order papers on a sale or return basis and keep a percentage of the selling price.

We try to increase the proportion of deliveries as these orders are reliable and predictable.

Appoximately one-third of the company's revenue is achieved from the cover price.

Three sales managers at each of the three evening titles control both full and part-time sales staff. The sales managers report directly to me.

There are three key areas in newspaper sales: canvassing, home delivery/newsagents and single copy sales.

As sales director I am responsible for formulating a marketing strategy to maintain and increase newspaper sales. The strategies have objectives and targets to complete the overall strategy. Each objective is broken down into key tasks and tactics. The strategies can be both long and short term.

My job is to ensure that these strategies are achieved so that the long-term future of the company is secured.'

How to prepare a marketing plan

The following case study shows how a professional advertising agency goes about preparing a marketing plan and developing a marketing strategy for a particular product or service.

CASE STUDY   Northern Electric - Super Tariff Campaign

The advertising agency which developed the Super Tariff campaign for Northern Electric was Martin Tait Redheads.

Identifying the problem

The Electricity industry was losing business to Gas especially in the Northern Electric area. The main reasons for this were:

- There was a strong consumer preference for gas home heating.
- Negative attitudes to electric storage heaters produced by problems with the systems in their early stages of development still prevail.
- Consumers perceive electricity to be high cost and to lack controllability.
- Storage heaters are not perceived by the consumer as a genuine central heating system.
- New house builders install the heating system they think appeals more to consumers, which is gas.

Why had this situation developed? Research findings were studied to discover the reasons.

The factors which created this situation were:

1. A higher gas advertising budget led to a low share of 'voice' (amount of advertising messages) for electric.
2. The gas advertising message 'Cookability – that's the beauty of gas' was very effective.
3. Gas is the preferred fuel. Given the choice, 54% of customers would prefer to use gas cookers, while only 21% would prefer electric.

Marketing

KEY FACTORS

1. HIGHER GAS ADVERTISING SPENDS
   – LOW SHARE OF VOICE FOR ELECTRIC

UK FREESTANDING MARKET – SHARE OF VOICE

	85	86	87	88	89	90
ELECTRIC	33%	44%	40%	47%	43%	37%
GAS	65%	56%	60%	53%	57%	63%

Figure 14.2 Key factors

4 These preferences are entrenched and reinforced by parents' preferences and school.

Figure 14.3 shows graphically the market situation for electric cooker sales compared with gas cooker sales.

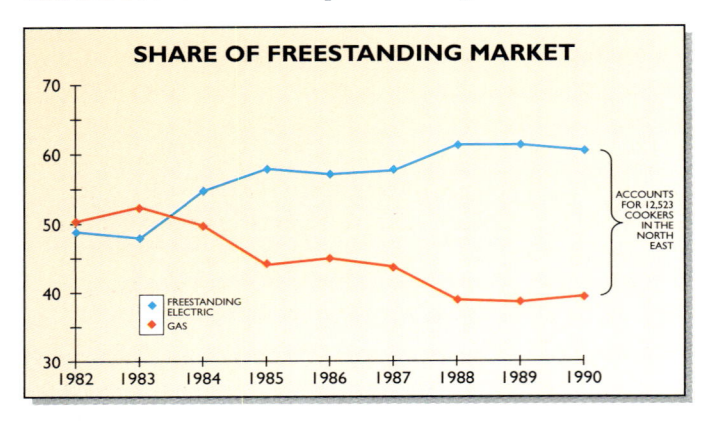

Figure 14.3 Share of the free-standing market

Next, a strategy for the advertising campaign had to be devised.

The campaign objectives

The campaign objectives were:
1 To halt the preference towards using gas for cooking and heating in the home.
2 To develop a growth in the use of electricity for heating and cooking.
3 To establish electricity as the preferred fuel for cooking.

The challenge was to reposition electric cookers and heating systems in the minds of the consumers. This was seen as a long-term process.

The advertising agency identified four **positioning statements** for electric cookers, that is the basic messages they wanted consumers to remember. These positioning statements were backed up by a rationale, that is the reasoning behind the statements.

POSITIONING STATEMENTS

1. YOU'LL ENJOY COOKING WITH ELECTRIC
2. IT'S SO EASY TO USE
3. CLOSE RELATIONSHIP BETWEEN COOK AND COOKER
4. ELECTRIC COOKERS ARE COOKERS OF TODAY

Figure 14.4 Positioning statements

RATIONALE

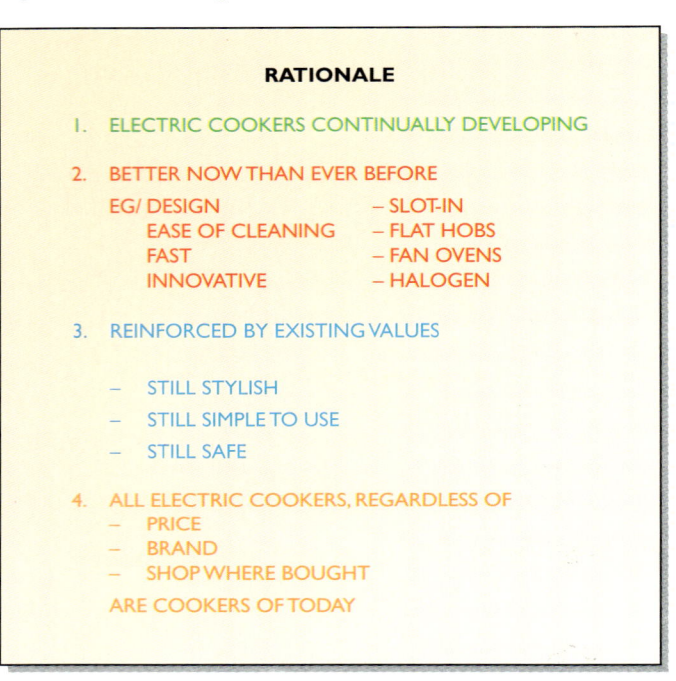

1. ELECTRIC COOKERS CONTINUALLY DEVELOPING

2. BETTER NOW THAN EVER BEFORE
   EG/ DESIGN   – SLOT-IN
   EASE OF CLEANING   – FLAT HOBS
   FAST   – FAN OVENS
   INNOVATIVE   – HALOGEN

3. REINFORCED BY EXISTING VALUES
   – STILL STYLISH
   – STILL SIMPLE TO USE
   – STILL SAFE

4. ALL ELECTRIC COOKERS, REGARDLESS OF
   – PRICE
   – BRAND
   – SHOP WHERE BOUGHT
   ARE COOKERS OF TODAY

Figure 14.5 Rationale

The desired responses were:

DESIRED RESPONSE

ELECTRIC COOKERS GIVE ME CONFIDENCE

"GEORGE, WE MUST HAVE A LOOK AT ELECTRIC COOKERS".

Figure 14.6 Desired response

The atmosphere of the advertising messages was:

ATMOSPHERE

1. WARM AND FRIENDLY
2. MODERN BUT NOT PRETENTIOUS
3. NOT OVER ASPIRATIONAL
4. ACCESSIBLE AND COMFORTABLE

Figure 14.7 Atmosphere

On an image map the desired result looked like this:

IMAGE MAP
REPOSITIONING ELECTRIC:

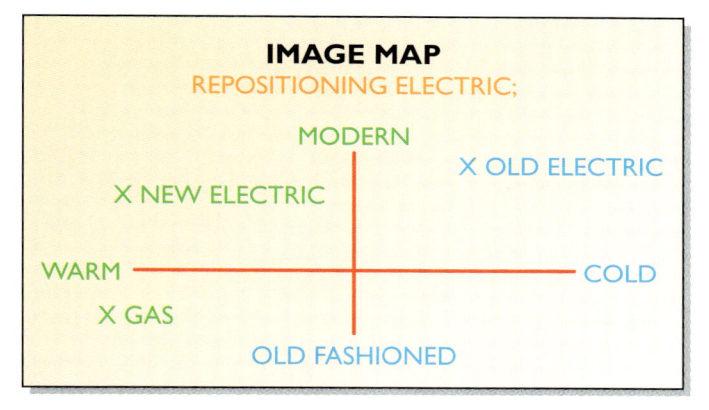

```
              MODERN
                        X OLD ELECTRIC
  X NEW ELECTRIC

WARM ─────────────┼───────────── COLD
  X GAS
            OLD FASHIONED
```

Figure 14.8 Image map

A multi-media campaign was suggested. The advertising message was to be built around the image of Cilla Black. She was chosen because she had already been used by Northern Electric in their previous heating adverts, because she was well known from her high rating television shows and because 'she commands attention whenever she appears'.

A Activity

Collect current examples of personalities used in advertising campaigns and discuss with your group why these people have been chosen. Which personalities would you choose to sell/publicise:
- a new alcoholic drink targeted at males aged 18-25
- the New Labour Party
- an anti-drug campaign
- a new teenage magazine for girls which concentrates on pop music and sex.

The marketing activities decided on now had to be scheduled.

Media schedule

There were two important criteria which determined the scheduling of the campaign. One was that electric cooker sales patterns had two peaks – April and September to November. The other was that gas advertising always predominated from April to September.

The agency decided to advertise in two bursts – one in April and the other from September to October.

Television advertising would be used for an initial impact. Adverts in the local press would be used to add frequency and maintain momentum to the campaign. The main advantages of television advertising are that it gives a 95% coverage of the target area and has high impact.

Posters using high coverage and frequency and top sites would act as **reminder advertising**. The top 48 poster sites in the region were chosen because they enabled 'strong coverage and frequency'.

The regional press was selected in preference to the national press because it has 'local authority of voice', is tightly targeted, has high household penetration and is cost efficient.

This coverage is graphically illustrated in Figure 14.9 a **laydown schedule**.

The effect of this coverage in terms of numbers of people being exposed to the advertising is calculated in 'impacts'. Martin Tait Redhead calculated that in the sixth week of the campaign, which was the last week of its first television 'burst' and the first week of its poster campaign, that the impacts had been as follows:

Television impacts (roughly speaking the number of viewers)	4 544 000
Newspaper impacts (number of readers)	2 018 000
Poster impacts (number of motorists and pedestrians who have the opportunity to see the posters)	7 668 000

The costing, negotiating and purchasing of this advertising space is done by the media buying department of the agency.

The details of the campaign were worked on by the creative department of the agency.

Marketing

LAYDOWN SCHEDULE

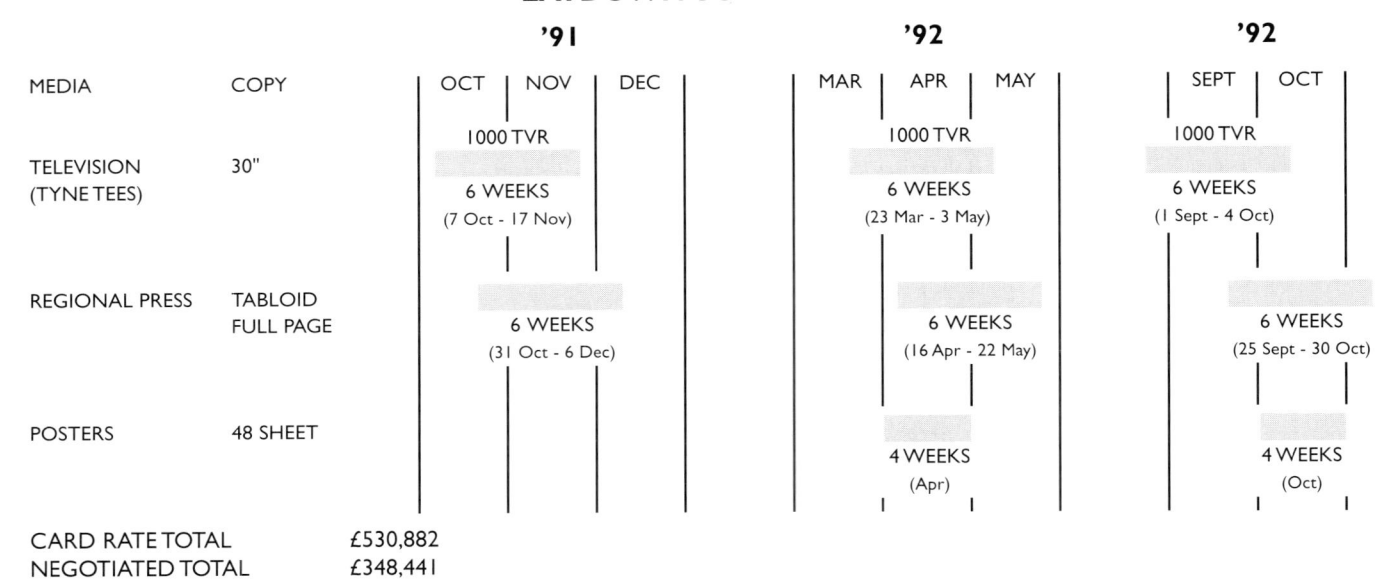

MEDIA	COPY	'91 OCT	NOV	DEC	'92 MAR	APR	MAY	'92 SEPT	OCT
TELEVISION (TYNE TEES)	30"	1000 TVR 6 WEEKS (7 Oct - 17 Nov)			1000 TVR 6 WEEKS (23 Mar - 3 May)			1000 TVR 6 WEEKS (1 Sept - 4 Oct)	
REGIONAL PRESS	TABLOID FULL PAGE		6 WEEKS (31 Oct - 6 Dec)			6 WEEKS (16 Apr - 22 May)			6 WEEKS (25 Sept - 30 Oct)
POSTERS	48 SHEET					4 WEEKS (Apr)			4 WEEKS (Oct)

CARD RATE TOTAL £530,882
NEGOTIATED TOTAL £348,441
NATIONAL EQUIVALENT £8,000,000

Figure 14.9 A laydown schedule

Creative strategy

This team had weekly work-in-progress meetings which were reported to the client within forty-eight hours. The reports showed what action had been decided on and who was responsible for doing it.

The creative department had to produce draft scripts for television commercials as shown in Figure 14.10. They also had to produce full-page adverts to go in the local press, posters, banners for the sides of buses, point-of-sale display signs and brochures.

An example of a standard creative brief which one of the team would be given is shown in Figure 14.11.

Figure 14.10 Draft script for television commercial

```
CLIENT:      Northern Electric           2nd October 1991
CAMPAIGN:    30" TV – Electric Cooking   NEE 09T 1077

VISION: Cilla in kitchen set  AUDIO
                              Cilla: Lets face it
                              chucks, when it comes to
                              cookin' I say the easier
                              the better ...

                              And that's gorra mean
                              cooking' with electric!
                              It's so easy to use...

Mixture of a series of        And talk about easy
cutaway shots of Cilla        control - nifty eh!
demonstrating features and
Cilla close-ups.              And so safe too.

                              It's dead easy to clean -
                              who needs all these fiddly
                              bits?

                              And isn't it Superlookin'
                              too?

                              And with electric, you get
                              a lorra cooker for your
                              money!

Cilla removes meal from       So see what Super cookin'
cooker.                       can do for you!

She smells food and looks     Mmmm ... Well, worra
up.                           you waiting' for?

Freeze frame. Super 5
retail logos
```

Figure 14.11 The creative brief

```
                         CREATIVE BRIEF
CLIENT:  NORTHERN ELECTRIC ENERGY       JOB NO: 2525 797
SUBJECT: SUMMER STORAGE HEATER PROMOTION  DATE: 4.4.90
REQUIREMENT (Campaign, One-off Ad, Brochure, Mark-up, etc)
Press advertisement targeted at older householders (50+) at the middle
lower end of the housing market.
(NB: All ads. will be part of a campaign aimed at a variety of different
audiences, so a generic theme should run throughout).
TECHNICAL DATA (Publications/Sizes, etc)
Half-page landscape (broadsheet 280x366mm), in a range of local press.
DESCRIPTION/BACKGROUND
During May 1st-July 31st, all storage heaters will carry a £50
discount.
Using 'cheapness' as the hook, we need to promote the low cost aspects
of electric heating. If you're looking for low-cost heating, electric
storage heaters combine easy, low cost installation (especially with
the discount), with economical running costs (as cheap to run as any
comparable system). You can install a complete electric home/water
system for as little as £750.
MARKETING OBJECTIVE           ADVERTISING OBJECTIVE
To sell 2,500 storage heaters i. To make the audience aware that
during May 1st-July 31st.        storage heaters are inexpensive
                                 to install and can be run
                                 economically.
                              ii. To stimulate enquiries for
                                  field sales force to follow up.
SINGLE MINDED MESSAGE
You could install a complete electric heating system for as little as
£750.
SUBSTANTIATION FOR THE MESSAGE
i.   £50 discount on all heaters.
ii.  Run on less than half price night-time electricity.
iii. Can be bought on 'special payment' terms.
MANDATORY INCLUSIONS          BUDGET RESTRAINTS
(Logos,Dealers,etc)
i. Northern Electric logo.    £200,000 campaign.
ii. Call to action: Freefone number  Allow 10% (£20,000) for production
and coupon.                          of all campaign elements.
iii. Deferred payment/interest free
credit offer.
TIMING - TO ACCOUNT GROUP:    TO CLIENT:    COPY DATE:
                                            Monday 30th April

SIGNED:
```

254

Marketing

Figure 14.12 *'It's New, it's Cheap...' An example of one of Northern Electric's adverts*

Once the campaign was running, researchers checked its effectiveness. Surveys of cross-sections of the community were made as in Figure 14.13, which shows the numbers of people who claimed to recall television, press and poster advertising for any of the electricity categories – electricity, electric storage heaters, electric water heating and electric cooking. Martin Tait Redheads' own publicity brochure expressed great satisfaction at the 'spectacular recall figures'.

'In a difficult commodity market where gas domination seemed unchallengeable, the Liverpool lass has delivered her Super Cheap Electric Heating message with devastating effect.

Within weeks of the launch, the commercials achieved a spectacular 84% recall; and Northern Electric achieved over 9 000 enquiries in the same few weeks – almost equal to the number of installations carried out in the whole of the previous year.'

Figure 14.13 Media awareness survey

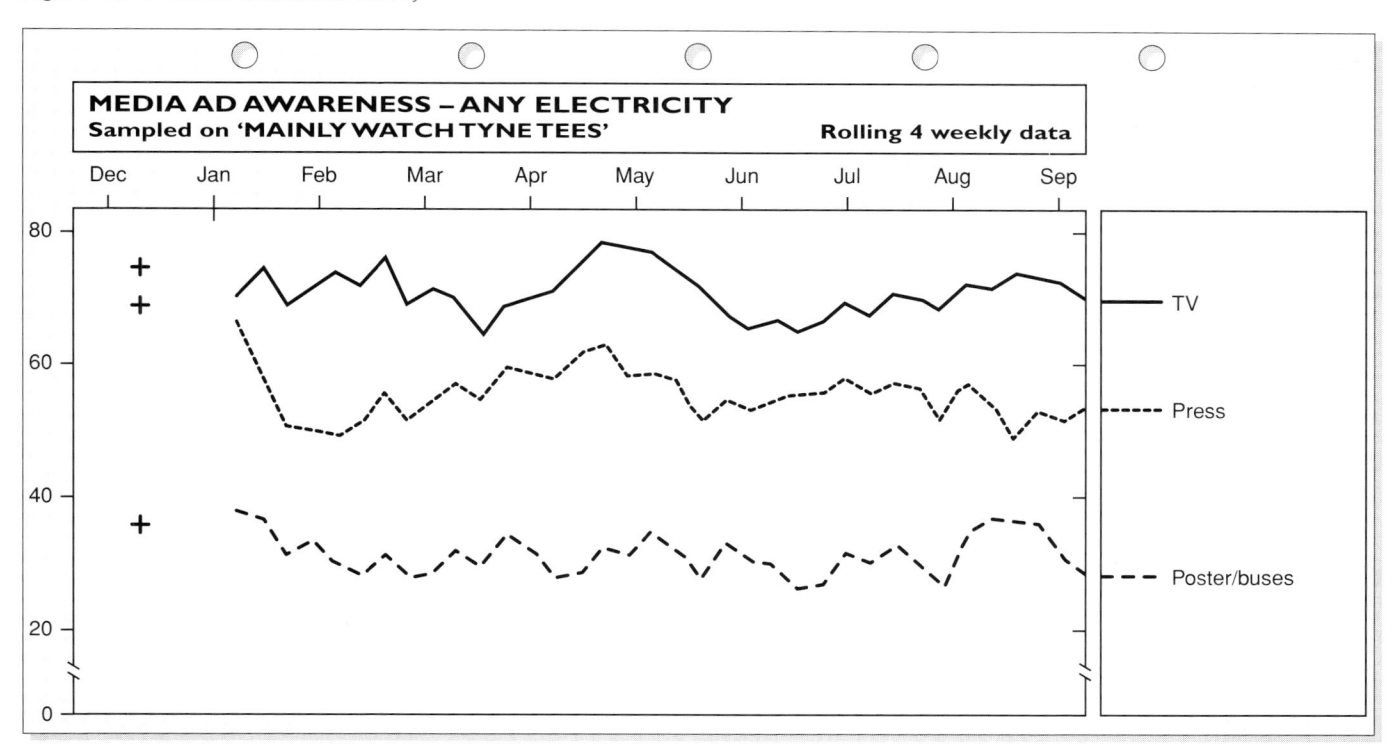

Ethical considerations

Any advertising campaign has to obey certain codes of practice. British Gas complained to the Advertising Standards Authority about the following in one of the leaflets produced for Northern Electric during the campaign examined in the case study above : '...a super heating system is now super easy to install – with no boilers and flues to bother about...The smart Super Heaters themselves cost much less than any other equivalent system...Super Heating is now Super Affordable. Cheaper than gas in most homes...can that be true?...maintenance costs are non-existent having no complex boilers, pumps or flues to be serviced. Take a closer look at our new intelligent meter and at the cost savings of Super Tariff electric heating. You save from the start and you keep on saving.'

British Gas argued that the leaflet implied that running costs would be lower than those of gas. They questioned whether this claim could be supported with evidence. As it could not, the advertisers were obliged by ASA to amend their advertising and to ensure that future claims could be supported.

The Advertising Standards Code

The Advertising Standards Authority, which was set up by the advertising industry, operates a voluntary code which covers the content of all forms of advertising in newspapers, magazines, sales and promotions literature and adverts shown in the cinema. Television and radio advertising are checked by the Independent Television Commission and the Independent Radio Authority.

The basic ASA code, called the *British Code of Advertising and Sales Promotion Practice*, says that adverts should be legal, honest, decent and true. They must not give the wrong information and they must not downgrade competitors.

Here are some of the rules:
- No advert should contain matter which is likely to cause grave or widespread offence.
- No advert should exploit people's inexperience, lack of knowledge or credibility in a way which is detrimental to them.
- No advert should mislead by being inaccurate, ambiguous or exaggerated.
- Opinions about a product can be expressed as long as they are obviously opinions.
- The word 'free' cannot be used if payment is only deferred.
- No advert should play on fear or excite distress.
- Adverts should not incite or condone violence or anti-social behaviour.
- Adverts should be designed so that anyone who looks at them closely can see that they are adverts.
- Adverts should not exploit the credulity, lack of experience or sense of loyalty of children.
- Adverts for alcohol should not encourage excessive drinking and particular care should be taken with adverts which feature powered vehicles of any kind and especially motor cars.

▶ More detail can be obtained from The Advertising Standards Authority, Brook House, 2–16 Torrington Place, London WC1E 7HN)

▶ The Radio Authority's Code of Advertising Standards can be obtained free from The Radio Authority, Holbrook House, 14 Great Queen Street, London WC2B 5DG.

▶ The Independent Television's leaflet *Advertising and Sponsorship on Commercial Television* can be obtained from The ITC, 33 Foley Street, London W1P 7LB.

Marketing a film

Before a film can be seen by the public it has to be *distributed*. Distributors buy the rights to show and publicise a film. Some distributors can be small organisations which specialise in certain types of film. Others will be large multinational organisations which combine production and distribution.

Distributors have to consider when is the best time to release a film. A *schedule* of release time has to be prepared, usually months in advance of the showing. Obvious choices would be to release an animated cartoon aimed at a family audience during the school holidays or a film with seasonal themes such as *Miracle on 34th Street* just before Christmas. The controversial *Reservoir Dogs* was re-released after it attracted publicity but was shown only late at night in many cinemas.

The pattern of release has to be worked out. Sometimes films will be released in London and then shown in the regions, though with multiplex cinemas it is now more likely that popular films will have a nationwide launch.

Some films whose popularity is hard to gauge will be released in a limited number of places to see how the public react to them. *Four Weddings and a Funeral* was released in this way. A film print is expensive (in excess of £1000) to make so distributors have to be careful about how many prints to make, and therefore how many outlets to use, or they could run up big losses.

A Activity

You can begin to think about how a film reaches its audience by asking your group how and why they went to see a recent film. The factors could be:

- other people recommended it
- its stars
- its subject matter
- good reviews
- a trailer
- a poster
- winning awards.

Films can be sold through *advertising*. This involves buying advertising space in the media which are likely to be read, seen or heard by the target audience. Most films are advertised in newspapers and magazines and radio is also used widely because it is cheaper than television and can back up press and poster campaigns. It is especially useful if the film has a strong soundtrack. Television advertising is usually too expensive for all but high budget films. Posters depict key moments from a film and emphasise the film's genre and its stars. Sometimes quotations from critics are included as are references to any awards the film has won.

The advertising campaign starts roughly two weeks before the release date of the film and continues for the first week of its release.

Press releases are sent to journalists in radio, television and the press. They consist of information about the film, such as a plot synopsis and

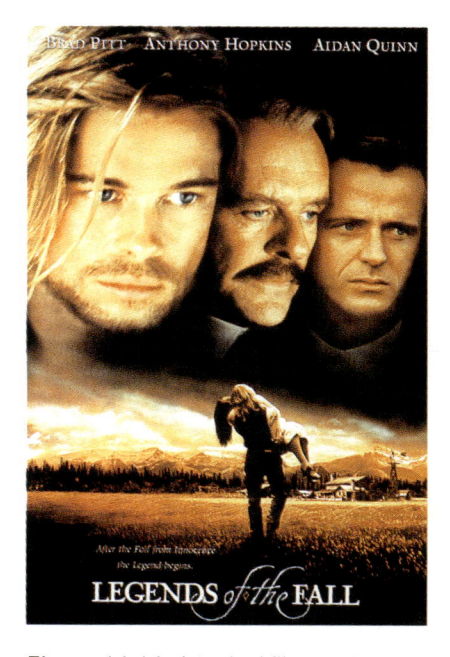

Figure 14.14 A typical film poster

notes about the cast, the director and the production. Stills from the film are included as are video clips of the film, interviews for television and audio clips for radio. Journalists are invited to preview showings of films several days before they are released.

The *trailer* is shown in cinemas a few weeks before the film is released. Trailers aim to show the audience what type of film they are advertising, fix the stars' names and the title in their minds and create a desire to see the film by making people curious.

Star interviews are organised to create maximum publicity. The interviews, across a spectrum of newspapers, magazines, radio and television, are organised by the distributor and are carefully scheduled to reach the target market. The objective is to get the public to be aware of a forthcoming film.

This can also be done by special *preview screenings*. Sometimes specialist audiences are invited, so that when *Backdraft* was shown members of the fire services were invited to the screenings. On other occasions occupational groups with a close contact with the public, such as hairdressers or taxi drivers, are invited. Again the objective is to get people talking about the film.

Merchandising

Merchandising a film means selling products that have their designs based on that film. This can be a lucrative spin off of a popular film, so much so that some production companies, such as Disney and Warner Brothers, have their own retail chains.

In Britain the merchandising sometimes precedes the release of an American film. This happened with *The Lion King*, an animated Disney film aimed at children. *Lion King* products such as pencils, scrapbooks, models and books, were available before the film was released and so acted as advertising for the film.

The same thing can happen with music where the popularity of a record enhances a film's popularity as with Whitney Houston's *I Will Always Love You* in *The Bodyguard*. Sometimes there is a circularity where the music sells the film and the film sells the music as happened with *The Commitments*.

You can study a marketing campaign by tracking a newly released film. You will need to read the press and collect any examples of reviews, previews and any stories about the stars involved in the film. You should also look for specialist film magazines such as *Empire*, and record film review programmes on television and radio. Look for trailers of the film in your local cinema and for posters on display. It might also be possible for your media group to get special permission to attend preview screenings.

Marketing your own product

If you follow the industry model given on pages 251–255, your marketing plan for your own product should be organised under these headings:
- the problem
- campaign objectives
- media schedule
- creative strategy
- evaluation.

As you do not have to actually market your products, this can be a theoretical exercise. However, some students, such as those referred to on page 99 who produced and sold their fanzine, have gone on to sell or at least distribute to a real audience.

▶ Case Study. page 99

One of your main challenges will be making your target audience aware that your product will be available, so you will need some advanced publicity. You will need to know the costs of buying media space. Depending on the scale of your operation this could vary from booking space on a school/college notice board at no cost to buying a primetime television slot. You can find out current costs by asking media organisations for copies of their rate cards.

You should also think about the logistics of distribution. A publication with a small print run can be sold or distibuted by the production group to their peers. On the other hand, you might have to distribute thousands of copies if you are publishing your own community newspaper, in which case you may have to pay a delivery firm.

Dissemination of audio-visual products can simply mean arranging for another group of students to hear or see them. But there are more ambitious possibilities. A group of media studies students from Fulton Manor School in Sittingbourne marketed their CD-ROM *Investigating Newspapers* at a conference of newspaper professionals and educators where they hired an exhibition space. Amber films, an independent co-operative which produces documentaries, hired a cinema for a week to show one of its films, while a group of students who produced an audio tape for children had it played in the intervals of a pantomime at their local theatre.

Assignment

Marketing a video

Devise an advertising campaign for a video you have made showing parents how to help their young children to read.

First of all decide which people or organisations are likely to find the video useful. Then decide which of these might buy your video.
Find out how much it would cost to make copies of the video so that you can price it. (You will also need to add the cost of marketing it.)

Visit some potential buyers and find out what would make them more likely to buy the video and how they would use it.

Discuss with your group what the possible selling points of your video are and how you would use visual images and words to convey these most effectively.

Discuss with your group the means of disseminating your message. You should consider each medium, even television (though you will not be able to buy advertising space, there are slots on some regional channels for public service announcements which are free. You might interest a television editor in your project as a news story which would give you free publicity.)

Draw up a media schedule to show how and when your message will be disseminated.

Design rough drafts of advertising material, such as newsletters, brochures and posters. Work out the costs of your campaign and add these to the price of your video.

15 An overview of United Kingdom media industries

This chapter is intended as a resource and a stimulus for your own research into the situation of the media industries in the United Kingdom. It concentrates on the United Kingdom, but United Kingdom media industries operate in a context of multi-national media organisations and global operations.

The chapter is organised into the following sections:
- Introduction
- Print media
- Broadcasting
- Film and video
- Access and regulation

Introduction to media industries

The media industries in the United Kingdom vary from small businesses, offering services such as the design and writing of advertising copy, to huge companies with international links. Size is important, however, and the media economy is dominated by groups of companies, with a variety of different interests, called 'conglomerates'. This chapter gives an overview across a selection of principal organisations, with a bias towards the larger national media producers.

The operations of these industries reflect various aspects of the geography, history and culture of the United Kingdom. Most of the population resides in the metropolitan areas of England, and there is a concentration of media industries and corresponding employment opportunities in and around London. Although Britain has a very centralised system of communication, Scotland, Wales, Northern Ireland and the 'regions' of England have a very distinctive identity which is reflected in the media. Scotland and Northern Ireland have their own print and broadcast media. Some media producers in Wales produce print and broadcast media in Welsh instead of, or as well as, English.

The United Kingdom is a major trading nation, and a member of the European Union, with nearly half its trade overseas going outside Europe. Britain was once the 'mother country' of the largest empire in history, and worldwide links with most former colonies are maintained through the Commonwealth.

In its relations with the world, Britain is still adjusting to the fact that it no longer has the same world role as in the imperial past, but the world role of English and post-imperial links mean that media organisations, like the BBC, and publications, such as the *Financial Times*, still have particular influence and opportunities in global media. Britain is also subject to American influ-ences, which people tend to take for granted. Films set and made in the US are not even recognised as 'foreign films', and the British film industry has suffered, near fatally, from such competition. There is also increasing evidence that continental European influences, supported by British membership of the European Union, are changing Britain's media industries and markets.

This chapter will look at the principal producers in the three areas of Print Media, Broadcasting, and Film/Video, followed by a short section looking at how these industries are regulated, or controlled. The information will be broken down according to the following headings:
- Print Media and News Agencies (broken down into Newspapers and Magazines, with some cross reference between the two, and the agencies).
- Broadcasting (broken down into a view of the major broadcasters).
- Film and Video (with reference to production, distribution, cinema and video).
- Access and Regulation.

This situation is constantly changing and therefore you need to update your own knowledge and this information.

Print media

No sector of the British newspaper and periodical press is state-owned, state-subsidised, or state-controlled apart from by the controls of the law and the influence of regulatory bodies (e.g. The Press Complaints Commission and The Advertising Standards Authority). The United Kingdom has, in theory, a *free press* which operates in a capitalist market of businesses and their consumers. On the other hand, as you will see, the press operates in a market where *big business* usually dominates. Large organisations which have financial resources, integration between different media and production processes, and links with other companies, are at a definite advantage and can squeeze other players out of the market. There has also been a tendency in Britain for large media businesses to support right-wing politicians and the Conservative Party.

Newspapers

The ownership of national, regional and local newspapers shows concentration into the hands of relatively few large corporations with interests in other areas of media and communications markets. Newsprint forms over 25% of national newspaper costs on average. Labour costs are usually more than 50%. The press is still the largest advertising medium in the country, with a total yearly spend by advertisers of over £5 billion.

The biggest presence in the British national newspapers is News International plc. News International is the United Kingdom arm of the NewsCorp 'empire' controlled by Rupert Murdoch.

News International owns the five national newspapers: the *Sun*, the *Times*, *The Sunday Times* and *The News of the World*. Together, these newspapers take about 35% of the United Kingdom national market. Newspaper publishing remains the most profitable part of News

International's business, operating on a profit margin of 21% in 1992. News International owns the book publisher HarperCollins, and a 50% shareholding in British Sky Broadcasting (BSkyB).

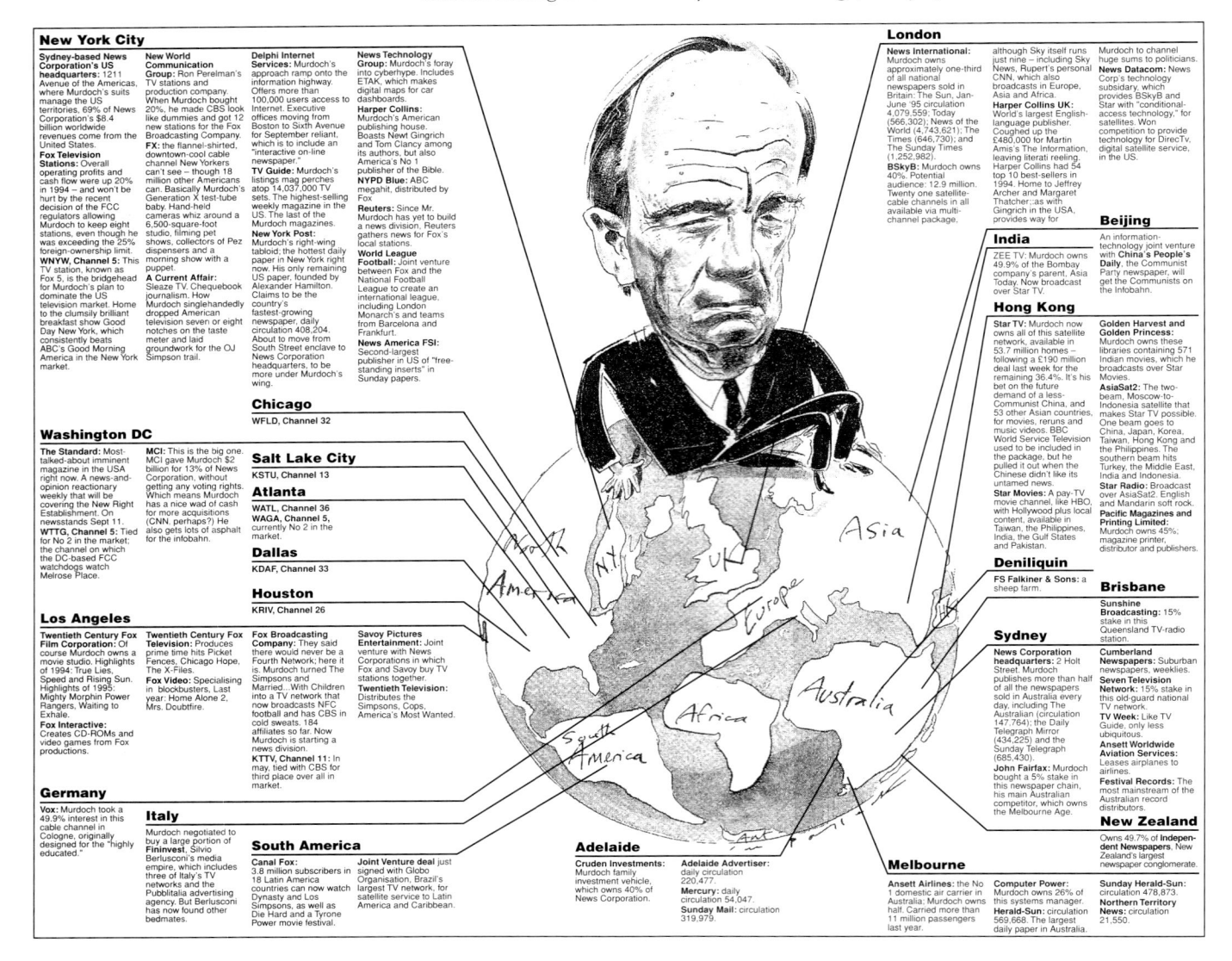

New York City

Sydney-based News Corporation's US headquarters: 1211 Avenue of the Americas, where Murdoch's suits manage the US territories, 69% of News Corporation's $8.4 billion worldwide revenues come from the United States.
Fox Television Stations: Overall operating profits and cash flow were up 20% in 1994 – and won't be hurt by the recent decision of the FCC regulators allowing Murdoch to keep eight stations, even though he was exceeding the 25% foreign-ownership limit.
WNYW, Channel 5: This TV station, known as Fox 5, is the bridgehead for Murdoch's plan to dominate the US television market. Home to the clumsily brilliant breakfast show Good Day New York, which consistently beats ABC's Good Morning America in the New York market.

New World Communication Group: Ron Perelman's TV stations and production company. When Murdoch bought 20%, he made CBS look like dummies and got 12 new stations for the Fox Broadcasting Company.
FX: the flannel-shirted, downtown-cool cable channel New Yorkers can't see – though 18 million other Americans can. Basically Murdoch's Generation X test-tube baby. Hand-held cameras whiz around a 6,500-square-foot studio, filming pet shows, collectors of Pez dispensers and a morning show with a puppet.
A Current Affair: Sleaze TV. Chequebook journalism. How Murdoch singlehandedly dropped American television seven or eight notches on the taste meter and laid groundwork for the OJ Simpson trail.

Delphi Internet Services: Murdoch's approach ramp onto the information highway. Offers more than 100,000 users access to Internet. Executive offices moving from Boston to Sixth Avenue for September reliant, which is to include an "interactive on-line newspaper."
TV Guide: Murdoch's listings mag perches atop 14,037,000 TV sets. The highest-selling weekly magazine in the US. The last of the Murdoch magazines.
New York Post: Murdoch's right-wing tabloid; the hottest daily paper in New York right now. His only remaining US paper, founded by Alexander Hamilton. Claims to be the country's fastest-growing newspaper, daily circulation 408,204. About to move from South Street enclave to News Corporation headquarters, to be more under Murdoch's wing.

News Technology Group: Murdoch's foray into cyberhype. Includes ETAK, which makes digital maps for car dashboards.
Harper Collins: Murdoch's American publishing house. Boasts Newt Gingrich and Tom Clancy among its authors, but also America's No 1 publisher of the Bible.
NYPD Blue: ABC megahit, distributed by Fox
Reuters: Since Mr. Murdoch has set to build a news division, Reuters gathers news for Fox's local stations.
World League Football: Joint venture between Fox and the National Football League to create an international league, including London Monarch's and teams from Barcelona and Frankfurt.
News America FSI: Second-largest publisher in US of "free-standing inserts" in Sunday papers.

Chicago
WFLD, Channel 32

Washington DC
The Standard: Most-talked-about imminent magazine in the USA right now. A news-and-opinion reactionary weekly that will be covering the New Right Establishment. On newsstands Sept 11.
WTTG, Channel 5: Tied for No 2 in the market; the channel on which the DC-based FCC watchdogs watch Melrose Place.

MCI: This is the big one. MCI gave Murdoch $2 billion for 13% of News Corporation, without getting any voting rights. Which means Murdoch has a nice wad of cash for more acquisitions (CNN, perhaps?) He also gets lots of asphalt for the infobahn.

Salt Lake City
KSTU, Channel 13

Atlanta
WATL, Channel 36
WAGA, Channel 5, currently No 2 in the market.

Dallas
KDAF, Channel 33

Houston
KRIV, Channel 26

Los Angeles
Twentieth Century Fox Film Corporation: Of course Murdoch owns a movie studio. Highlights of 1994: True Lies, Speed and Rising Sun. Highlights of 1995: Mighty Morphin Power Rangers, Waiting to Exhale.
Fox Interactive: Creates CD-ROMs and video games from Fox productions.

Twentieth Century Fox Television: Produces prime time hits Picket Fences, Chicago Hope, The X-Files.
Fox Video: Specialising in blockbusters. Last year: Home Alone 2, Mrs. Doubtfire.

Fox Broadcasting Company: They said there would never be a Fourth Network; here it is. Murdoch turned The Simpsons and Married...With Children into a TV network that now broadcasts NFC football and has CBS in cold sweats. 184 affiliates so far. Now Murdoch is starting a news division.
KTTV, Channel 11: In May, tied with CBS for third place over all in market.

Savoy Pictures Entertainment: Joint venture with News Corporations in which Fox and Savoy buy TV stations together.
Twentieth Television: Distributes the Simpsons, Cops, America's Most Wanted.

Germany
Vox: Murdoch took a 49.9% interest in this cable channel in Cologne, originally designed for the "highly educated."

Italy
Murdoch negotiated to buy a large portion of Fininvest, Silvio Berlusconi's media empire, which includes three of Italy's TV networks and the Pubblitalia advertising agency, but Berlusconi has now found other bedmates.

South America
Canal Fox: 3.8 million subscribers in 18 Latin American countries can now watch Dynasty and Los Simpsons, as well as Die Hard and a Tyrone Power movie festival.

Joint Venture deal just signed with Globo Organisation, Brazil's largest TV network, for satellite service to Latin America and Caribbean.

London

News International: Murdoch owns approximately one-third of all national newspapers sold in Britain: The Sun, Jan-June '95 circulation 4,079,559; Today (566,302); News of the World (4,743,621); The Times (646,730); and The Sunday Times (1,252,982).
BSkyB: Murdoch owns 40%. Potential audience: 12.9 million. Twenty one satellite-cable channels in all available via multi-channel package.

although Sky runs itself just nine – including Sky News, Rupert's personal CNN, which also broadcasts in Europe, Asia and Africa.
Harper Collins UK: World's largest English-language publisher. Coughed up the £480,000 for Martin Amis's The Information, leaving literati reeling. Harper Collins had 54 top 10 best-sellers in 1994. Home to Jeffrey Archer and Margaret Thatcher:,as with Gingrich in the USA, provides way for

Murdoch to channel huge sums to politicians.
News Datacom: News Corp's technology subsidiary, which provides BSkyB and Star with "conditional-access technology," for satellites. Won competition to provide technology for DirecTv, digital satellite service, in the US.

India
ZEE TV: Murdoch owns 49.9% of the Bombay company's parent, Asia Today. Now broadcast over Star TV.

Hong Kong
Star TV: Murdoch now owns all of this satellite network, available in 53.7 million homes – following a £190 million deal last week for the remaining 36.4%. It's his bet on the future demand of a less-Communist China, and 53 other Asian countries, for movies, reruns and music videos. BBC World Service Television used to be included in the package, but he pulled it out when the Chinese didn't like its untamed news.
Star Movies: A pay-TV movie channel, like HBO, with Hollywood plus local content, available in Taiwan, the Philippines, India, the Gulf States and Pakistan.

Beijing
An information-technology joint venture with China's People's Daily, the Communist Party newspaper, will get the Communists on the Infobahn.

Golden Harvest and Golden Princess: Murdoch owns these libraries containing 571 Indian movies, which he broadcasts over Star Movies.
AsiaSat2: The two-beam, Moscow-to-Indonesia satellite that makes Star TV possible. One beam goes to China, Japan, Korea, Taiwan, Hong Kong and the Philippines. The southern beam hits Turkey, the Middle East, India and Indonesia.
Star Radio: Broadcast over AsiaSat2. English and Mandarin soft rock.
Pacific Magazines and Printing Limited: Murdoch owns 45%; magazine printer, distributor and publishers.

Deniliquin
FS Falkiner & Sons: a sheep farm.

Sydney
News Corporation headquarters: 2 Holt Street. Murdoch publishes more than half of all the newspapers sold in Australia every day, including The Australian (circulation 147,764); the Daily Telegraph Mirror (434,225) and the Sunday Telegraph (685,430).
John Fairfax: Murdoch bought a 5% stake in this newspaper chain, his main Australian competitor, which owns the Melbourne Age.

Brisbane
Sunshine Broadcasting: 15% stake in this Queensland TV-radio station.
Cumberland Newspapers: Suburban newspapers, weeklies.
Seven Television Network: 15% stake in this old-guard national TV network.
TV Week: Like TV Guide, only less ubiquitous.
Ansett Worldwide Aviation Services: Leases airplanes to airlines.
Festival Records: The most mainstream of the Australian record distributors.

New Zealand
Owns 49.7% of **Independent Newspapers**, New Zealand's largest newspaper conglomerate.

Adelaide
Cruden Investments: Murdoch family investment vehicle, which owns 40% of News Corporation.

Adelaide Advertiser: daily circulation 220,477.
Mercury: daily circulation 54,047.
Sunday Mail: circulation 319,979.

Melbourne
Ansett Airlines: the No 1 domestic air carrier in Australia; Murdoch owns half. Carried more than 11 million passengers last year.

Computer Power: Murdoch owns 26% of this systems manager.
Herald-Sun: circulation 569,668. The largest daily paper in Australia.

Sunday Herald-Sun: circulation 478,873.
Northern Territory News: circulation 21,550.

Figure 15.1 The Global Visage

MGN (Mirror Group Newspapers) produces six newspapers in England and Wales. It owns the *Mirror*, the *Sunday Mirror*, the *People*, *Sporting Life*, and the Scottish newspapers, the *Daily Record* and the *Sunday Mail*, giving it over 25% of the market. The processes of concentration can be seen in the moves of the Mirror Group into television. Mirror Group has interests in cable, and owns the maximum 20% holding in ITV franchises allowed under the present rules limiting cross-media ownership. In addition, the Mirror Group owns a large stake in Newspaper Publishing plc. The *Independent* and the *Independent on Sunday* (market share about 2%) are owned by Newspaper Publishing plc.

The Daily Mail and General Trust plc is a group which includes Associated Newspapers, Northcliffe Newspapers and publishing interests. National newspapers, the *Daily Mail* and *the Mail on Sunday*, and a regional paper, the *Evening Standard*, are owned by Associated Newspapers. This represents 12.5% of the national market. Northcliffe Newspapers has 23 regional centres producing regional and local titles. The group has shareholdings in other media, including the GWR local radio business and Reuters, the global news agency.

United Newspapers publishes three national tabloid papers in the United Kingdom: the *Daily Express*, the *Star* and the *Sunday Express*. It has a 12% market share. In addition, this group owns seven regional dailies, 43 weekly paid for papers, 65 free, local papers and a magazine publisher.

The Daily Telegraph group is owned by a conglomerate called Hollinger Inc. based in Canada. The Daily Telegraph group produces the *Daily Telegraph*, the *Sunday Telegraph*, and a magazine, the *Spectator*. It has a 5.4% share of the national newspaper market.

The Scott Trust has a 3% national market share. It owns Guardian Newspapers, which also publishes the Sunday paper, the *Observer*, and the *Manchester Evening News*. The company owns local papers around the Manchester area and in the south-east. It also has interests in broadcasting and owns 15% of GMTV, the ITV breakfast time franchise holder.

Pearson plc is a conglomerate which incorporates local and regional newspapers, a national newspaper, publishing, television and interests outside the media. Pearson owns the *Financial Times*, a United Kingdom national daily with 1% of the national market, and significant international sales. It also owns Westminster Press, a large regional and local newspaper producer with a total circulation of more than 3 million for its titles. Pearson has significant interests in television, including ownership of the production company Thames television, and holdings in BSkyB and cable.

Figure 15.2 'National Newspapers'

Title and foundation date	Controlled by	Circulation[a] average February–July 1994
National dailies		
'Populars'		
Daily mirror (1903)	Mirror Group Newspapers (1986) plc	2,497,076
Daily Star (1978)	United Newspapers	671,373
The Sun (1964)	News International plc	4,101,988
'Mid market'		
Daily Mail (1896)	Associated Newspapers Ltd	1,796,795
Daily Express (1900)	United Newspapers	1,358,246
'Qualities'		
Financial Times (1888)	Pearon	296,634
The Daily Telegraph (1855)	The Telegraph plc	1,013,860
The Guardian (1821)	Guardian Media Group plc	400,856
The Independent (1986)	Mirror Group consortium[b]	275,447
The Times (1785)	News International plc	507,894
National Sundays		
'Populars'		
News of the World (1843)	News International plc	4,769,105
Sunday Mirror (1963)	Mirror Group Newspapers (1986) plc	2,560,234
The People (1881)	Mirror Group Newspapers (1986) plc	2,006,393
'Mid market'		
The Mail on Sunday (1982)	Associated Newspapers Ltd	1,972,012
Sunday Express (1918)	United Newspapers	1,544,404
'Qualities'		
Sunday Telegraph (1961)	The Telegraph plc	633,112
The Independent on Sunday (1990)	Mirror Group consortium[b]	327,689
The Obsever (1791)	Guardian Media Group plc	495,483
The Sunday Times (1822)	News International plc	1,205,457

[a]Circulation figures are those of the Audit Bureau of circulations (consisting of publishers, advertisers and advertising agencies) and are certified average daily or weekly net sales for the period.
[b]The consortium comprises Mirror Group Newspapers (1986) plc, Promotra de Informaciones and Espresso International Holding.

The ownership of local newspapers is complex. In addition to the local newspaper ownership indicated above, there are very large media companies with interests in newspapers such as EMAP, DC Thomson and Trinity International Holdings. You will find some details of the ownership of your local papers printed at the foot of one of the pages towards the front or the back of the paper. You can use *Benn's Media Guide* (United Kingdom) and/or the *Guardian Media Guide* to look further into the ownership of the local papers in your own area. The ownership of media organisations and print media titles is in constant change. At the time of writing, the Thomson Organisation is in the process of selling off local media interests, and Reed Elsevier, one of the largest media conglomerates in Europe, has offered its regional newspaper division for sale.

Reed lays future on-line

Emily Bell explains why Winnie the Pooh is being auctioned off by Britain's biggest publisher

REED Elsevier's out-with-the-old, in-with-the-new strategy saw the majority of its consumer publishing properties put up for sale last week.

The £800 million auction, including the Hamlyn books division and the company's regional newspaper division – which owns the world's oldest newspaper, the Worcester Journal – will attract a host of other media owners.

Reed Regional Newspapers could draw the attention of established press barons such as Conrad Black and Tony O'Reilly, as well as regional newspaper specialists such as Midland Independent Newspapers and Emap.

The books division, whose imprints include Hamlyn, Heinemann and Mandarin, could be targeted by the ambitious Hodder Headline company, or Pearson, which owns Penguin, or even an overseas interest such as Bertelsmann. The City also identifies 'rank outsiders' Virgin and Carlton Communications.

As Britain's largest publishing company, Reed's sheer dullness has stopped it attracting the same attention as its far smaller rivals. Yet its strategy of divesting 'user friendly' assets such as the publishers of Winnie the Pooh and Barbar the Elephant in favour of impenetrable scientific journals and business titles such as Farmers Weekly show it has a talent to prosper, if not to amuse.

The areas Reed Elsevier wants to focus on are those easily distributed through new technology – the potential for online distribution of academic and professional publications is far higher than for consumer titles.

Reed is selling just as paper prices are rising at their fastest rate for 20 years – a 30 per cent increase so far this year. It is clear from Reed's orientation that its ultimate wish is to become a paperless publisher. The pur-chase of the predomin-

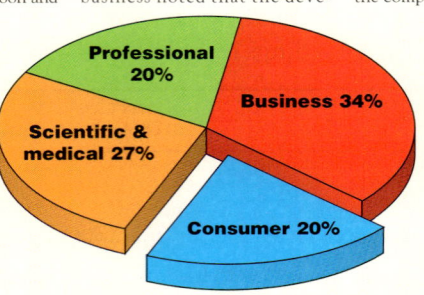

Reed Elsevier operating profits 1994
- Business 34%
- Scientific & medical 27%
- Professional 20%
- Consumer 20%

antly on-line news and professional information service Lexis-Nexis last year for $1.5 billion (£1bn) cornerstone of the company's new strategy.

Electronic publishing is still an immature market, but a Goldman Sachs circular on the impact it may have on Reed Elsevier's business noted that the developing on-line market gives a publisher two streams of revenue – one for a library subscription and one for users.

Others are less convinced that the shift to on-line publishing will be a money-spinner. David Forster, an analyst at Smith New Court, says: 'The one thing everybody remains unsure of is how the migration to on-line will affect existing businesses.'

The inevitable question raised by the sell-off of other non-specialist divisions is how long the company intends to keep IPC Magazines, which carries titles such as Loaded and Ideal Home, as its sole surviving consumer division. Although margins on the consumer division of the company are expected to be in the order of 15 per cent for 1995, this is less impressive than the scientific and medical division which will deliver a whopping 35 per cent, while business and professional publishing is projected at 21.4 per cent and 22.4 per cent respectively.

But one analyst believes: 'It's profitable, high profile and glamorous, so there is probably little pressing reason for them to get rid of IPC.'

One wider question the Reed sale raises is whether there are more sellers than buyers currently in the printed media market. Monopolistic restraints prevent some of the richer companies such as Associated Newspapers augmenting their local newspaper interests, leaving scattered buyers for the Reed portfolio.

Thomson Regional Newspapers sold off most of its local interests two weeks ago to Trinity International Holdings, and is seeking a separate buyer for its prize assets of the Scotsman, Scotland on Sunday and the Aberdeen Press & Journal.

There is some speculation that Pearson, publisher of the Financial Times, may also sell Westminster Press, its own regional newspaper subsidiary, if it was offered the right price.

According to one analyst: "The fact that two multinational publishers [Reed and Thomson] have both decided to sell their regional portfolios probably tells us that they have done their sums and seen diminishing returns against the increasing competition from local radio and even cable TV in advertising terms.'

Figure 15.3 Excerpt: newspaper article from Observer 23 July 1995, 'Reed lays future on line'

Magazines

The magazine market is dominated by a small number of very large media groups.

In 1996, Reed Elsevier is the largest magazine publisher. Reed Elsevier owns both IPC Magazines Ltd and Reed Business Publishing, in addition to its other media interests in book publishing and regional newspapers. IPC magazines has 54 magazine titles of the more general lifestyle and special interest varieties. This includes *What's On TV* and *TV Times*, two of the best selling British magazines. As explained above, Reed Elsevier is in the process of restructuring, and it remains to be seen how much of its publishing interests will be offered for sale, or sold.

The second largest British magazine publisher is EMAP, a company based in Peterborough and London. Consumer magazines include *Big!*, *Match*, *More!*, *Smash Hits* and many other familiar titles. The company has interests in radio broadcasting, and has been expanding into Europe. It owns a 99% share in Kiss FM Radio Ltd, and a 24% shareholding in Home Counties Newspapers Ltd.

Other prominent owners include Bauer, the BBC, Conde Nast, and the National Magazine Company. The BBC has been increasing in importance as a magazine publisher with titles *BBC Good Food* and *BBC Gardener's World*. The Radio Times (circ 1 463 942) has declined slightly under competition from other television guides. The National Magazine Company is owned by the American Hearst Corporation. It publishes titles such as *Cosmopolitan*, *Country Living*, *Esquire*, *Good Housekeeping*, and *Harpers and Queen*.

News agencies

The principal news agencies in Britain are Reuters, the Press Association and Extel. Associated Press and United Press International are British subsidiaries of news agencies in the United States.

Reuters is an international news agency with more than 11 000 employees in 80 countries and links with a further 70 nations. The Press Association is the national news agency, not only for Britain but also the Irish Republic, providing information services in the form of news, sport, photographs and graphic data. Extel is an international news agency part owned by Agence France Presse and Pearson through the Financial Times Group. Although newspapers are their principal customers, these agencies also provide services to broadcasters and business. The provision of financial information to companies, banks and other financial institutions is an important source of business and revenue for both Reuters and Extel.

Broadcasting

Britain has four terrestrial television channels, with a fifth about to be licensed, five BBC national radio networks, 38 BBC local radio stations, three national commercial radio stations and more than 150 independent local radio station services. The ownership and control of British Broadcasting can be understood in terms of three influences: 'public service', commercialism and 'change'. The first two refer to the possibilities that broadcasting may be used to serve the public as a whole, or to make money with popular products. The last refers to the changing situation of broadcasting, which may be changed by government decisions or new technologies.

The ideas that broadcasting should serve the public good, the nation, and higher ideals such as notions of education and cultural improvement, are most evident in the existence of the BBC. The BBC still attempts to serve the whole population by maintaining a large market share of national audiences, and to have a regional presence in radio and television. It also produces educational television and works with the Open University.

The second influence is that of big business and commercialism. The ITV franchises allow large media companies to bid for the profits to be made from the regional franchises, within a framework which shows the remains of some public service in the 'light touch' regulation and the tender fees returned to the taxman. Channel Four, the forthcoming Channel Five, and satellite and cable broadcasters, all function as commercial television broadcasters.

The third influence is that of change driven by a changes in politics and public policy, and/or changes in technology. As explained in chapter 16, periodic changes in British Broadcasting have been influenced by the recommendations of government committees. An example of policy change is that of 'deregulation', the political decision starting in the 1980s to get rid of rules which limited the role of commerce and free operation of big business. This also included forcing big monopolies like the BBC and the ITV companies to open themselves up to the publication of the work of smaller independent production companies. Examples of technological change are the technologies of cable and satellite, which have added a new tier of television to the old terrestrial television as represented by the BBC and ITV. These are now linked with the *digital revolution* which means that print media, radio, television, video and most other media technologies are coming together as part of a new digital communications system.

The BBC

The British Broadcasting Corporation is a public body which carries out radio and television broadcasting 'as public services'. The BBC is managed by the Director General, at present John Birt, and a Board of Governors (for further details see the section on regulation below). The BBC's main source of revenue is the television licence fee, administered by a Post Office subsidiary, which every viewing household must pay by law. In May 1994, over 20 million licences were held. The BBC also makes money from publishing, the commercial sales of videos and other merchandise, and from selling programming to other organisations in the United Kingdom and abroad.

In 1994 a government white paper on the future of the BBC, *The Future of the BBC: Serving the Nation, Competing Worldwide*, renewed the BBC Charter for ten years. It laid down that the funding of the BBC by licence fees would continue until 2001. It also proposed that the BBC should develop its commercial activities, without any use of the licence fee to subsidise these. The BBC was also allowed to launch cable and satellite services on the recommendation of the white paper. In January 1995 the BBC launched two European satellite channels, BBC Prime and BBC World, with backing from Pearson and a US company, Cox Communications. These channels are part of BBC Worldwide, which also includes World Service Television.

The BBC has a structure of six regions, in addition to its London base. The three English regions are BBC North, BBC Midlands and East, and BBC South. BBC Scotland, Wales and Northern Ireland represent their areas. The regions make programmes for their own audiences, and contribute to the national network. The two national channels, BBC 1 and BBC 2, transmit over 12 800 hours of programmes per year for national and regional audiences. These are produced mainly in London. In 1993–94 about one quarter of programme production expenditure was commissioned with the BBC regions.

BBC Radio

BBC Network Radio still dominates national radio with Radios 1, 2, 3, 4 and 5. BBC Network Radio broadcasts approximately 38 000 hours of programmes on the five networks:

- BBC Radio 1 is mainly a rock and pop channel, broadcasting 24 hours a day.
- BBC Radio 2 broadcasts a mixture of popular, often middle of the road, music and light entertainment 24 hours a day.
- BBC Radio 3 is a high culture channel with an emphasis upon classical music.
- BBC Radio 4 is probably the most varied of all, with a soap (*The Archers*), plays, news, quiz shows, magazine programmes, coverage of parliament etc.
- BBC Radio 5 (now known as 'Five Live') is a 24-hour service based around continuous news and sport coverage.

The BBC also has 39 regional radio stations covering most of the United Kingdom.

BBC Worldwide

The BBC has an international reputation, and broadcasts and exports programmes to other countries. In May 1994 external operations took on the structure of BBC Worldwide with three divisions: BBC World Service, BBC International Television and BBC publishing. BBC World Service is contracted by the Foreign Office to maintain overseas radio broadcasts in English and 38 other languages, subsidised by a government grant. The 130 million listeners to these services are estimated to tune in regularly. BBC International Television is a self-funding company set up to establish a worldwide television service. It has formed a partnership with Pearson plc to develop satellite services, and has launched two European channels. BBC Publishing produces books, tapes and other BBC consumer products, both for the home and international markets.

ITV

ITV (Channel Three) and Channel Four deliver the two commercial terrestrial television channels which all households are entitled to receive. Their main source of funding is the sale of advertising and commercial sponsorship.

ITV consists of the ITV Network Centre, ITN, and the 16 commercial companies which deliver national and regional programming through the network. The ITV Network Centre is jointly owned by the 16 ITV companies it services. It commissions and schedules the programmes shown on ITV. The top committees of the Network Centre supervise, and allow the ITV and other production companies to compete for production of, the schedule. In 1995, ITV had a network budget of £570 million. However, this amount was under review at the time of writing. Independent Television News (ITN) is the common news service subscribed to by the ITV network.

The 16 ITV companies consist of 13 serving their own regions, two serving the London region, and the franchisee for the national breakfast television service. The 16 companies are Anglia (East Anglia), Border (Isle of Man and the western side of the Scottish borders), Carlton (London), Central (Midlands), Channel Television (Channel Islands), GMTV (breakfast), Grampian (North of Scotland), Granada (North West England around Manchester), HTV (serving Wales and HTV West), London Weekend Television, Meridian (South and South East England), Scottish Television (Central Scotland), Yorkshire/Tyne Tees (North East

England), Ulster Television (Northern Ireland) and West Country Television (South West England). All franchisees are under an obligation to show some regional programming, mainly in the form of regional news, current affairs and sport.

There is much evidence to support the division between those companies in the dominant 'Big Five' and the rest. The Big Five are Carlton, Central, Granada, LWT and Yorkshire. These companies have the greatest resources because they serve areas with large populations and can earn the most from advertisers. They also tend to produce a greater proportion of the network output than the remaining smaller franchisees.

A Activity

What effects do you think the domination of the 'Big Five' has on the types of programmes we tend to see on ITV and their representation of the United Kingdom?

Can you find any evidence in the published schedules for your guesses and expectations?

Channel Four

Channel Four is now an independent body, set up as the Channel Four Television Corporation under the 1990 Broadcasting Act. The Independent Television Commission has issued Channel Four with a ten-year licence. The ITC regulates Channel Four and supervises its programming policy. The Channel Four Corporation is charged to continue the role of the fourth channel in terms such as 'innovation', 'experiment' and those tastes not catered for by ITV. In addition to meeting demands for entertainment, the channel is under requirements to provide information and educational material.

The principal source of revenue for Channel Four is its revenues from advertising. At present, this is set at a target of 14% of the total income of ITV, Channel Four and the Welsh S4C. ITV takes half of any earnings above 14%, and provides a subsidy of up to 2% if the earnings of Channel Four fall below this target.

Channel Four is not allowed to make its own programmes. It is a kind of publisher of television products, and it is compelled to ensure that a 'substantial proportion' of its programmes come from independent production companies. In 1993, Channel Four became the third largest broadcaster in Britain with an average audience share of nearly 11%.

S4C

Sianel Pedwar Cymru (S4C), based in Cardiff, is the name of Channel Four Wales. S4C broadcasts 23 – 30 hours a week of programmes in the Welsh language, together with over 85 hours of English Channel Four programmes. About 10 hours of the programmes in Welsh are produced by the BBC. S4C has a government grant which is its main source of revenue. In addition, S4C sells its own advertising which at present covers about 10% of its revenue.

Satellite and cable broadcasting

The alternatives to terrestrial television (BBC, ITV and Channel Four) come from satellite broadcasters, received either through home satellite dishes, or through a central receiving dish on a cable network. Revenue is normally raised from channels through subscriptions charged to households and other receivers, advertising, or a mix of the two. British satellite and cable operations are regulated by the Independent Television Commission (ITC). Satellite and cable offer access, not only to general entertainment such as Sky, Superchannel and UK Gold, but also to more specialised services aimed at specific audiences such as TV Asia and the Chinese Channel.

The main groups of satellites transmitting services to Britain are Astra, Eutelsat and Intelsat. These satellite owners lease channels on the satellites to other broadcasting companies supplying programmes. The principal satellite broadcaster providing services to Britain is British Sky Broadcasting (BSkyB), which is part owned by Rupert Murdoch's News International (50%) and Pearson (16%). Other satellite broadcasters include the Cable News Network (CNN), MTV and TV Asia. The BBC is also an important satellite broadcaster. In 1993, BBC International Television, a branch of BBC worldwide, joined forces with Thames Television to set up the UK Gold channel which carries 'golden oldies' and other programmes from the past.

Cable services are delivered through underground cables, paid for by subscription. Cable systems serving more than 1 000 homes are licensed by the ITC. These are usually broadband franchises carrying a range of television channels (up to 45 in number), phone and telecommunications, and interactive services such as home shopping and banking. They are allocated areas of the country on a franchise basis. In 1994, 66 broadband franchises were in operation, with nearly 650 000 homes actually connected to the cables passing the doors of about 3 million in total. North American companies own approximately 80% of all United Kingdom cable delivery systems.

Independent radio broadcasters

It is possible to identify seven types of independent radio: local, national, satellite, cable, community, restricted service and pirate. The first four are mainly commercial operations. Over 155 independent local radio stations have been established and licensed since London's LBC first appeared in 1973. Independent national radio includes the stations Classic FM, Virgin and Talk Radio UK. Satellite and cable also carry radio broadcasting services including both independents and BBC radio channels. Community radio refers to non-profit making organisations who want to run local radio stations for the local community. A few such organisations have received licences to run low-powered local services; at least 100 further groups have placed applications. Restricted service refers to small-scale, low-power broadcasts which are limited to a short space of time or to a particular institution, and are non-profit making. They include, for example, hospital and college radio stations. Pirate broadcasting refers to unlicensed, illegal broadcasting by groups who are pursued and sometimes raided by the government Radiocommunications Agency.

National Transcommunications Limited (NTL) owns the transmission networks which transmit Channel 4, S4C and 100 independent local radio stations.

Film and video

Most of Britain's home grown film studios have closed, and production has declined. Production and distribution for the British market is dominated by the Hollywood major studios and distributors. Only one film in the top 20 at the British Box Office in 1993 was made in the United Kingdom: *Much Ado About Nothing*. The average budget of a mostly British film was £1.32 million in 1993, as compared with £11.54 million on average in a Hollywood film. The film *Shallow Grave* (1993), backed by Channel Four, had a budget of less than a million pounds. US films also dominate the video rentals market, and take the highest prices when they reach television.

There was an increase from 47 films made in Britain in 1992 to 69 in 1993. However, those films which were mostly British in terms of their finance and/or making remained fairly stable rising from 28 in 1992 to 32 in 1993. In 1993, 10 films 'made in Britain' were Hollywood Productions including *In the Name of the Father* (Universal), *Interview with a Vampire* (Warner) and *Mary Shelley's Frankenstein* (Tristar/Zoetrope). Co-production with other countries supported the remaining films made in Britain. For example, *The War of the Buttons*, with a budget of £5 million was made in partnership with backers from France, Japan and Ireland.

Television has become the major investor in, and sales outlet for, most British films. The largest single investor in the British film industry is Channel Four. Channel Four is also the major investor in British Screen Finance Ltd, a company in the private sector which invested £2.7 million in new British films in 1992. The European Co-production Fund has become increasingly important, investing over £2 million in films made in Britain with European partners in 1992.

The major US distributors at the United Kingdom box office are UIP, Warner, Columbia Tristar, Buena Vista and 20th Century Fox. These five account for sales of over £260 million, or 82% of total takings.

The leading cinema chain is MGM/Cannon owned by Pathe Communications Corp, USA, with over 400 screens at 125 sites in 1993. The others in the top 5 are Rank/Odeon owned by Rank UK (322 screens, 75 sites), UCI whose parent company is Viacom USA (219 screens, 25 sites), Warner whose parent company is the US giant Time Warner (84/9), and Showcase, an affiliate of National Amusements, USA (127/10). These five own over 60% of screens and account for something like 85% of all box office takings. This is a far greater concentration of ownership than in the USA where the top six chains make up 38% of all screens.

The United Kingdom video market continues to grow. Rentals stood at a total of £528 million, and sales totalled £643 million in 1993. American films and distributors almost dominate the video rental market. The top three distributors of sell-through videos were Buena Vista (distributor of Disney titles), PolyGram and the BBC. These statistics also include television material, comedy, music and children's programmes. The top distributor of feature films on sale through video was Warner Home Video.

Access and regulation

Access

Access refers to the opportunities available to people, groups or organisations to have their voices or views heard through those media products which concern them, or to make their own media products. Newspapers have letters pages, and complaints may be dealt with internally or through the Press Complaints Commission. Broadcasters have access programmes, either where the audience may put points of view, or where access programmes putting a particular view may be made. They also record complaints, and give them airtime, as in BBC Radio 4's *Feedback* programme, or Channel Four's *Right to Reply*. Channel Four has a remit to broadcast the work of independent producers and to schedule programmes for minorities. The recent television 'video diaries' are an interesting example of programming with an access dimension. In addition, the various regulatory bodies have a responsibility to ensure that producers are accountable and to answer complaints from members of the public. The media are accountable not only to the powers that be, but also to their audiences, and members of the public with serious complaints.

The history and current situation of radio show examples of how the existing producers have not always provided what people want, and so-called pirates have gained 'illegal' access to the airwaves and given listeners sounds and opinions they have wanted to hear.

Access programmes on television are scheduled out of prime time, and with the assumption that they will attract small audiences. For example, the BBC facilitates open access educational and training programmes for public bodies and charities through BBC Select which transmits on the late night-time hours free on BBC 1 and BBC 2. The corporation justifies this arrangement with the rationale that the programmes are designed for video recording and for specialist audiences.

Regulation

The regulation of the media in Britain comes from four sources:
- the law
- government action
- self regulation
- regulatory bodies.

Media production takes place in the context of limits placed by law. Broadcasting is controlled by government licences, and those who ignore this such as radio pirates are pursued, and, if caught and found guilty, punished. The licences set out limits in terms of 'good taste' and 'not giving offence'. Otherwise, most laws relevant to the media are not specific 'media laws', but part of other legislation. The most important are:
- Contempt of Court (controls publication of material about court cases with the intention of stopping the media from influencing the outcome of a trial).
- Defamation of character (slander covering the spoken word, libel covering writing).
- Obscene Publications Act (publication may be stopped if material blasphemes Christianity, is indecent etc.).
- Official Secrets Act (allows the government to stop the publication of material deemed to threaten national security).

- The Prevention of Terrorism Act (allows the government to censor material relating to Northern Ireland).

As you can see, the government has the power to censor material, although most observers take the view that most media activity takes place free of such direct government intervention. However, the British government has directly and frequently censored coverage of Northern Ireland. With this exception, most legal action against the media pursues libel and is taken by individuals. Nevertheless, the law could be seen as simply part of government action since the government through parliament makes laws. Laws relevant to the media give the government a strong hold over broadcasting in particular. In addition, the government has influence through their control over appointments to important jobs such as the Chairman and Governors of the BBC. Whichever political party is in government can bring strong influence to bear upon the media because of their powers, and all mainstream political parties have a right to demand some broadcasting time for the use of party political broadcasts.

When people and organisations impose upon themselves certain limits and standards they undertake *self-regulation*. Self-regulation begins with the individual worker and extends to organisations set up by the industries themselves. The making of media products is influenced by professional standards, editorial control and the limits which institutions place on themselves. In the case of journalists who belong to the union, The National Union of Journalists has a code of professional conduct. The code includes duties to avoid misrepresentation, falsification, intrusion into private grief and distress, and a prohibition on the acceptance of bribes. In practice, the greatest influence on self-regulation probably comes from the employer. Newspapers have greater freedom than broadcasters to take sides politically and in disputes, but this freedom usually results in a bias towards the interests of the organisation or the individual owner. The ownership and management of media organisations have influence over the internal guidelines and filters within their organisations. In addition to internal self-regulation, the media industries have external bodies to watch over their output of material; most of these regulatory bodies were set up by the industries themselves.

The regulatory bodies which regulate the media are as follows:
- Newspapers: the Press Complaints Commission. Established in 1991, the PCC is perhaps the last chance for the press to regulate itself. 'The Commission was set up by the newspaper and periodical industry in a final attempt to make self regulation of the press work properly. It is funded by PRESSBOF (the Press Standards Board of Finance) which was set up in 1990 to co-ordinate and promote self regulation in the industry. These measures were prompted by growing criticism of press standards, with allegations of unjustified invasion of privacy and inaccurate and biased reporting, among other abuses, resulting in calls for government regulation of the press.'

Central Office of Information, 1994, *Britain 1995, An official handbook*, HMSO.

- Radio and Television: the Radio Authority, the Independent Television Commission (ITC), the BBC Governors, The Broadcasting Standards Council. These bodies were set up by government statute.

    The Radio Authority took over responsibility for independent radio from the Independent Broadcasting Authority (IBA) in 1991. It monitors independent local radio output in terms of quality and the range of material broadcast. It awards licences by competitive tender to the highest bidder. It also gives restricted service licences (for a maximum of 28 days).

    The ITC is responsible for the licensing and regulation of all television services apart from those provided by the BBC. The ITC covers Channels 3, 4 and the impending Channel 5, teletext services, cable and satellite.

    The BBC is regulated through committees and a management hierarchy answerable to the Governors. The Board of Governors are twelve in number, and nominated by the government. The BBC operates under a royal charter outlining its aims, powers and obligations. It also has a licence and agreement set by the government which gives some detail about how it should operate. These documents give the BBC some freedom from government interference, although there are clauses which allow the government to take over transmitters and direct programming in 'an emergency'. The BBC is not allowed to accept broadcast advertising or payment for broadcasts, or to express its own opinion on news.

    The Broadcasting Standards Council has powers over radio and television. These powers refer mainly to the portrayal of sex and violence, and the limits of 'taste and decency'. It sets a policy or code which broadcasting organisations must pay attention to in their own codes of practice. You, and any other member of the public, may take a complaint on such issues to the Council.

- Film and video: the British Board of Film Certification.

    The BBFC issues certificates for films, and may decline to award a certificate for distribution at all. Local Authorities usually accept these as evidence of a film's suitability for cinema exhibition, but they may if they wish forbid exhibition as has happened to certificated films such as *Straw Dogs*.

- Advertising: the Advertising Standards Authority.

    The content of advertising, is regulated by the Advertising Standards Authority, which elicits, investigates and answers complaints from the public.

A Activity

All the regulatory bodies here will send out material in answer to requests from the public. Look up the address of any regulatory body which interests you in the library, and send a letter asking for details of their activities, and how you might complain about an area they regulate.

Assignment

The Company Game

Introduction

Playing this game will help you to:
- understand media ownership
- understand the way in which companies in the media industries function
- put forward your own ideas about where the money goes and how companies can be marketed
- understand how companies merge or take one another over to form larger, more diverse and more complex groups of companies, called conglomerates
- prepare to research, analyse and report on a real company.

To play the game you will need two stacks of cards:
- a Company Description stack
- a Company Asset stack.

The information to be written on the two sets of cards is given at the end of this assignment, and it must be written on the two sets of cards and the two stacks shuffled before you start the game.

Outcomes

At the end of the game you will have engaged in discussion, made a presentation and mounted an exhibition. You will also have produced two reports, one justifying your bid for another company, and the other about the operations of an imaginary company based on the cards. You will submit the assignment in the form of the two reports, and a recording of the game (in a format which you can decide).

Rules

Each member of the class or group plays the part of a representative of a media company. Each player then takes two cards: one card from each stack.

The group then divides up into pairs. Each player discusses with one other player the contents of their two cards. The pairs then swop around so that there are two new partners in each pair to discuss their companies and their assets. This continues until everyone has spoken to everyone else in the group.

Each player should take notes about what the other players have on their cards.

Once all the information has been shared, each representative will make a bid for another company. These bids must be referred to an adjudicator, probably played by a teacher or supervisor, who will decide on which pairs of companies can merge.

It is then up to the new merged companies to write up a report (the content of which is realistic, but fictional) detailing the viability of the company after the first year of operations. These reports will then be exhibited and discussed.

Playing the game

1. Read the rules and set up the game.
2. Play the discussion phase of the game through.

3 Decide which company you want to bid for and write a report justifying your bid in terms of the profitability and welfare of both companies.
4 Submit the report to the adjudicator.
5 Make a presentation to the rest of the class making your bid and justifying it in terms of the profitability and welfare of both companies.
6 The adjudicator will discuss all the bids with all the representatives in the group.
7 The adjudicator will announce a decision on which pairs of companies will merge.
8 The paired companies discuss their plans for their first year of operations.
9 They present their plans to the adjudicator.
10 The paired companies agree with the adjudicator on the likely scenario for their first year of operations.
11 Each company produces a report on their first year of operations using the format detailed in the advice below.
12 The reports are displayed in an exhibition showing the results of the game.

Company descriptions

a You represent a company which owns a chain of local newspapers in the North East of England and also in Hampshire. You have benefited in profitability from new print technology. At the moment, your profits have increased, but newspaper sales are falling and you want to expand into another area.
b You represent a company which produces television programmes for your own and others' franchises. You also have a majority shareholding in two regional television franchises (Central and LWT). Your company is now interested in making links with other media outlets.
c You represent a company which owns a number of highly profitable radio stations. Your advertising revenue and audience figures are healthy. You are looking for ways to expand or diversify.
d You represent a company which buys out the top magazines in their field. This strategy has worked and profits keep growing. You have a majority shareholding in the company printing your magazines. You are finding it difficult to expand further in the magazine industry and want to 'put your eggs into more baskets'.
e You work for an independent company which publishes a broadsheet national newspaper. You have small interests in other fields: a political magazine, and a small television production company. You do not want to be eaten up by a large conglomerate and are looking for a partner company which would help you to fight off such unwelcome bids.
f You are a media business person running a company which includes a middle-ranging advertising agency, and a small production company in the business of making corporate and training videos. You have the staff and expertise to expand into other areas if you can find the right partner.

g You run a media business working mainly in the music industry. You have an independent record label. You hire out studio recording facilities. You also run a music venue which has a reputation for showcasing new ideas and talent. Your business is small but very profitable.
h You represent a small print production house and publisher which specialises in graphic productions and comics. Despite your small size as a business you have an international reputation, you export to Japan, and there are obvious possibilities to market titles and characters from your comics in other media, and other products.
i You work for a production company which specialises in animation and special effects for film and television. Recently, one of your animation titles has received successful international distribution resulting in a rise in profits. You need to branch out, but where, with whom?
j You represent a book publisher and printing company. The publishing house specialises in travel guides. Your publications include guides and other books about localities within the UK, as well as a chain of titles, 'The Adventurer' series, which covers countries abroad. The printing works prints leaflets and brochures for the travel industry as well as your own publications. Your guides have an established brand image and audience, but you are now seeking a partner who can help you make links with other media.

Company assets

1 Your most important asset from the point of view of a business partner is your production plant and equipment, into which you have poured money, so that you now have the capacity to make media products in your area for other companies.
2 Your most attractive asset for any business partner is the talented staff who work for you. They are already famous names, but they have star possibilities which could be exploited in other media.
3 Your most attractive asset for any partner is your name. You have a tradition for trustworthiness and quality of products which many others envy.
4 Your most attractive asset is your property. By accident, you happen to occupy buildings which have great potential because of recent changes in their localities and use.
5 Your most attractive asset is your audience. You have attracted loyalty which resembles cult status. Your audience reach is also wide, taking in a wide span of ages and spending patterns.
6 Your most attractive asset is your reputation for taking on all competitors and winning because of the quality of your management.
7 Your most attractive asset is cash. You have made a lot of money which has gone into investments rather than the business. This is now out of proportion and money could be redirected into investing in media products.
8 You have a reputation for tight financial management which maximises profits but minimises risk. You also have small shareholdings in many other media companies which gives you useful links and would help future projects.

9 You are famous for the creative and writing talent in your organisation. This could be exploited in other media.
10 You have popular appeal which has the potential for a wider audience. Your staff and your products have attracted such wide attention outside your target audience that you need to think how you can exploit this for the good of the company.

Advice on report formats

Your report should open with an introduction explaining the purpose and scope of the report, and then list the rest of the headings it will be organised under.

The report justifying your bid should be presented in the form of answers to question headings you decide upon. An example would be a heading, 'What benefits will such a merger have for our prospective partner?'

The 'fictional' report about your paired companies should follow a format you also devise yourselves, but which includes answers to the following questions:
- Who are you? (names etc.)
- What do you produce?
- Where do you get your money from?
- Who consumes your products?
- What do you spend your money on?
- How do you market your products?

16 | A historical sketch of mass media in the United Kingdom

▶ The production history of the *Sun*, page 21

▶ The production history of the magazine, page 41

▶ Looking at film genre and production context, page 128

The development of the mass media in Britain is a huge subjects which cannot be covered thoroughly in a single chapter. Our aim here is to pick out some of the most important development and these are divided into four periods.
- Before 1914
- 1914 – 1949
- 1950 – 1969
- 1970 onwards.

This history concentrates on newspapers, radio, television and cinema. Other areas of importance in the development of the mass media such as the music industry and advertising are not investigated.

Before 1914

The radio, the television, the cinema, the video, the hi-fi and the computer are twentieth-century products. In the nineteenth century, live popular entertainment might be enjoyed at the music hall or through spectator sport (the F.A. Cup was first contested in 1872), but audiences had to go outside the home to enjoy such pleasures. Before 1900, the only truly *mass* media, in the modern sense, in Britain were those provided by books, newspapers and magazines. The first such publications appeared as mass produced products in the sixteenth and seventeenth centuries following the invention and development of the printing press. Most of the so called 'serious' or *quality* broadsheet papers read today were founded before 1896: *The Times* (1785), the *Manchester Guardian* (1821), the *Daily Telegraph* (1855), the *Financial Times* (1888). The *Observer*, the oldest national Sunday paper in the world, first appeared in 1791. (There are some exceptions to this generalisation about the popular/ quality divide. The *News of the World* first appeared as a newspaper in 1843, and has moved downmarket since.) For much of the nineteenth century, newspapers were targeted at the better off, the privately educated, and the elite. The building of mass audiences for print media did not take place until universal education late in the nineteenth century made it possible for the mass of the population to be able to read and write.

The news agencies which distribute and sell news nationally and internationally appeared in the nineteenth century. The establishment of these agencies was facilitated by the new technology of the electric telegraph, carrying coded messages by wire, which appeared around the middle of the century. Reuters News Agency opened in London in 1851.

The Press Association was established as the British national news agency in 1868. Both these agencies, and most national newspaper offices, were located in an area between Holborn and Blackfriars Bridge known by the name of its central street, Fleet Street.

Figure 16.1 A guide to Fleet Street in its heyday. Newspaper production has since moved out of the immediate area.

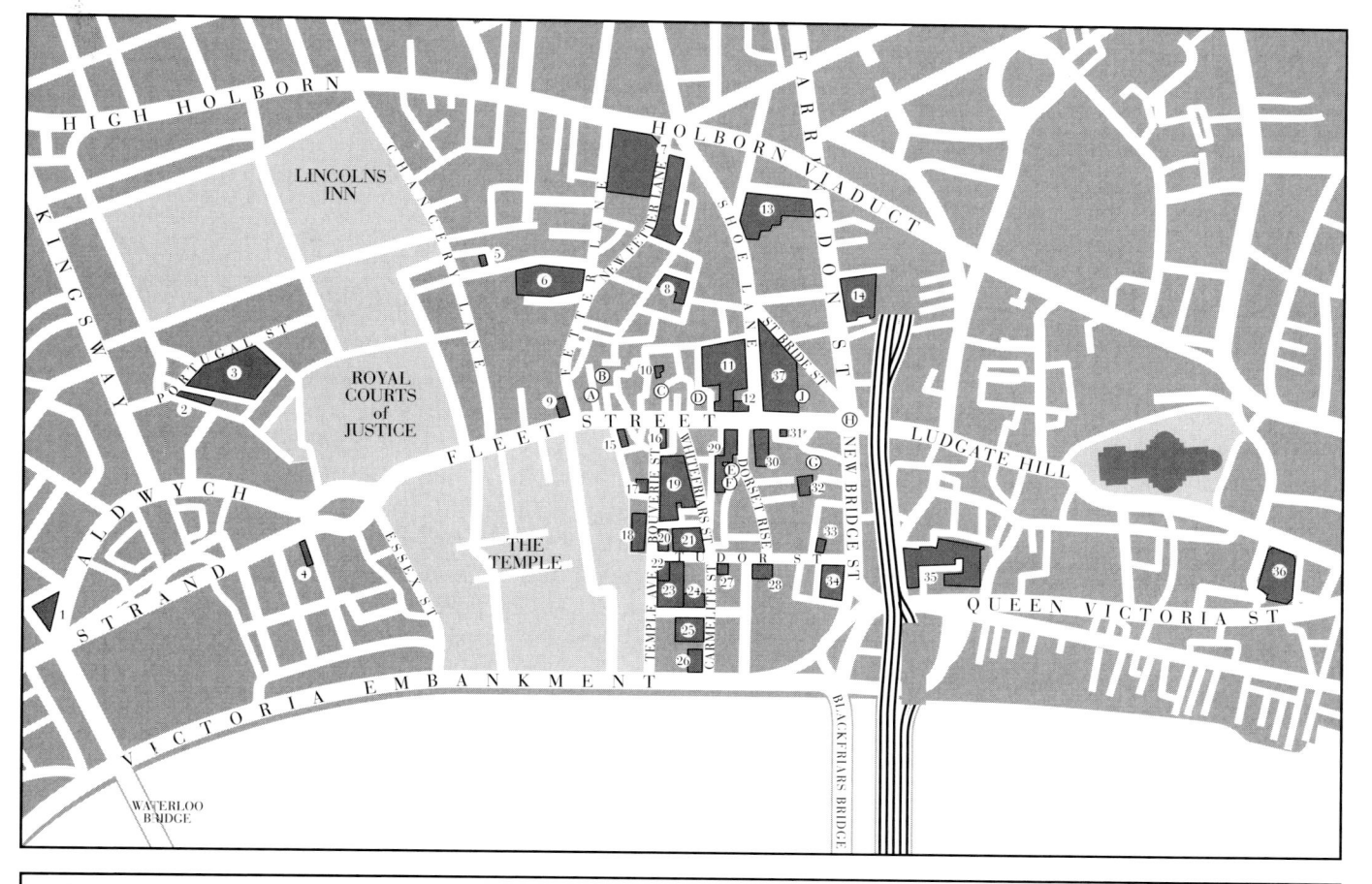

A	Crane Court	7	Dail Mirror (since (1960)	23	Temple House (Horace Marshall and Sons)
B	Red Lion Court	8	Newspaper House (Westminster Press)	24	National Press Agency
C	Bolt Court	9	*Sheffield Daily Telegraph*	25	Carmelite House (*Daily Mail* and *Evening News*)
D	Wine Office Court	10	Bolt Court School	26	New Carmelite House
E	Salisbury Court	11	*The Daily Telegraph*	27	*The Daily Telegraph* reserve printing works
F	Salisbury Square	12	*Liverpool Daily Post*	28	Co-operative Printing Society
G	Bride Lane	13	*Evening Standard*	29	*Daily Chronicle* and *Lloyd's Weekly News*
H	Ludgate Circus	14	Fleetway House (Amalgamated Press)	30	Reuters and Press Association
J	Poppins Court	15	*Glasgow Herald*	31	*Birmingham Daily Post*
		16	*The Scotsman*	32	St Bride Foundation Institute
1	*Morning Post*	17	*Punch*	33	Institute of Journalists
2	*Church Times* and *The Financial Times*	18	*News Chronicle*	34	Blackfriars House (Spicer Brothers)
3	W H Smith (from 1920)	19	News of the World	35	Printing House Square (*The Times* and *The Observer*)
4	W H Smith (before 1920)	20	*Daily News* and *The Star*		
5	*The Athenaeum*	21	Northcliffe House (Associated Newspapers)	36	Bracken House (*The Financial Times* from 1959)
6	*Dail Mirror* (before 1960)	22	Argus Printing Company	37	Express Newspapers

At the end of the nineteenth century, Alfred Harmsworth (later Lord Northcliffe), a newspaper owner with a vision of popular newspapers which built mass audiences with a mix of entertainment, human interest and news, introduced the *Mail* in 1896. The *Daily Express* first appeared in 1900, followed by the *Daily Mirror* in 1903. The popular journalism which these newspapers developed is the historical background to the development of the *tabloid journalism* of today.

Lord Northcliffe is also an example of the *press baron* and *media mogul*, phenomena which are a feature of twentieth-century media history (as exemplified more recently by figures such as Rupert Murdoch and the late Robert Maxwell).

'Northcliffe had all the mogul characteristics; he took risks, he built his holdings by launching new titles as well as rescuing old ones. He personally was the dominant operator and owner, although he also pioneered the stock market flotation of his enterprise as a public company. He was highly controversial (attacking the war leadership in 1916), politically interventionist, and idiosyncratic to the point of ultimate insanity.'

> Tunstall and Palmer, 1991, *Media Moguls*, Routledge, page 114

By 1910, Northcliffe owned six London papers including the *Daily Mail*, *Daily Mirror*, *The Times* and the *Observer*. For the next forty-five years no more than eight companies and their press barons owned most of Britain's newspapers.

The first moving images were to be seen in the silent films produced at the turn of the century. At this time the showing of moving images on film had not yet developed into a medium available to mass audiences. In October 1894, a parlour offering the public the chance to experience the Edison kinetoscope, a film viewing machine which the solitary viewer looked into, opened at 70 Oxford Street in the centre of London. The earliest films produced in Britain were non-fiction and based upon real events. At the first projection screen performance at the Royal Photographic Society in 1896, film maker Birt Acres showed films with titles such as *The Opening of the Kiel Canal*, *The Derby* and *Rough Seas at Dover*.

The first purpose-built cinemas appeared from 1908. For example, the first cinema with a sloping floor was the Picture Palace at St Albans, Hertfordshire, opened in 1908. By 1910, cinema was established as a form of mass entertainment and the British film industry was successful in competing with the United States. The first British feature films released 1912–13 included titles such as *Oliver Twist*, *Lorna Doone* and *Ivanhoe*, showing the influence of literary culture in British film from the beginnings of the industry. One of the many problems that the British film industry has constantly faced is a certain British snobbery about popular film. The government, and the establishment in British culture, have never fully recognised cinema as an art form in its own right, as important to national identity as literature or the theatre.

The first Cinematograph Act of 1909 was a government measure to ensure the public safety of cinemas. The responsibility of this was handed over to local authorities. However, the local authorities used their powers with gusto to control everything from opening hours to the content of what was shown. By 1913, cinema owners, film makers and distributors were so concerned about censorship of cinema programmes by local authorities that they formed a self-regulatory body, the British Board of Film Censors in order to keep the councils quiet.

1914 – 1949

The period 1914 – 1949 takes in the two World Wars, and the inter-war period, which includes the economic depression from 1929 through most of the thirties. During this time the mass circulation newspapers were the predominant news medium, the cinema became a mass entertainment system of stars and film genres led in the main by the Hollywood studios, and radio developed as public service broadcasting in Britain.

During the First World War (1914–18), the newspapers were influenced by the war effort as vehicles for propaganda and anti-German feeling, and came under direct censorship. After the war, the newspaper industry grew massively and continued to reach peaks in its influence and success through the 1920s, 1930s and 1940s. Newspapers with a national distribution gained ground against the regional newspapers. In 1923, the circulation of national newspapers overtook that of regional morning and evening newspapers for the first time. By 1945, the national papers sold twice as many copies as the provincial press.

The use of radio waves for sending telegraph signals had been shown by the inventor Marconi in as early as 1896. Wireless telegraphy developed during the First World War. After the war, pressure to develop radio broadcasting developed under three influences: amateur radio operators (many of them ex-servicemen); manufacturers who needed new markets for radio equipment; and government concern to centralise and regulate the new communications medium. In 1922, the British Broadcasting Company was formed by radio equipment manufacturers in order to exploit the possibilities of national radio broadcasting. In 1923, the Sykes committee, the first of the British government committees which have guided national broadcasting policy, recommended that 'the control of such a potential power over public opinion and the life of the nation ought to remain with the state'. In 1926, the BBC was nationalised, the organisation became the British Broadcasting Corporation, and received its first royal charter setting out its object as a public service broadcaster. As a monopoly, the BBC was not allowed to *opinionate* on its own behalf, or *editorialise*, as the commercial free press were. It was formally obliged to be impartial. BBC Radio developed a service which offered coverage of national events, with a bias towards the importance of the monarchy, 'high culture' such as plays and concerts, and some light entertainment with an emphasis on music. The BBC was financed through a tax on radio owners who had to buy a licence from the Post Office.

Figure 16.2 The new Broadcasting House, London

Figure 16.3 A page from the Radio Times from 1925

Hollywood dominance of the film market goes back as far as the competitive advantage it gained during the First World War. Many European film workers and stars took their talents to America. The British film industry was hard hit by the 1914–18 war and production fell back after 1916. In 1918, Britain produced 76 feature films compared with 841 produced by the USA. During the 1920s the British film industry suffered from American competition; by 1926, 95% of British cinema screentime was occupied by American films. In 1929, British International Pictures produced the first British talking feature film at Elstree Studios, *Blackmail* (directed by Alfred Hitchcock). This was two years after Warner Brothers' *The Jazz Singer*, the first 'talkie'.

In 1928, the government enacted a further Cinematographic Films Act which made it a matter of law that distributors and exhibitors should show a quota of British-made films. This helped the British film industry to compete with imported American films. Large cinema chains such as

Associated British Corporation (ABC), British Gaumont and the Odeon group spread across the country. Most people became regular cinema-goers. In 1933, Alexander Korda, based at Denham Studios west of London, made an international hit with *The Private Life of Henry VIII* starring Charles Laughton.

The Second World War (1939 – 45) once again meant that the mass media had an important role in the war effort, and newspapers were censored by the wartime Ministry of Information. Newsprint was rationed, but despite fewer pages, sales of newspapers rose. The BBC had started one of the world's first television services in 1936, broadcasting from Alexandra Palace in North London. In September 1939, BBC television closed, for fear that the broadcasts would be a navigational aid for German bombing planes. Television in America stayed on air throughout the war.

BBC radio developed in importance as 'the voice of the nation'. BBC staff more than doubled in size during the war, from 5 000 in 1938 to 11 000 in 1946. Listeners could choose between the General Forces programme (renamed the Light Programme in 1945) and the Home Service. The Third Programme, the precursor of Radio 3, was set up in 1946. The BBC World Service has its origins in the wartime Overseas Service which developed a reputation for giving more truthful accounts of the events of the war than the propagandist broadcasts of other nations.

'It was during the war and for the ten years or so after it that radio enjoyed its heyday, providing programmes of distinction in every genre to audiences of many millions. This was the period of what were regarded as radiogenic 'features' programmes – programmes of a factual, often documentary, nature but partly created through imaginative scripting which blended narration, actuality, dramatic dialogue, and sound effects.'

▶ Crisell, A., 1994, *Understanding Radio*, Routledge, page 25

Although the British film industry produced propagandist films of a popular nature, and production recovered in the late forties, the Second World War also assisted in the domination of Hollywood. The US studios benefited from the disruption of European production, and from the expertise of the refugee film makers who brought their talents to America. After the war, however, there was some recovery in British film production. Ealing Studios, for example, which had taken over at Ealing from another company at the end of the 1930s, produced some of the most memorable and successful British films of the forties and fifties, including *Whiskey Galore* and *Kind Hearts and Coronets*. In 1949, the National Film Finance Corporation (NFFC) was started with government money to stimulate national production.

1950 – 1969

The 1950s and 1960s are seen as peace time, but they were dominated by an arms race on a world scale. During the Second World War, as during the First, new technologies developed which were to influence communications media. These included the development of rocket propulsion and the electronic computer. The Second World War was followed by a Cold War between the Communist eastern bloc and the West, during which communications technologies developed in the context of a nuclear arms race.

'Every household name which shared in the post war boom in electric and electronic consumer durables – Marconi, Phillips, Decca, Westinghouse, General Electric, AT & T – was also deeply implicated in the arms race and to a very great extent dependent on military contracts.'

Lewis and Pearlman, 1986, Media and Power, Camden Press, page 110

The period 1950–69 also marks out two decades when television took off and established itself as the dominant mass medium. The newspapers continued to boom until 1957 when competition from commercial television started off a decline in advertising revenue. Newspaper rationing continued until 1955, but this limited costs and was not a problem while advertising space was in demand. Certainly newspaper circulations have not kept up with the increases in population in Britain since the late fifties, and sales of national Sundays, evening papers and the local weekly (paid for) categories went into an unsteady decline after 1957. Competition from television influenced the further diversification of newspapers away from hard news towards the inclusion of entertainment and features.

The 1950s was the decade of a consumer boom, the arrival of television as a mass medium, and the 'invention' of the teenager. From about 1953, the year of the televising of the coronation of the Queen, television took off as a successful rival to other media. Following the recommendations of the Beveridge committee (1950), a commercial television channel was set up, but regulated by a public corporation (the Independent Television Association or ITA). In 1955, the BBC's monopoly was replaced by a *duopoly* between the BBC and a group of commercial broadcasters broadcasting as Independent Television (ITV). By 1957, ITV had captured 80% of the audience, influencing the BBC to become more populist in its approach in order to win audiences back. Opinions vary as to whether ITV represented a commercial alternative to public service broadcasting.

'The terms under which commercial broadcasting was established by the government made it part of the public service system from the beginning. A public corporation, the Independent Television Authority, was created by Act of Parliament with general responsibilities to establish a commercial television service that would inform, educate and entertain. This service, known as Independent Television (ITV), was subject to state regulation and control by an authority charged with maintaining high standards of programme quality. It was an extension of public service broadcasting, not an alternative.'

Scannel, P., 'Public Service Broadcasting: the history of a concept', in Goodwin, A., and Whannel, G., 1990, Understanding Television, Routledge

The Pilkington committee (1960) criticised ITV for triviality, lack of variety or innovation. The third television channel was allocated to the BBC, and in 1964 BBC 2 began. Colour television broadcasts began in 1967. During the 1960s satellites for television communication developed; the first trans-Atlantic link beginning with the relay of live television pictures via the Telstar satellite in 1962. In 1967, the Beatles sang *All You Need is Love* on a worldwide satellite link-up.

The 1960s was a decade of a revolutionary expansion in youth culture. 'Pop' music, and its various branches, such as rock and roll, Tamla and soul, developed a presence on the radio. In 1964, the first radio pirate, Radio Caroline, dropped anchor in order to broadcast from outside UK territorial waters. The radio pirates directly resulted in the BBC setting up its own pop channel, Radio 1, in September 1967. The Light Programme became Radio 2, the Third Programme Radio 3, and the Home Service Radio 4. On the recommendation of the Pilkington Committee, the BBC had a monopoly of local VHF (FM) radio, and between 1966 and 1970 there were 20 local stations established.

Figure 16.4 Publicity still from an early episode of Coronation Street, the world's longest running television soap opera, first broadcast 1960.

At the beginning of the 50s, the Eady Levy, a percentage tax on cinema ticket sales, was set up to recycle profits back into film production. The NFFC and the Eady Levy assisted the production of many films, but the British film industry of the 1950s and 1960s continued to lose out against competition from Hollywood, and the new medium of television. In 1951, British censorship regulations were relaxed, and the 'X certificate' excluding admission to anyone under 16 was introduced for more adult films. Film studios in Ealing and Lime Grove were bought by the BBC in the mid-1950s. Warner's Teddington studios were bought up by an ITV company. In 1954, a small studio, Hammer, found that it could no longer produce 'B' films for the American market when its American partner pulled out. Hammer's *The Quatermass Experiment* (1955) was a cinema adaptation of an already successful BBC serial. It broke box office records in the UK and America. Capitalising on the success of *Quatermass*, Hammer then turned to a formula exploiting X-certificate material and the novelty of colour film, which gave the company an edge against the competition from black and white television. *The Curse of Frankenstein* (1957) was an international success and began a cycle of gothic horror films which became Hammer's trademark. At the end of the 1950s a new kind of British film with a gritty 'social realism' emerged. *Room at the Top* (1959), *Look Back in Anger* (1959) and *Saturday Night and Sunday Morning* (1960) were made by independent film production companies and criticised the barriers of social class.

American investment in British films in the 1960s backed the growth and success of studios at Elstree and Pinewood. *Dr No* (1962) was the first in the successful series of James Bond films. However, British-made film production began to show signs of decline during the 1960s.

1970 onwards

The newspaper industry has changed radically over the last twenty five years. The so-called decline of the newspaper is sometimes exaggerated.

The total circulation of national dailies has fallen from the 1957 high point of 16.7 million, but still hover, around the 15 million mark today. Ownership has become concentrated in relatively few hands. Locally, 'free sheets' have increased steadily in numbers since they first gained ground in the 1970s. They boomed from 1977 onwards, until by the late 1980s they outnumbered the paid for local weeklies. Nationally, the division between 'popular' and minority or 'quality' papers has grown, with the popular press becoming increasingly controversial in their activities. From about 1969, when the *Sun* converted from broadsheet format to tabloid, the popular broadsheet newspaper began to disappear.

Date of adopting tabloid format by national newspapers	
Before 1945	*Daily Mirror* (1935)
	Daily Sketch (1908)
	Sunday Pictorial/Sunday Mirror (1915)
1962	*Sunday Citizen*
1969	*Sun*
1971	*Daily Mail*
1974	*Sunday People* (*The People* from 1986)
1977	*Daily Express*
1978	*Daily Star* (at launch)
1982	*Mail on Sunday* (at launch)
1984	*News of the World*
1986	*Today* (at launch; closed 1995)
	Sunday Today (at launch; closed 1987)
	Sunday Sport (at launch)
1987	*News on Sunday* (at launch; closed 1987)
1988	*The Post* (at launch; closed 1988)

Figure 16.5 Table showing date of adopting tabloid format by national newspapers

Some new national newspaper titles appeared in the late 1970s and the 1980s, not all of which survived. The survivors include the *Daily Star* (1978), the *Mail on Sunday* (1981) and the *Independent* (1986).

In 1972, the government authorised the Independent Broadcasting Authority (forerunner of the ITC and the Radio Authority) to license commercial local radio stations. LBC and Capital Radio in London were the first to broadcast in 1973, and there are now more than fifty stations across the country. Independent local radio was soon incorporated into media conglomerates such as Crown Communications and the ITV companies.

Throughout the 1980s Britain was governed by the conservative government led by Margaret Thatcher. The 1980s was a time of 'deregulation', a loosening of the rules and government limitations which had previously controlled the commercial development of the mass media. Deregulation had the stated aims of 'extending freedom of choice', and opening up media industries to the free market. The politics of the free market combined with the implementation of new media technologies spurred changes in all media.

In 1986, News International, part of the 'empire' of Australian-American Rupert Murdoch, took all its national titles (*The Times, The Sunday Times,* the *Sun,* the *News of the World*) from Fleet Street to a new plant at Wapping. The aims of this move were to break the power of the print unions, and to use new electronic printing technologies to dramatically lower labour and printing costs. Despite a bitter dispute, and mass picketing by those who had lost their jobs, the move succeeded in its aims.

Figure 16.6 *'Fortress Wapping'*

The Annan committee (1977) proposed an open broadcasting authority, which would act as a publisher rather than a production company, for the proposed fourth television channel. The fourth television channel was allocated to the independent sector, and, in November 1982, Channel Four and S4C of Wales were launched. At the time, Channel Four was a company wholly owned by the IBA, with a brief to buy in programmes from a range of independent companies, and to serve the needs of minorities not fully served by existing services. Arguably, the idea that public service broadcasting could serve a common national audience, or *consensus*, had collapsed, and the new broadcasting was *pluralistic*, that is, it now tried to serve many audiences with different needs. In 1983, *breakfast time* television appeared on both BBC and ITV providing a rival medium at radio's peak listening time. The Peacock committee (1985) recommended greater use of independent production on all channels and the extension of choice for consumers. Broadcasting was now being seen as a commodity to be bought and sold, rather than a public service. Peacock's recommendation of a subscription system to finance the BBC was not taken up, however.

Soon viewers in some areas, prepared to pay subscriptions, could expand their choice to many more than four channels via cable and/or satellite. In America and Canada the cabling up of homes to a powerful aerial had been around from the earliest days of television. In the 1980s, cable technology linked to satellite broadcasting began to take off in Europe. In the UK, the newly formed Cable Authority began to allocate franchises from 1984. Satellite television appeared in its own right with Sky Television in 1989, and its short-lived rival British Satellite Television in 1990. They merged as BSkyB in 1991. In the same year the BBC set up an international division which included a company with the objective of establishing a worldwide television service, World Service Television.

The move to American dominance of the British film studios, which had helped finance the mini-boom of the 1960s, proved to be disastrous for the industry. In 1960, Britain produced 110 feature films; in 1987 production fell to 30. In 1970 there were only three major British studios:

ABPC Elstree, Pinewood and Shepperton. By the mid-1970s cinemas were closing and the American money was moving out. In 1979, 38 films were produced by British registered companies. In 1985, the NFFC and the Eady Levy were abolished. In the late 1980s, the British film industry was treated by government as a lame duck. The only bright spot was the co-operation between television, Channel Four in particular, and independent companies producing mainly low budget productions, such as *My Left Foot* (1991), co-produced by Channel Four and Granada.

Conclusion

The history of the mass media in Britain is part of a much larger history of events and social change, and connects with many factors. These include: the development of the USA and the relative decline of the UK as a world power; new technologies; new cultural phenomena and audience needs; the pressures from commercial organisations to make profits and compete; the desire of government to intervene in and control the power of communications media; the effects of war and relations between media industries and military production.

In the 1990s, the convergence of media through digital technologies, satellite and fibre optic networks has shrunk the world in communications terms. In 1964, a university professor called Marshall McLuhan coined the phrase, 'the global village' in order to describe the revolutionary new possibilities which electronic communications technologies offered. Over the decades since, not only the mass media but also the industries and economies with which they connect have become increasingly global. The media moguls of the 1990s, such as Bertelsman of BMG, or Murdoch of Newscorp, operate on an international or continental scale rather than within one country. The media industries in the UK are part of a business world dominated by multi-national conglomerates. The theory of dominance by America in media markets as a new kind of empire building, or 'US media imperialism', has been discussed since the 1960s, and remains relevant.

Index

academic research 16-17, 233, 238-9
access to media 271
accountability of media 271
action planning 185-7
advertising 24, 45, 247, 248, 251
    of films 257-8
    market research and 233
    marketing strategy and 251-6
    selling 92
    in teenage magazines 49-50, 58
Advertising Standards Authority 256, 273
alignment of text 95
analysis 10-14, 204
anchorage 47, 55
Annan Committee (1977) 287
Archers, The 212
assembly editing 198
assembly script 197
assessment, of GNVQ assignments 4-5
Associated British Corporation (ABC) 283
Associated Newspapers 263
Associated Press 265
audience 16-17, 68, 116
    classification of 17
    of horror films 131-2
    market research and 233, 236
    for quiz shows 153, 157, 158
Audience Appreciation service 234
audience participation quiz shows 156-9

Babe 99
backgrounds, in comics 126-7
'Bash Street Kids' 107-8
    narrative structure of 110-11
Baxendale, Leo 106-8
BBC (British Broadcasting Corporation) 265, 266, 270, 281, 284
    Board of Governors of 273
    educational broadcasting 271
    as magazine publisher 265, 267
    radio 266-7, 283, 284
    in World War II 283
    worldwide 266, 267
BBC International Television 267, 269
BBC World Service 267, 287

Beano 103-108
    'Bash Street Kids' 107-8
    'Calamity James' 111-13, 125
    narrative structure in 110-11
Bhaji on the Beach 137-9
Birds, The 131, 132, 140-1
Blankety Blank 162
Bolam, Silvester 25
brainstorming 172-3
breakfast time television 287
brief, for video production 171
British Board of Film Certification 273
British Broadcasting Corporation
    see BBC
British Code of Advertising and Sales Promotion Practice 256
British Gaumont 283
British International Pictures 282
British Screen Finance Ltd 270
British Sky Broadcasting (BSkyB) 269, 287
Broadcasters Audience Research Board (BARB) 233-4
broadcasting 265-9, 271, 287
    see also cable services; radio; satellite services; television
Broadcasting Standards Council 240, 273
broadsheet newspapers 25, 278, 286
BSkyB 269, 287
buzz track 188
Byrne, David 171
Cable Authority 287
Cable News Network (CNN) 269
cable services 266, 269, 287
camera cards 166
camera logic 166
camera operators 185
cameras 188
Capital Radio 286
capitals/lower case 94
captions 98
cardioid microphones 227
caricatures 83
categorisation 29
celebrity quiz shows 155-6
censorship 272, 285
Centre for Mass Communication 239

Chambers, Steve 211, 212-13
Channel Four 268, 270, 271, 287, 288
character roles 144, 147
characters
    in horror films 129-30
    in radio drama 212
cinemas 280, 282-3, 288
    ownership of 270
Cinematograph Act 1909 280
Cinematographic Films Act 1928 282
circulation 22, 23, 24
clapperboards 189
clip microphones 228
close-ups 179, 190, 192-3
closed endings 140
codes 13, 210
column width 94, 95
Comic Book Confidential (CD-ROM) 102
comic conventions 120-25
comics
    analysis of 102-8
    as genre 108-10
    production of 114-27
commercialism, broadcasting and 265, 284
community radio 269
competitions, in local newspapers 248
computers, video on 199-202
conflict 34, 37
connotation 11-12, 46-7, 133-5
contempt of court 271
content 91
    of magazines 44-5, 48-9
content analysis 32, 46-7, 240-41
contents page 48-9
continuity, shooting for 190-91
continuity of direction 191
contracts 176
control track 197, 198
copyright 76, 176, 201
Coronation Street 233
cover pages 46, 50-51
    image analysis of 54-5
cover price 23, 92
creative brief 171-2
creative strategy 254-5

Crisell, Andrew 207, 211
critical listening 205
crossfade 229
crossing the line 190-91
Cudlipp, Hugh 21
Curse of Frankenstein, The 133, 134-5, 285
cutaway shots 166, 191
cutting on action 190

Daily Express 263, 279
Daily Mail 24, 71-4, 263, 280
Daily Mail and General Trust plc 263
Daily Mirror 21, 262, 279, 280
Daily Star 286
Daily Telegraph 24, 278
Daily Telegraph Group 263
Dandy 103, 105
deadlines 93
defamation 74-6, 271
denotation 11-12, 46-7, 133-5
depth interviews 242-3
deregulation 266, 286
design/art director 184-5
design, set 164
design of product 93-8
digital revolution 266, 288
digital skill cameras 201
director 184, 213
distribution 16, 91, 247, 259
Dixon, Bob 106
dramatisation 34

Eady Levy 285, 288
Ealing Studios 283, 285
editing 16, 163
    equipment for 228-9
    shooting for 189
    of videos 197-9
editor 185
editorials 30, 31
    tabloid 30-2
educational programmes 271
effectiveness, of advertising campaigns 255
Elstree Studios 282, 285, 288
EMAP 43, 48, 264-5
emotional appeal 34, 35, 36
English Illustrated Magazine 42
Englishwoman's Domestic Magazine, The 42
equipment
    for audio productions 227-9
    for drawing 119
    for editing 228-9
    for video productions 188-9
establishing shot 135-7, 180, 189
ethics 76-7, 175, 229
European Co-production Fund 270
evaluation 63-4, 89, 173-4
Evening Standard 263

evidence indicators 6
Extel 265

factual programming 225-7
fading 229
fairytales, films as 144-5
features 68-71
Fifteen to One 147-9, 162
film fiction 128-49
film images
    analysis of 133-5
    in *Four Weddings and a Funeral* 147-8
film industry, British 270, 280, 282,3, 285, 287-8
film magazines 42
films
    distribution of 257
    endings of 139-42, 147
    genres of 13, 128-32, 146,7
    marketing of 257-8
    middles of 142-3, 147
    openings of 135-9, 147
    pre-1914 280
    release of 257
finance 91-2
Financial Times 263, 278
Fleet Street 279
floor plans 164
focus groups 241
football coverage 33-6, 205
format radio 207-8
Four Weddings and a Funeral 146-9, 257
Fowler, Roger 29
framing 120-21, 192, 194-5
Frankenstein 133
free newspapers 286
Future of the BBC, The 266

Gale, George 106
game shows 153, 154
games, in quiz shows 154
genre 13-14, 153
    and comics 108-9
    and films 128-32, 146-7
    and quiz shows 153, 162
    on radio 210-11
Gentleman's Magazine, The 42
Glasgow University Media Group 238-9
GNVQ 3-6
    Media qualification 7-8
government, and the media 271-2
grants 91
graphics 82-6
    software for 201
Greenslade, Roy 22
Guardian Media Guide 44, 67-8, 264
Guardian Newspapers 263

Hall, Stuart 71
Hammer Studios 132, 133, 285

Harmsworth, Alfred, Lord Northcliffe 279-80
headlines 26, 28
health and safety 176, 187
Herts Herald 250
Hitchcock, Alfred 132, 282
Hollywood 128-9, 270, 282, 283
horror films 129-32, 134-5
house style 26, 69
Hyperstudio 199, 200

icons 120, 125
ideas
    evaluation of 63-4, 89, 173-4
    generation of 170-74
    sources of 65-6
image analysis 10-13, 29, 46-7, 54-5, 133-5
    in teenage magazines 52-6, 59
Independent 262, 286
Independent on Sunday 262
Independent Broadcasting Authority 286
independent production 268, 287
independent radio 269
Independent Radio Authority 256
Independent Television (ITV) 265, 266, 267-8, 284
Independent Television Association (ITAS) 284
Independent Television Commission 256, 268, 269, 273
Independent Television News (ITN) 267
induction loop AM 224-5
information sources 65-6, 91
insert editing 198
intertextuality 154
interviews 66-8
    shooting 195-6
IPC Magazines Ltd 264
ITV 265, 266, 267-8, 284
ITV Network Centre 267

jump cuts 191
Just Seventeen 43

kerning 94, 95
Korda, Alexander 283

Ladies Mercury, The 42
Lamb, Larry 21
language 13, 28, 46, 59
    in editorials 30
    of female teenage magazines 52
    images and 47-8, 55-6
Lasses' Night Out 114-16
law, and the media 271-2
laydown schedule 253-4
layout, of teenage magazines 45-6, 50, 51, 58
LBC 286
lead paragraphs 28

Index

leading 94, 95
legibility 94-6
letter spacing 94, 95
lettering 127
libel 74-6
lighting 165, 188-9
literacy 25
local newspapers
    marketing activities of 246-9, 250
    ownership of 264
local radio 269, 286
long shots 179

Macaulay, Sean 22
McCloud, Scott 121
Mackenzie, Kelvin 20, 22
McLuhan, Marshall 288
magazines 40, 44-60
    ownership of 264-5
    production history of 41-4
Mail on Sunday 263, 286
Manchester Evening News 263
Manchester Guardian 278
Manorisms 100
maps 83
market research 207, 232-6, 248
    techniques of 239-43
marketing 246-59
marketing plan 251-6
mass media
    pre-1914 278-80
    1914-1949 280-3
    1950-69 283-5
    after 1970 285-8
master plan 89-92
master shot 180, 190
Masterman, Len 10
Mastermind 153, 154, 162
Match 57-60
meaning 11, 17, 40
media industries 26078
    research organisations of 233-8
    standards of 15-16
medium sots 179
merchandising 258
MGM 133, 270
microphone technique 229
microphones 165, 188, 227-8
Minogue, Kylie 71-4
Mirror Group Newspapers (MGN) 262
mise en scene analysis 133
mixing desk 228
Moonie, George 106
More! 43, 48-57
movement, in comic art 122-5
MTV 269
multimedia 199-202
multiple images 122
Murdoch, Rupert 29, 21, 22, 261, 280

music radio 207-8
narrative, film as 135-43, 147
narrative structure 14, 27, 110-11
National Film Finance Corporation
    (NFFC) 283, 285, 288
National Magazine Company 265
National Readership Survey 234-6
National Theatre of Brent 171
National Transcommunications Ltd 269
National Union of Journalists 272
news agencies 265, 278-9
News International plc 21, 23, 261-2, 269, 286
News of the World 262, 278
News Quiz 155-6
news story analysis 25-9
newspaper reporter 86
newspapers
    history and development of 278-80, 281, 283, 284, 285-6
    ownership of 261-4, 280
    sales of 251
    see also broadsheet newspapers; local newspapers; tabloid newspapers
noddy shot 191
Northcliffe, Lord 279-80
Northcliffe Newspapers 263
Northern Electric, marketing plan for 251-6

objectives 90, 175
Obscene Publications Act 271
Observer 263, 278, 280
Odeon Group 283
Official Secrets Act 271
omni-directional microphone 228
On the Waterfront 136, 142-3, 144-5
open endings 140
opening paragraphs 58-9
origination 15

painting packages 199
panning 192
paper edit 197
parallel action 191
passage of time, in comics 122, 124
Peacock Committee (1985) 287
Pearson plc 263, 267, 269
People 262
performance criteria 5
personalisation 28-9, 33-4, 35-6
phone-in 211
photographs 77-81, 83
    use of 96-8
picture-led 47, 55, 59
pictures for comics 117-19
Pilkington Committee (1960) 284
Pinewood Studios 285, 288
pirate radio 269, 271, 284

plagiarism 76
planning 165-6
    of audio productions 225
    of print material 93
    of studio productions 163-7
    of video productions 170-87
popular culture 43, 152, 159
portfolios 6-7
positioning statements 252
posters 253, 257
pot cut 229
practice shoot 189
presenters, on radio 208-10
Press Association 265, 279
Press Complaints Commission 271, 272
    Code of Practice 76-7
press releases 257-8
Prevention of Terrorism Act 272
preview screening 258
print material
    planning of 62-86
    production of 88-99
print media, British 261-5
printing 92
Private Eye 156
producer 184, 213
product 90-1
    design of 93-8
    development of 248
product specification 174
production 15-16, 92-3
production assistant 185
production history, importance of 19, 41-2, 102
production scripts 176-83
production team 164
professional conduct, code of 272
promotional brief 174, 177-8
promotional events 247-8
Propp, Vladimir 144, 147
public service broadcasting 265, 287

Quatermass Experiment, The 285
quiz shows 152-9
    formulas for 161-2
    production of 163-8
    script for 162-3

radio 204-13
    BBC 266-7, 283, 284
    development of 206, 284, 286
    history of 281, 283
    listeners to 206-7
    presenters on 208-10
    producing programmes for 224-9
Radio 1 207-8
Radio Authority 273
radio drama 211-13
Radio Handbook, The 305, 207, 210

Radio Joint Audience Research 206, 236-8
radio journalist 230
radio microphone 228
radio station, setting up 224-5
range statements 5
'reach' 236
reader offers 248
readership 248-9, 251
    of *Beano* 103-4
    and market research 234-6
    of the *Sun* 24-5
reconnaissance 187
Redhead, M T 251, 253
Reed Elsevier 264
regional newspapers *see* local newspapers
regulation of media 271-3
reminder advertising 253
representation 27, 43, 71-5, 132
    in Four Weddings and a Funeral 148-9
    quiz shows and 154, 156
    in teenage magazines 53
representative sampling 240
research 5, 66-8, 117
    into media 232-43
    for video production 174-5
Research Services Ltd 236
resources 185
restricted service radio 269
Reuters 265, 278
reverse print 95
ribbon microphone 227
rituals, of quiz shows 154, 158
roles
    for studio production teams 164
    for video production 184-5
run through 166-7

S4C (Sianel Pedwar Cymru) 268, 287
Sagacity 236
sales departments 247-8
satellite services 266, 268-9, 284, 287
scanning 200-201
Scott Trust 263
script editor 185
scripts
    for comics 117
    for quiz shows 162-3, 166
    for radio drama 212-13
self-regulation 272
semiotics 10-11
sequential graphics 83
serif/sans serif 94
set design 164
setting, of horror films 130-31
Shepperton Studios 288
shooting 186, 189-96
shooting script 166
shopping discount cards 248

shot allocation 166
shot list 163, 171
shot/reverse shot 141, 180
shots, planning 179-81
signs 11-12
silent films 280
slideshows 199
Smash Hits 43, 44
social classes 16-17, 241
sound 165, 196, 197-8
    computers and 201
sound recordist 185
special effects 199
specification 15
Sporting Life 262
sports coverage 32-6
star interviews 258
still images 200-201
storyboard 163, 166, 171-3
storyline, of horror films 131
storytelling 14
strapline 48
streaking 122
studio managers 213
studio production 163-8
style 69-70, 132
subscription television 269, 287
Sun 19, 262, 286
    competitive market and 22-5
    production history of 21-2
    textual analysis of 25-37
Sunday Express 263
Sunday Mirror 262
Sunday Telegraph 263
Sunday Times 262
Super Profiles 236
surveys 239-40
Sykes Committee (1923) 281
synopses 178-9

tabloid newspapers 18-39, 279, 286
talent 185
tape recorders 227
target audience 89-90
    for quiz shows 154
teamwork 15, 63, 88
technical details 71
technical team 164
teenage magazines 42, 43-4, 46, 47
    female 48-56
    male 57-60
television 24, 265-6, 267-9, 284, 287
    advertising on 253, 257
text-led 47
Thames Television 269
Thatcher, Margaret 22
Thomson Organisation 264
Times, The 23, 262, 278, 280
timeshift viewing 233

Titbits 42
today 24
tracking 248
trailers 258
transition between frames 121
travel schemes 248
treatment 174, 177-8
Trinity International Holdings 264
tripod 188
Tunstall, Jeremy 207
TV Asia 269
typography 30, 51, 94-6

UK Gold 269
United Kingdom, media industries in 260-88
United Newspapers 263
United Press International 265
Universal Studios 132, 133

Victoria Station 213
video-in board 200
video market 270
video production 170, 188-202
    planning 184-7
    pre-production 170-87
    scripts for 176-83
visual material 77-86

Wapping 286
Warner Brothers 133, 270, 282
Westminster Press 263
wildtrack sound 229
women's magazines 42, 43
word limit 68
Working Title Productions 146
World War II
    Beano and *Dandy* in 104
    mass media during 283
writing for visual material 176

youth culture 284

zoo format radio 209
zooming 192